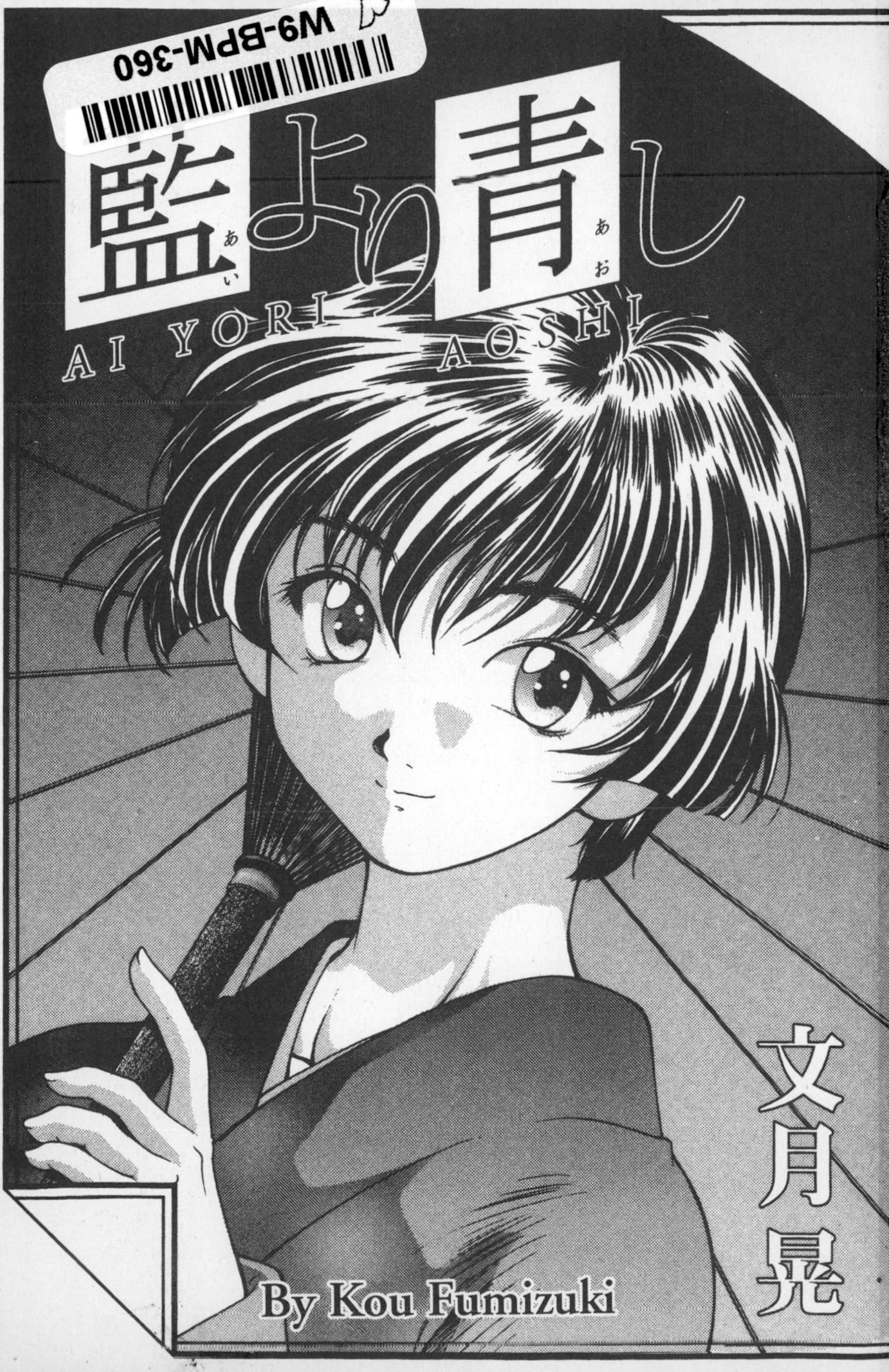
藍(あい)より青(あお)し
AI YORI AOSHI
文月晃
By Kou Fumizuki

Translators - Alethea Nibley, Athena Nibley
English Adaptation - Jamie Rich
Copy Editor - Carol Fox
Retouch and Lettering - John Lange
Cover Layout - Gary Shum
Graphic Designer - Deron Bennett

Editor - Jake Forbes
Managing Editor - Jill Freshney
Production Coordinator - Antonio DePietro
Production Managers - Jennifer Miller, Mutsumi Miyazaki
Art Director - Matt Alford
Editorial Director - Jeremy Ross
VP of Production - Ron Klamert
President & C.O.O. - John Parker
Publisher & C.E.O. - Stuart Levy

Email: editor@TOKYOPOP.com
Come visit us online at www.TOKYOPOP.com

A TOKYOPOP® Manga

TOKYOPOP Inc.
5900 Wilshire Blvd. Suite 2000
Los Angeles, CA 90036

Ai Yori Aoshi Vol. 2

ISBN: 1-59182-646-2

First TOKYOPOP printing: March 2004

10 9 8 7 6 5 4 3 2 1

Printed in the USA

藍より青し

AI YORI AOSHI™

VOLUME 2

STORY & ART
BY
KOU FUMIZUKI

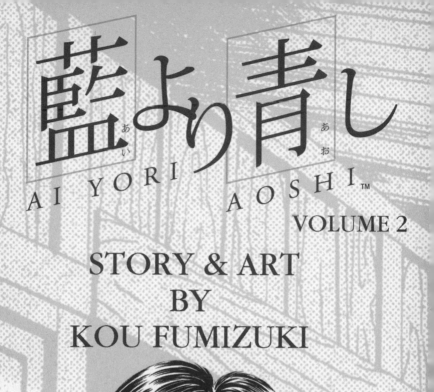

藍より青し

<ruby>藍<rt>あい</rt></ruby>より<ruby>青<rt>あお</rt></ruby>し

AI YORI AOSHI ™

CONTENTS

藍(あい)より青(あお)し

AI YORI AOSHI

CHAPTER 11 DOUSEI COHABITATION

第十一話 同棲—どうせい—

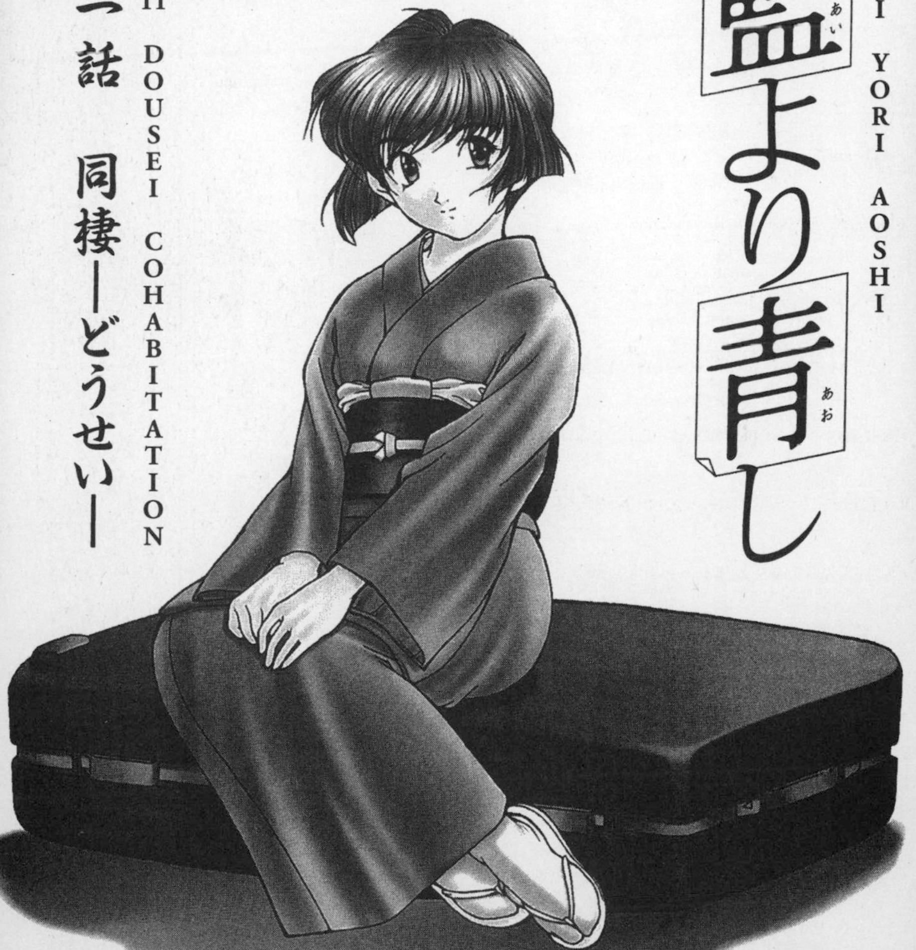

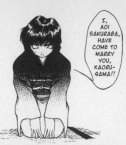

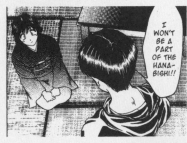

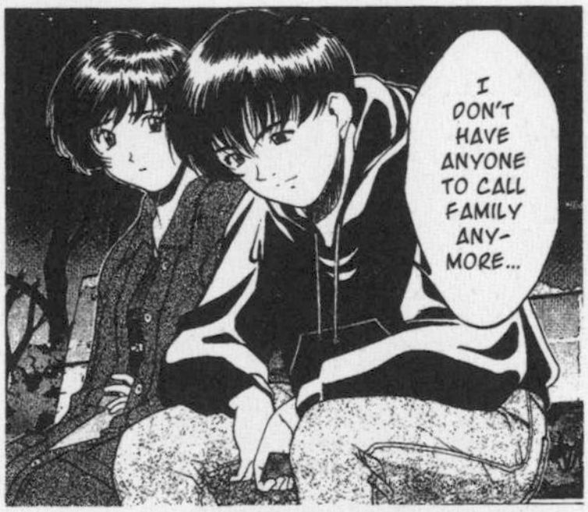

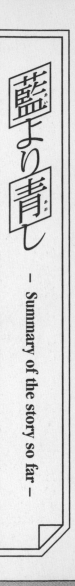

藍より青し

- Summary of the story so far -

I, AOI SAKURABA, HAVE COME TO MARRY YOU, KAORU-SAMA!!

On his way home from school one day, Kaoru Hanabishi, a sophomore in college, spotted a girl wearing traditional Japanese clothing. She seemed lost, and Kaoru asked if she needed help. In doing so, he discovered that she was looking for someone and had to go to the same station to which he was heading, and they ended up searching for her friend together. However, the address she had written down turned out to be nothing but an empty lot. When Kaoru asked the discouraged young woman if she had any other clues to find this missing person, she handed him a photograph. The two children in the picture were younger versions of the girl and Kaoru himself. Then she, Aoi Sakuraba, told him something rather surprising.

I WON'T BE A PART OF THE HANA-BISHI!!

The eighteen years of Aoi Sakuraba's life had been devoted to preparing her for an adulthood as Kaoru's bride. But because Kaoru had been disowned by the Hanabishi family, the engagement was broken off. Aoi wanted to speak with her now ex-betrothed directly and ask him to return to the Hanabishi, so they could be together—and thus her current trip was born. Though impressed by Aoi's devotion, Kaoru had his reasons for being unable to return to his family.

I DON'T HAVE ANYONE TO CALL FAMILY ANY-MORE...

Kaoru's father was the heir to the Hanabishi Zaibatsu, but he was never married to Kaoru's mother. And when Kaoru was five years old, his father died. The family, concerned about how they would raise their heir, tore Kaoru from his mother's care and raised him themselves; unfortunately, Kaoru was unable to endure that harsh environment and ran away from home. As a result, no matter how much Aoi longed for him to return, he could never go back.

MOTHER...

Now knowing the full story, Aoi hardened her resolve to leave Kaoru behind. This was easier said then done, and ultimately she left the Sakuraba family to return to her formerly intended husband. After the couple spent one night together, Aoi's mother and Aoi's caretaker, Miyabi Kagurazaki, came to get her, but she convinced them to let her stay and the pair of childhood friends were finally allowed to be together.

Cast

Aoi Sakuraba

Kaoru Hanabishi

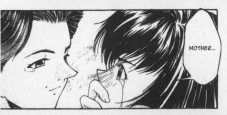

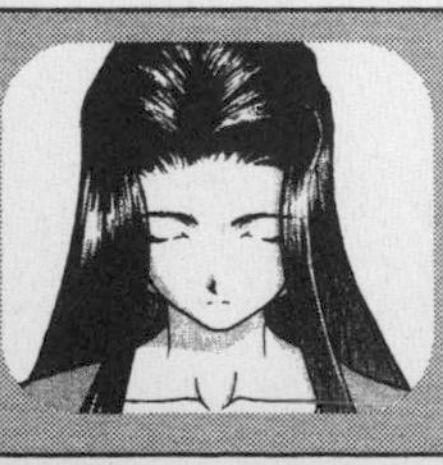

Miyabi Kagurazaki

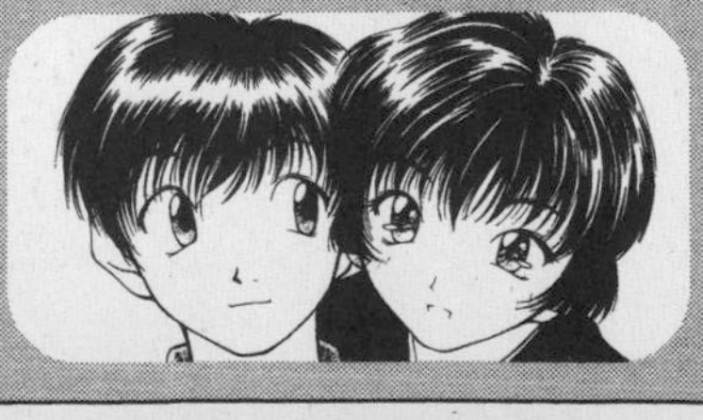

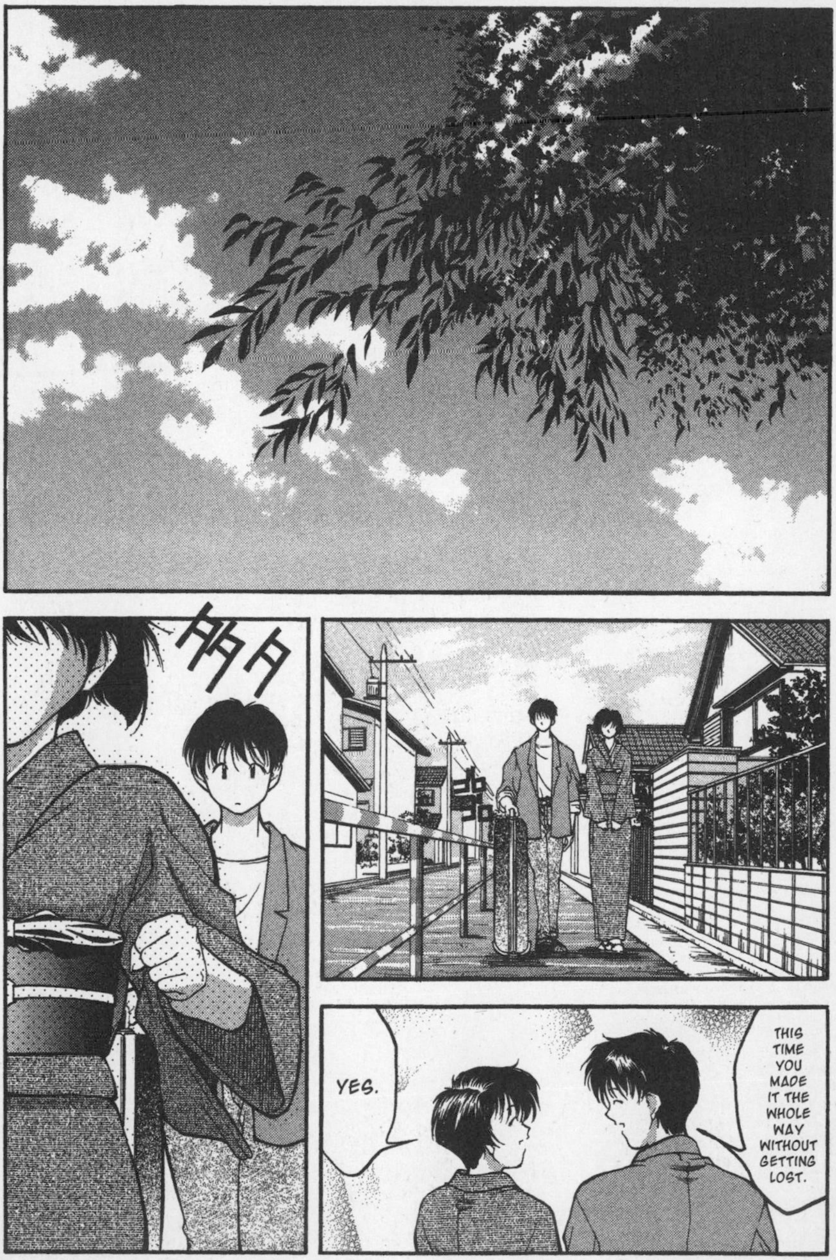
THIS TIME YOU MADE IT THE WHOLE WAY WITHOUT GETTING LOST.
YES.

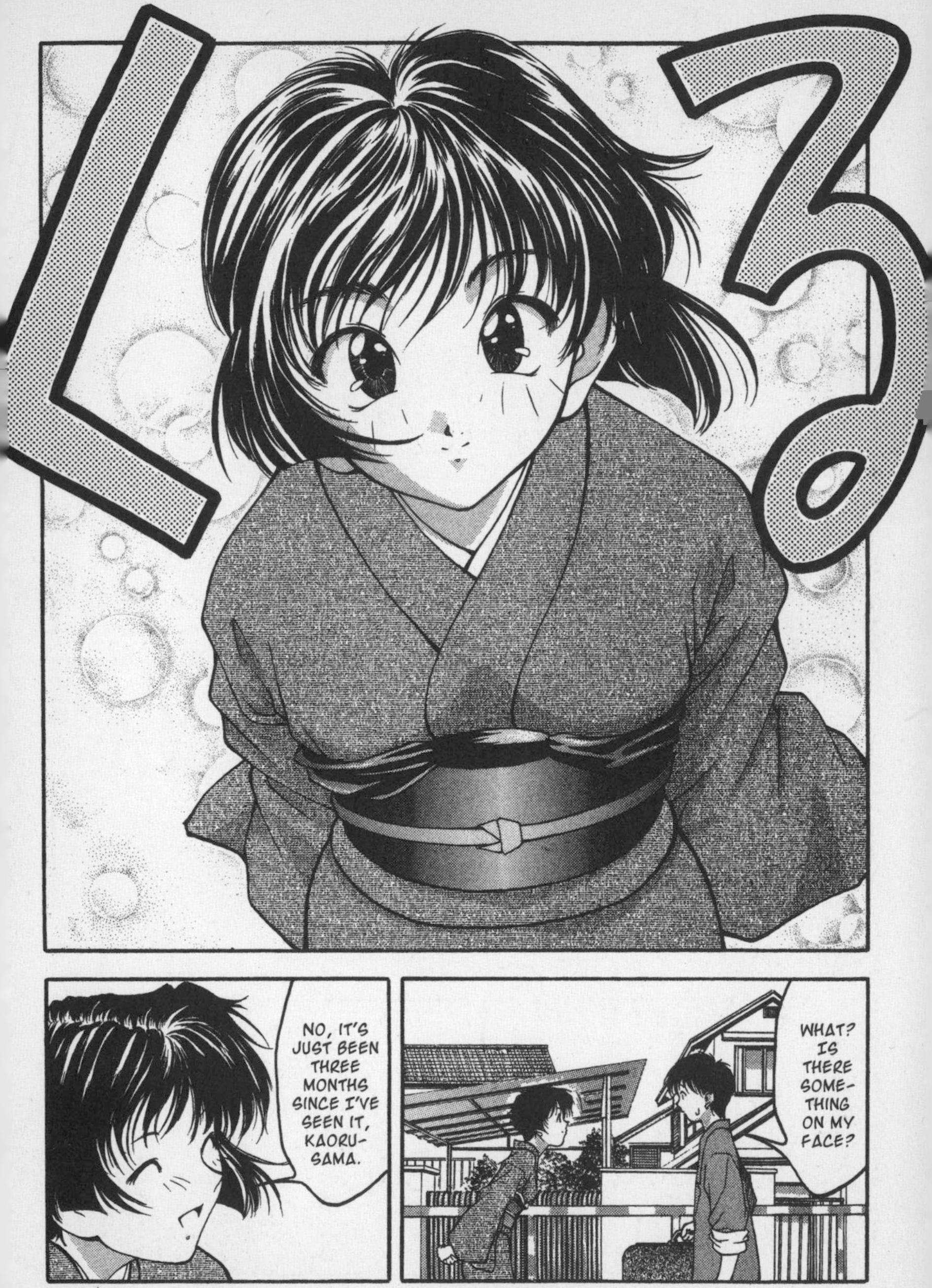
WHAT? IS THERE SOME-THING ON MY FACE?
NO, IT'S JUST BEEN THREE MONTHS SINCE I'VE SEEN IT, KAORU-SAMA.

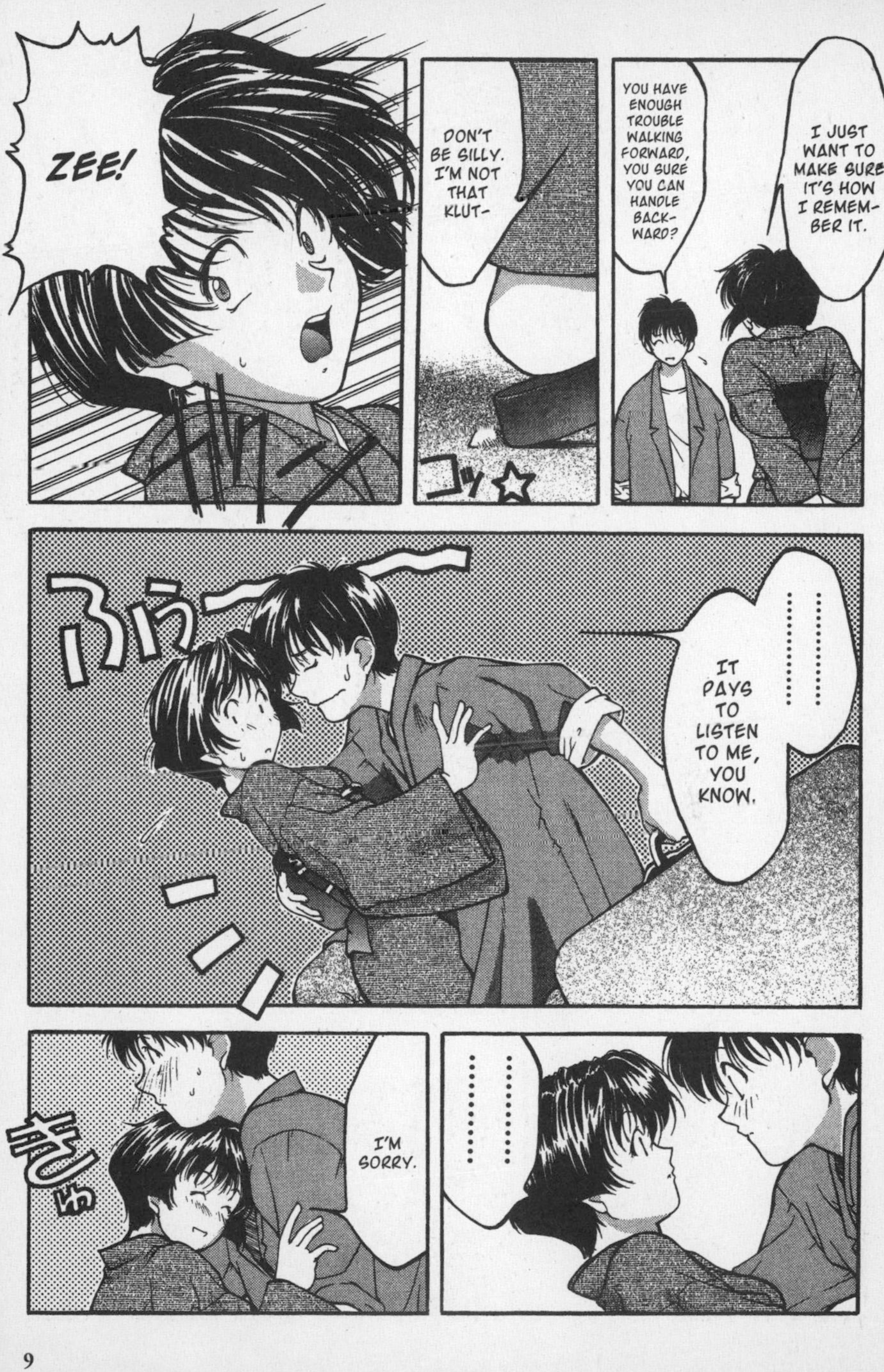
I JUST WANT TO MAKE SURE IT'S HOW I REMEMBER IT.
YOU HAVE ENOUGH TROUBLE WALKING FORWARD, YOU SURE YOU CAN HANDLE BACKWARD?
DON'T BE SILLY. I'M NOT THAT KLUT-
ゴッ☆
ZEE!
......
IT PAYS TO LISTEN TO ME, YOU KNOW.
ふぅーーー
......
I'M SORRY.
きゅ

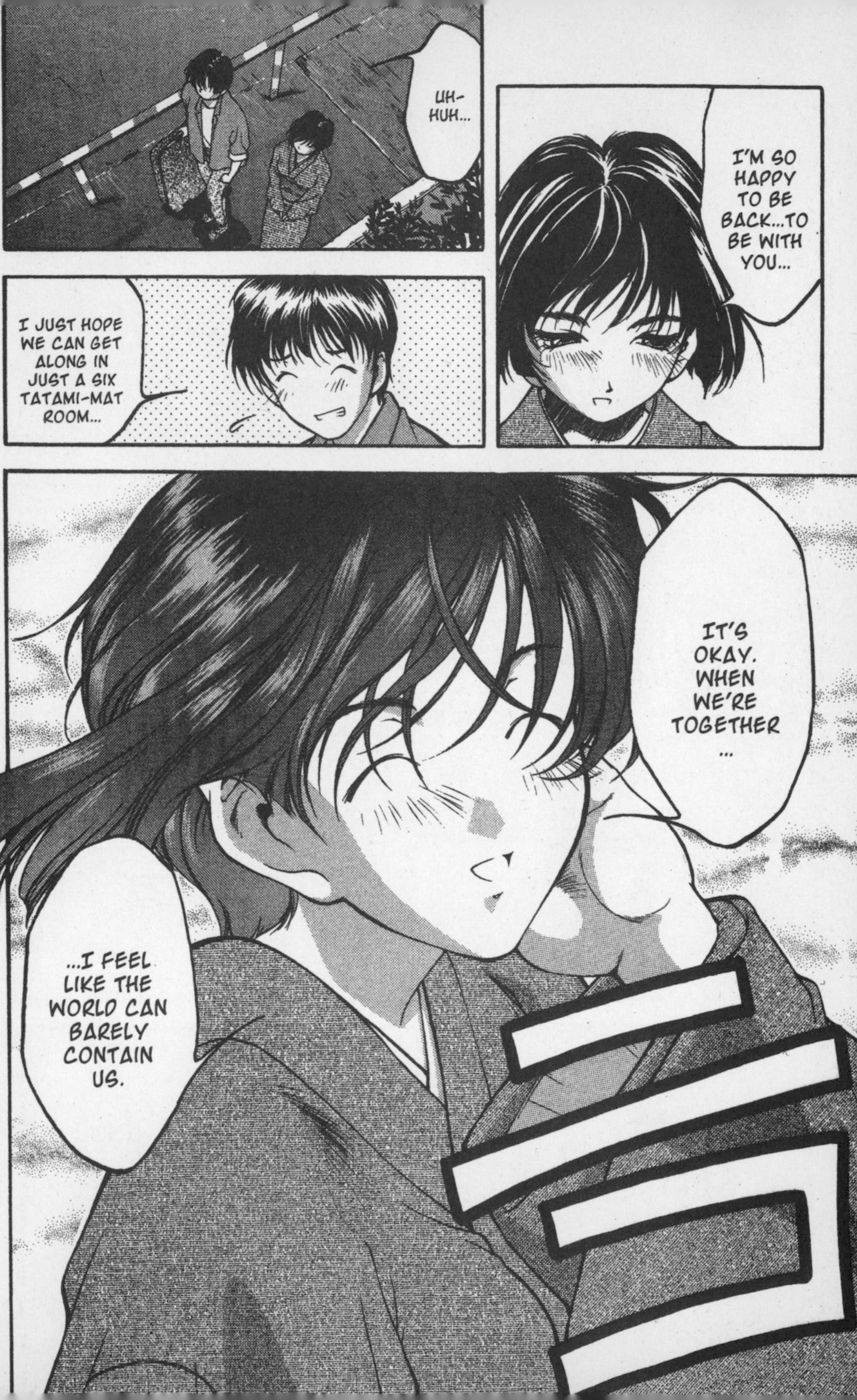
I'M SO HAPPY TO BE BACK...TO BE WITH YOU...
UH-HUH...
I JUST HOPE WE CAN GET ALONG IN JUST A SIX TATAMI-MAT ROOM...
IT'S OKAY. WHEN WE'RE TOGETHER ...
...I FEEL LIKE THE WORLD CAN BARELY CONTAIN US.

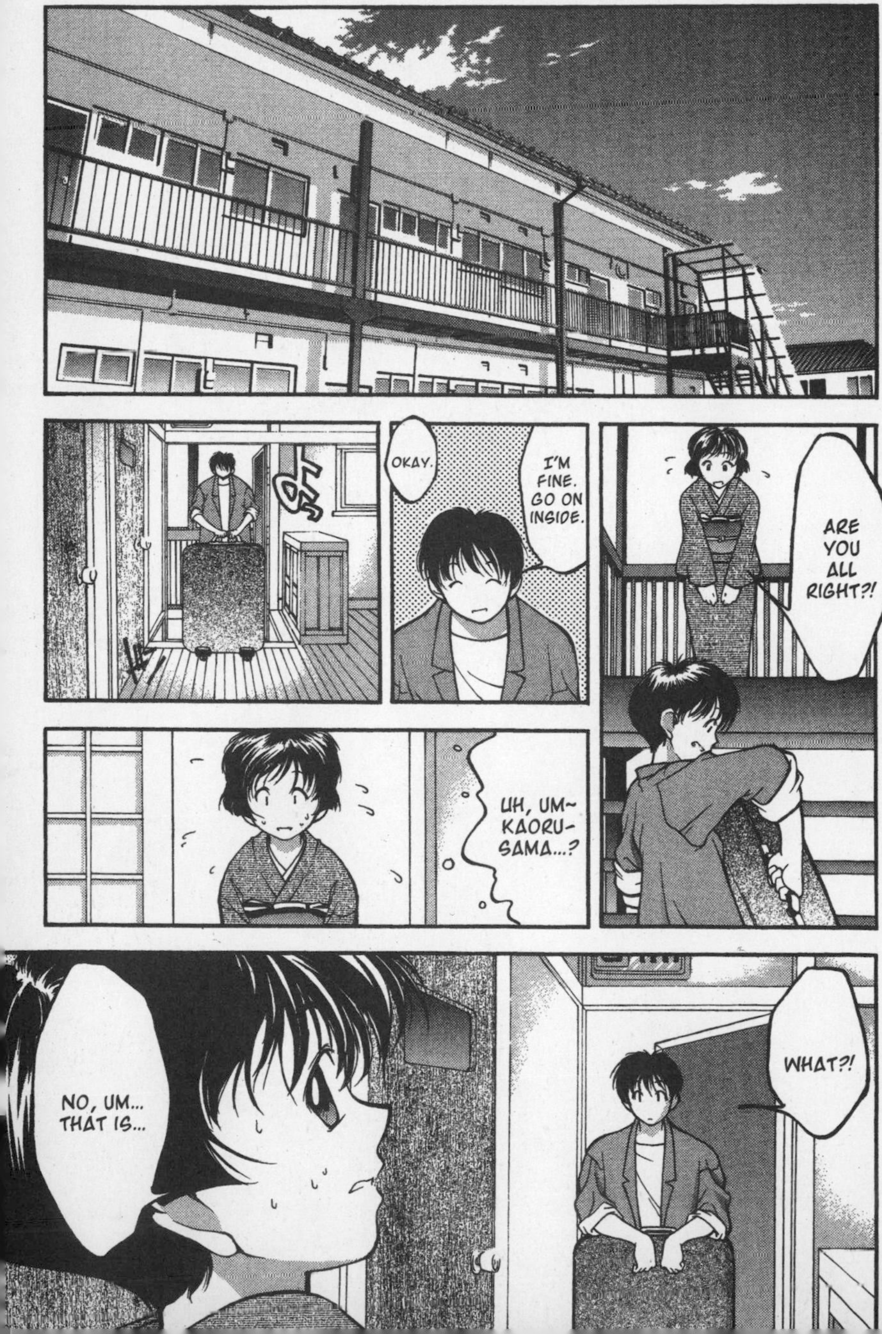
ARE YOU ALL RIGHT?!
I'M FINE. GO ON INSIDE.
OKAY.
UH, UM~ KAORU-SAMA...?
WHAT?!
NO, UM... THAT IS...

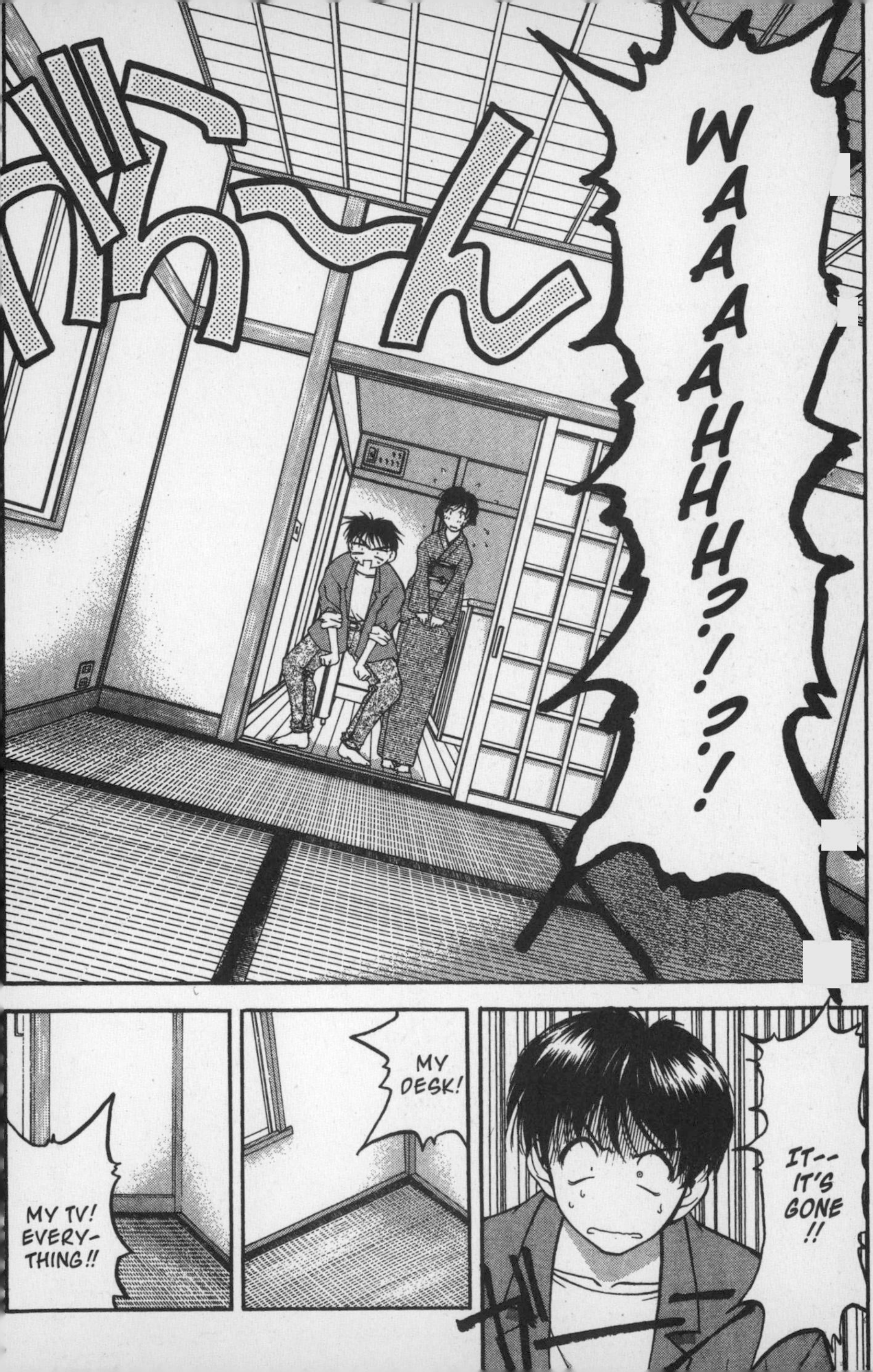
WAAAAHHH?!?!
IT-- IT'S GONE!!
MY DESK!
MY TV! EVERYTHING!!

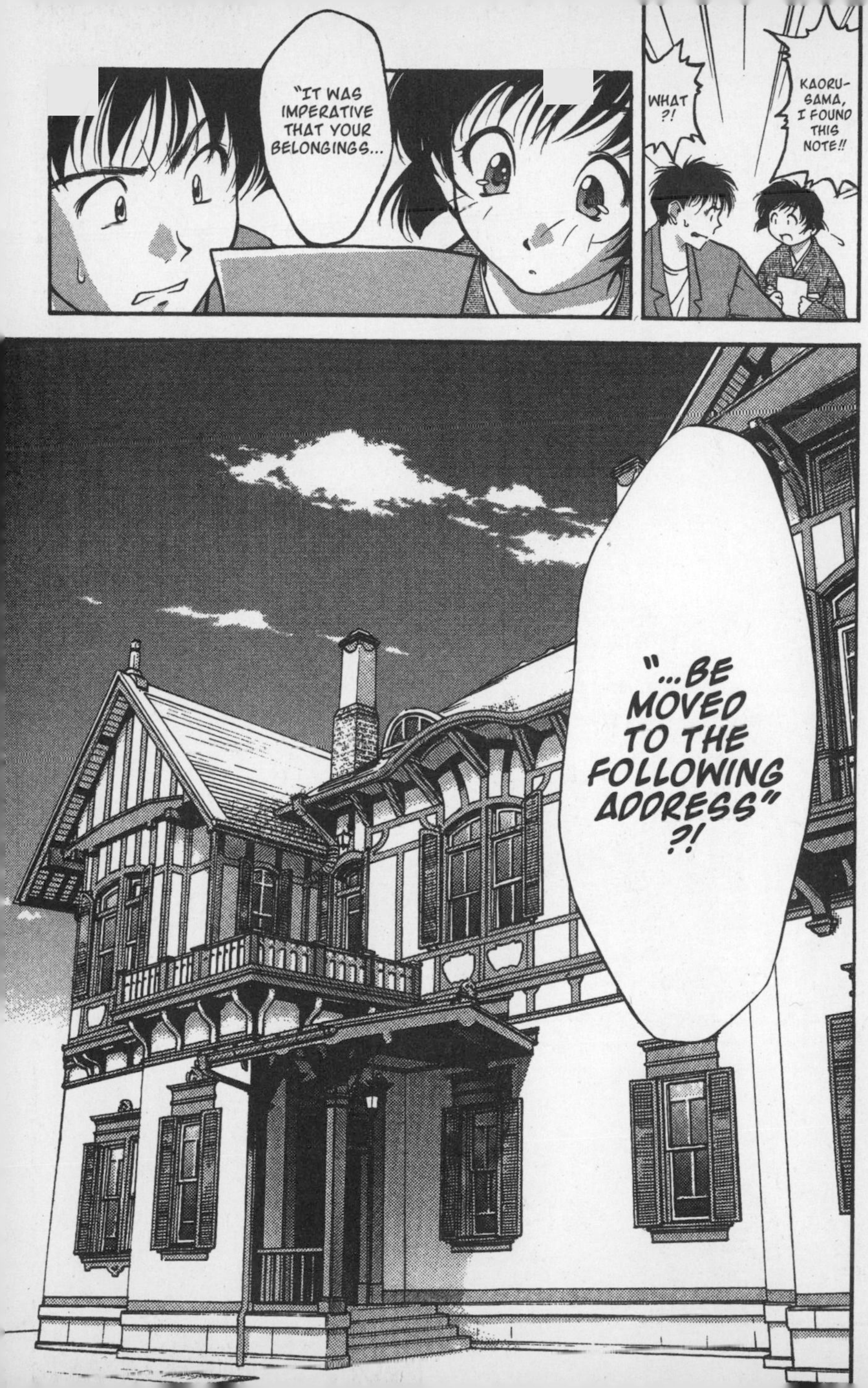
KAORU-SAMA, I FOUND THIS NOTE!!
WHAT ?!
"IT WAS IMPERATIVE THAT YOUR BELONGINGS...
"...BE MOVED TO THE FOLLOWING ADDRESS" ?!

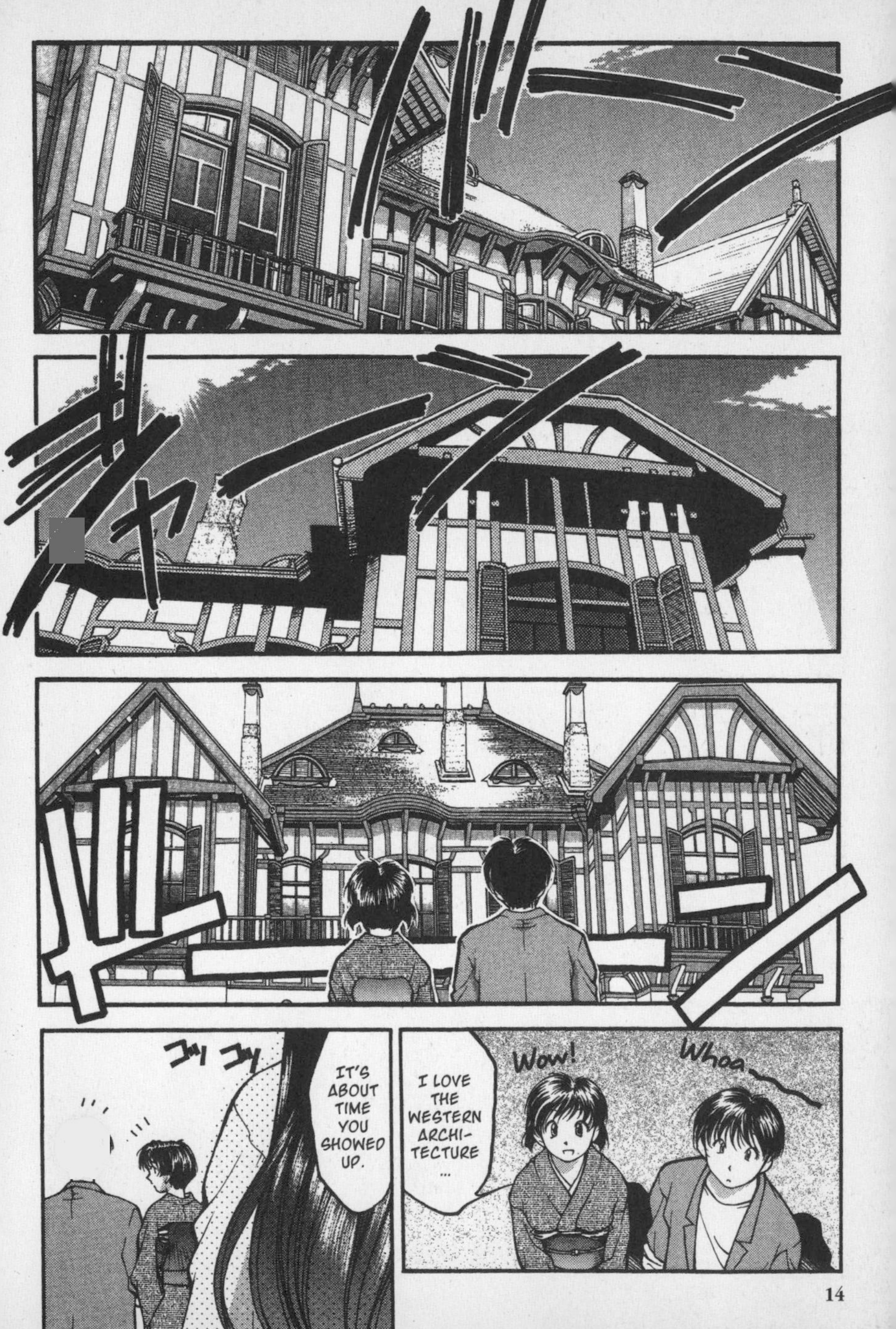
Whoa~
Wow!
I LOVE THE WESTERN ARCHITECTURE...
IT'S ABOUT TIME YOU SHOWED UP.

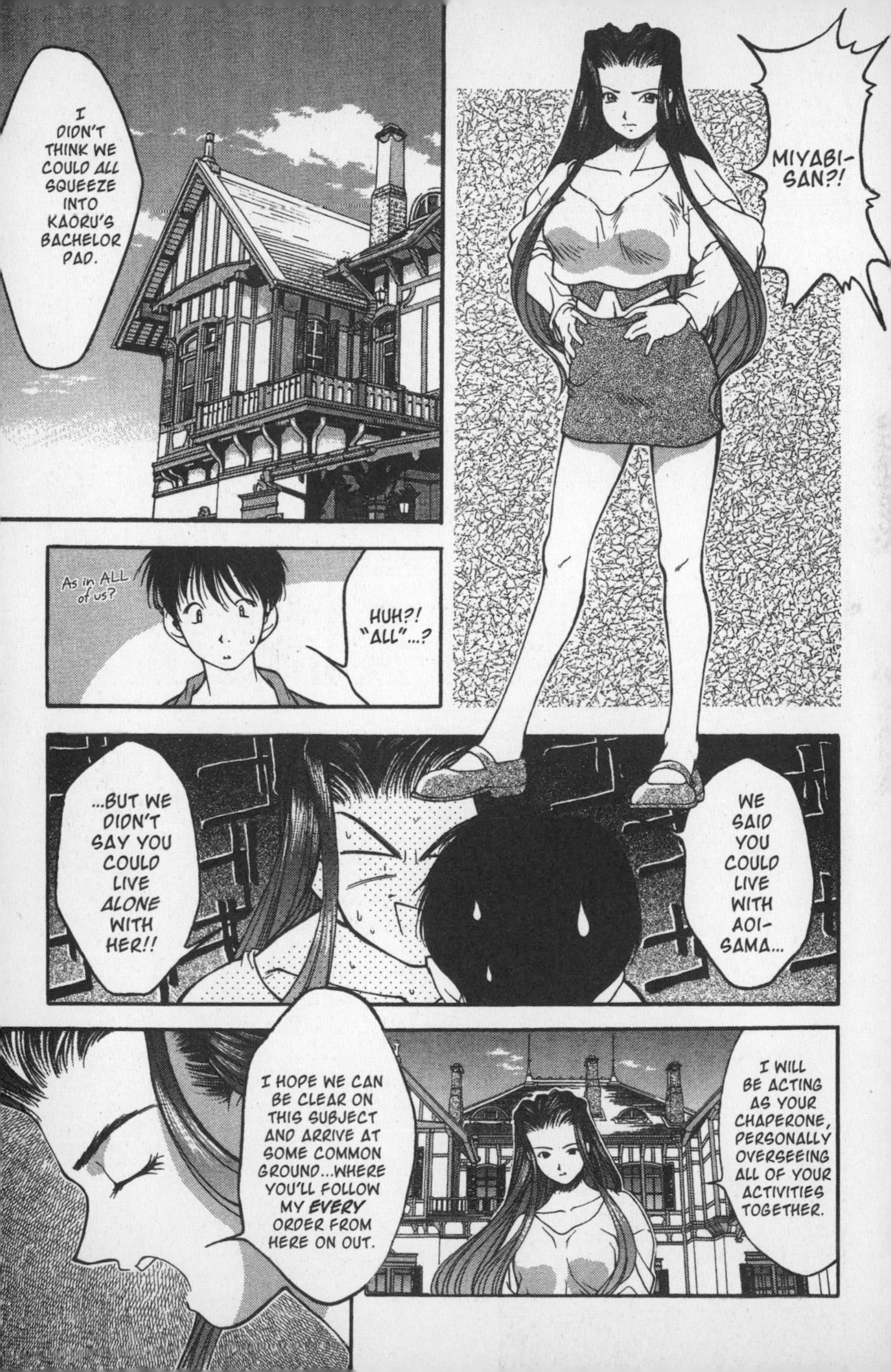
MIYABI-SAN?!
I DIDN'T THINK WE COULD ALL SQUEEZE INTO KAORU'S BACHELOR PAD.
HUH?! "ALL"...?
As in ALL of us?
WE SAID YOU COULD LIVE WITH AOI-SAMA...
...BUT WE DIDN'T SAY YOU COULD LIVE ALONE WITH HER!!
I WILL BE ACTING AS YOUR CHAPERONE, PERSONALLY OVERSEEING ALL OF YOUR ACTIVITIES TOGETHER.
I HOPE WE CAN BE CLEAR ON THIS SUBJECT AND ARRIVE AT SOME COMMON GROUND...WHERE YOU'LL FOLLOW MY *EVERY* ORDER FROM HERE ON OUT.

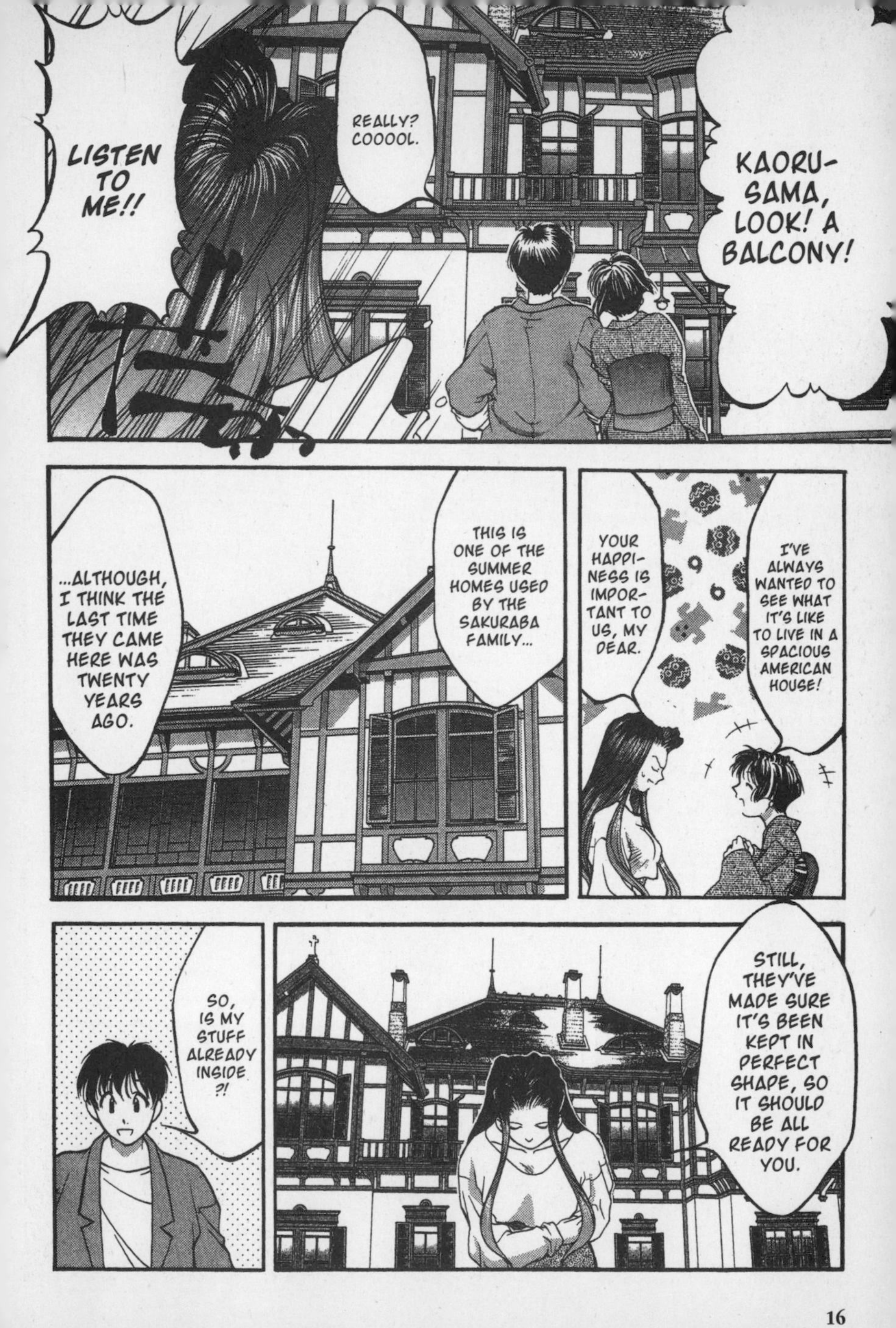
KAORU-SAMA, LOOK! A BALCONY!
REALLY? COOOOL.
LISTEN TO ME!!
I'VE ALWAYS WANTED TO SEE WHAT IT'S LIKE TO LIVE IN A SPACIOUS AMERICAN HOUSE!
YOUR HAPPINESS IS IMPORTANT TO US, MY DEAR.
THIS IS ONE OF THE SUMMER HOMES USED BY THE SAKURABA FAMILY...
...ALTHOUGH, I THINK THE LAST TIME THEY CAME HERE WAS TWENTY YEARS AGO.
STILL, THEY'VE MADE SURE IT'S BEEN KEPT IN PERFECT SHAPE, SO IT SHOULD BE ALL READY FOR YOU.
SO, IS MY STUFF ALREADY INSIDE ?!

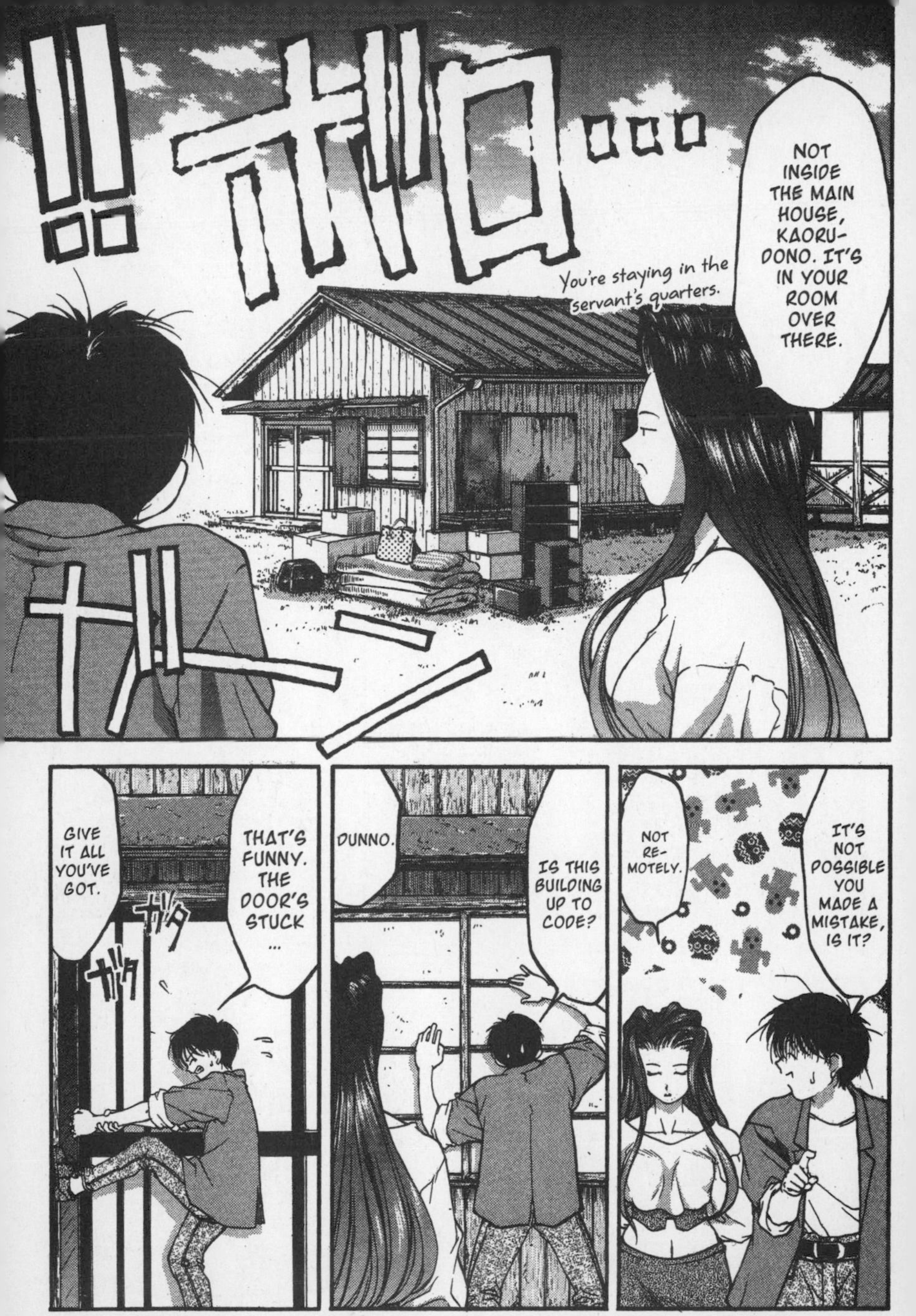

!!
ボロ...
NOT INSIDE THE MAIN HOUSE, KAORU-DONO. IT'S IN YOUR ROOM OVER THERE.
You're staying in the servant's quarters.
IT'S NOT POSSIBLE YOU MADE A MISTAKE, IS IT?
NOT RE-MOTELY.
IS THIS BUILDING UP TO CODE?
DUNNO.
THAT'S FUNNY. THE DOOR'S STUCK ...
GIVE IT ALL YOU'VE GOT.
ガタ
ガタ

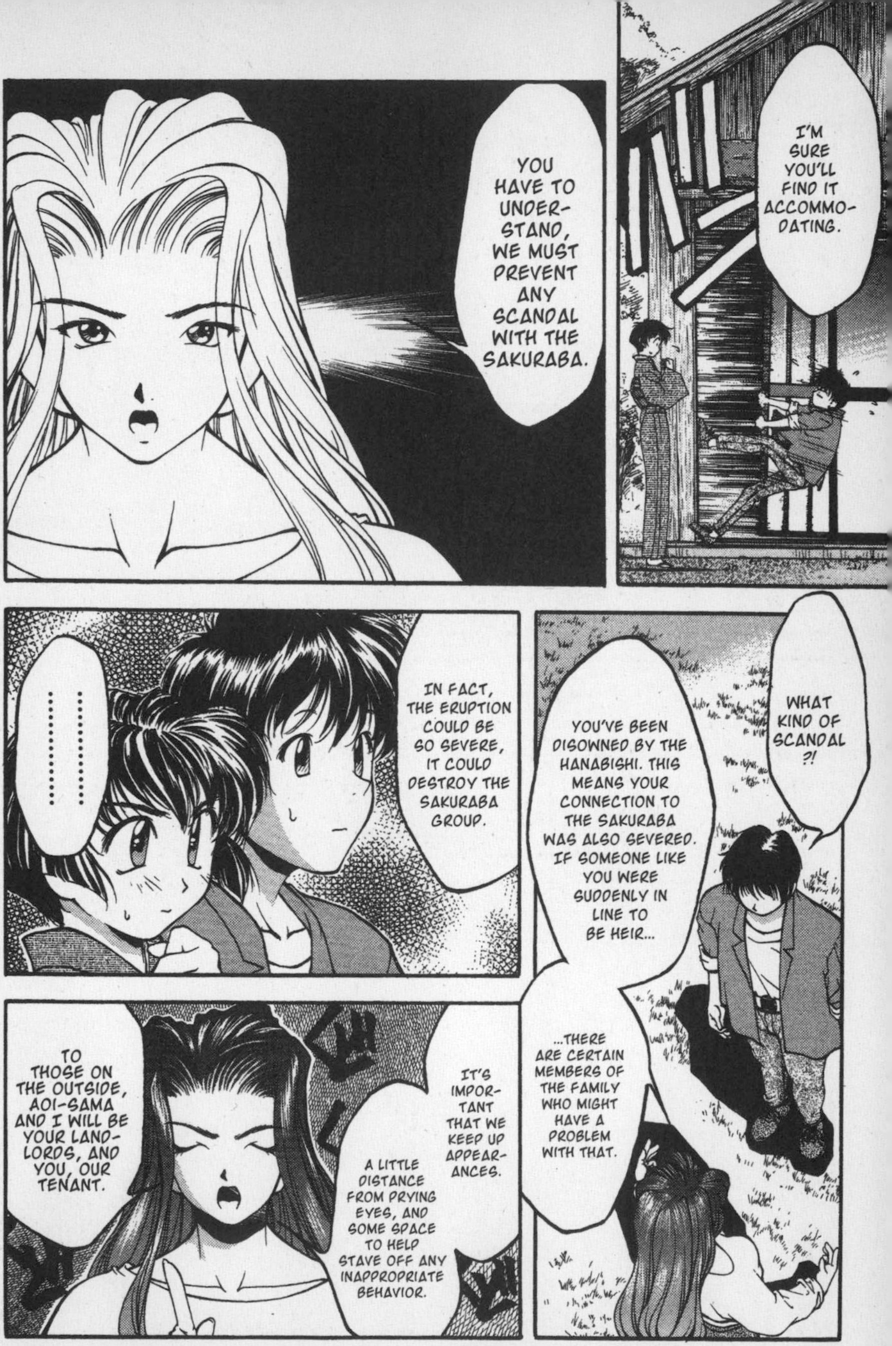
I'M SURE YOU'LL FIND IT ACCOMMODATING.
YOU HAVE TO UNDERSTAND, WE MUST PREVENT ANY SCANDAL WITH THE SAKURABA.
WHAT KIND OF SCANDAL ?!
YOU'VE BEEN DISOWNED BY THE HANABISHI. THIS MEANS YOUR CONNECTION TO THE SAKURABA WAS ALSO SEVERED. IF SOMEONE LIKE YOU WERE SUDDENLY IN LINE TO BE HEIR...
...THERE ARE CERTAIN MEMBERS OF THE FAMILY WHO MIGHT HAVE A PROBLEM WITH THAT.
IN FACT, THE ERUPTION COULD BE SO SEVERE, IT COULD DESTROY THE SAKURABA GROUP.
......
IT'S IMPORTANT THAT WE KEEP UP APPEARANCES.
TO THOSE ON THE OUTSIDE, AOI-SAMA AND I WILL BE YOUR LANDLORDS, AND YOU, OUR TENANT.
A LITTLE DISTANCE FROM PRYING EYES, AND SOME SPACE TO HELP STAVE OFF ANY INAPPROPRIATE BEHAVIOR.

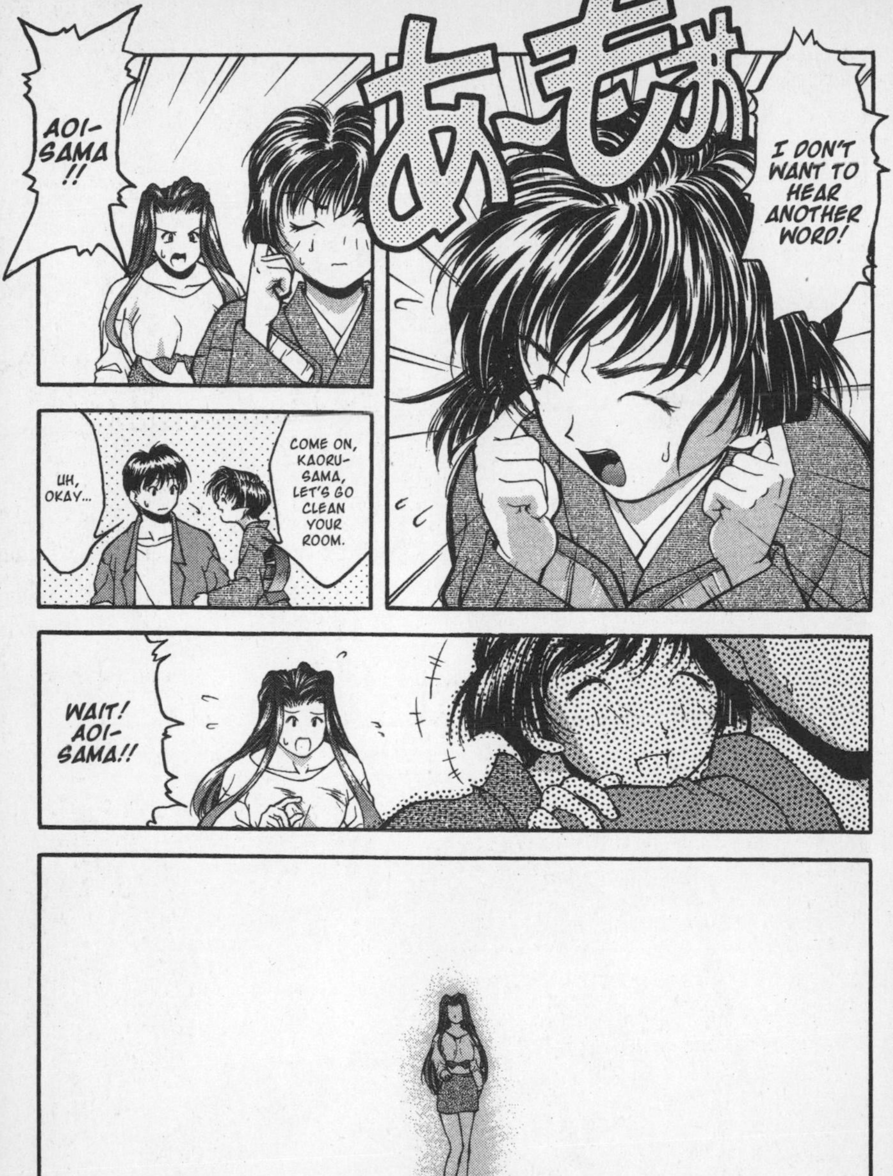
あーもぉ
I DON'T WANT TO HEAR ANOTHER WORD!
AOI-SAMA!!
COME ON, KAORU-SAMA, LET'S GO CLEAN YOUR ROOM.
UH, OKAY...
WAIT! AOI-SAMA!!

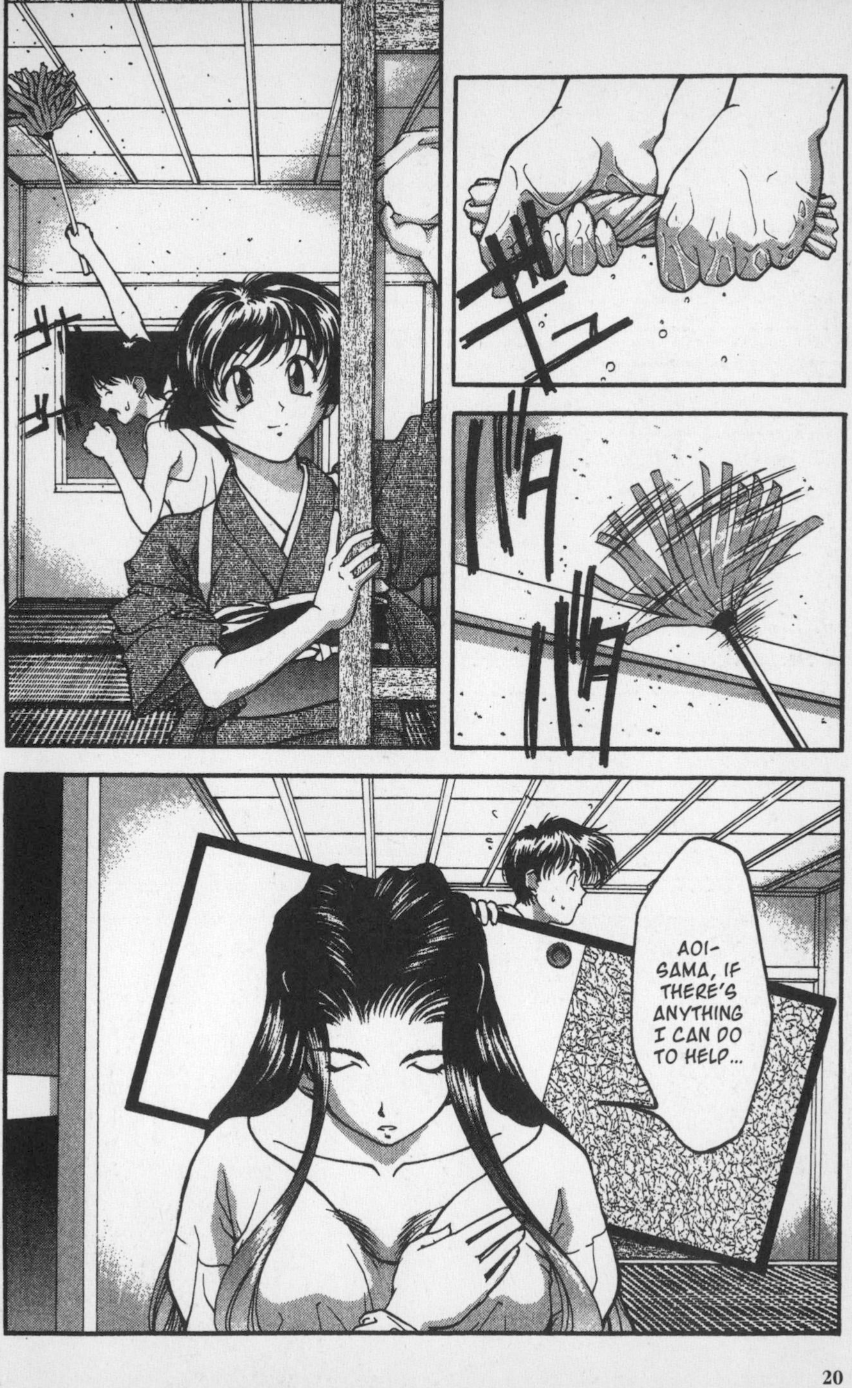
AOI-SAMA, IF THERE'S ANYTHING I CAN DO TO HELP...

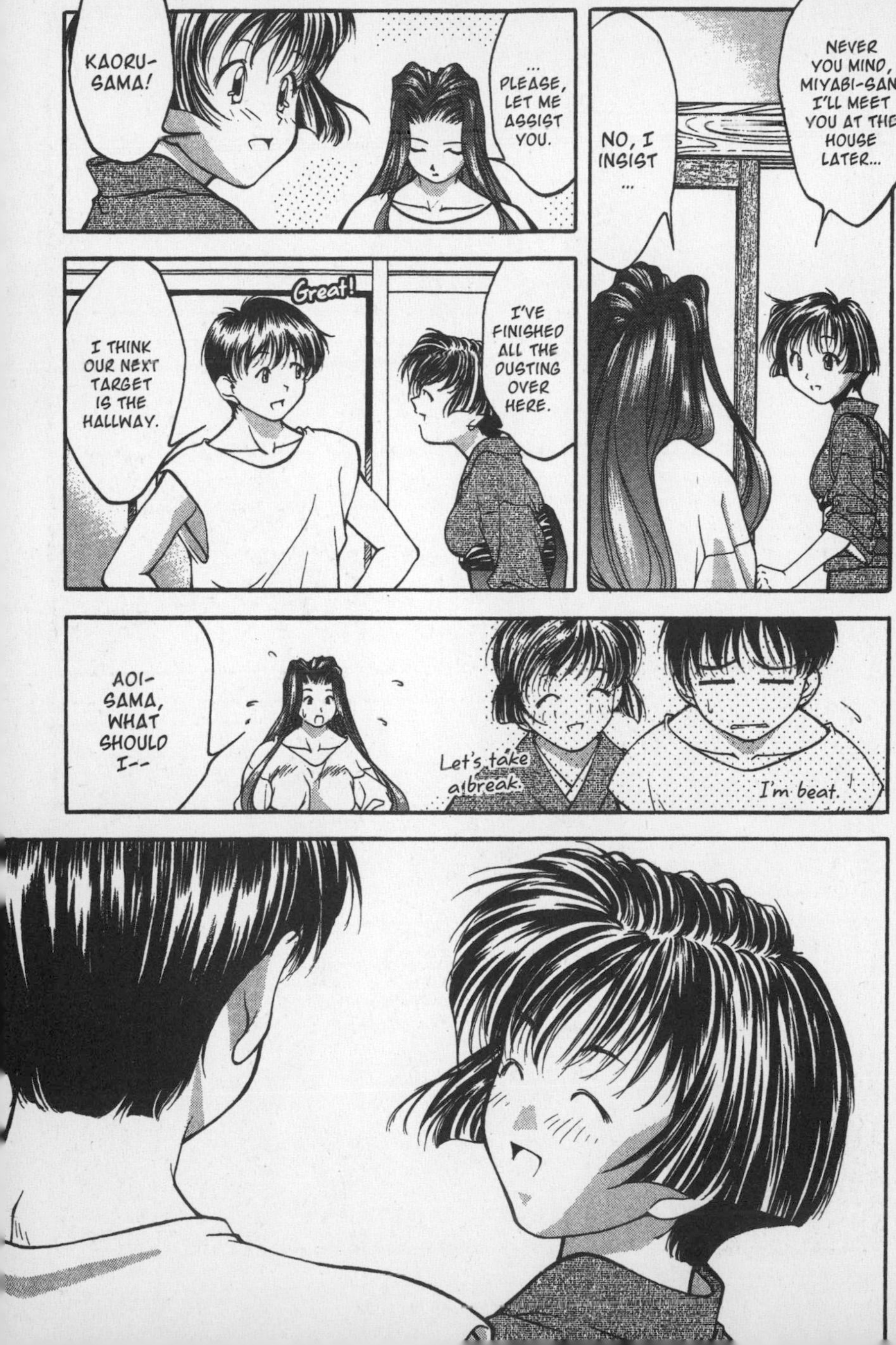
NEVER YOU MIND, MIYABI-SAN. I'LL MEET YOU AT THE HOUSE LATER...
NO, I INSIST ...
... PLEASE, LET ME ASSIST YOU.
KAORU-SAMA!
I'VE FINISHED ALL THE DUSTING OVER HERE.
Great!
I THINK OUR NEXT TARGET IS THE HALLWAY.
I'm beat.
Let's take a break.
AOI-SAMA, WHAT SHOULD I--

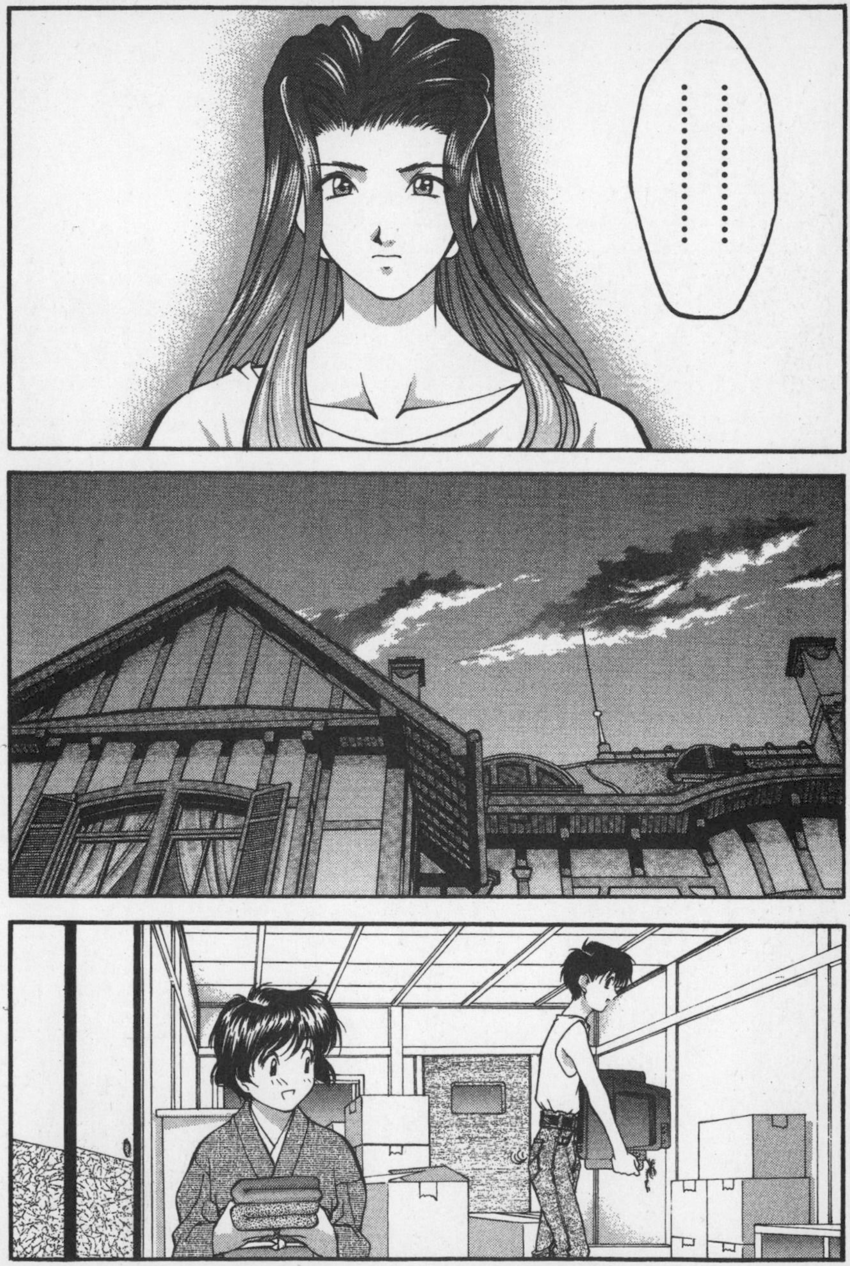
……

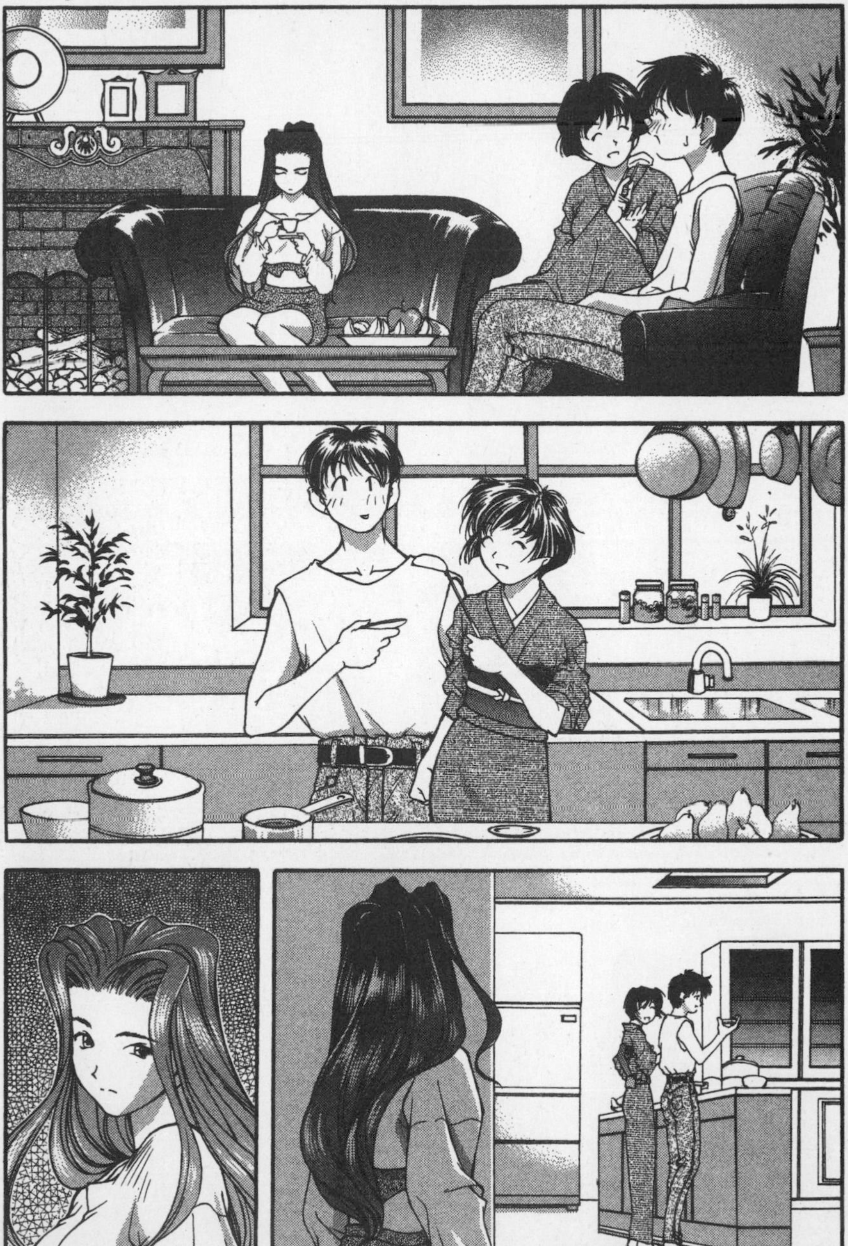

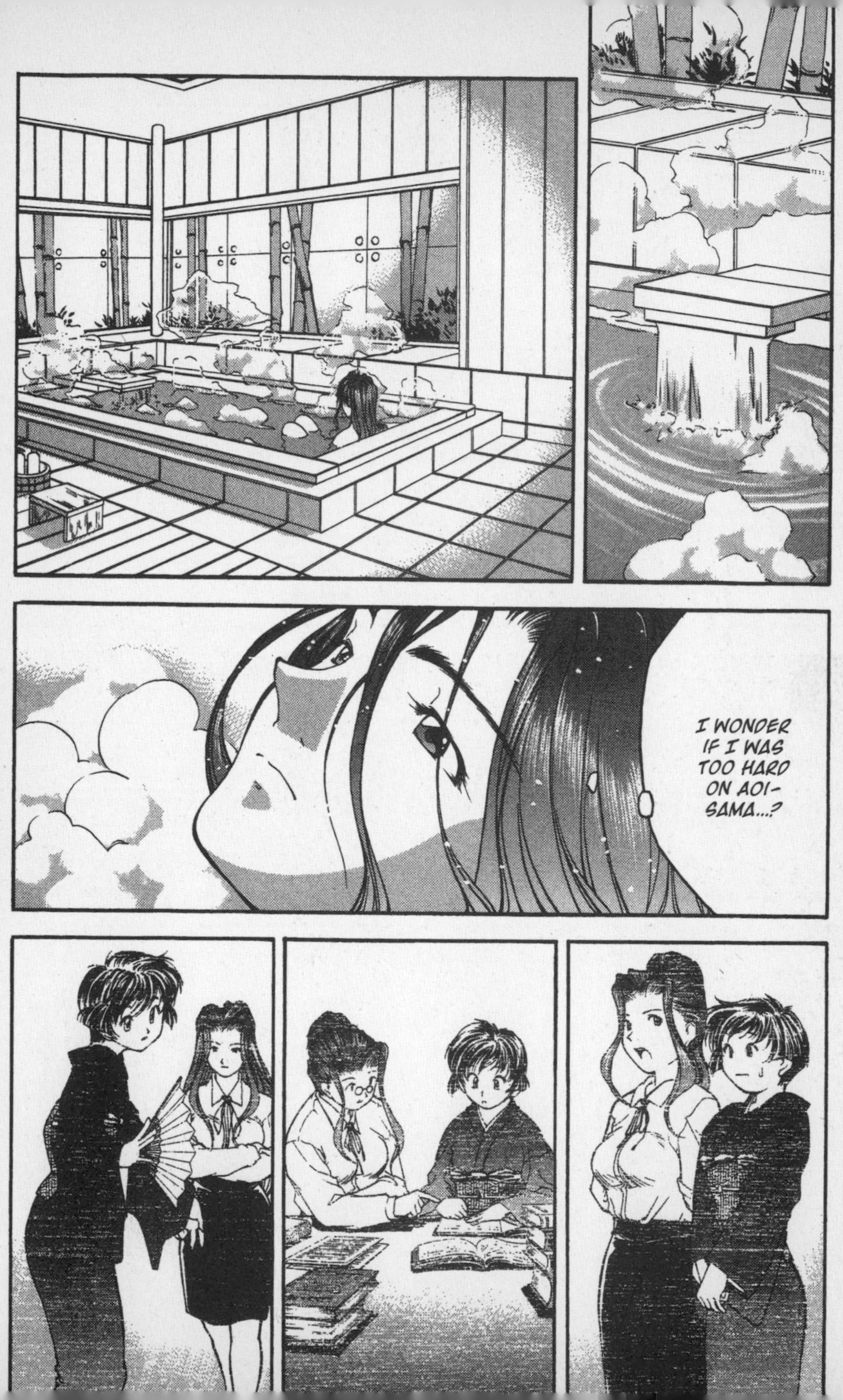
I WONDER IF I WAS TOO HARD ON AOI-SAMA...?

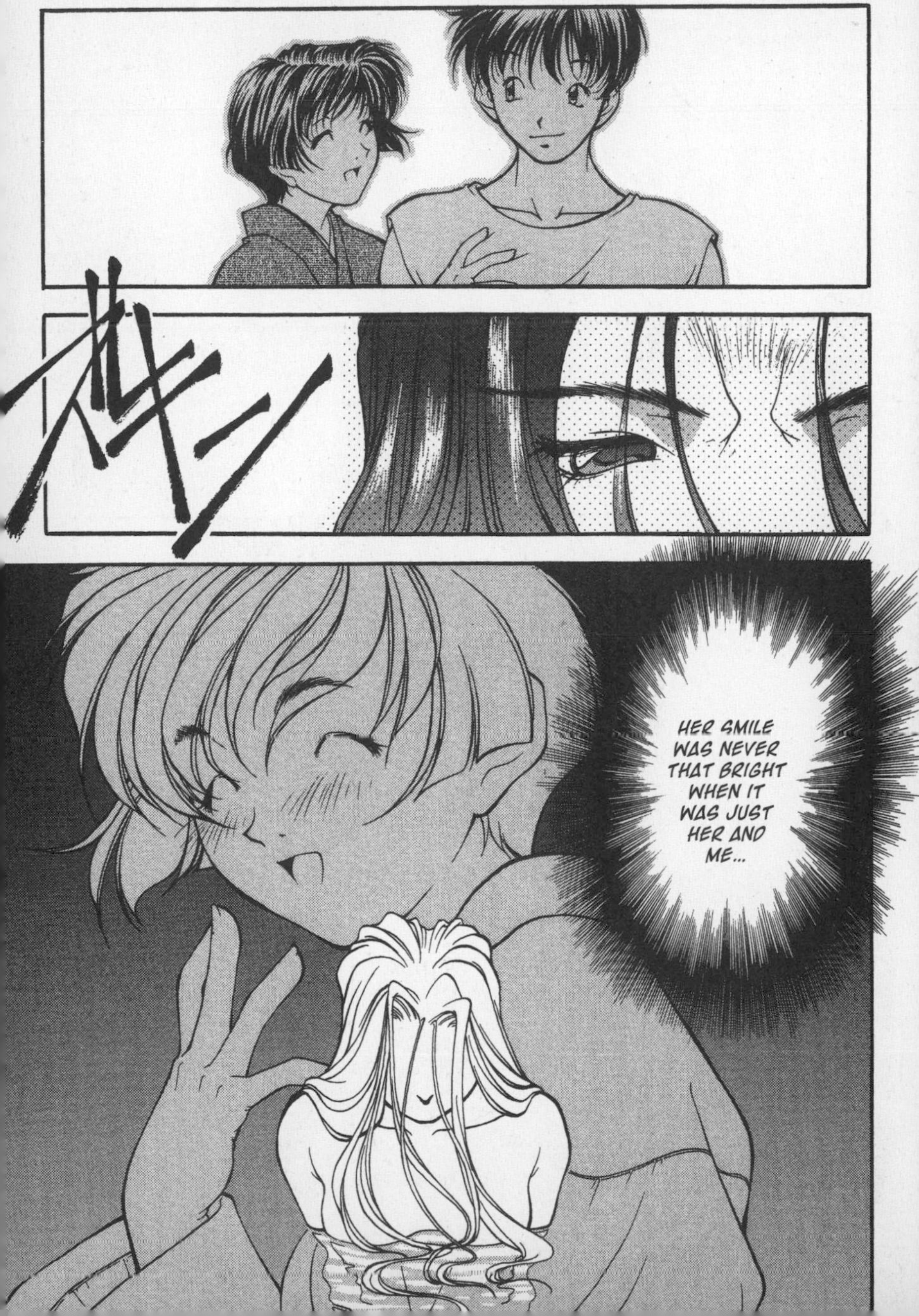
HER SMILE WAS NEVER THAT BRIGHT WHEN IT WAS JUST HER AND ME...

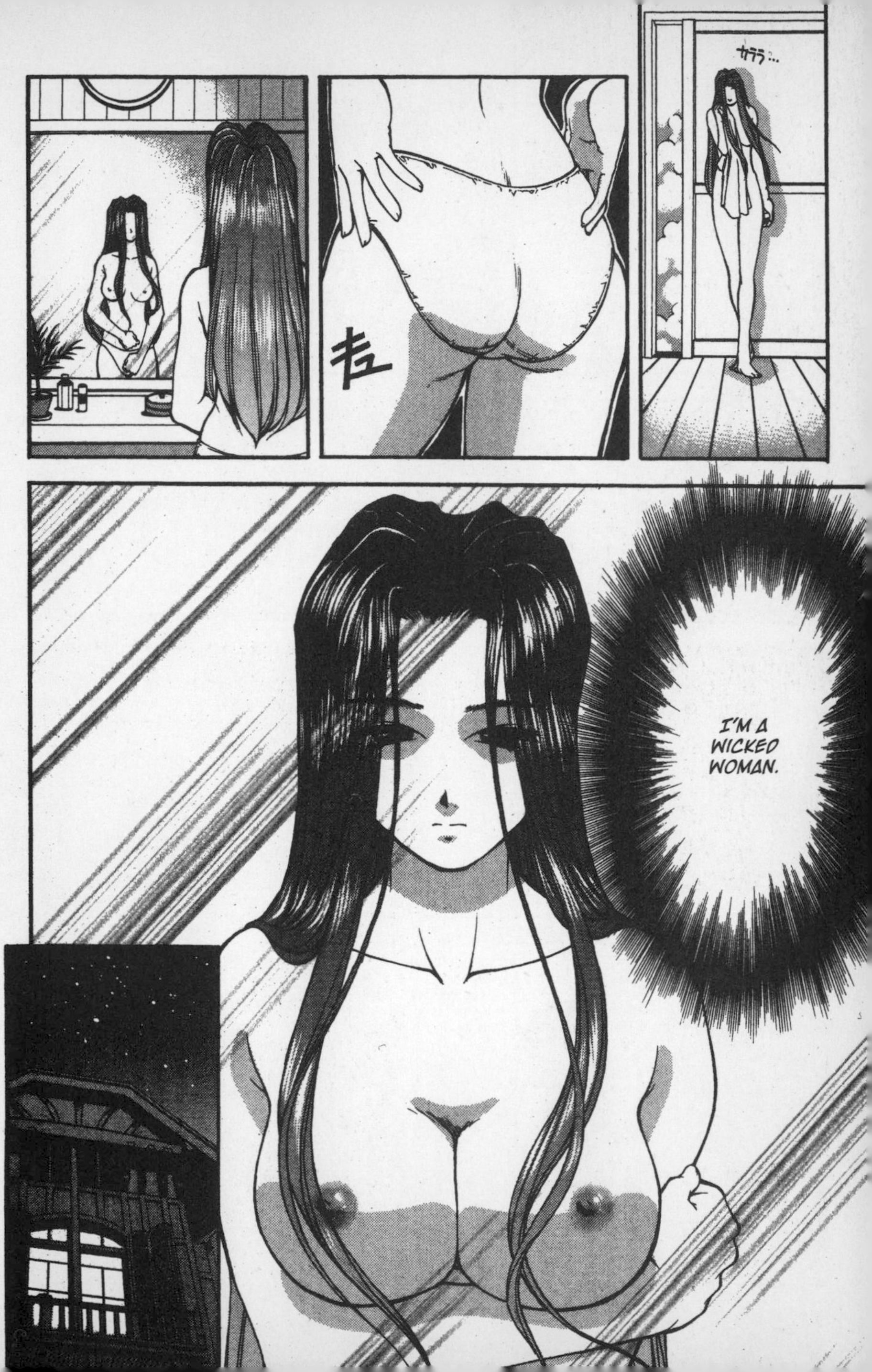
カララ…
I'M A WICKED WOMAN.

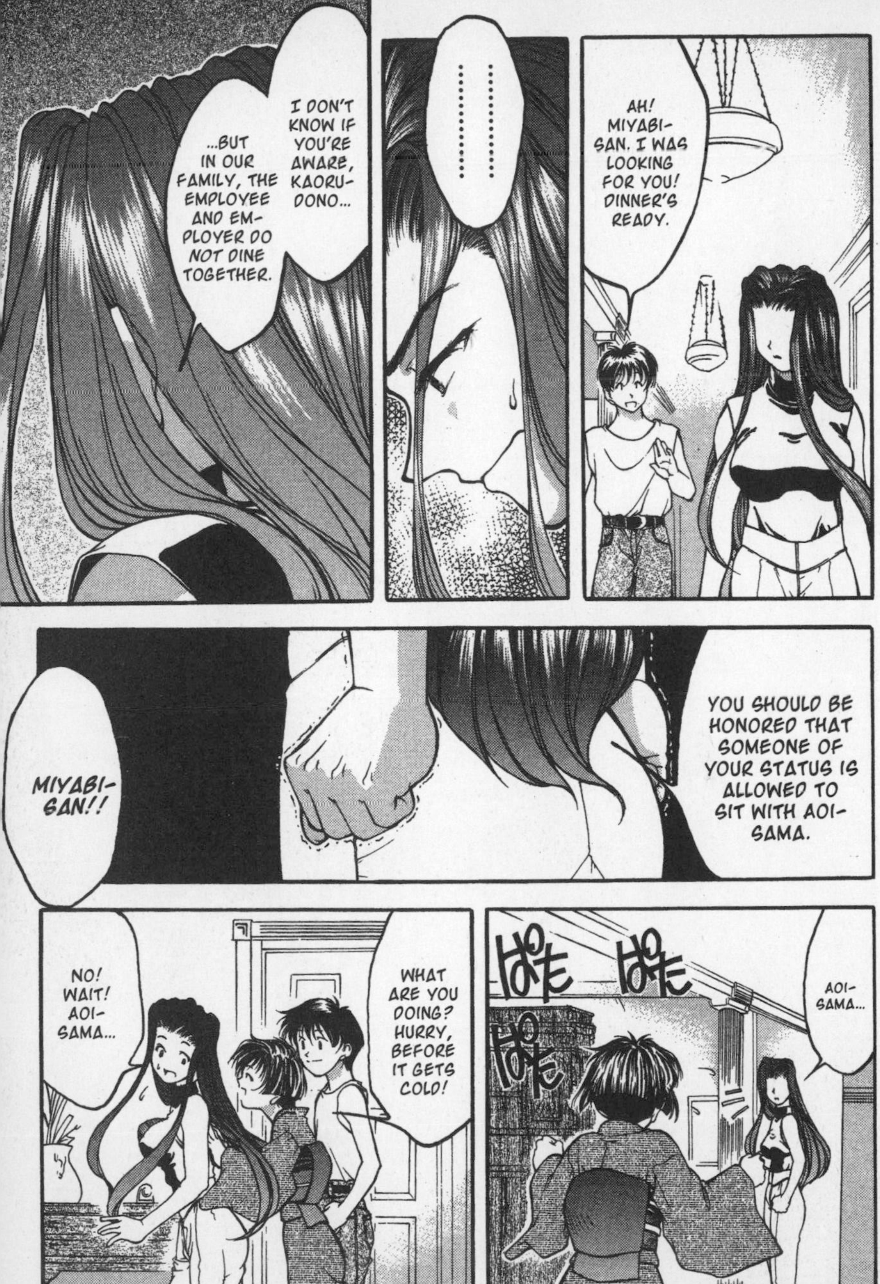
AH! MIYABI-SAN. I WAS LOOKING FOR YOU! DINNER'S READY.
......
I DON'T KNOW IF YOU'RE AWARE, KAORU-DONO...
...BUT IN OUR FAMILY, THE EMPLOYEE AND EMPLOYER DO NOT DINE TOGETHER.
YOU SHOULD BE HONORED THAT SOMEONE OF YOUR STATUS IS ALLOWED TO SIT WITH AOI-SAMA.
MIYABI-SAN!!
AOI-SAMA...
ぱた ぱた
ぱた
WHAT ARE YOU DOING? HURRY, BEFORE IT GETS COLD!
NO! WAIT! AOI-SAMA...

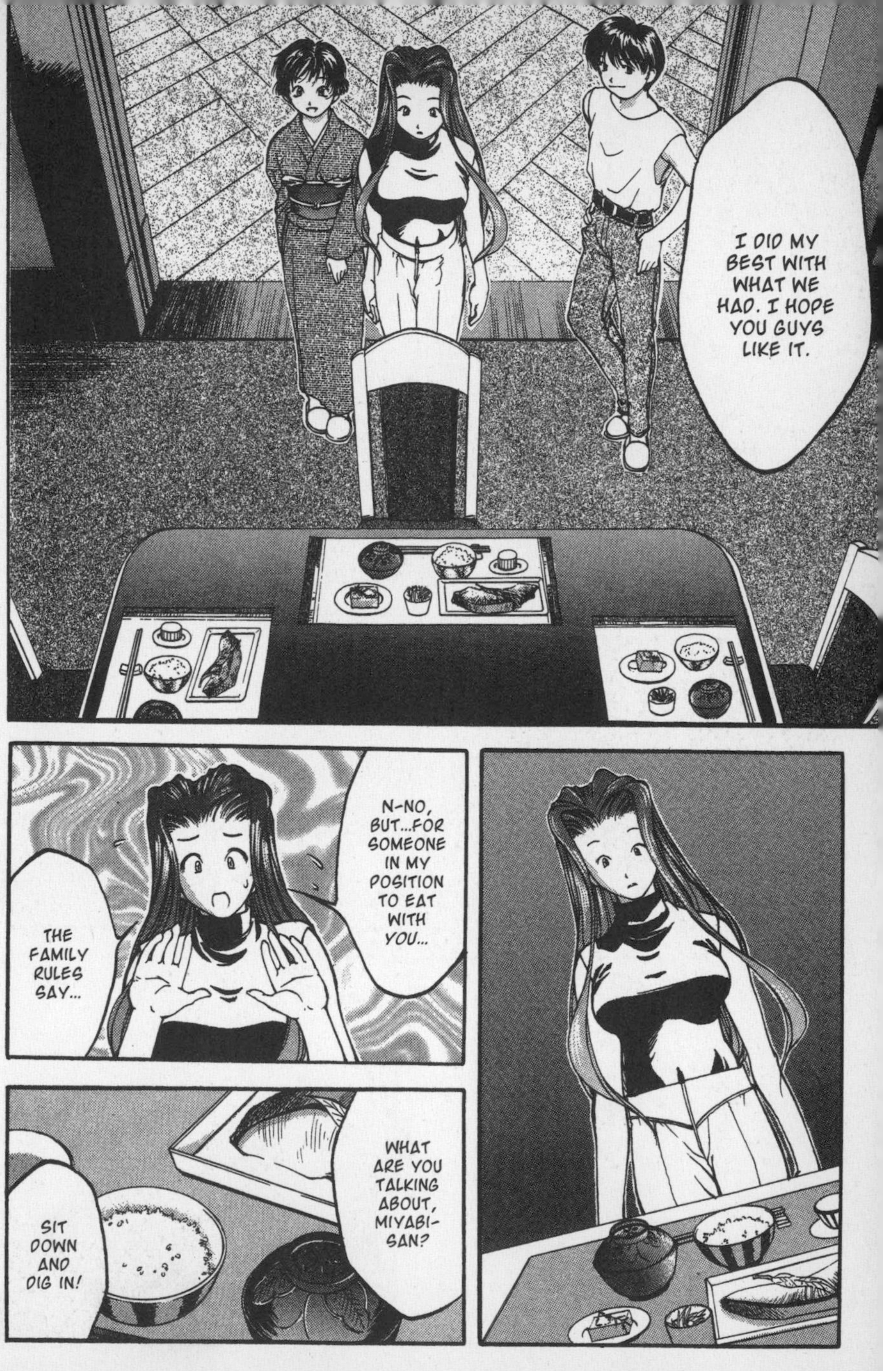
I DID MY BEST WITH WHAT WE HAD. I HOPE YOU GUYS LIKE IT.
N-NO, BUT...FOR SOMEONE IN MY POSITION TO EAT WITH YOU...
THE FAMILY RULES SAY...
WHAT ARE YOU TALKING ABOUT, MIYABI-SAN?
SIT DOWN AND DIG IN!

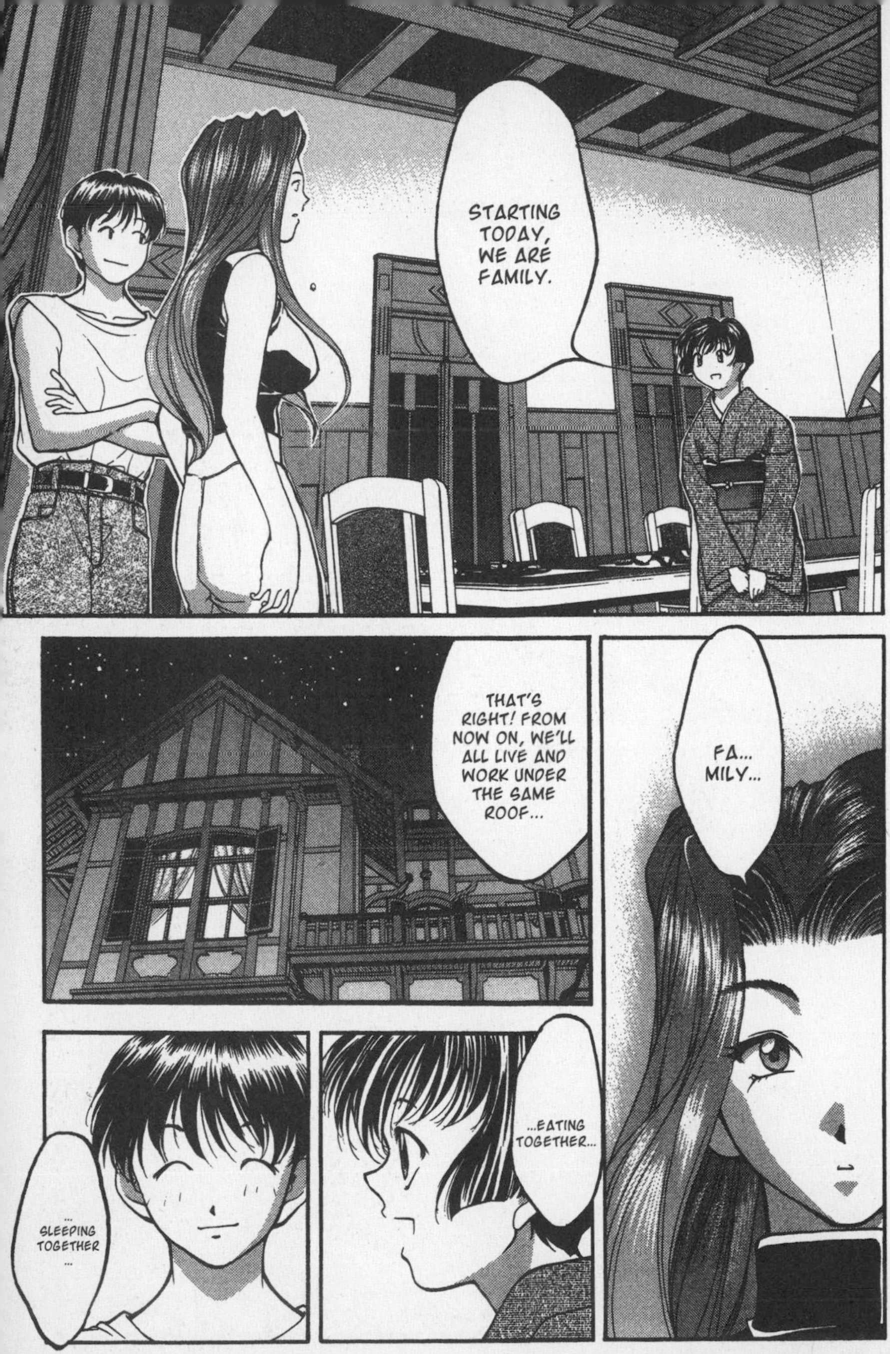
STARTING TODAY, WE ARE FAMILY.
FA... MILY...
THAT'S RIGHT! FROM NOW ON, WE'LL ALL LIVE AND WORK UNDER THE SAME ROOF...
...EATING TOGETHER...
...SLEEPING TOGETHER...

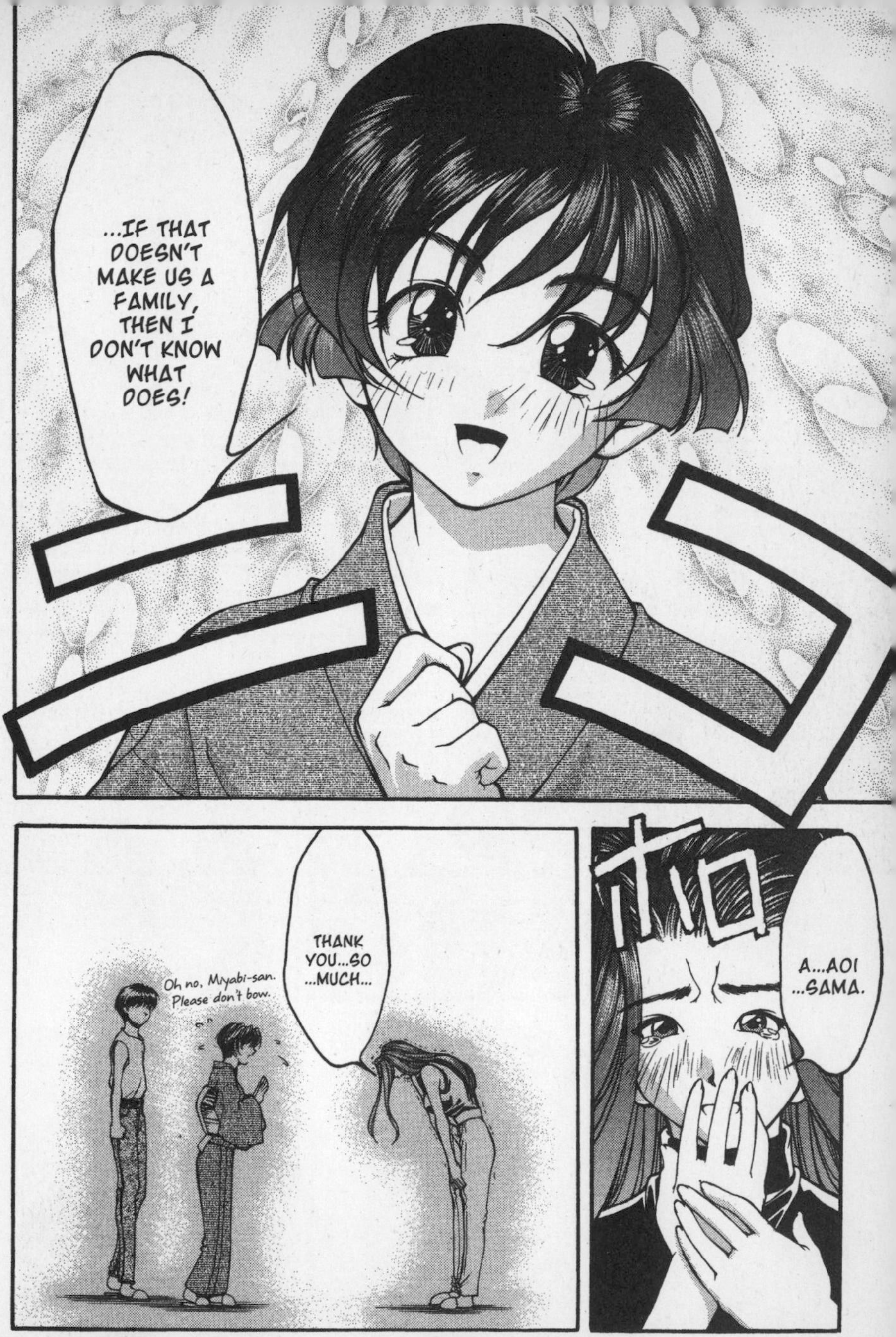
...IF THAT DOESN'T MAKE US A FAMILY, THEN I DON'T KNOW WHAT DOES!
A...AOI ...SAMA.
THANK YOU...SO ...MUCH...
Oh no, Miyabi-san. Please don't bow.

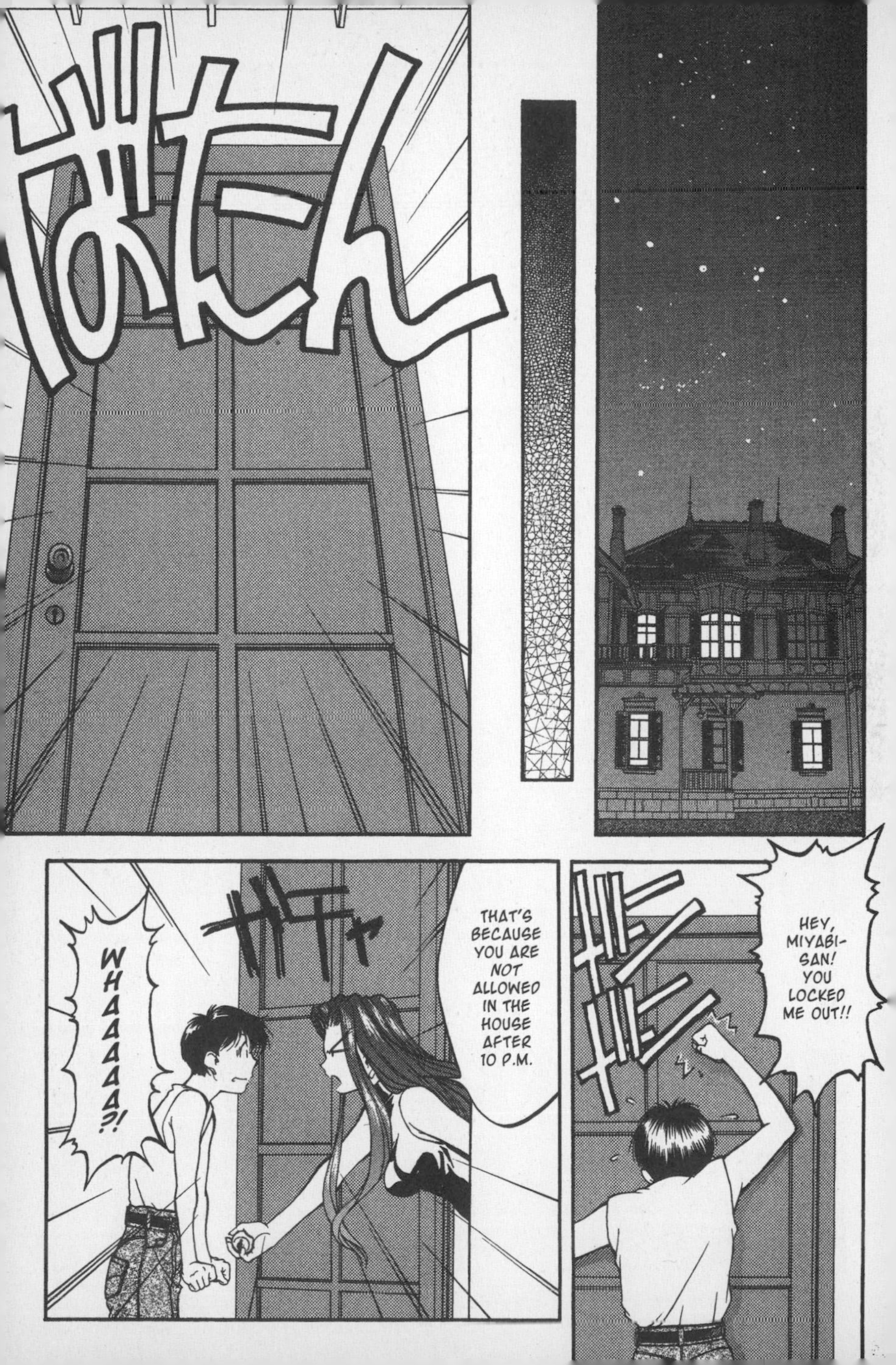
ばたーん
HEY, MIYABI-SAN! YOU LOCKED ME OUT!!
ガチャ
THAT'S BECAUSE YOU ARE NOT ALLOWED IN THE HOUSE AFTER 10 P.M.
WHAAAAAAA?!

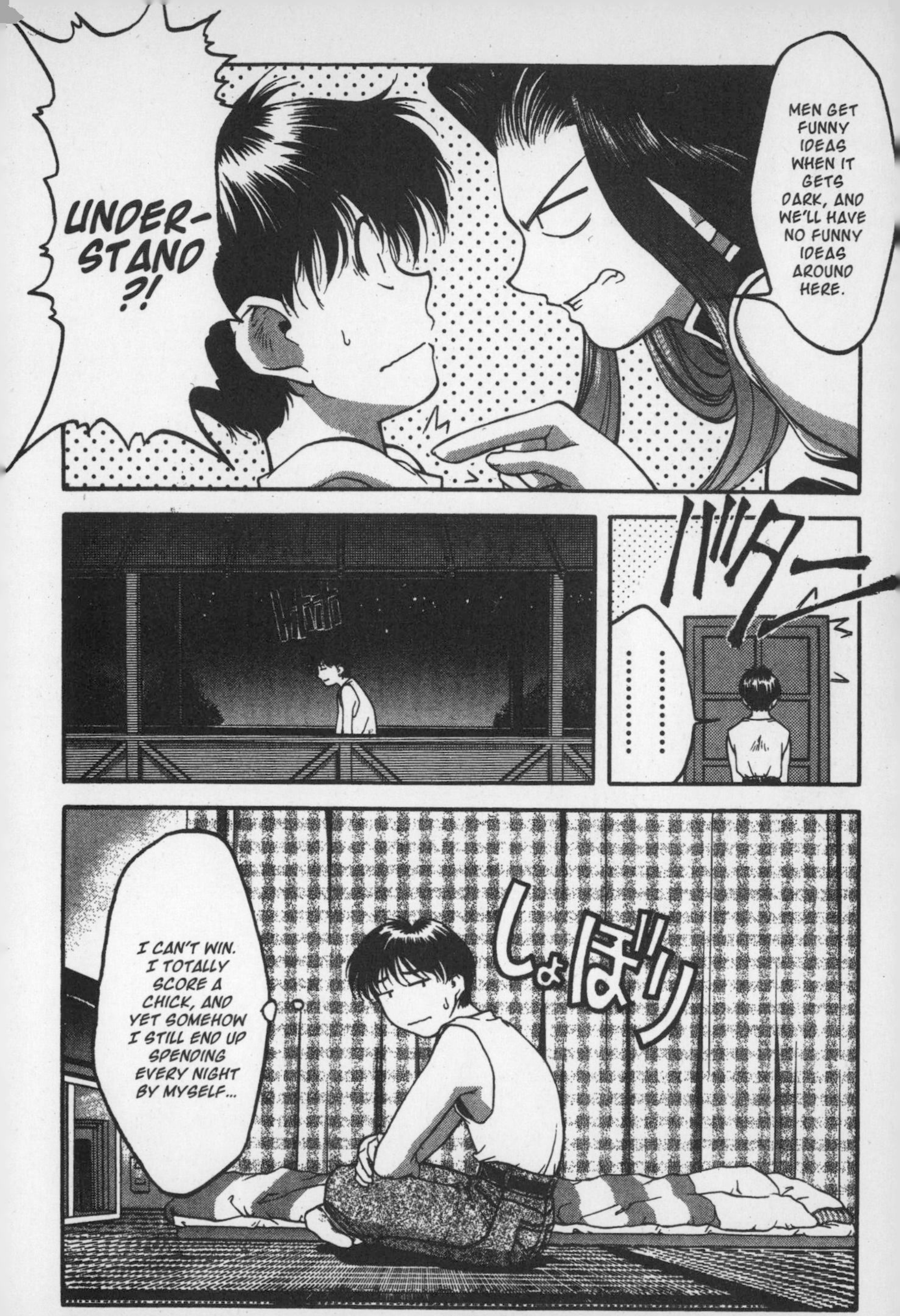
MEN GET FUNNY IDEAS WHEN IT GETS DARK, AND WE'LL HAVE NO FUNNY IDEAS AROUND HERE.
UNDER-STAND?!
バターー
しょぼり
I CAN'T WIN. I TOTALLY SCORE A CHICK, AND YET SOMEHOW I STILL END UP SPENDING EVERY NIGHT BY MYSELF...

End of Chapter 11: Dousei—Cohabitation

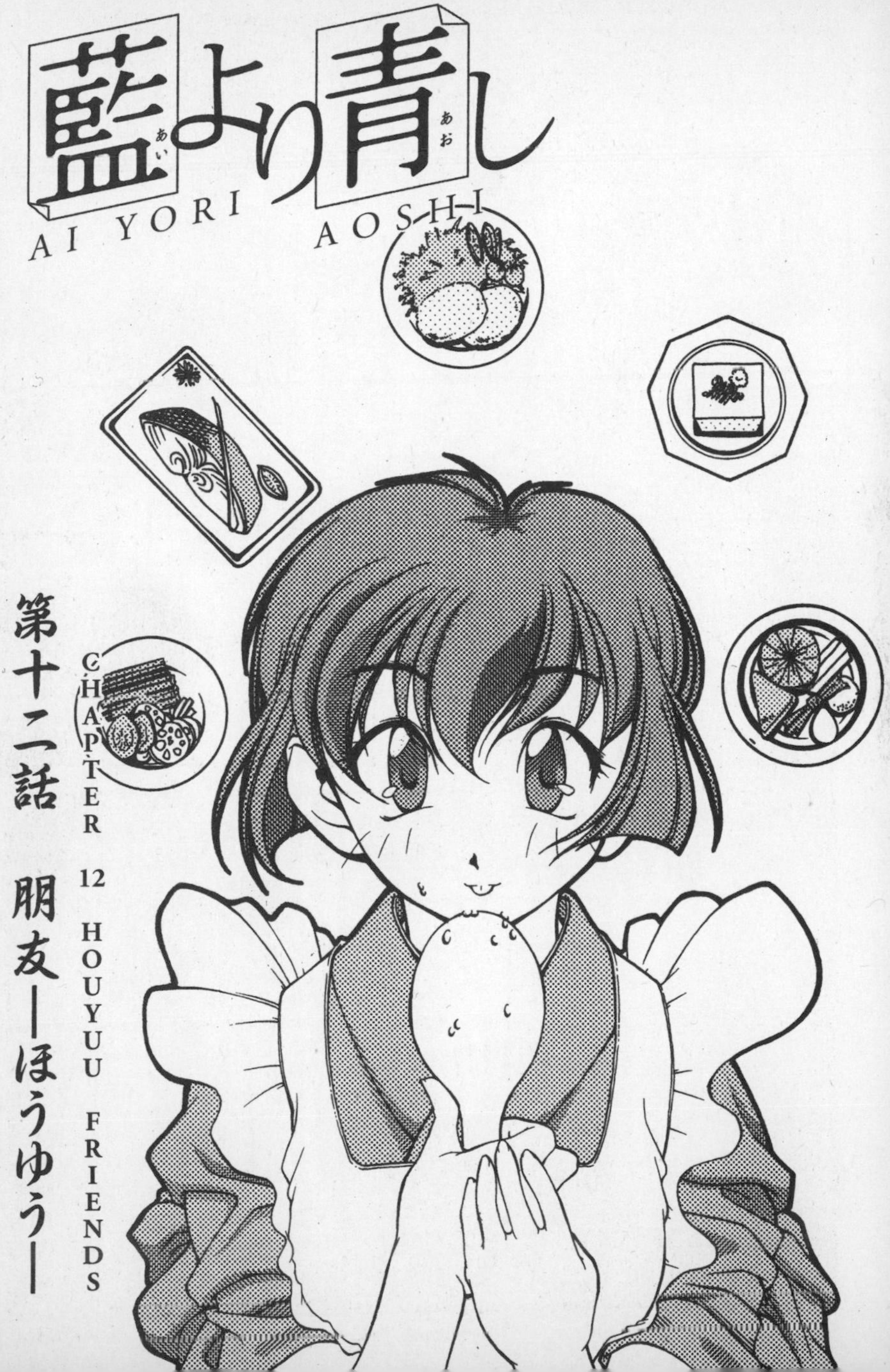
藍(あい)より青(あお)し
AI YORI AOSHI
第十二話
CHAPTER 12 HOUYUU FRIENDS
朋友—ほうゆう—

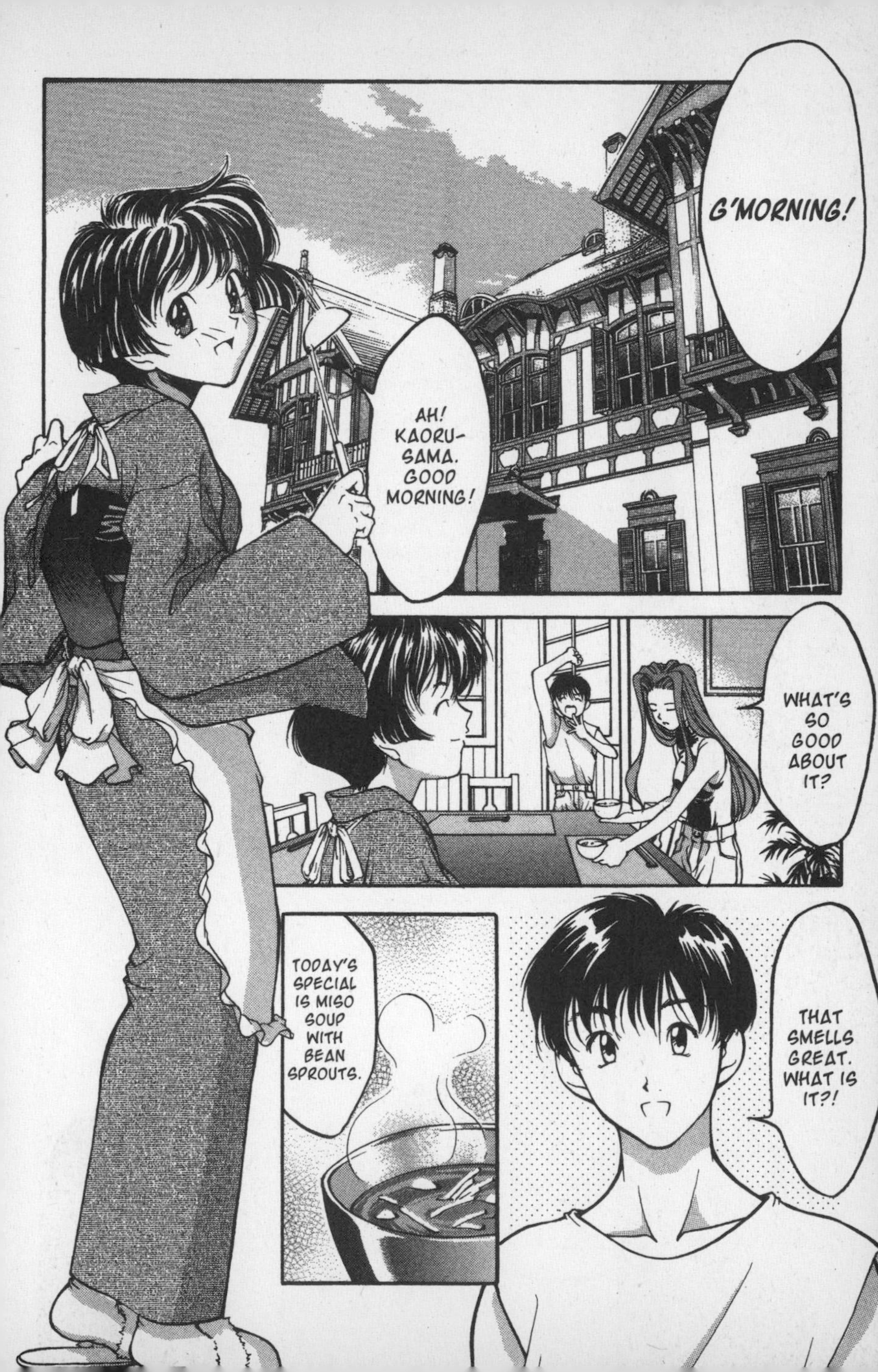
G'MORNING!
AH! KAORU-SAMA. GOOD MORNING!
WHAT'S SO GOOD ABOUT IT?
THAT SMELLS GREAT. WHAT IS IT?!
TODAY'S SPECIAL IS MISO SOUP WITH BEAN SPROUTS.

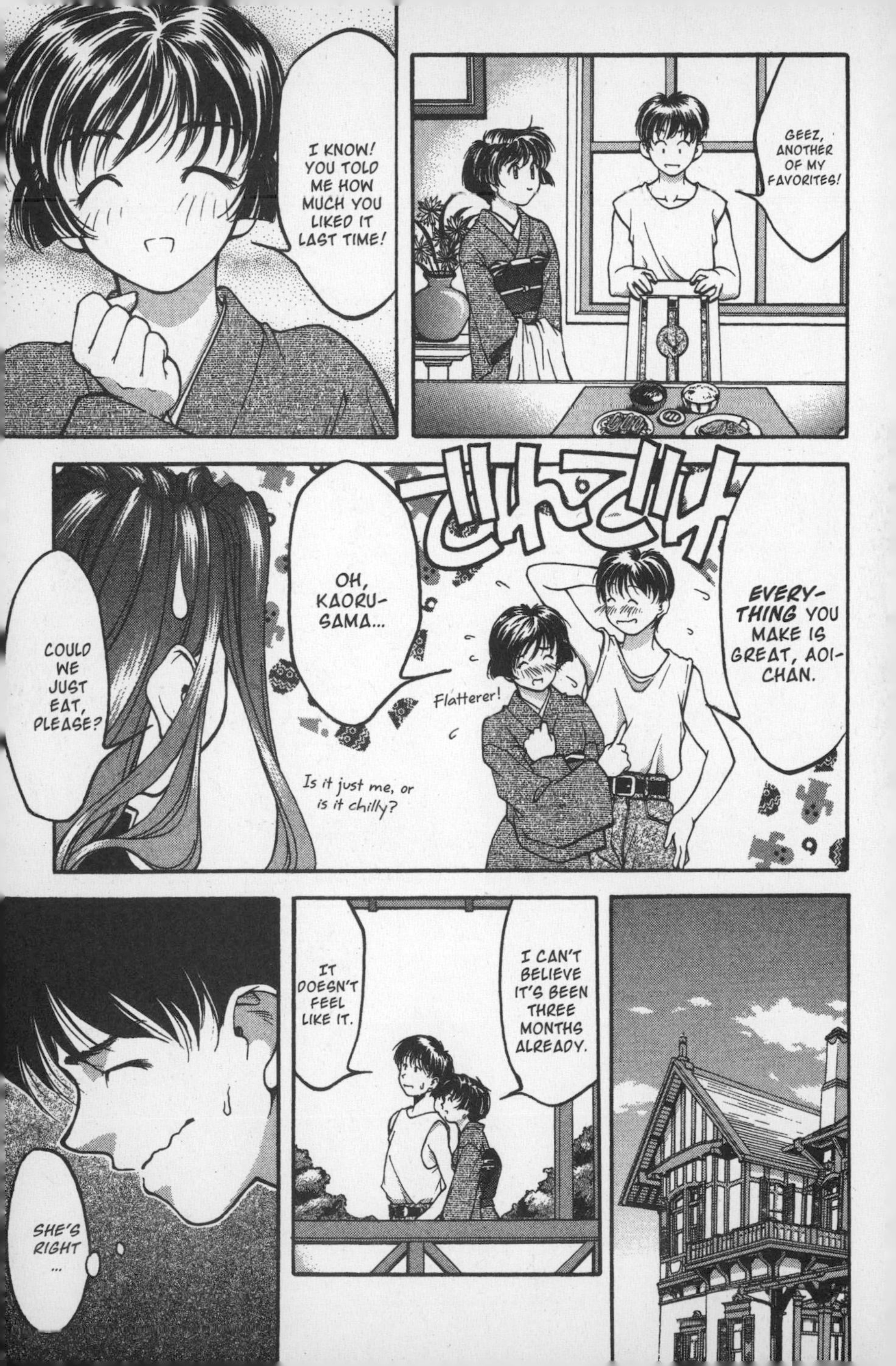
GEEZ, ANOTHER OF MY FAVORITES!
I KNOW! YOU TOLD ME HOW MUCH YOU LIKED IT LAST TIME!
EVERYTHING YOU MAKE IS GREAT, AOI-CHAN.
Flatterer!
OH, KAORU-SAMA...
Is it just me, or is it chilly?
COULD WE JUST EAT, PLEASE?
I CAN'T BELIEVE IT'S BEEN THREE MONTHS ALREADY.
IT DOESN'T FEEL LIKE IT.
SHE'S RIGHT ...

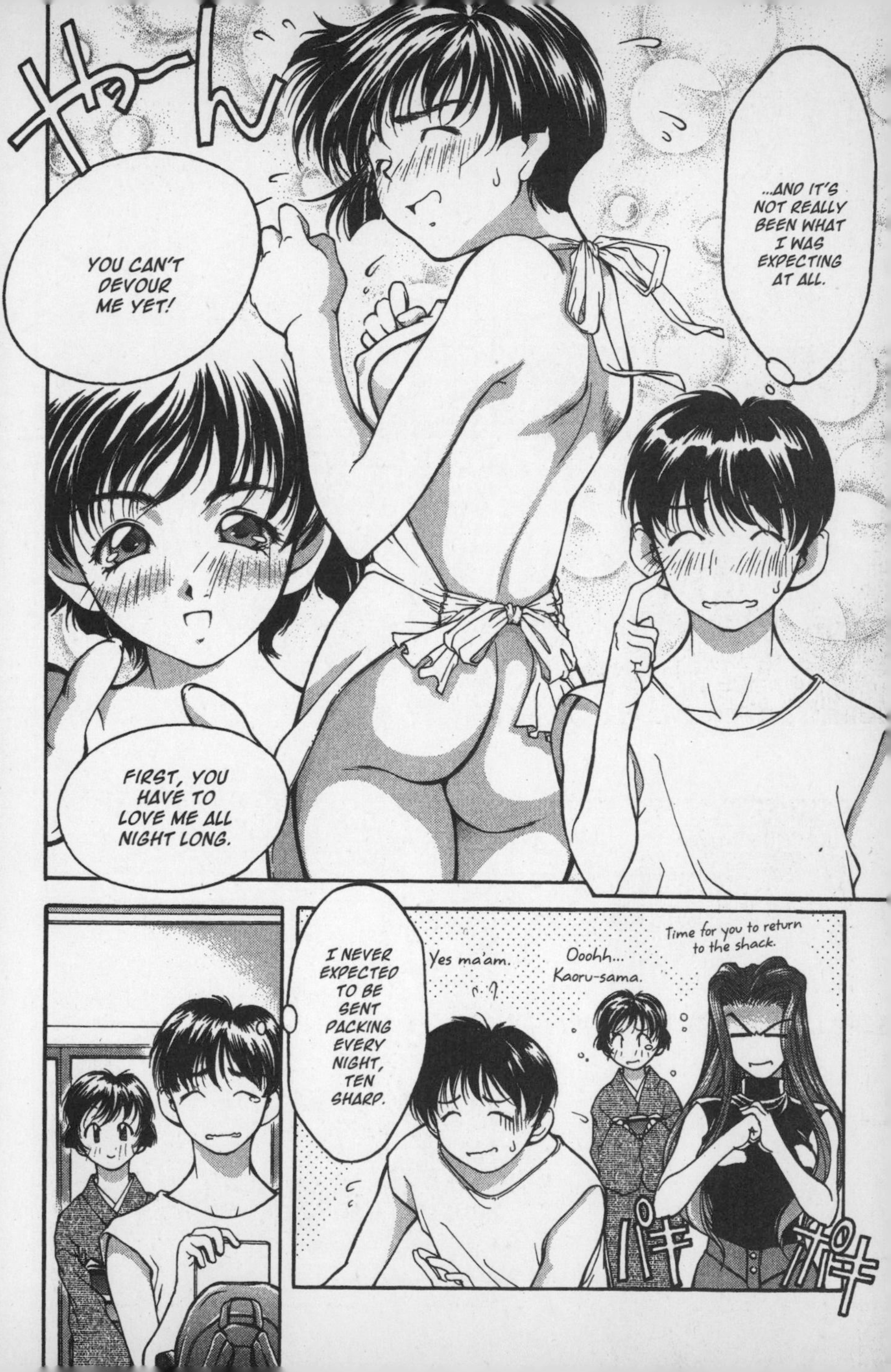
...AND IT'S NOT REALLY BEEN WHAT I WAS EXPECTING AT ALL.
YOU CAN'T DEVOUR ME YET!
FIRST, YOU HAVE TO LOVE ME ALL NIGHT LONG.
Time for you to return to the shack.
パキ ポキ
Ooohh... Kaoru-sama.
Yes ma'am.
I NEVER EXPECTED TO BE SENT PACKING EVERY NIGHT, TEN SHARP.

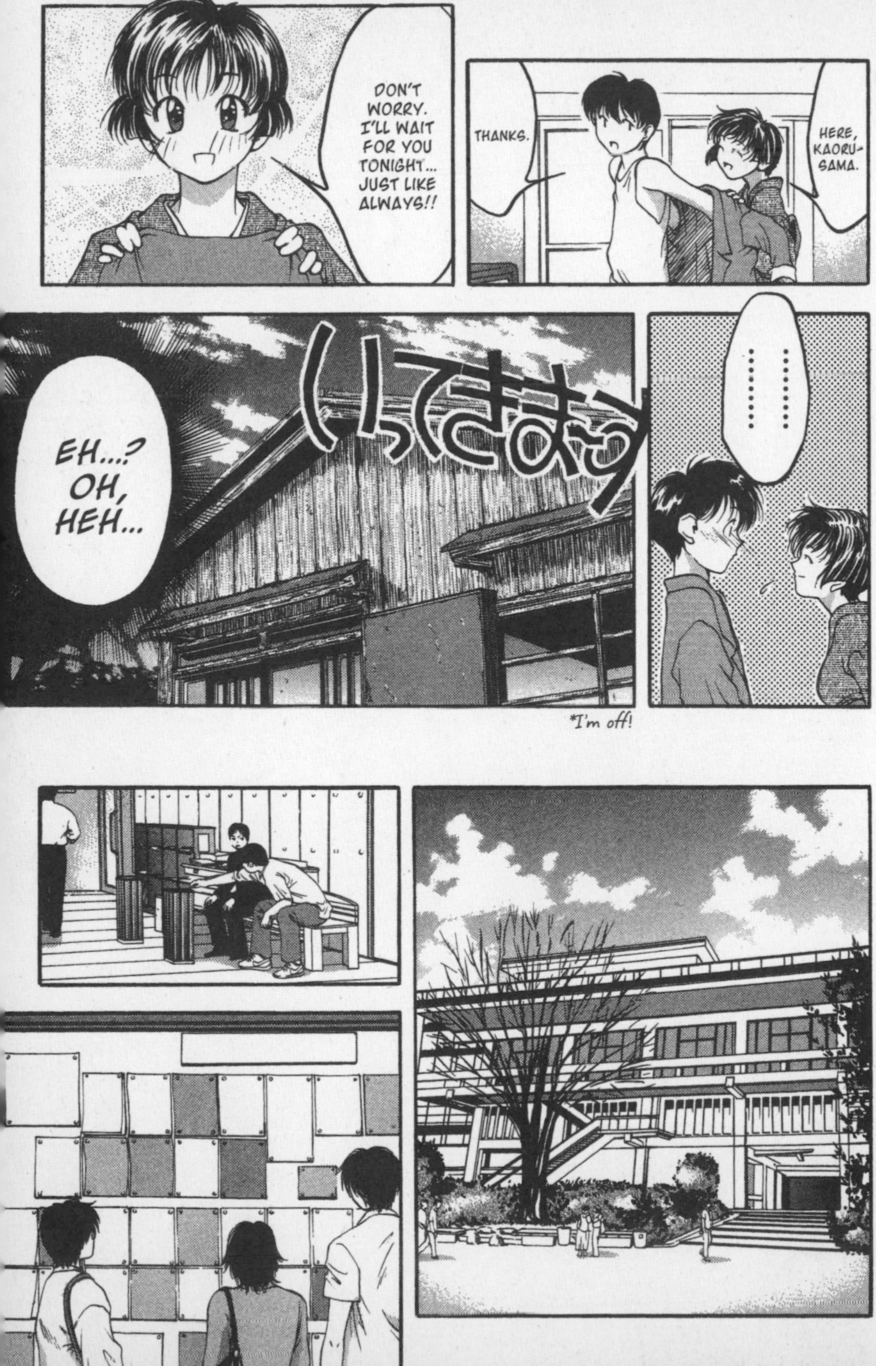
HERE, KAORU-SAMA.
THANKS.
DON'T WORRY. I'LL WAIT FOR YOU TONIGHT... JUST LIKE ALWAYS!!
......
いってきまーす
EH...? OH, HEH...

*I'm off!

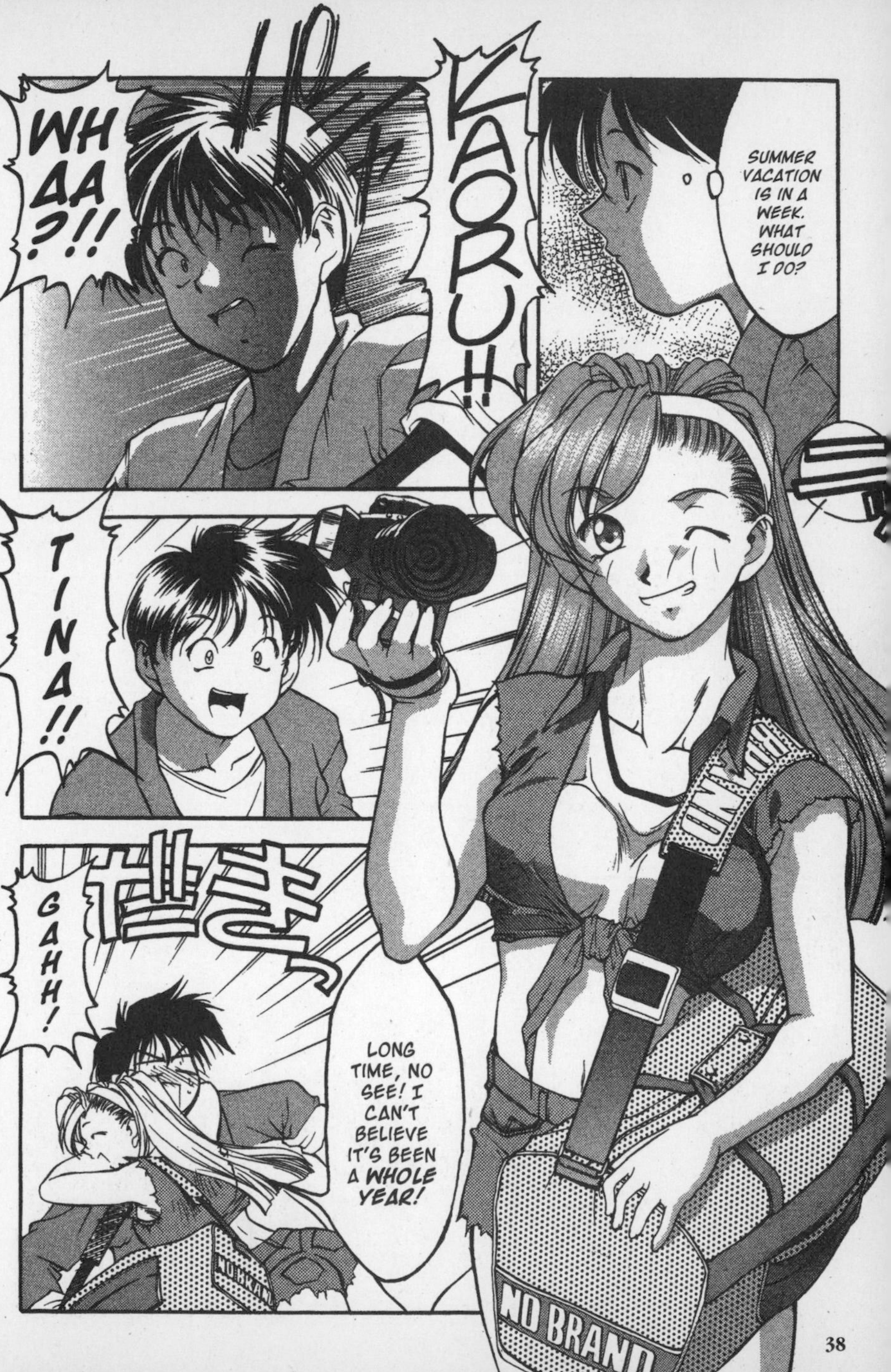
SUMMER VACATION IS IN A WEEK. WHAT SHOULD I DO?
KAORU!!
WHAA?!!
TINA!!
LONG TIME, NO SEE! I CAN'T BELIEVE IT'S BEEN A WHOLE YEAR!
GAHH!
NO BRAND

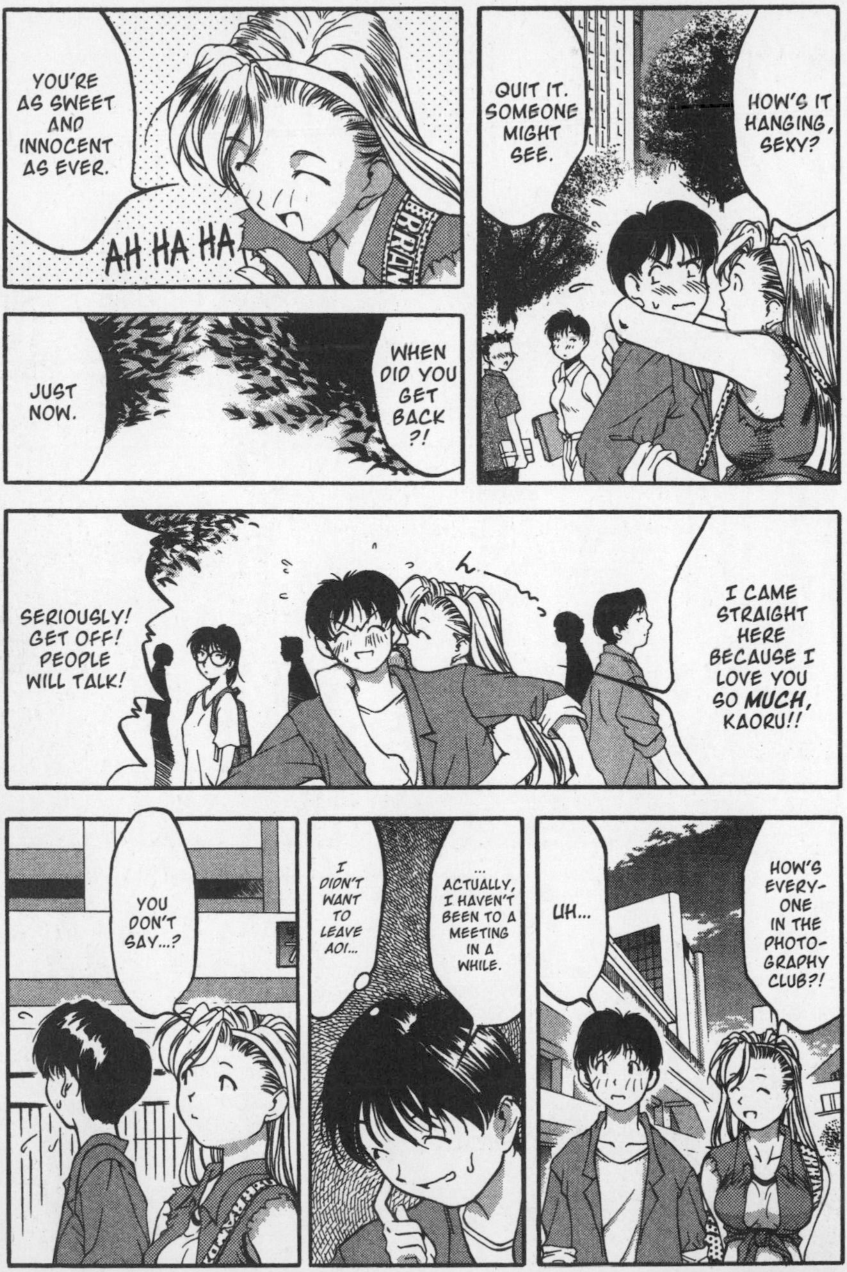
HOW'S IT HANGING, SEXY?
QUIT IT. SOMEONE MIGHT SEE.
YOU'RE AS SWEET AND INNOCENT AS EVER.
AH HA HA
WHEN DID YOU GET BACK?!
JUST NOW.
I CAME STRAIGHT HERE BECAUSE I LOVE YOU SO *MUCH*, KAORU!!
SERIOUSLY! GET OFF! PEOPLE WILL TALK!
HOW'S EVERYONE IN THE PHOTOGRAPHY CLUB?!
UH...
...ACTUALLY, I HAVEN'T BEEN TO A MEETING IN A WHILE.
I DIDN'T WANT TO LEAVE AOI...
YOU DON'T SAY...?

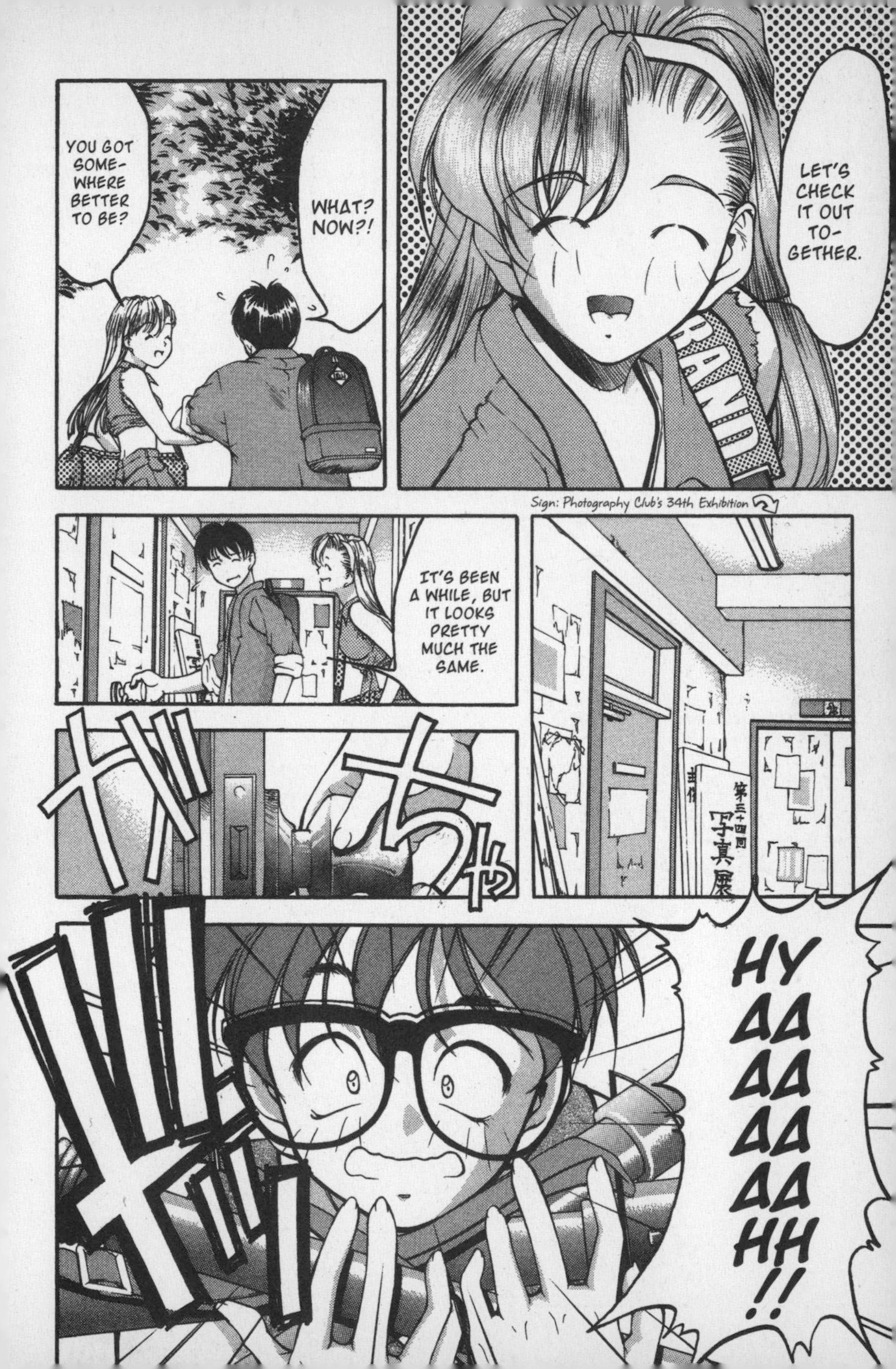
LET'S CHECK IT OUT TO-GETHER.
WHAT? NOW?!
YOU GOT SOME-WHERE BETTER TO BE?
Sign: Photography Club's 34th Exhibition
第三十四回 写真展
IT'S BEEN A WHILE, BUT IT LOOKS PRETTY MUCH THE SAME.
ガちゃ
HYAAAAAAAAAAAHH!!

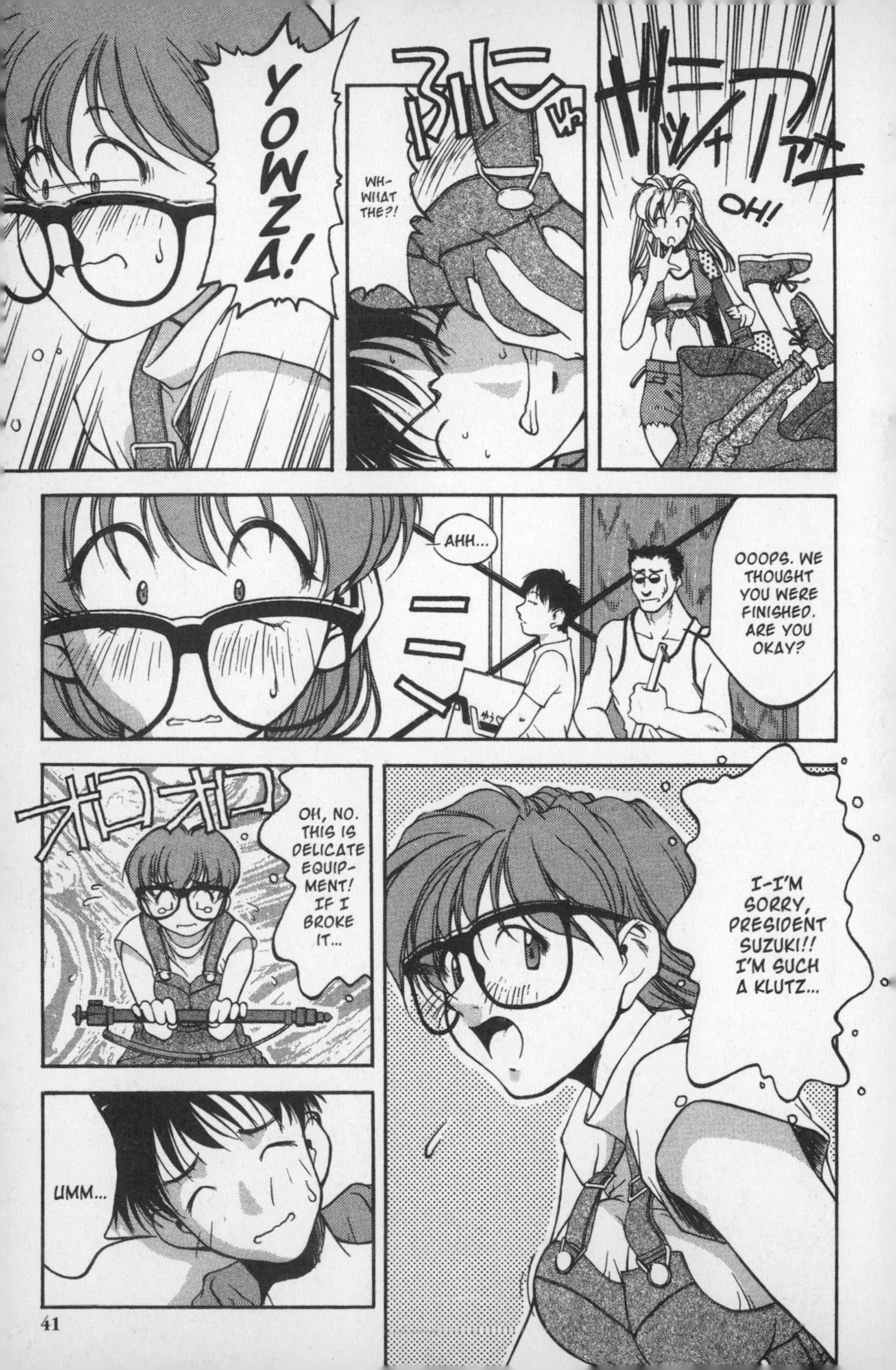
OH!
WH-WHAT THE?!
YOWZA!
OOOPS. WE THOUGHT YOU WERE FINISHED. ARE YOU OKAY?
AHH...
I-I'M SORRY, PRESIDENT SUZUKI!! I'M SUCH A KLUTZ...
オロオロ
OH, NO. THIS IS DELICATE EQUIP-MENT! IF I BROKE IT...
UMM...

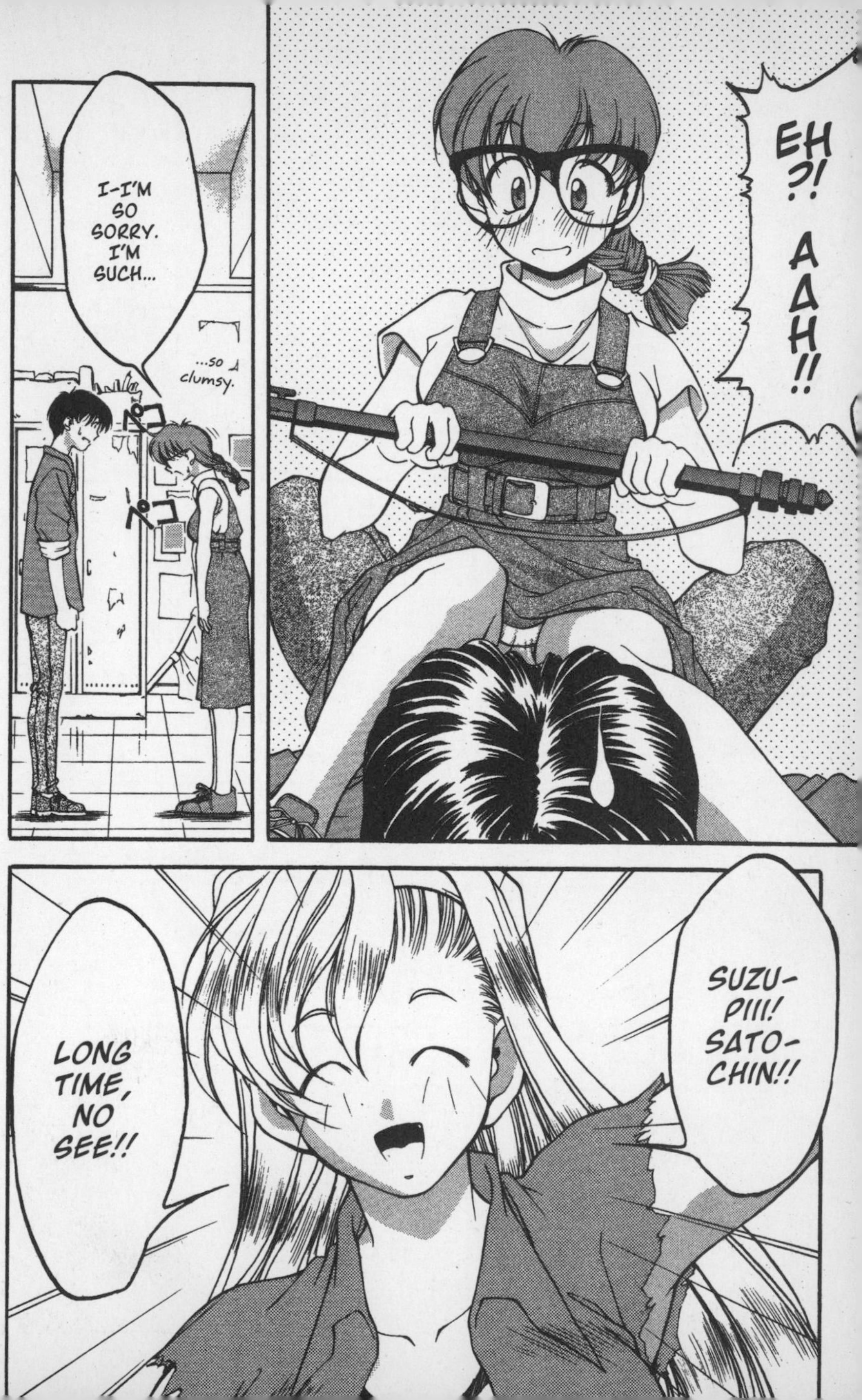
EH ?! AAAH!!
I-I'M SO SORRY. I'M SUCH...
...so clumsy.
SUZU-PIII! SATO-CHIN!!
LONG TIME, NO SEE!!

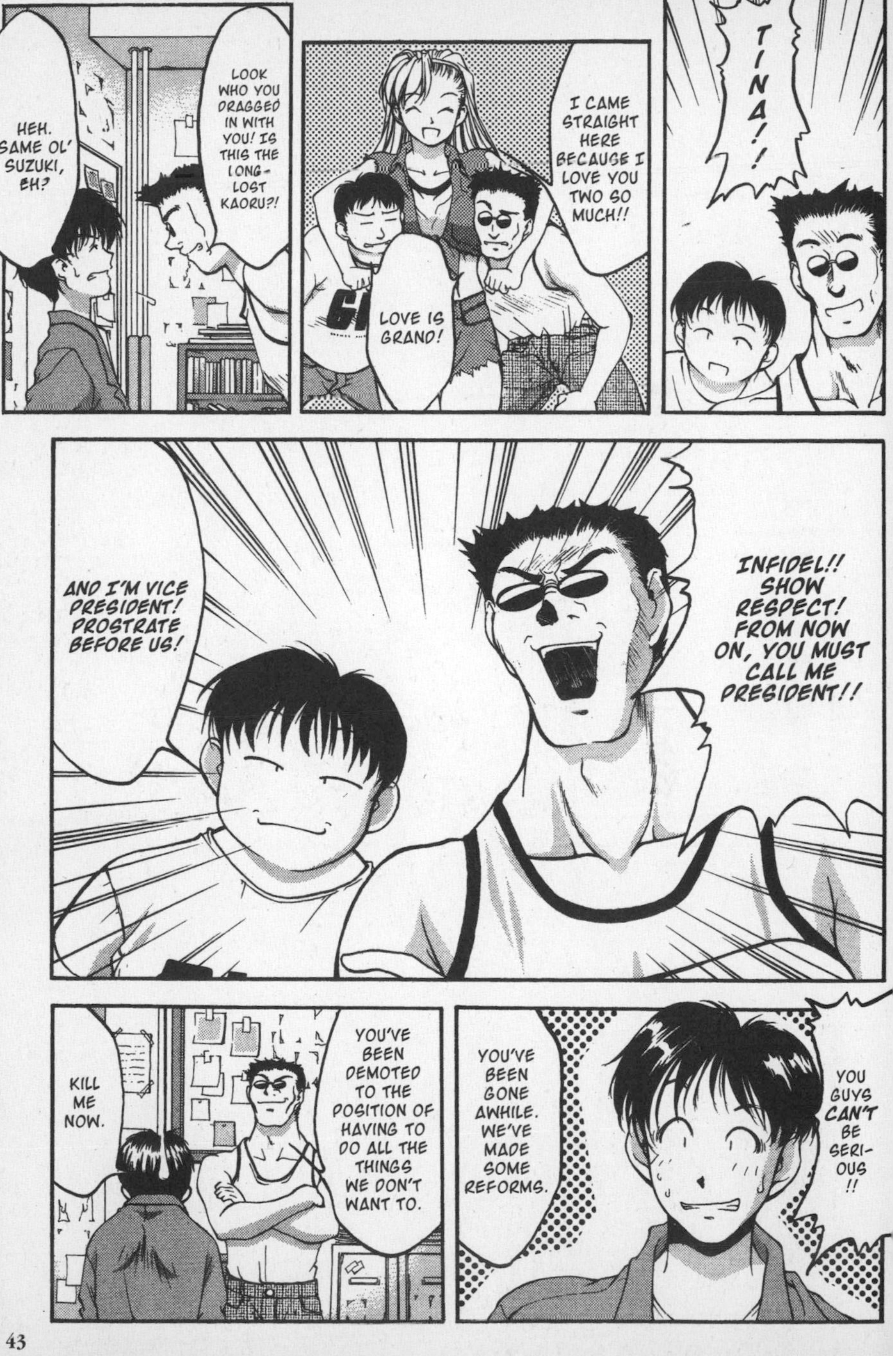
TINA!!
I CAME STRAIGHT HERE BECAUSE I LOVE YOU TWO SO MUCH!!
LOVE IS GRAND!
LOOK WHO YOU DRAGGED IN WITH YOU! IS THIS THE LONG-LOST KAORU?!
HEH. SAME OL' SUZUKI, EH?
INFIDEL!! SHOW RESPECT! FROM NOW ON, YOU MUST CALL ME PRESIDENT!!
AND I'M VICE PRESIDENT! PROSTRATE BEFORE US!
YOU GUYS CAN'T BE SERIOUS!!
YOU'VE BEEN GONE AWHILE. WE'VE MADE SOME REFORMS.
YOU'VE BEEN DEMOTED TO THE POSITION OF HAVING TO DO ALL THE THINGS WE DON'T WANT TO.
KILL ME NOW.

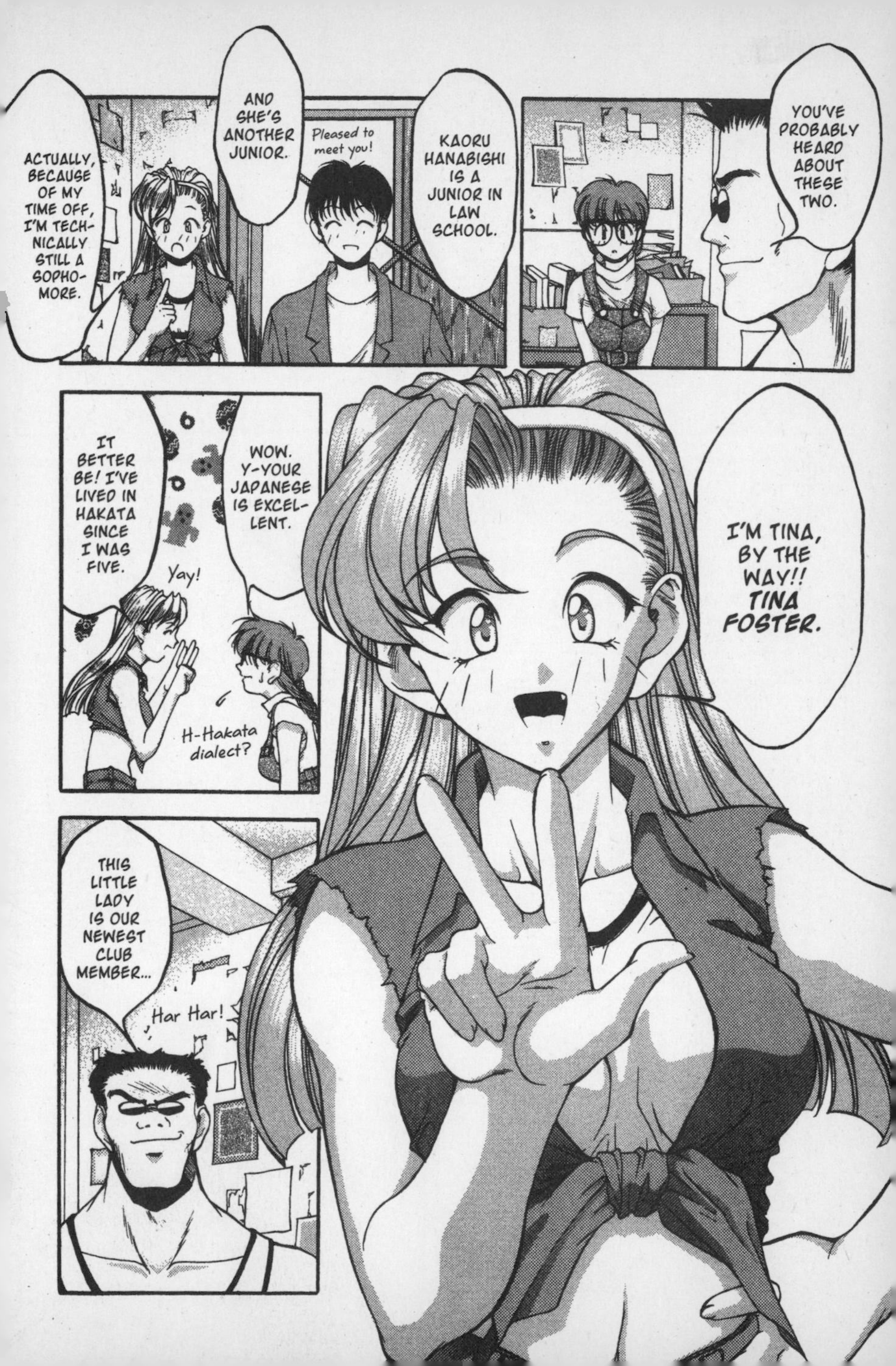
YOU'VE PROBABLY HEARD ABOUT THESE TWO.
KAORU HANABISHI IS A JUNIOR IN LAW SCHOOL.
Pleased to meet you!
AND SHE'S ANOTHER JUNIOR.
ACTUALLY, BECAUSE OF MY TIME OFF, I'M TECHNICALLY STILL A SOPHOMORE.
I'M TINA, BY THE WAY!! TINA FOSTER.
WOW. Y-YOUR JAPANESE IS EXCELLENT.
IT BETTER BE! I'VE LIVED IN HAKATA SINCE I WAS FIVE.
Yay!
H-Hakata dialect?
THIS LITTLE LADY IS OUR NEWEST CLUB MEMBER...
Har Har!

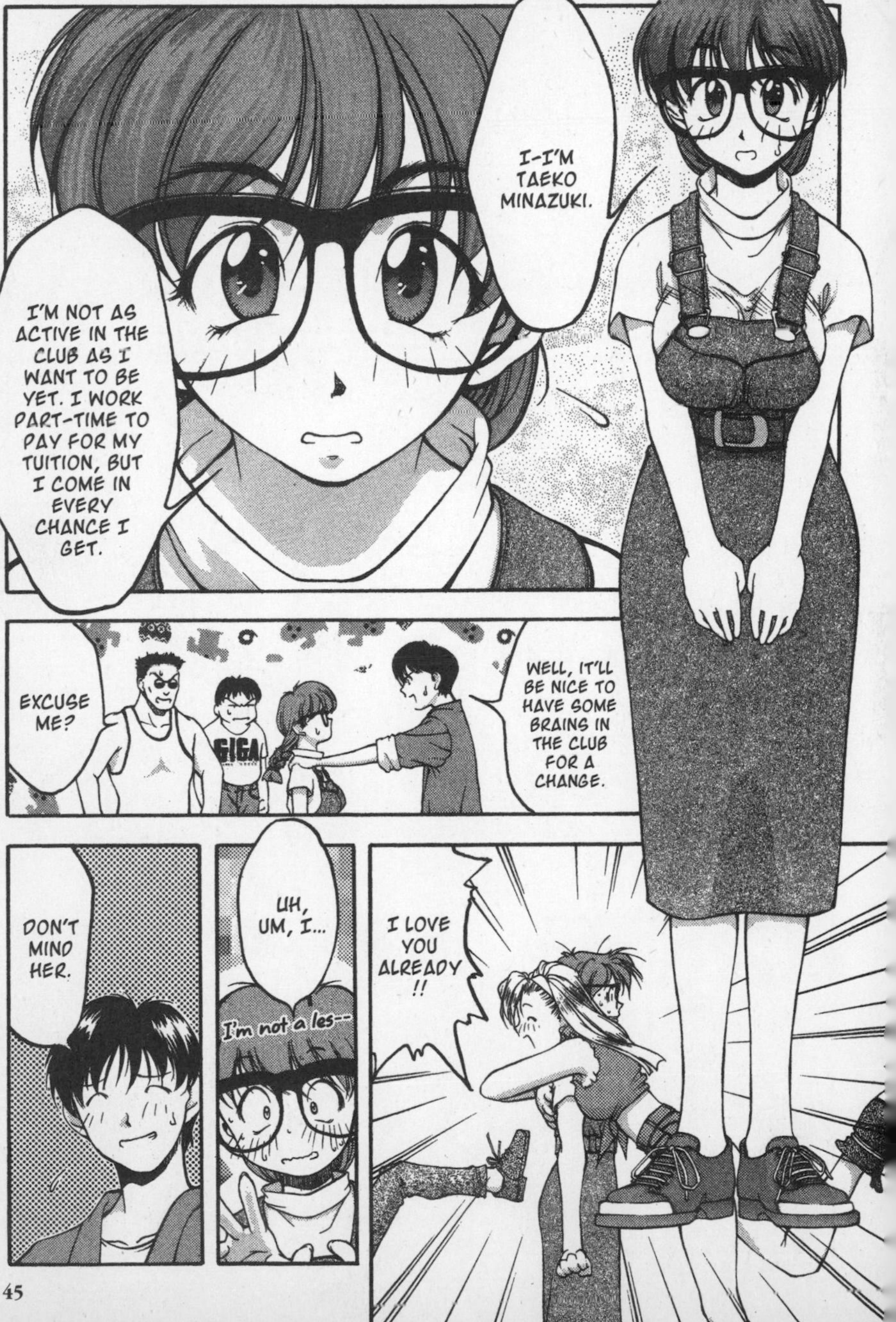
I-I'M TAEKO MINAZUKI.
I'M NOT AS ACTIVE IN THE CLUB AS I WANT TO BE YET. I WORK PART-TIME TO PAY FOR MY TUITION, BUT I COME IN EVERY CHANCE I GET.
WELL, IT'LL BE NICE TO HAVE SOME BRAINS IN THE CLUB FOR A CHANGE.
EXCUSE ME?
I LOVE YOU ALREADY !!
UH, UM, I...
I'm not a les--
DON'T MIND HER.

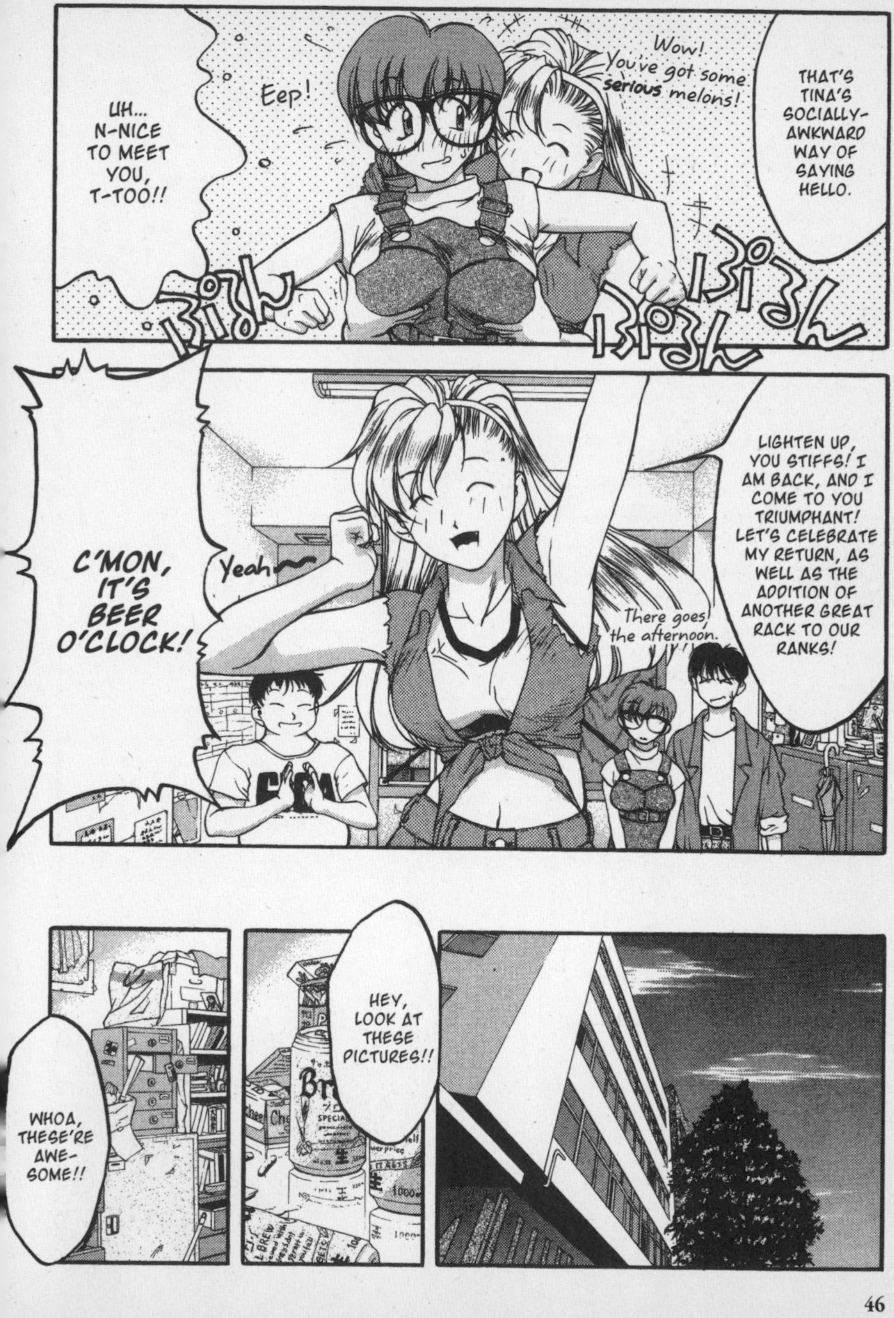
THAT'S TINA'S SOCIALLY-AWKWARD WAY OF SAYING HELLO.
Wow! You've got some **serious** melons!
Eep!
UH... N-NICE TO MEET YOU, T-TOO!!
ぷりん ぷりん
ぷりん
LIGHTEN UP, YOU STIFFS! I AM BACK, AND I COME TO YOU TRIUMPHANT! LET'S CELEBRATE MY RETURN, AS WELL AS THE ADDITION OF ANOTHER GREAT RACK TO OUR RANKS!
There goes the afternoon.
Yeah~~
C'MON, IT'S BEER O'CLOCK!
HEY, LOOK AT THESE PICTURES!!
WHOA, THESE'RE AWE-SOME!!

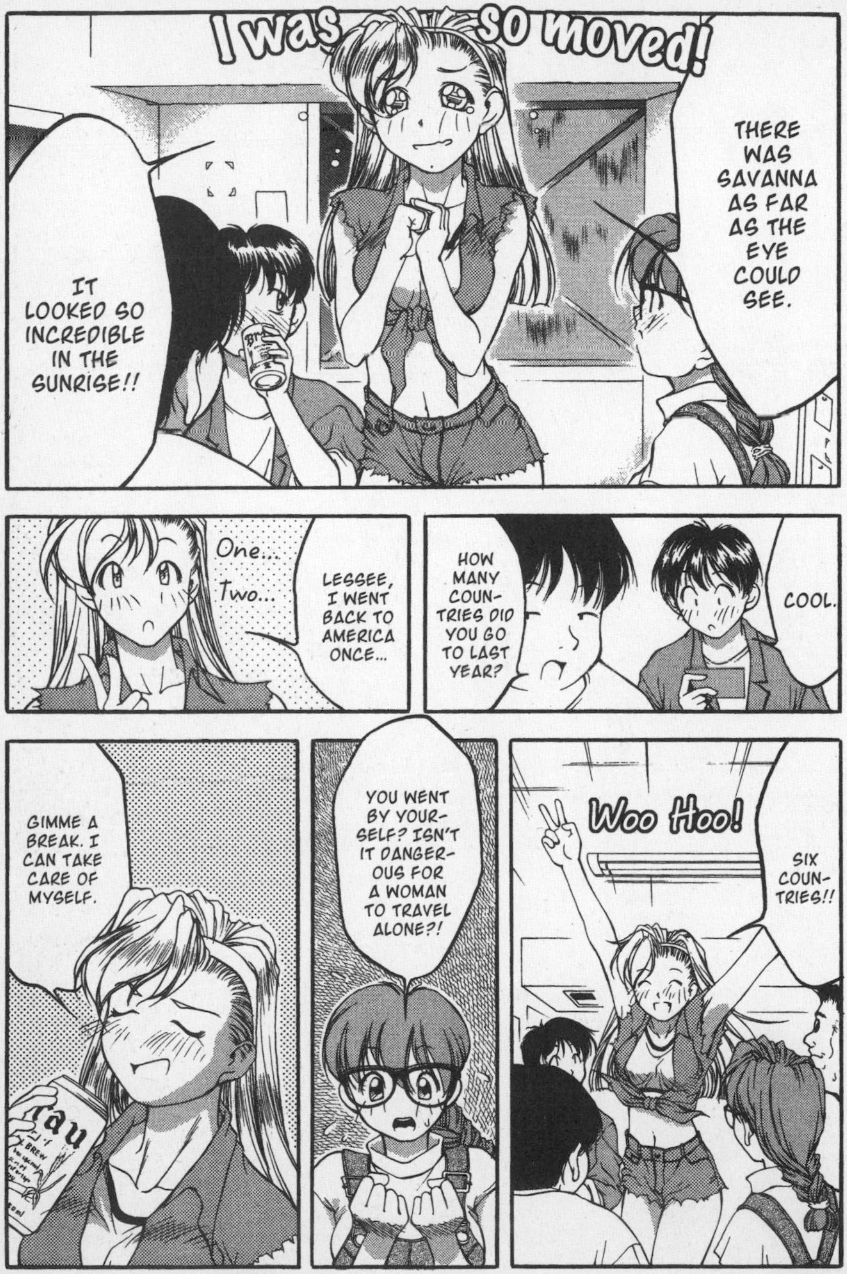
I was so moved!
THERE WAS SAVANNA AS FAR AS THE EYE COULD SEE.
IT LOOKED SO INCREDIBLE IN THE SUNRISE!!
COOL.
HOW MANY COUNTRIES DID YOU GO TO LAST YEAR?
LESSEE, I WENT BACK TO AMERICA ONCE...
One... Two...
Woo Hoo!
SIX COUNTRIES!!
YOU WENT BY YOURSELF? ISN'T IT DANGEROUS FOR A WOMAN TO TRAVEL ALONE?!
GIMME A BREAK. I CAN TAKE CARE OF MYSELF.

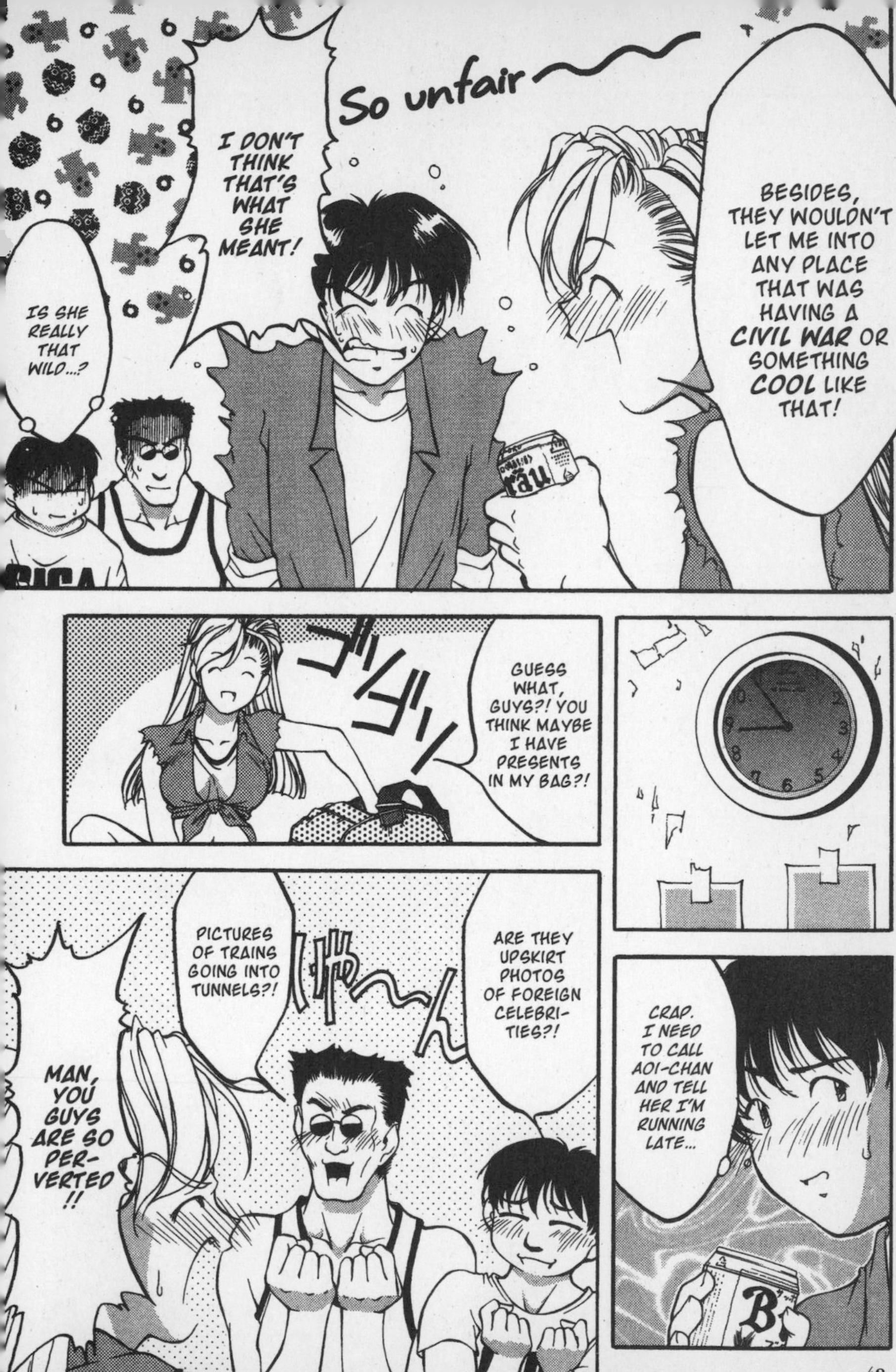
BESIDES, THEY WOULDN'T LET ME INTO ANY PLACE THAT WAS HAVING A CIVIL WAR OR SOMETHING COOL LIKE THAT!
So unfair
I DON'T THINK THAT'S WHAT SHE MEANT!
IS SHE REALLY THAT WILD...?
GUESS WHAT, GUYS?! YOU THINK MAYBE I HAVE PRESENTS IN MY BAG?!
CRAP. I NEED TO CALL AOI-CHAN AND TELL HER I'M RUNNING LATE...
ARE THEY UPSKIRT PHOTOS OF FOREIGN CELEBRITIES?!
PICTURES OF TRAINS GOING INTO TUNNELS?!
MAN, YOU GUYS ARE SO PERVERTED!!

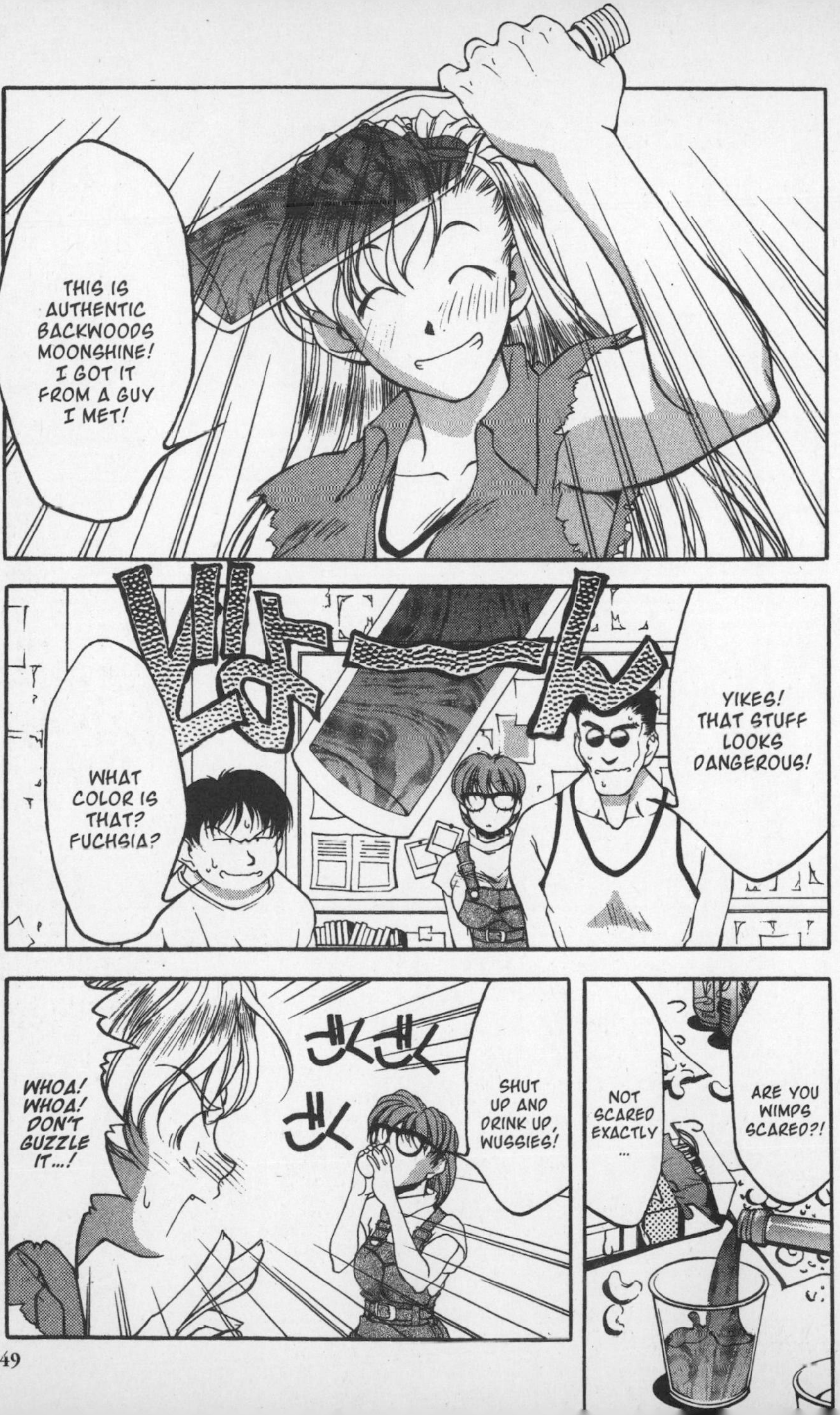
THIS IS AUTHENTIC BACKWOODS MOONSHINE! I GOT IT FROM A GUY I MET!
YIKES! THAT STUFF LOOKS DANGEROUS!
WHAT COLOR IS THAT? FUCHSIA?
ARE YOU WIMPS SCARED?!
NOT SCARED EXACTLY ...
SHUT UP AND DRINK UP, WUSSIES!
ごくごく
ごく
WHOA! WHOA! DON'T GUZZLE IT...!

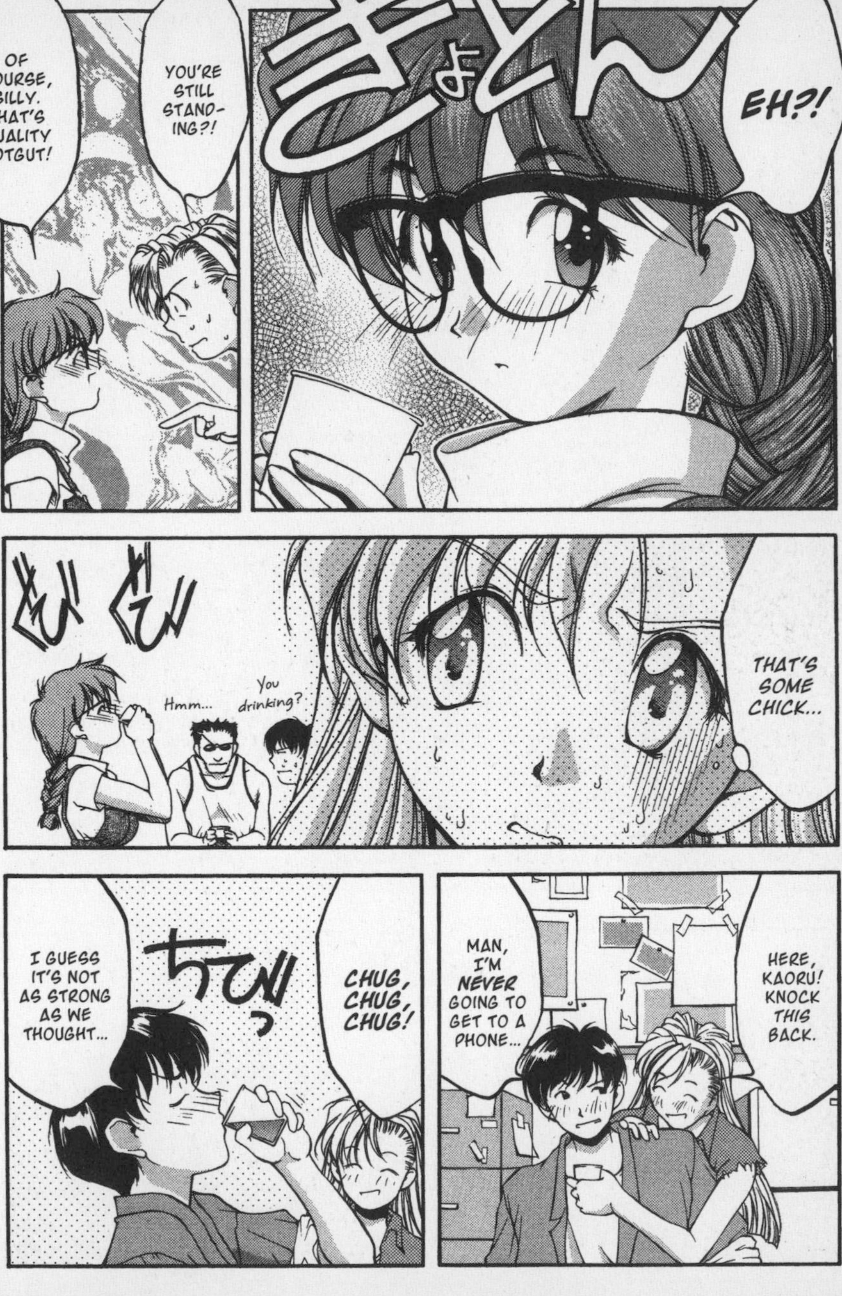
きょとん
EH?!
YOU'RE STILL STANDING?!
OF COURSE, SILLY. THAT'S QUALITY ROTGUT!
THAT'S SOME CHICK...
You drinking?
Hmm...
ぐびぐび
HERE, KAORU! KNOCK THIS BACK.
MAN, I'M ***NEVER*** GOING TO GET TO A PHONE...
CHUG, CHUG, CHUG!
ちびっ
I GUESS IT'S NOT AS STRONG AS WE THOUGHT...

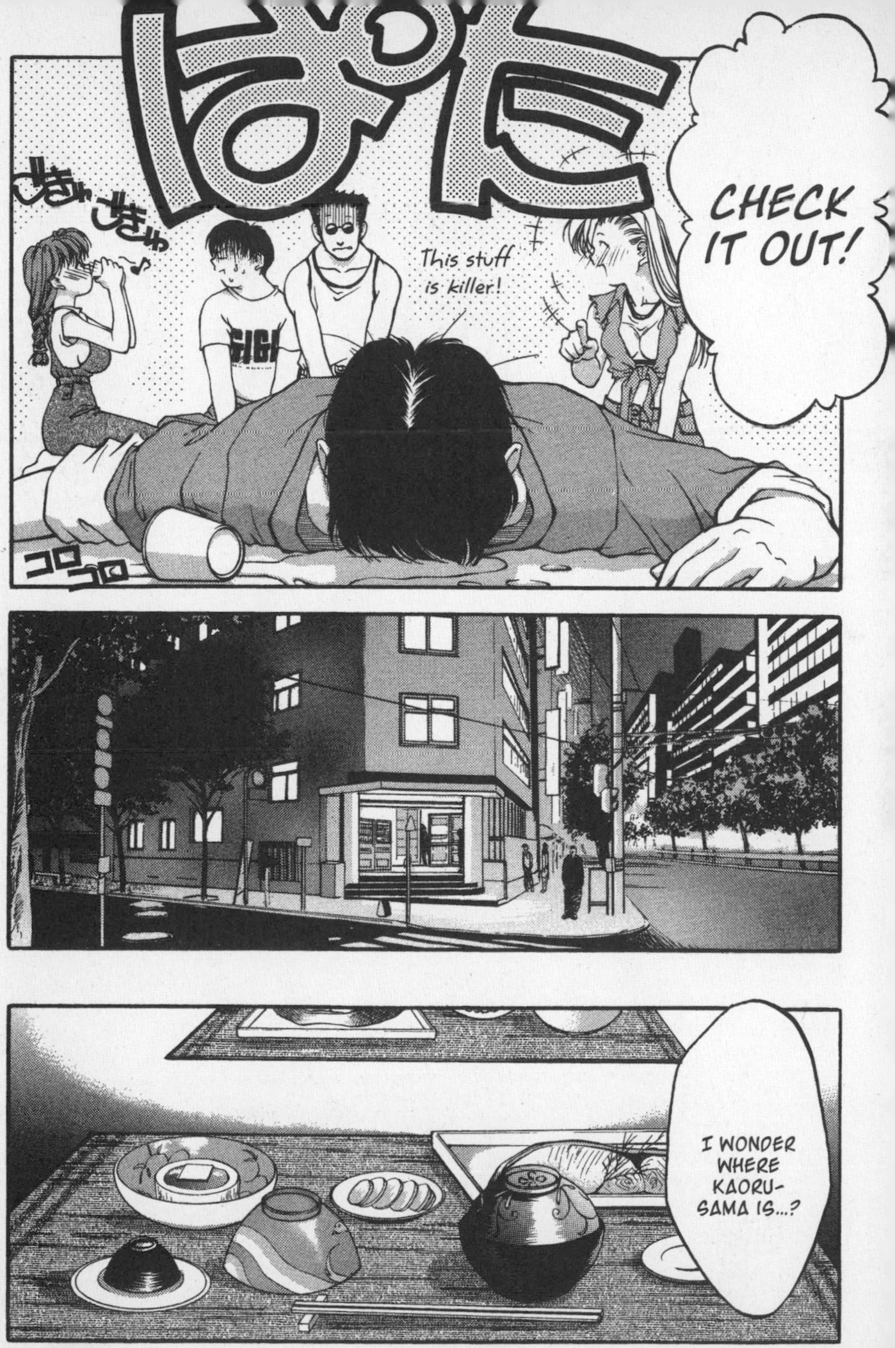
CHECK IT OUT!
This stuff is killer!
ごきゅ ごきゅ
コロコロ
I WONDER WHERE KAORU-SAMA IS...?

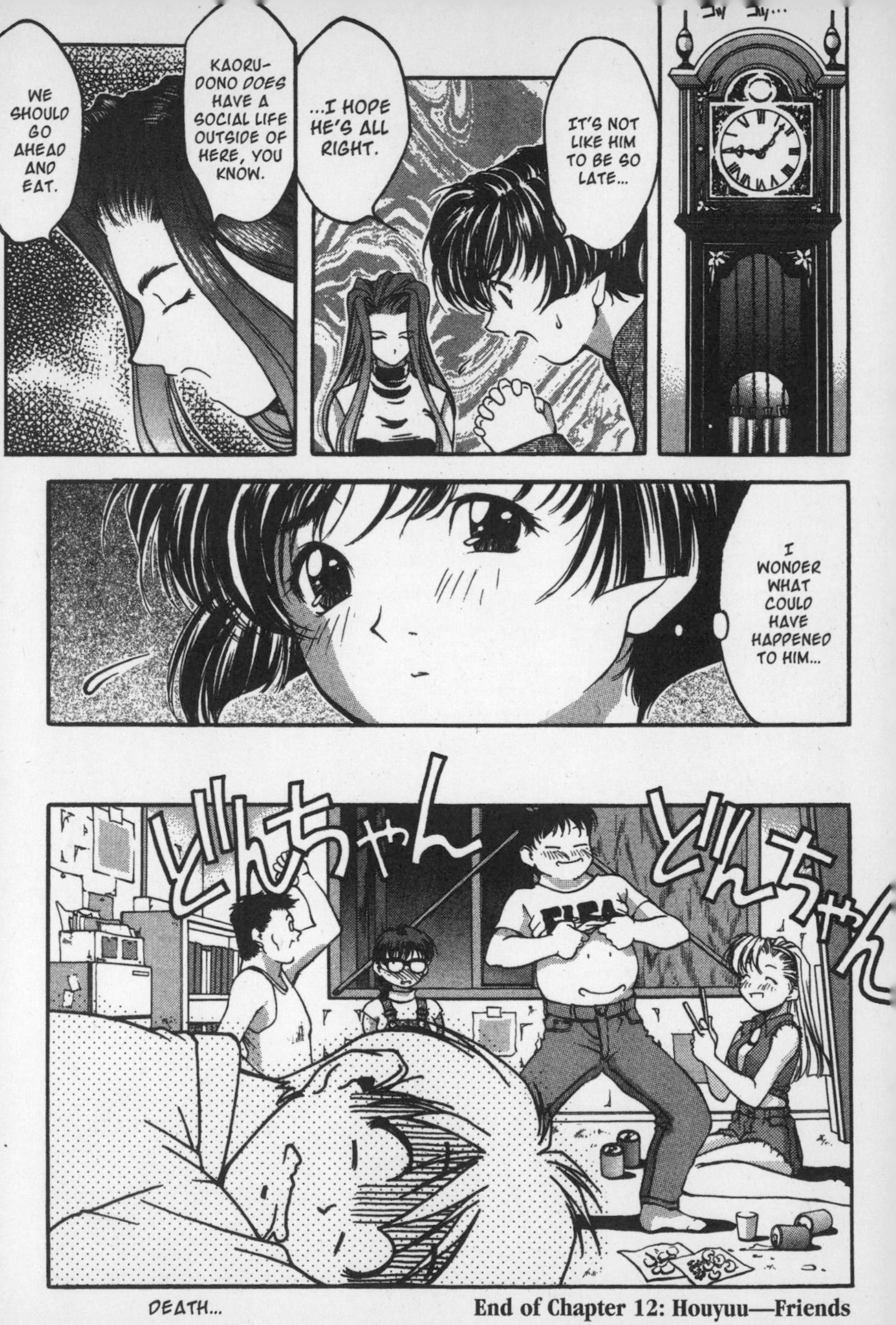
IT'S NOT LIKE HIM TO BE SO LATE...
...I HOPE HE'S ALL RIGHT.
KAORU-DONO DOES HAVE A SOCIAL LIFE OUTSIDE OF HERE, YOU KNOW.
WE SHOULD GO AHEAD AND EAT.
I WONDER WHAT COULD HAVE HAPPENED TO HIM...
どんちゃん
どんちゃん

DEATH...

End of Chapter 12: Houyuu—Friends

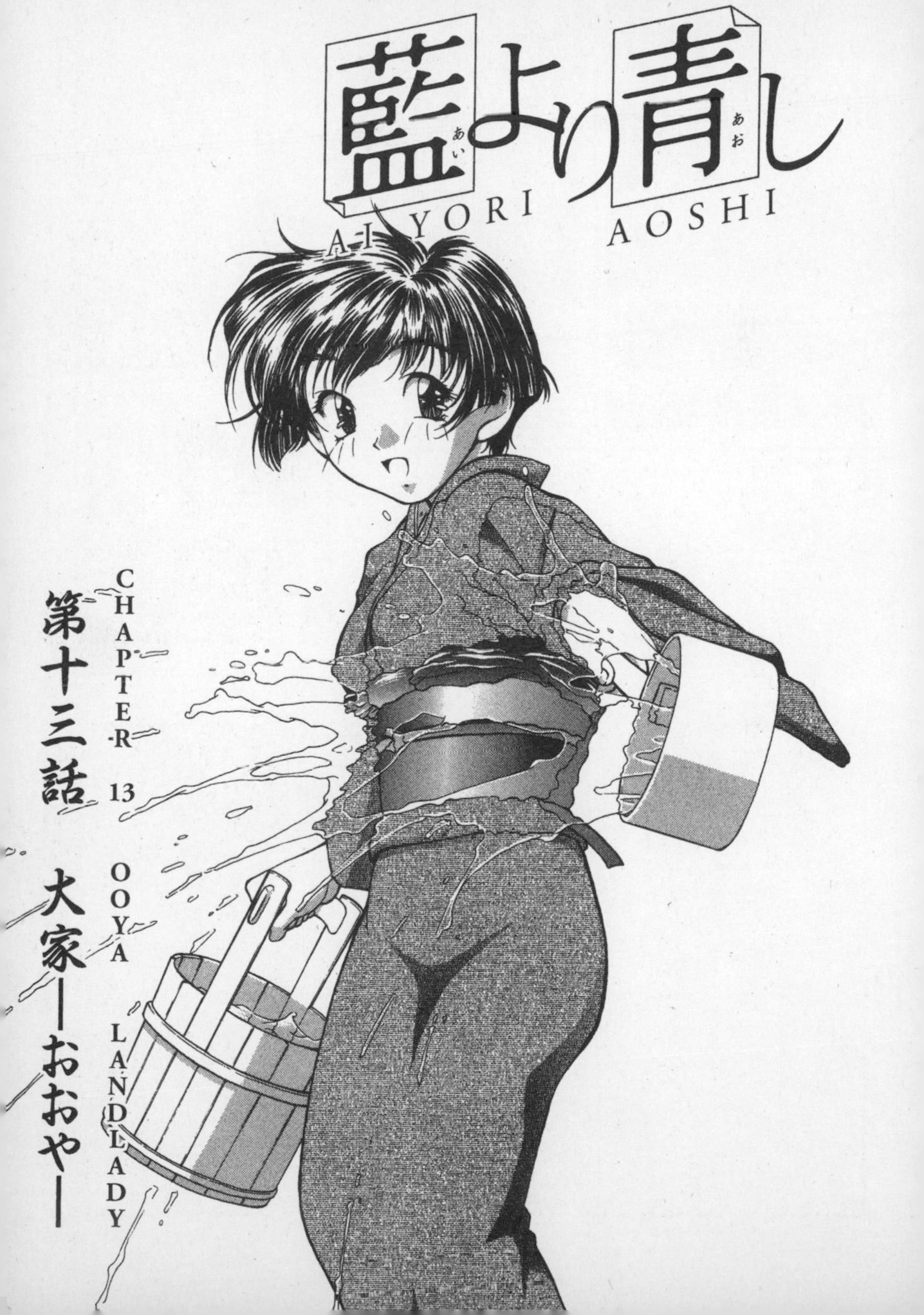

藍より青し
あい
あお
AI YORI AOSHI
CHAPTER 13
OOYA LANDLADY
第十三話
大家ーおおやー

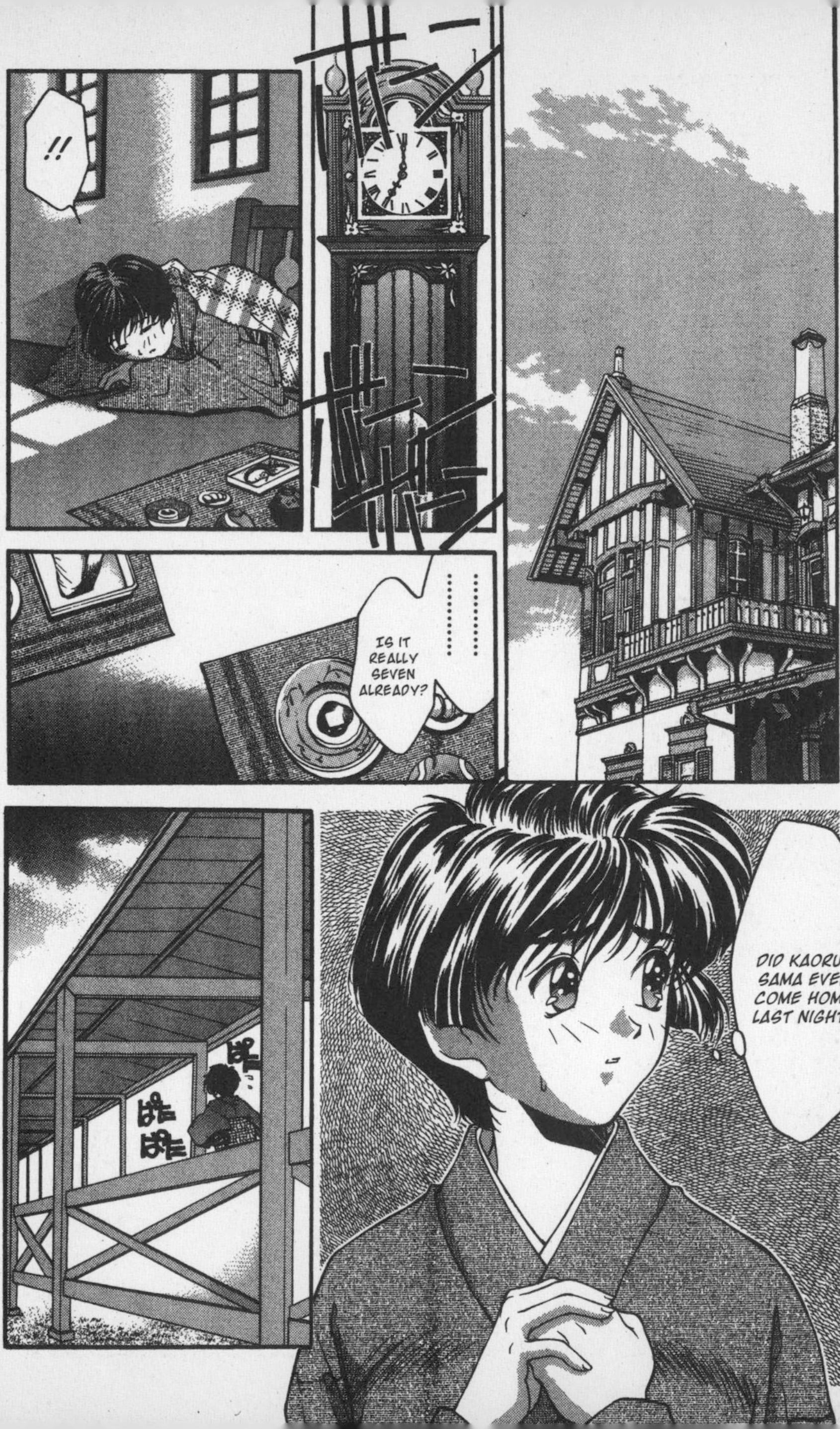

!!
......
IS IT REALLY SEVEN ALREADY?
DID KAORU-SAMA EVER COME HOME LAST NIGHT?

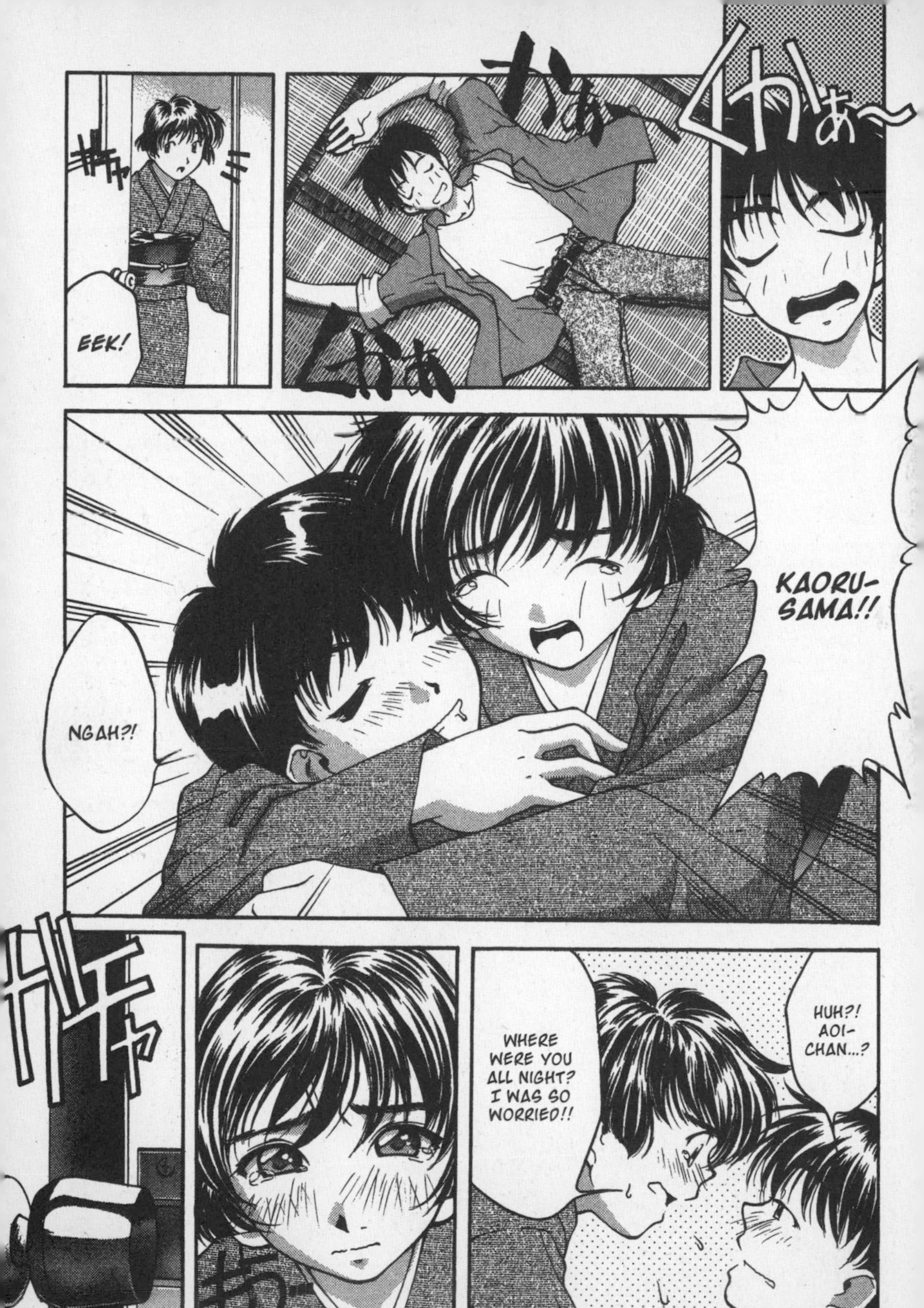
くわぁ~
EEK!
KAORU-SAMA!!
NGAH?!
HUH?! AOI-CHAN...?
WHERE WERE YOU ALL NIGHT? I WAS SO WORRIED!!
ガチャ

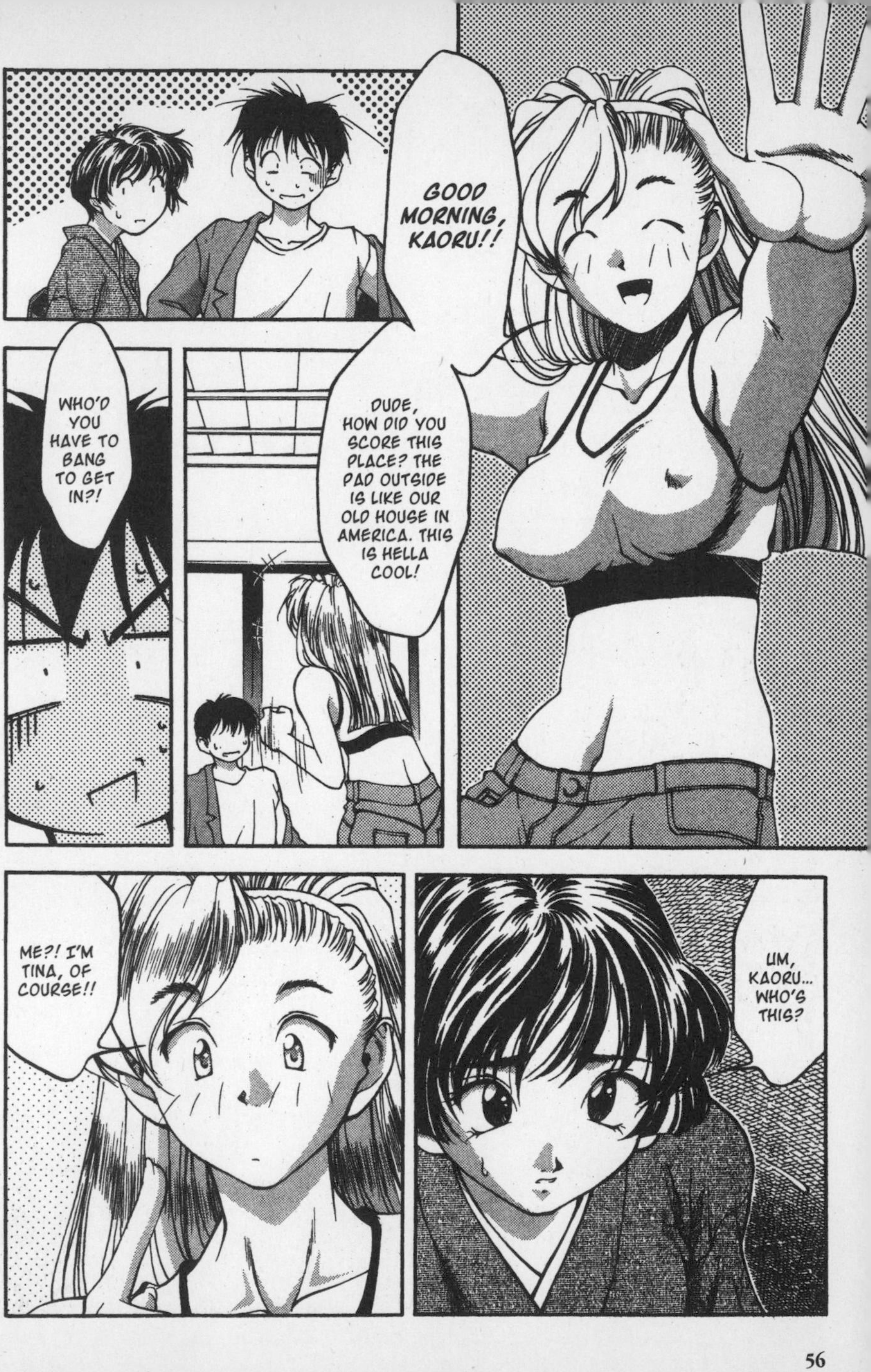
GOOD MORNING, KAORU!!
DUDE, HOW DID YOU SCORE THIS PLACE? THE PAD OUTSIDE IS LIKE OUR OLD HOUSE IN AMERICA. THIS IS HELLA COOL!
WHO'D YOU HAVE TO BANG TO GET IN?!
UM, KAORU... WHO'S THIS?
ME?! I'M TINA, OF COURSE!!

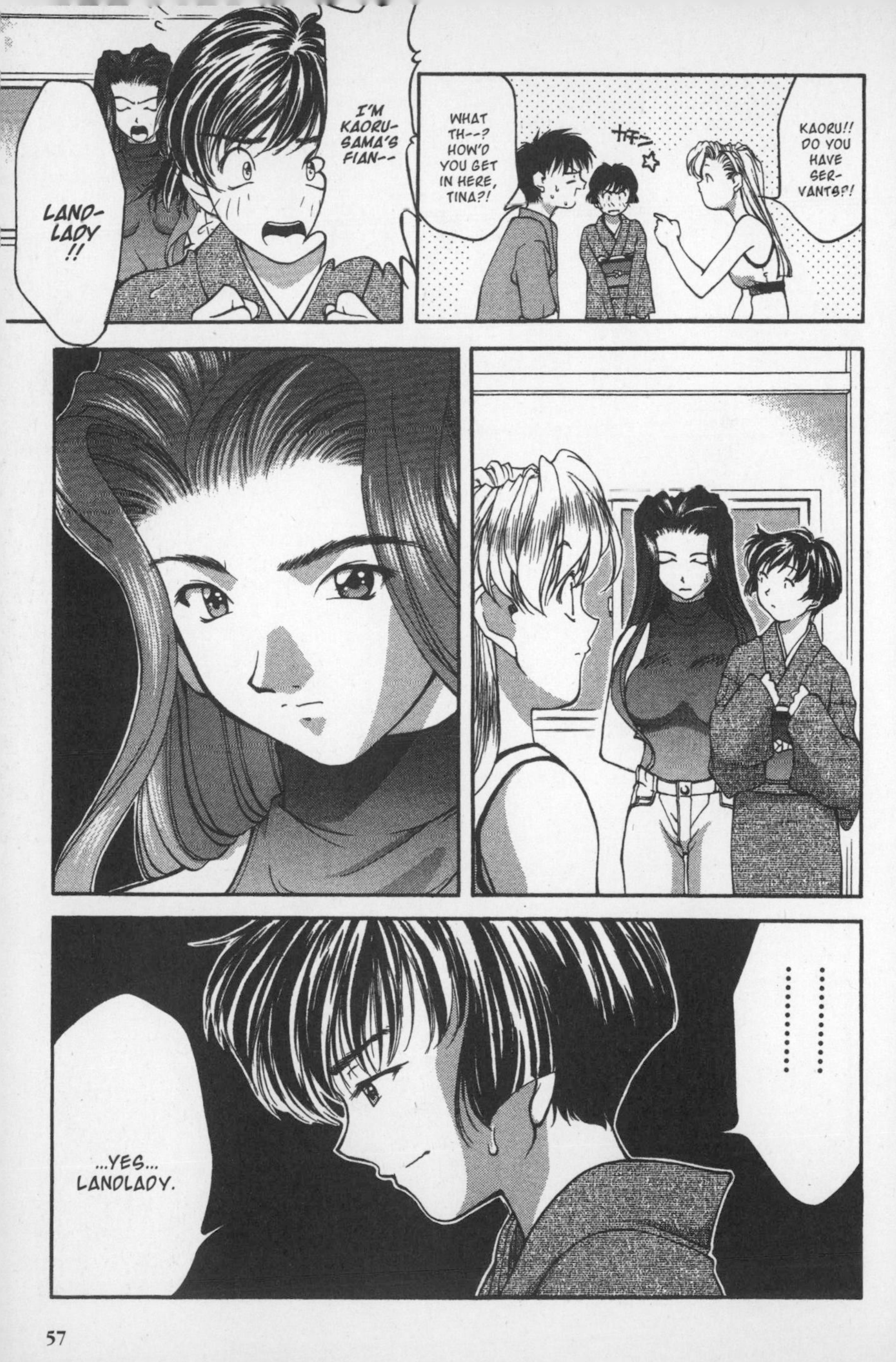
KAORU!! DO YOU HAVE SER-VANTS?!
WHAT TH--? HOW'D YOU GET IN HERE, TINA?!
I'M KAORU-SAMA'S FIAN--
LAND-LADY!!
......
...YES... LANDLADY.

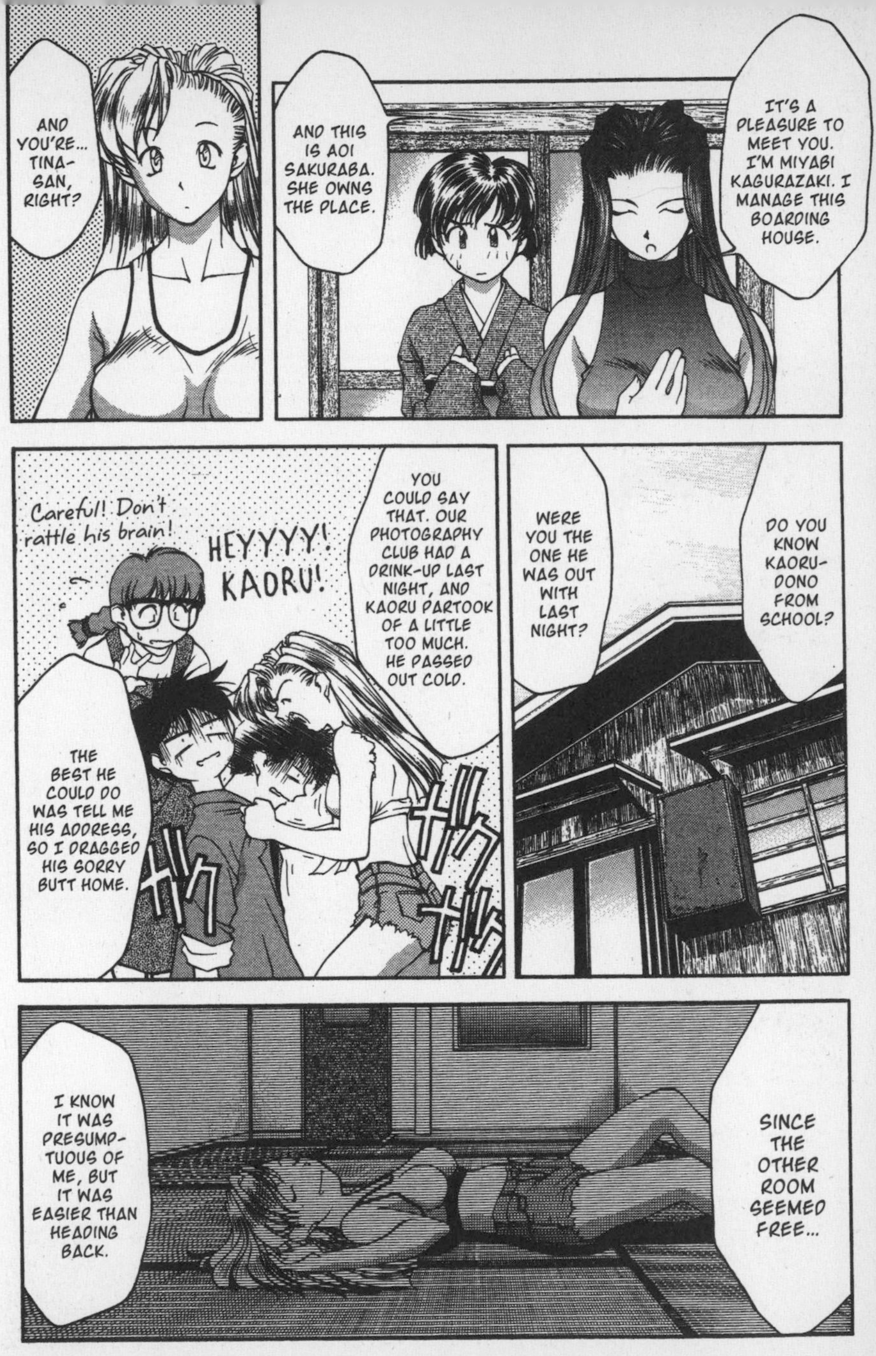
IT'S A PLEASURE TO MEET YOU. I'M MIYABI KAGURAZAKI. I MANAGE THIS BOARDING HOUSE.
AND THIS IS AOI SAKURABA. SHE OWNS THE PLACE.
AND YOU'RE... TINA-SAN, RIGHT?
DO YOU KNOW KAORU-DONO FROM SCHOOL?
WERE YOU THE ONE HE WAS OUT WITH LAST NIGHT?
YOU COULD SAY THAT. OUR PHOTOGRAPHY CLUB HAD A DRINK-UP LAST NIGHT, AND KAORU PARTOOK OF A LITTLE TOO MUCH. HE PASSED OUT COLD.
HEYYYY! KAORU!
Careful! Don't rattle his brain!
THE BEST HE COULD DO WAS TELL ME HIS ADDRESS, SO I DRAGGED HIS SORRY BUTT HOME.
SINCE THE OTHER ROOM SEEMED FREE...
I KNOW IT WAS PRESUMPTUOUS OF ME, BUT IT WAS EASIER THAN HEADING BACK.

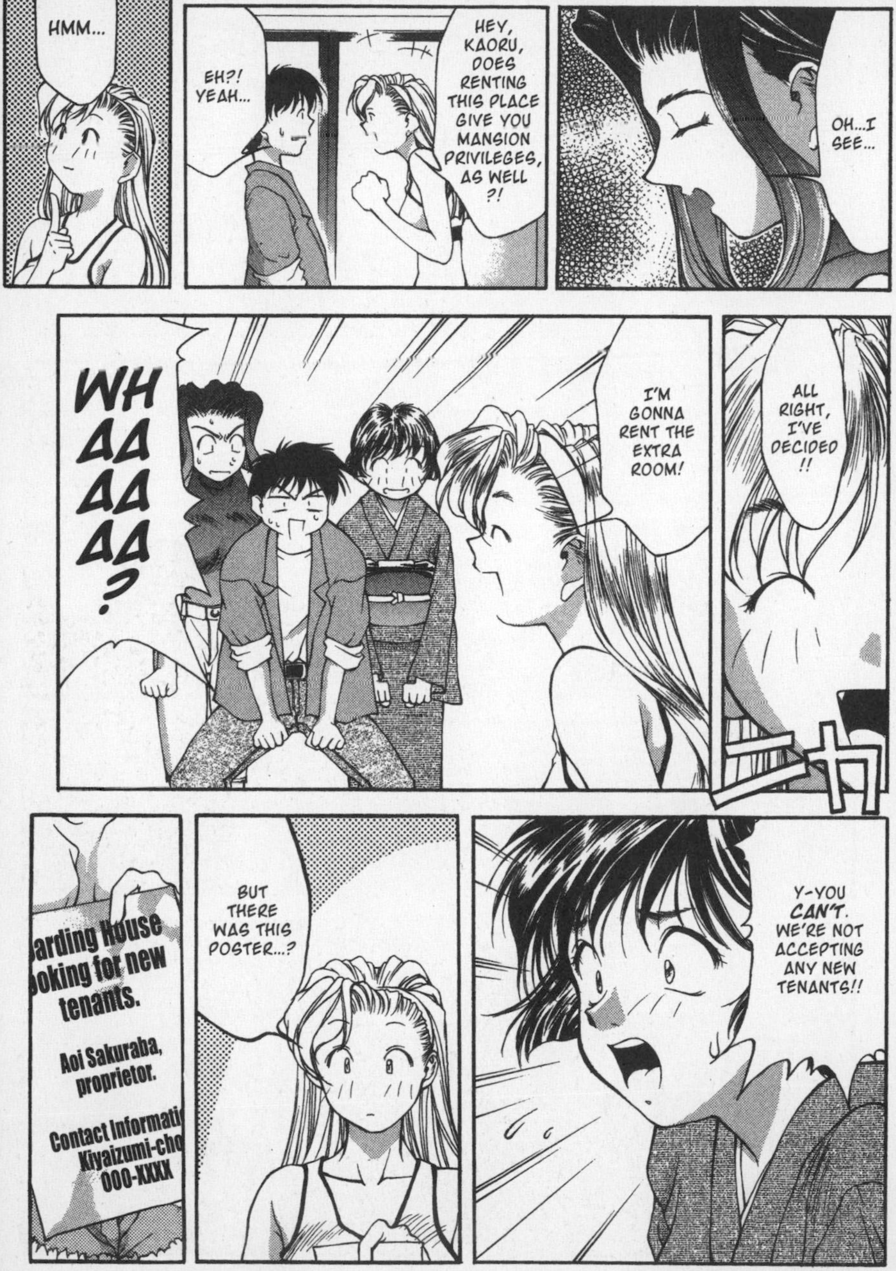
OH...I SEE...
HEY, KAORU, DOES RENTING THIS PLACE GIVE YOU MANSION PRIVILEGES, AS WELL ?!
EH?! YEAH...
HMM...
ALL RIGHT, I'VE DECIDED !!
I'M GONNA RENT THE EXTRA ROOM!
WHAAAAAAAA?
Y-YOU CAN'T. WE'RE NOT ACCEPTING ANY NEW TENANTS!!
BUT THERE WAS THIS POSTER...?
arding House
ooking for new
tenants.
Aoi Sakuraba,
proprietor.
Contact Informati
Kiyaizumi-cho
000-XXXX

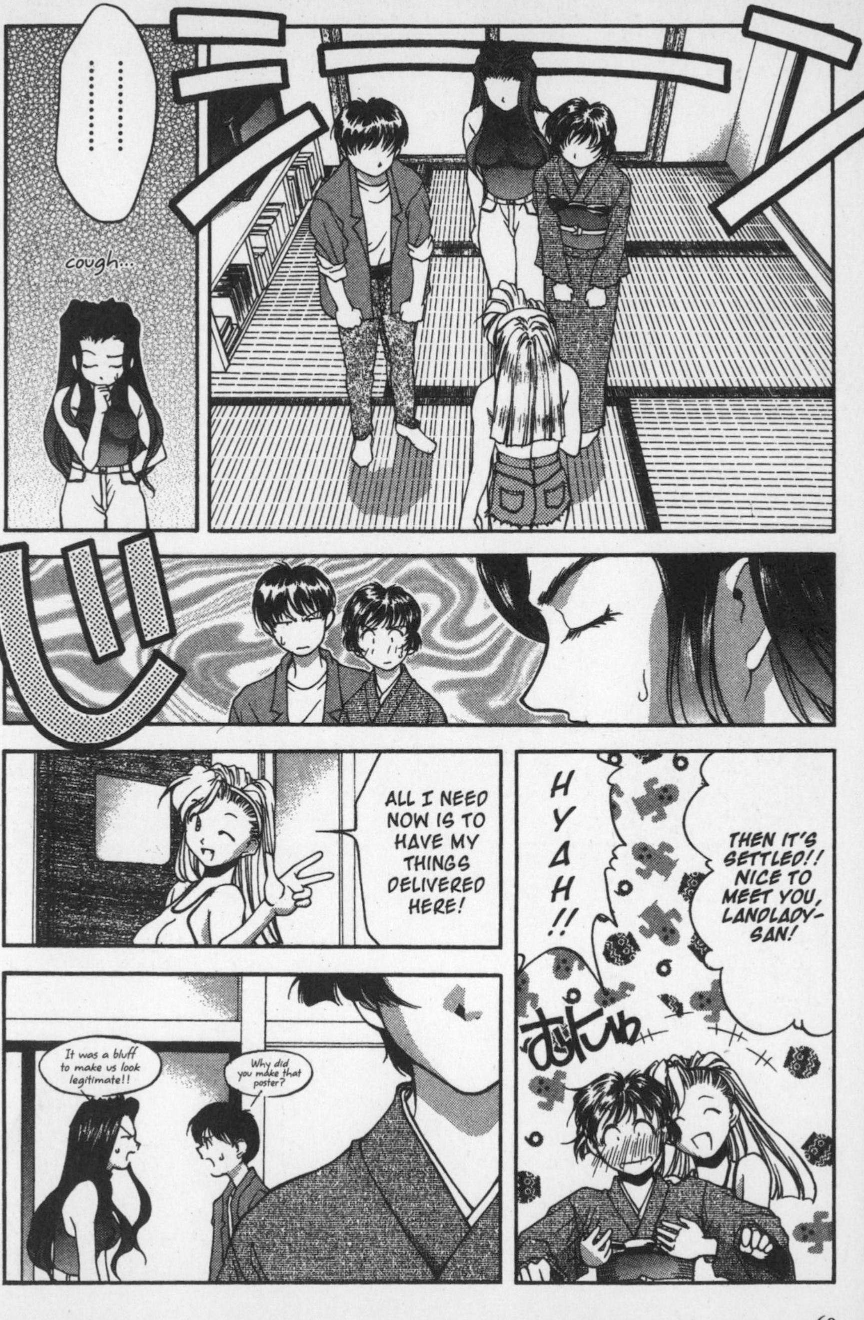
......
cough...
THEN IT'S SETTLED!! NICE TO MEET YOU, LANDLADY-SAN!
HYAAH!!
ALL I NEED NOW IS TO HAVE MY THINGS DELIVERED HERE!
Why did you make that poster?
It was a bluff to make us look legitimate!!

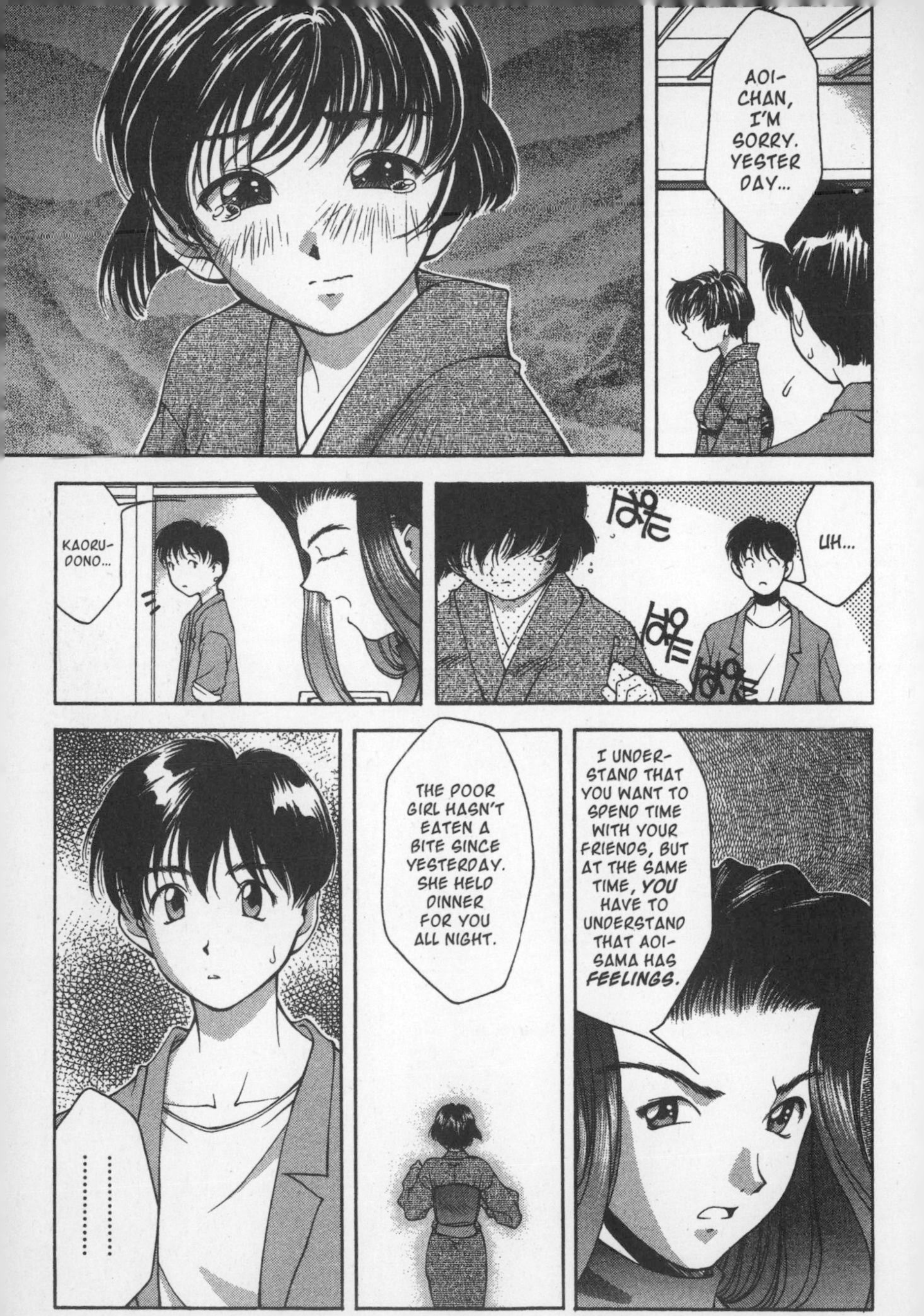
AOI-CHAN, I'M SORRY. YESTER DAY...
UH...
KAORU-DONO...
I UNDER-STAND THAT YOU WANT TO SPEND TIME WITH YOUR FRIENDS, BUT AT THE SAME TIME, *YOU* HAVE TO UNDERSTAND THAT AOI-SAMA HAS **FEELINGS.**
THE POOR GIRL HASN'T EATEN A BITE SINCE YESTERDAY. SHE HELD DINNER FOR YOU ALL NIGHT.
......

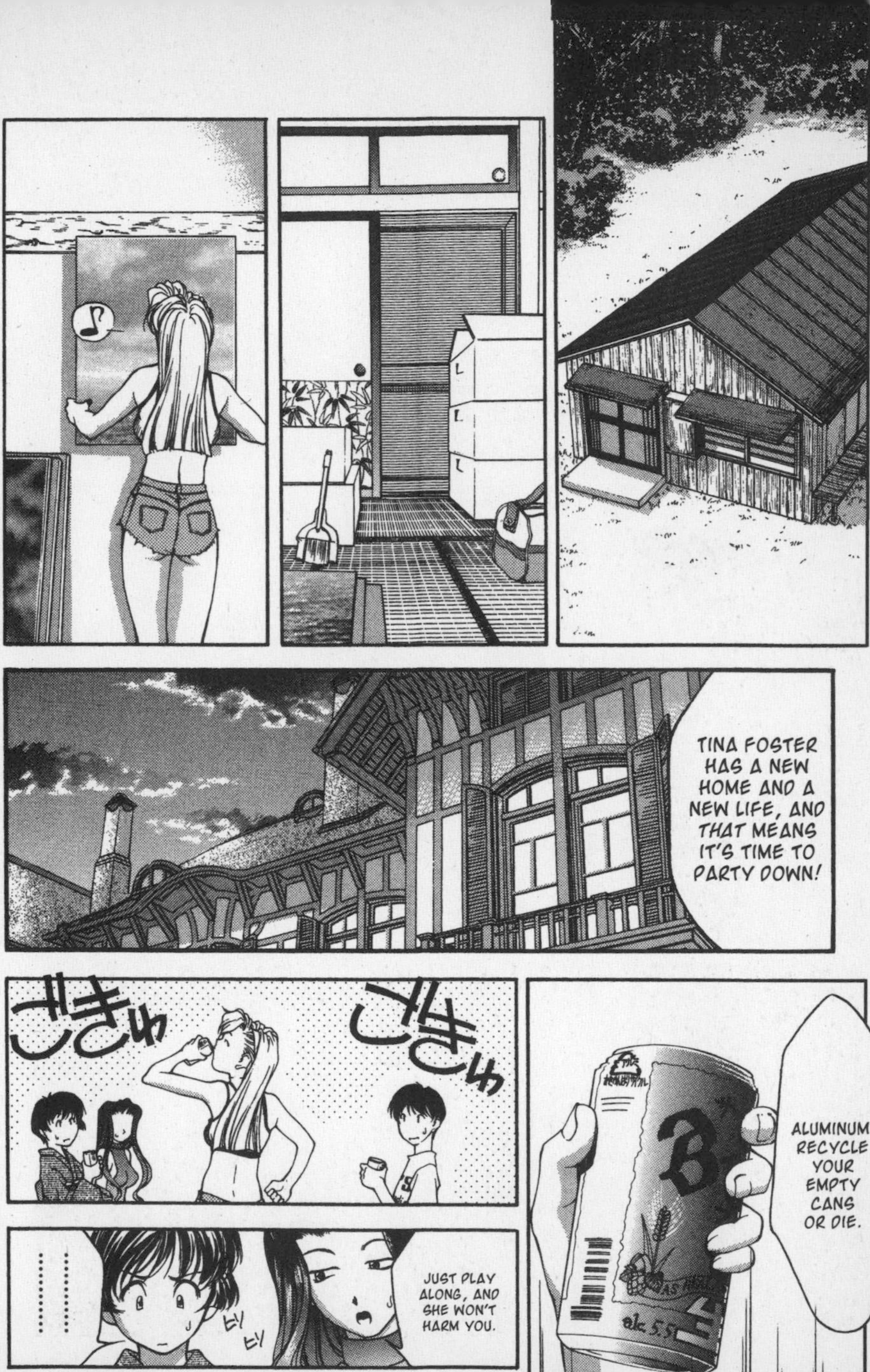
TINA FOSTER HAS A NEW HOME AND A NEW LIFE, AND THAT MEANS IT'S TIME TO PARTY DOWN!
ALUMINUM. RECYCLE YOUR EMPTY CANS OR DIE.
ごきゅ
ごきゅ
JUST PLAY ALONG, AND SHE WON'T HARM YOU.
ヒソ ヒソ

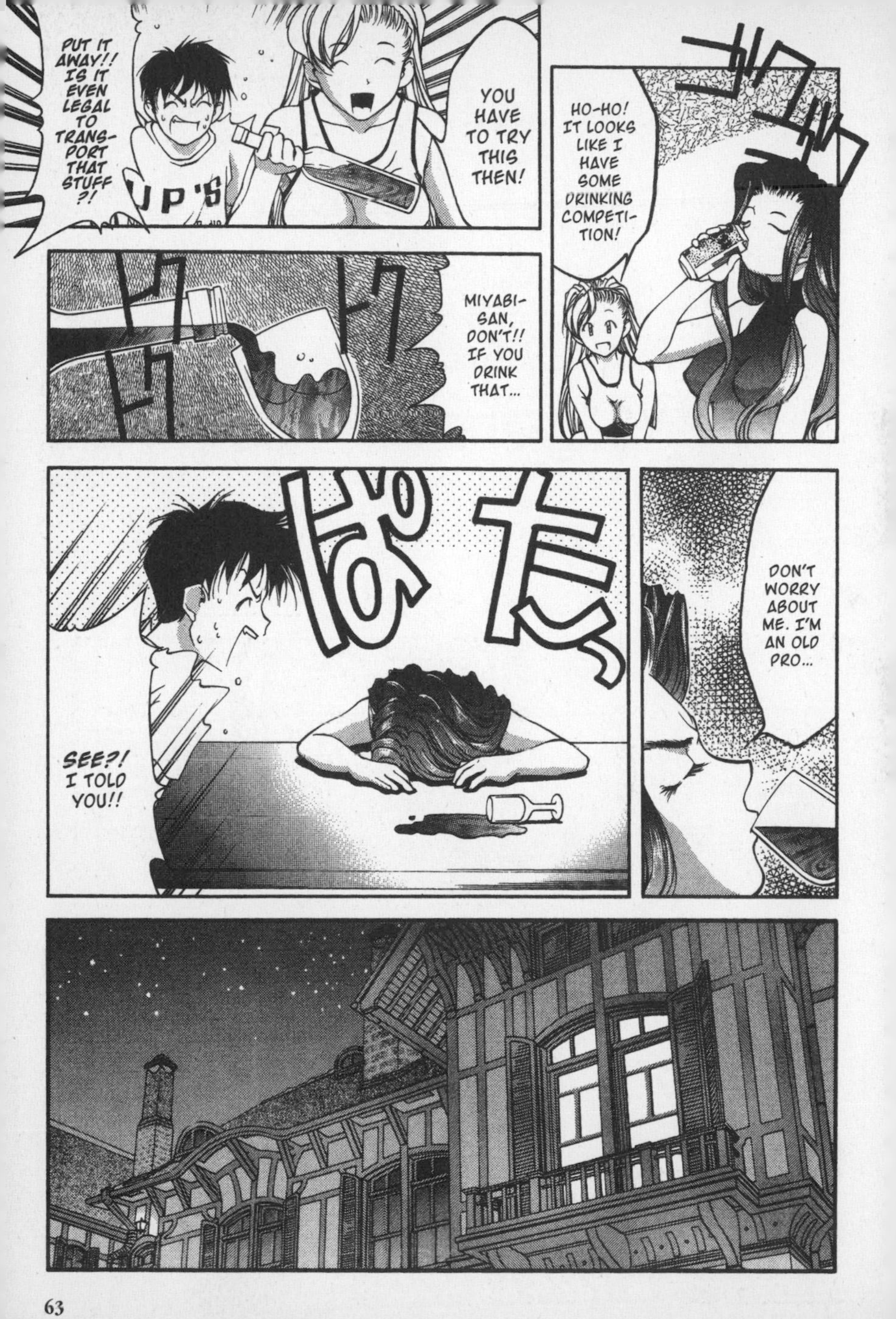

ゴクゴク
HO-HO! IT LOOKS LIKE I HAVE SOME DRINKING COMPETITION!
YOU HAVE TO TRY THIS THEN!
PUT IT AWAY!! IS IT EVEN LEGAL TO TRANS-PORT THAT STUFF?!
UP'S
トクトク
MIYABI-SAN, DON'T!! IF YOU DRINK THAT...
DON'T WORRY ABOUT ME. I'M AN OLD PRO...
ぱた
SEE?! I TOLD YOU!!

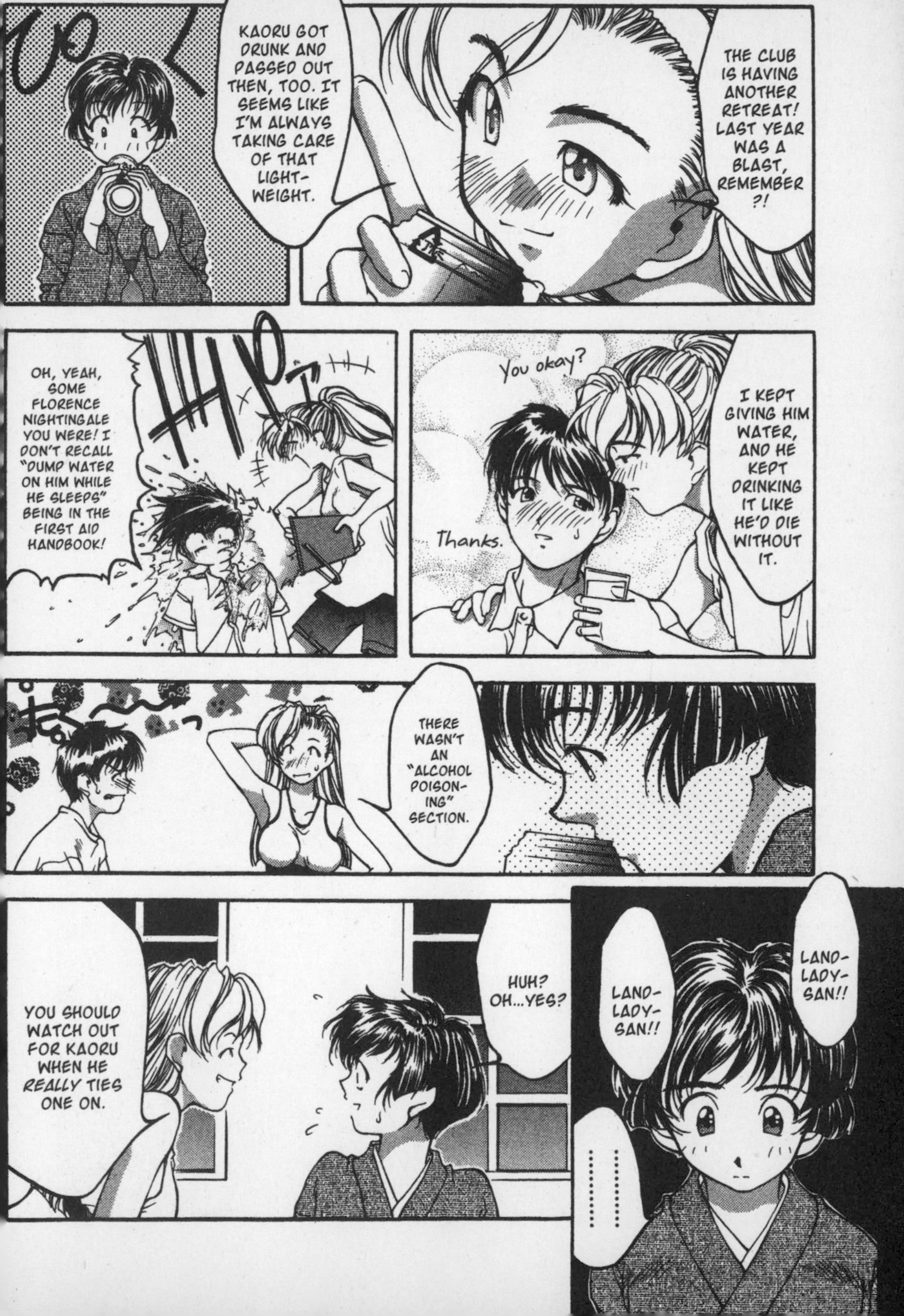
THE CLUB IS HAVING ANOTHER RETREAT! LAST YEAR WAS A BLAST, REMEMBER?!
KAORU GOT DRUNK AND PASSED OUT THEN, TOO. IT SEEMS LIKE I'M ALWAYS TAKING CARE OF THAT LIGHT-WEIGHT.
I KEPT GIVING HIM WATER, AND HE KEPT DRINKING IT LIKE HE'D DIE WITHOUT IT.
You okay?
Thanks.
OH, YEAH, SOME FLORENCE NIGHTINGALE YOU WERE! I DON'T RECALL "DUMP WATER ON HIM WHILE HE SLEEPS" BEING IN THE FIRST AID HANDBOOK!
THERE WASN'T AN "ALCOHOL POISONING" SECTION.
LAND-LADY-SAN!!
LAND-LADY-SAN!!
......
HUH? OH...YES?
YOU SHOULD WATCH OUT FOR KAORU WHEN HE *REALLY* TIES ONE ON.

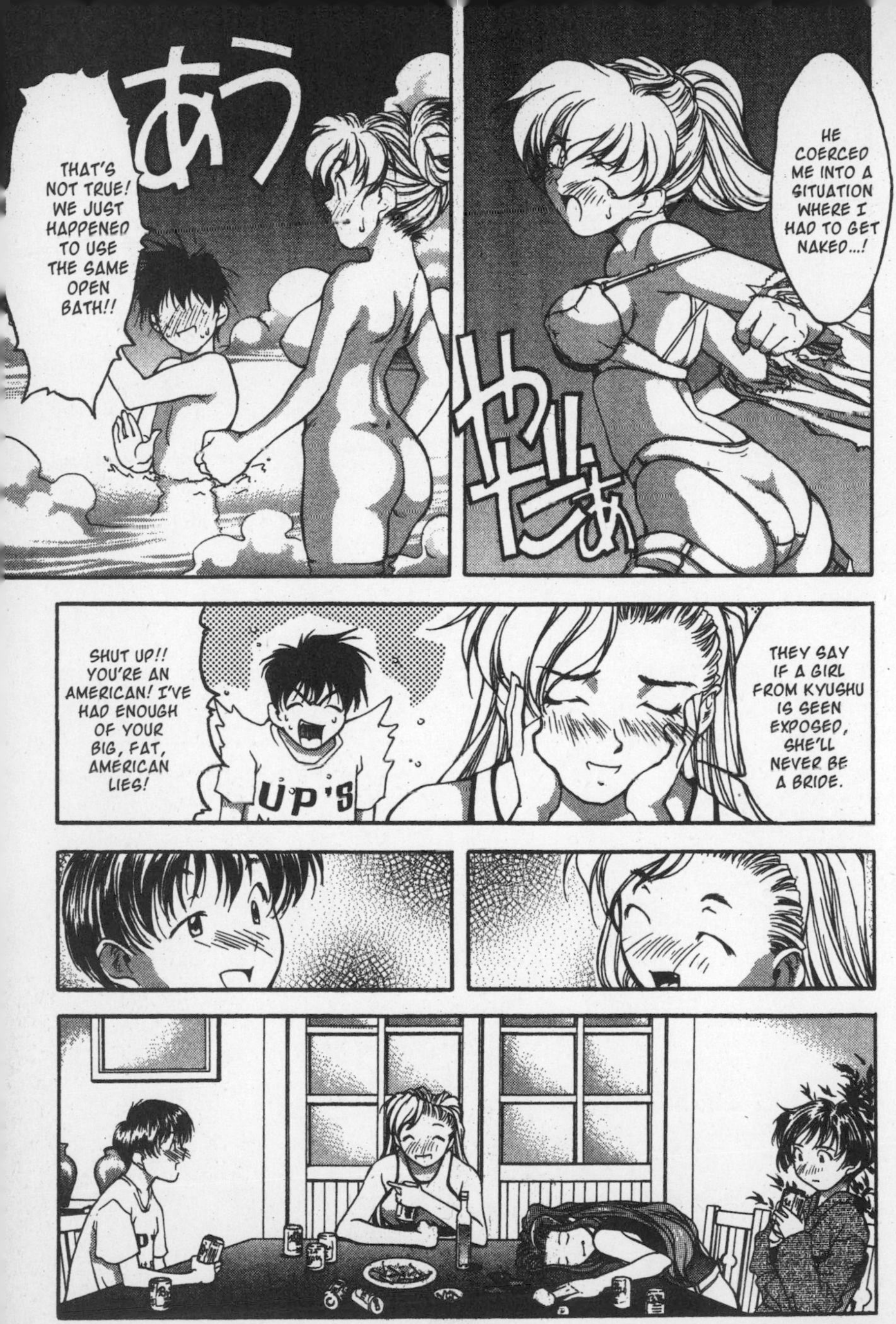

HE COERCED ME INTO A SITUATION WHERE I HAD TO GET NAKED...!
やーーあ
あう
THAT'S NOT TRUE! WE JUST HAPPENED TO USE THE SAME OPEN BATH!!
THEY SAY IF A GIRL FROM KYUSHU IS SEEN EXPOSED, SHE'LL NEVER BE A BRIDE.
SHUT UP!! YOU'RE AN AMERICAN! I'VE HAD ENOUGH OF YOUR BIG, FAT, AMERICAN LIES!
UP'S

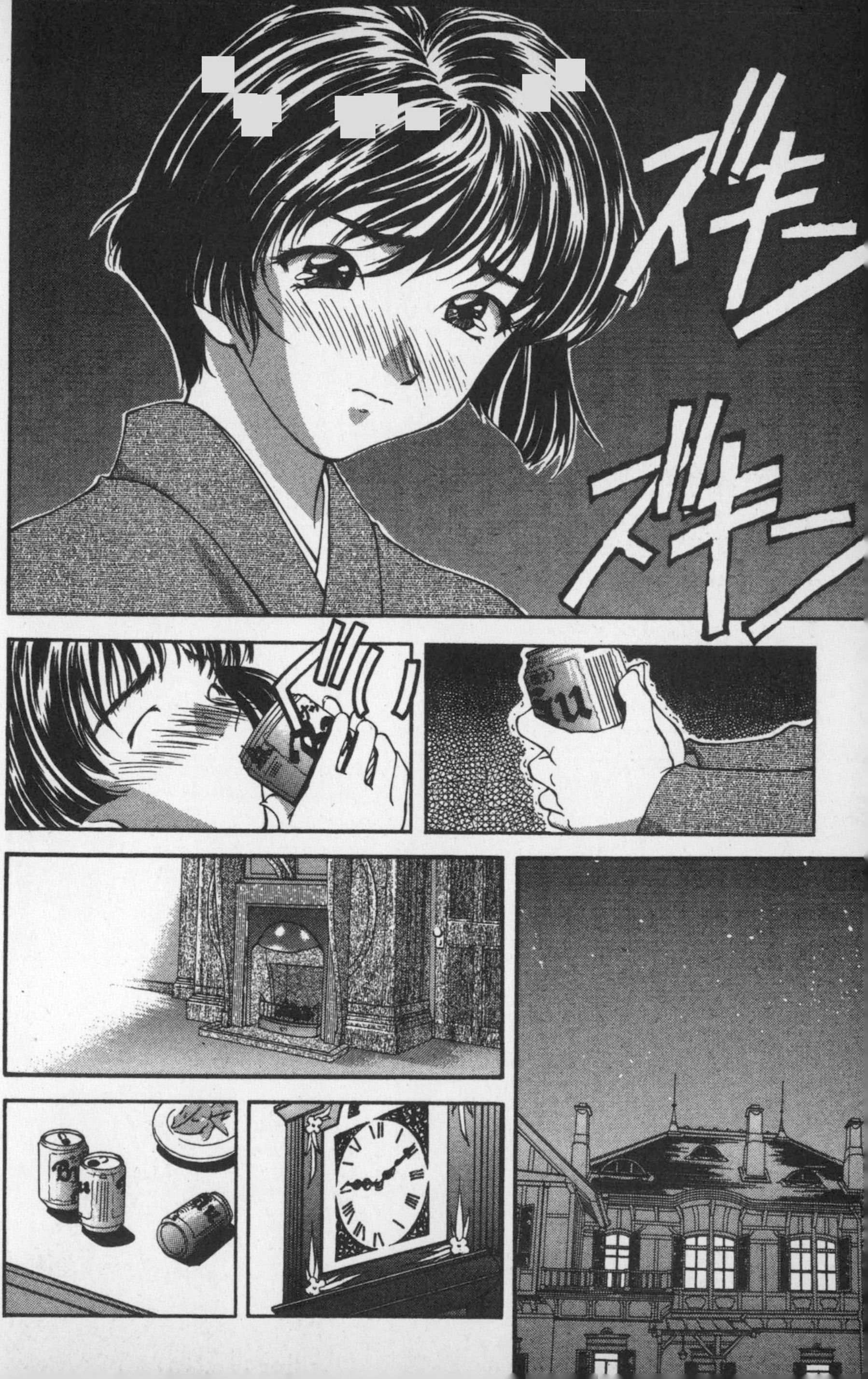
ズキン
ズキン
グー

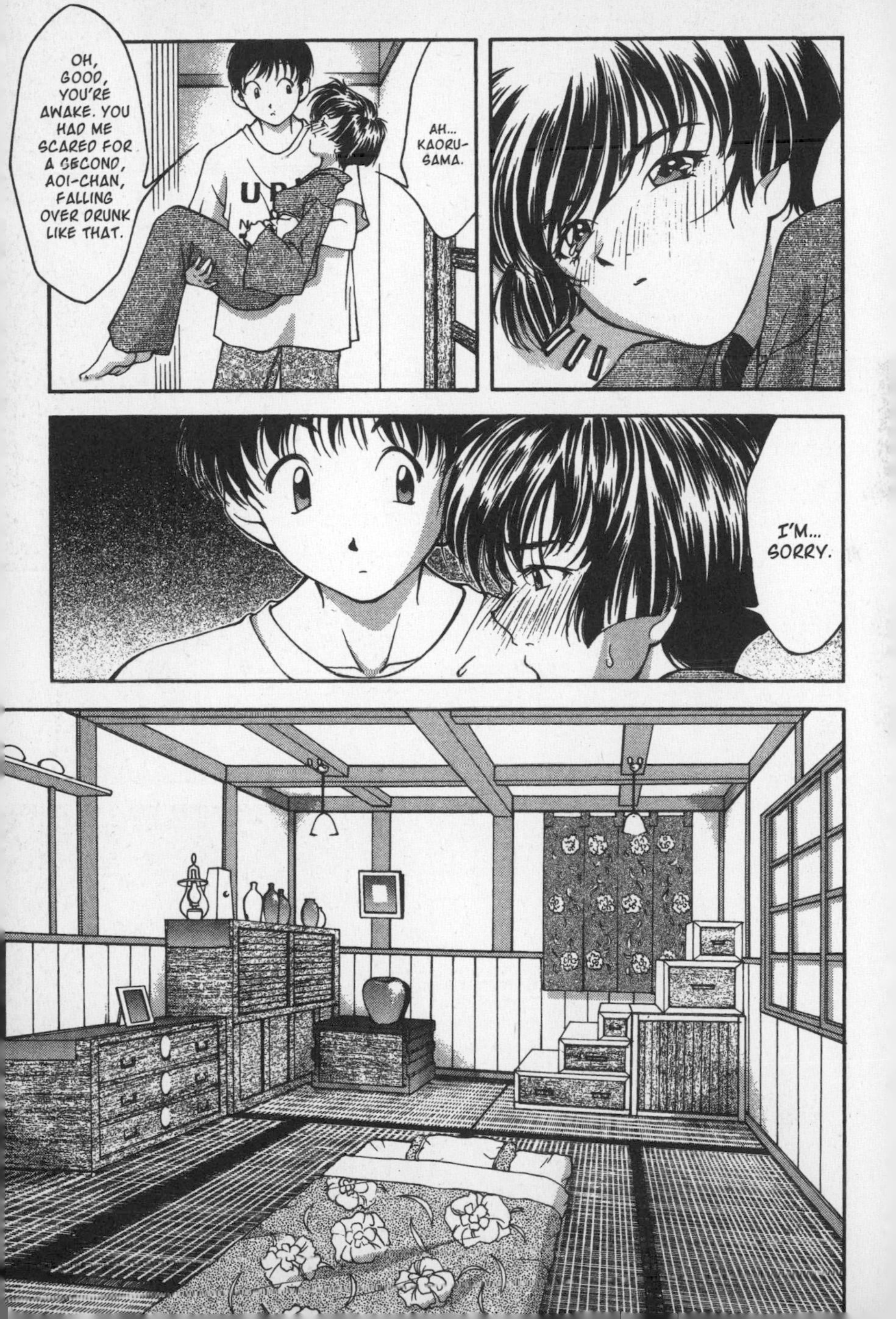
AH... KAORU-SAMA.
OH, GOOD, YOU'RE AWAKE. YOU HAD ME SCARED FOR A SECOND, AOI-CHAN, FALLING OVER DRUNK LIKE THAT.
I'M... SORRY.

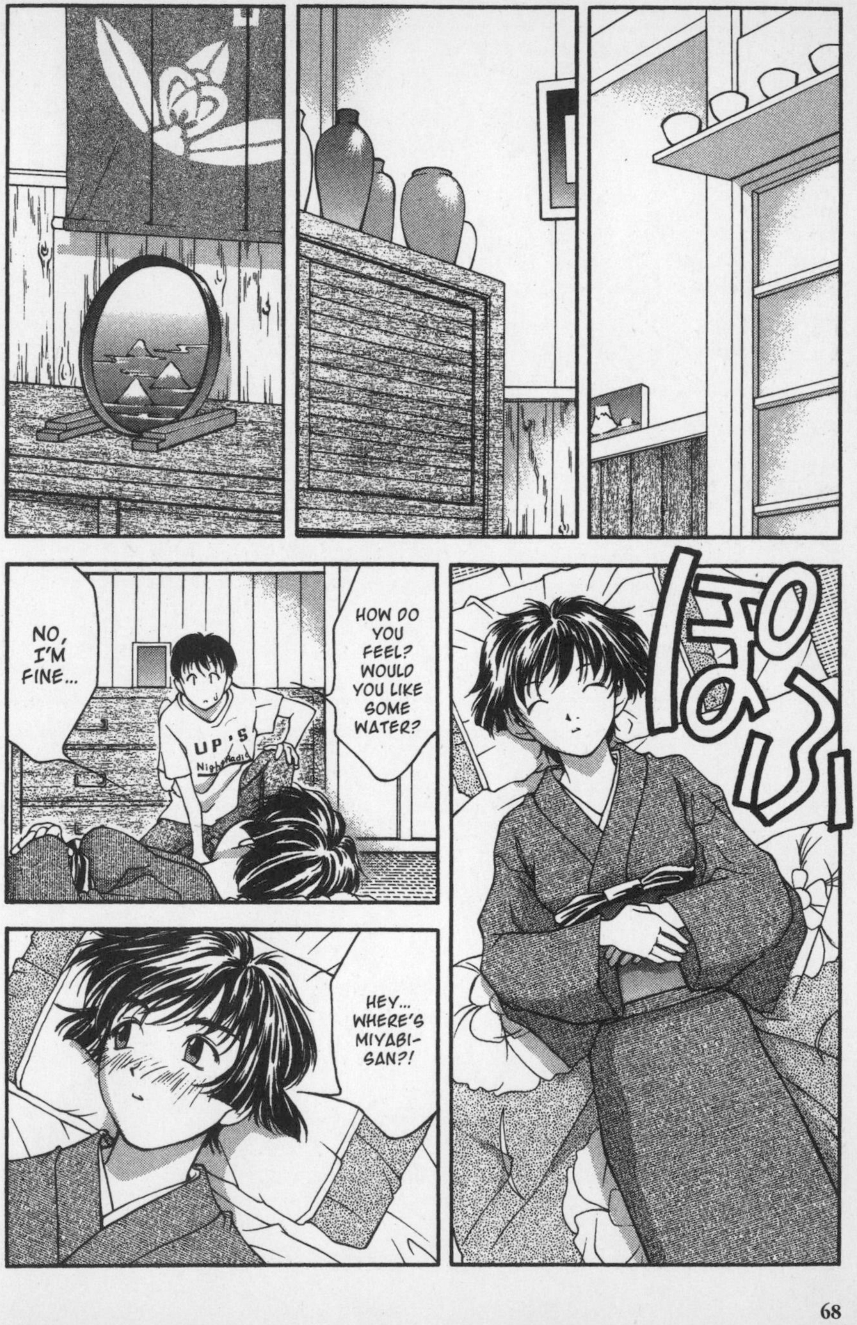
ぽふ
HOW DO YOU FEEL? WOULD YOU LIKE SOME WATER?
NO, I'M FINE...
HEY... WHERE'S MIYABI-SAN?!

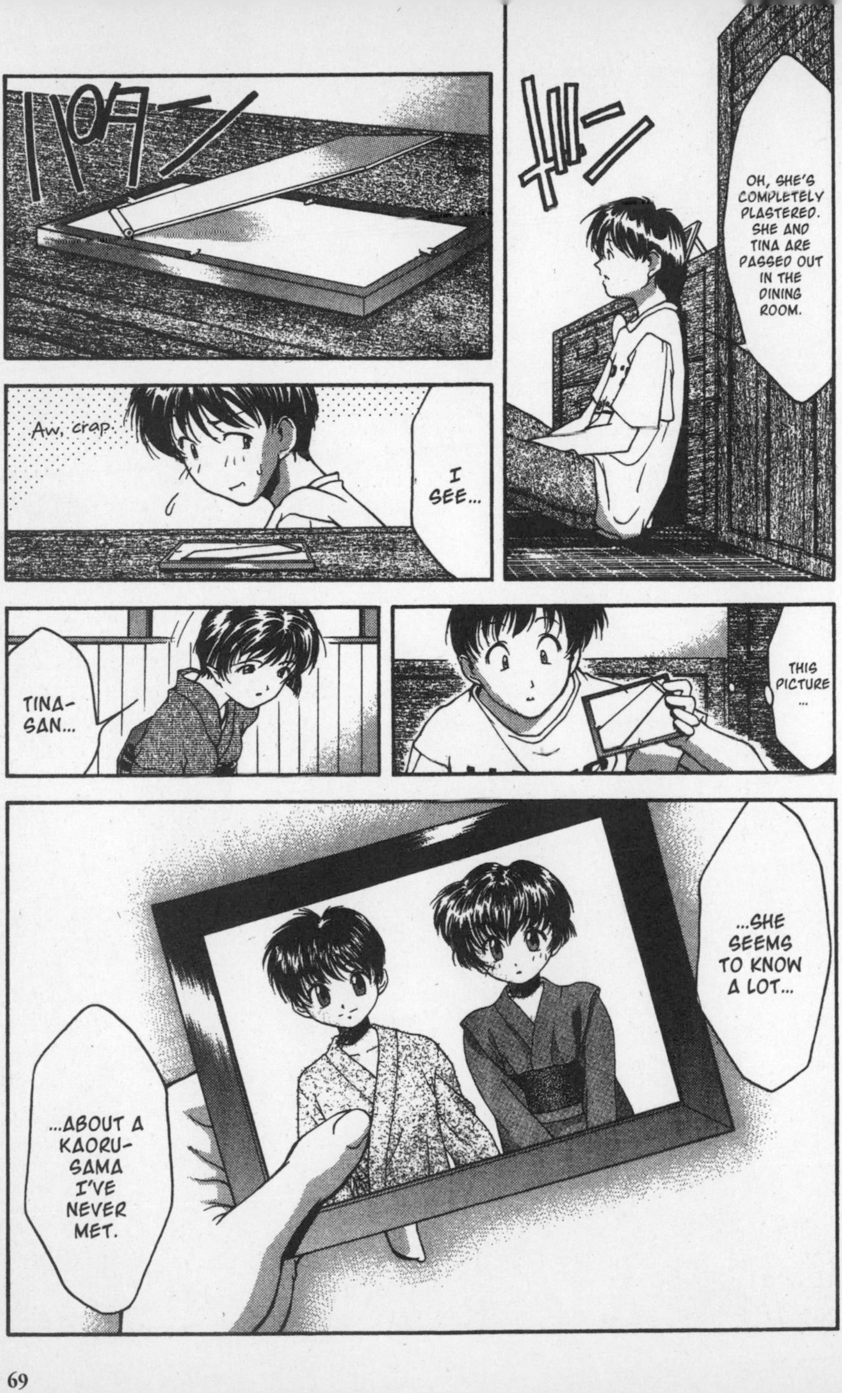
OH, SHE'S COMPLETELY PLASTERED. SHE AND TINA ARE PASSED OUT IN THE DINING ROOM.
I SEE...
Aw, crap.
THIS PICTURE ...
TINA-SAN...
...SHE SEEMS TO KNOW A LOT...
...ABOUT A KAORU-SAMA I'VE NEVER MET.

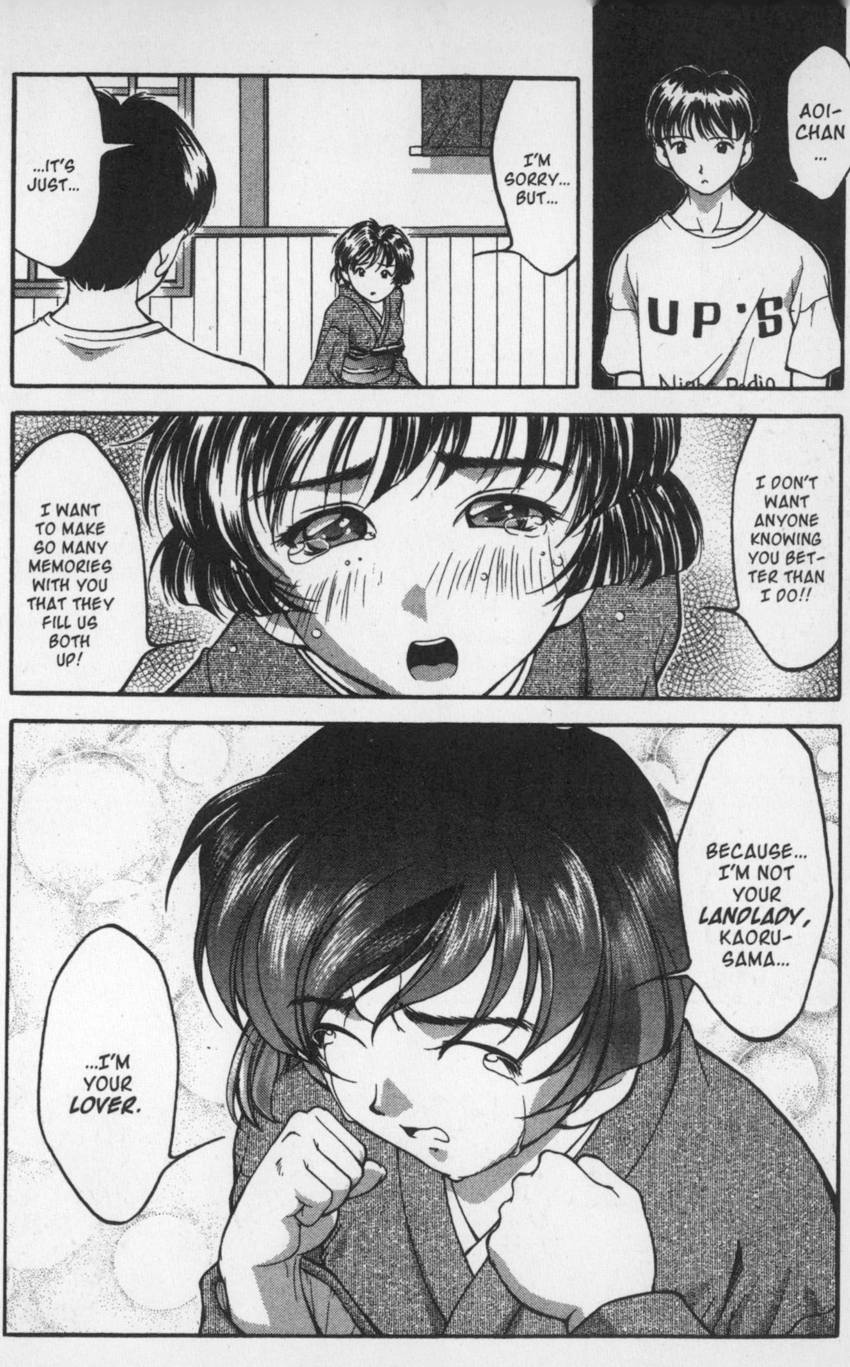
AOI-CHAN ...
UP'S
I'M SORRY... BUT...
...IT'S JUST...
I DON'T WANT ANYONE KNOWING YOU BETTER THAN I DO!!
I WANT TO MAKE SO MANY MEMORIES WITH YOU THAT THEY FILL US BOTH UP!
BECAUSE... I'M NOT YOUR LANDLADY, KAORU-SAMA...
...I'M YOUR LOVER.

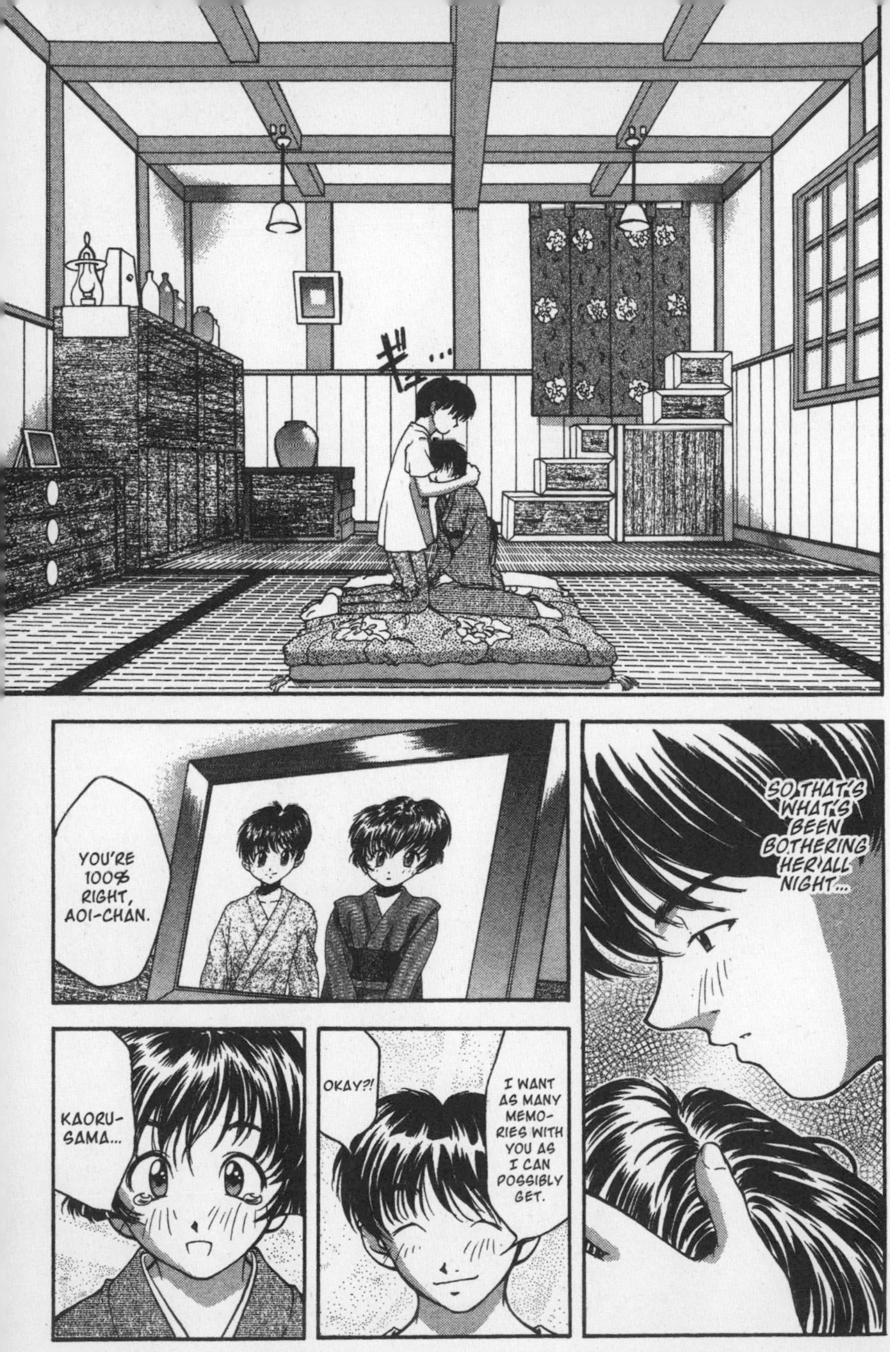

ギュ...
SO THAT'S WHAT'S BEEN BOTHERING HER ALL NIGHT...
YOU'RE 100% RIGHT, AOI-CHAN.
I WANT AS MANY MEMORIES WITH YOU AS I CAN POSSIBLY GET.
OKAY?!
KAORU-SAMA...

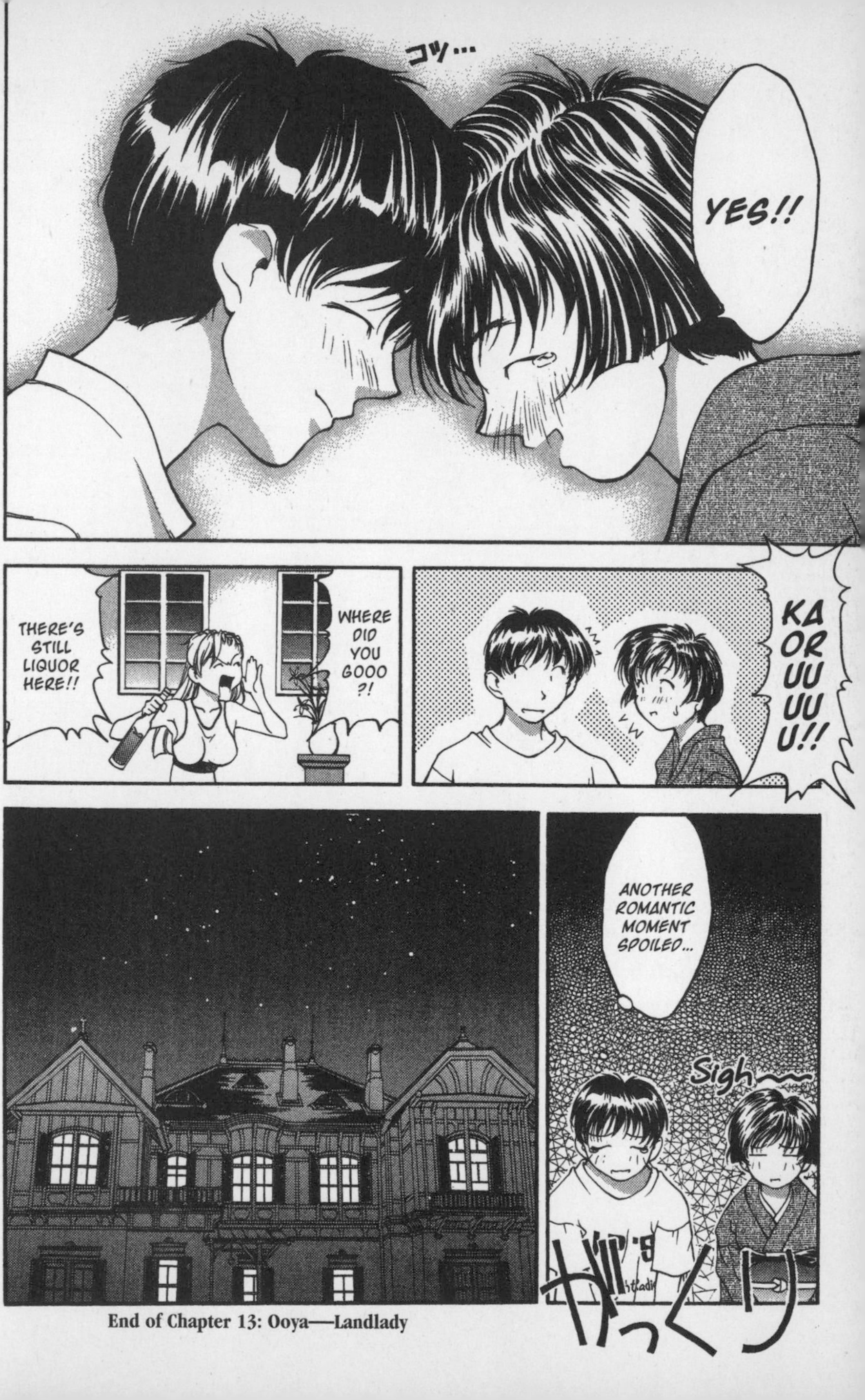
コツ…
YES!!
KAORUUUUUU!!
WHERE DID YOU GOOO?!
THERE'S STILL LIQUOR HERE!!
ANOTHER ROMANTIC MOMENT SPOILED...
Sigh
がっくり

End of Chapter 13: Ooya—Landlady

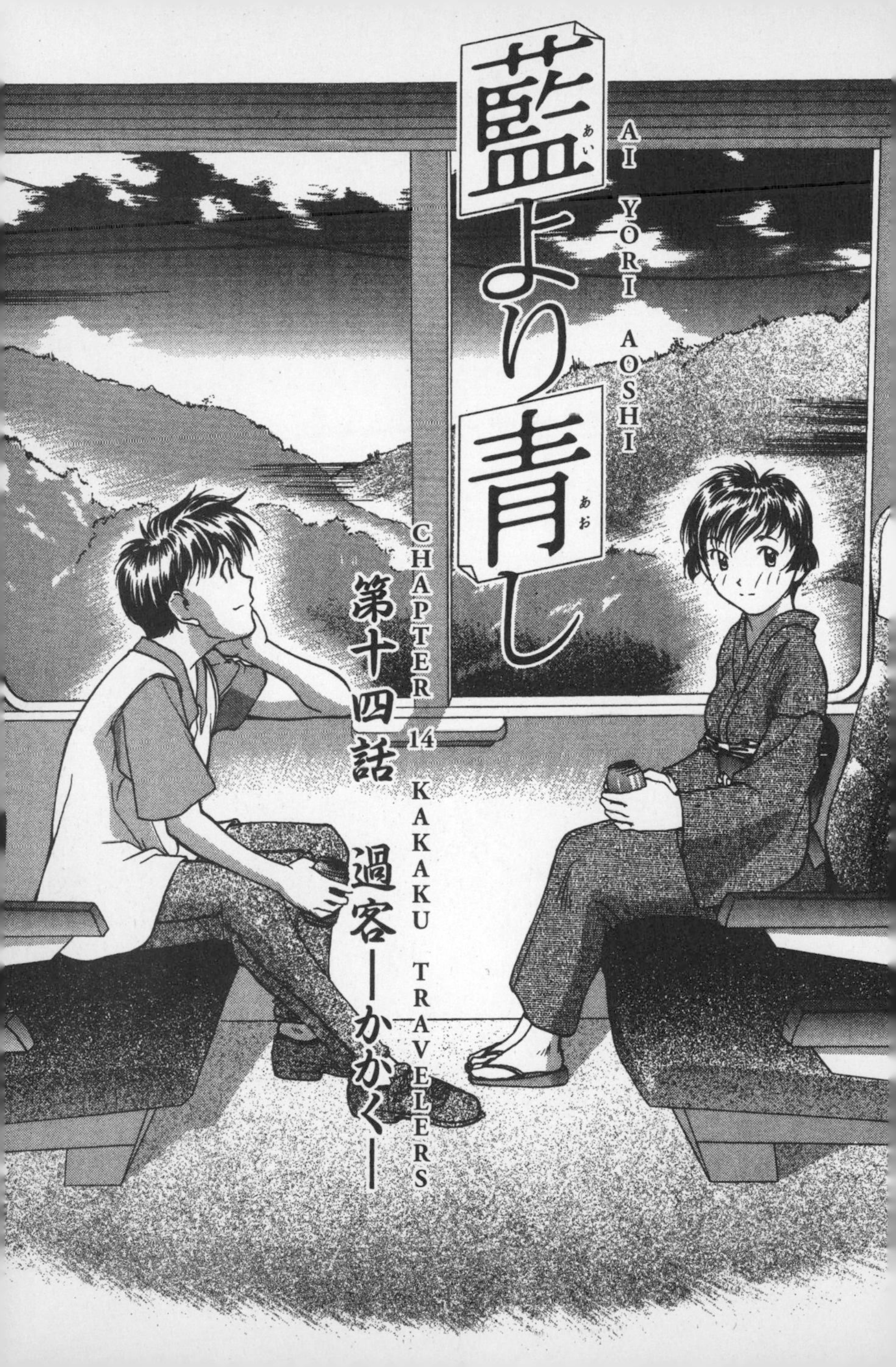

藍より青し
あい
あお
AI YORI AOSHI
第十四話
CHAPTER 14
過客―かかく―
KAKAKU TRAVELERS

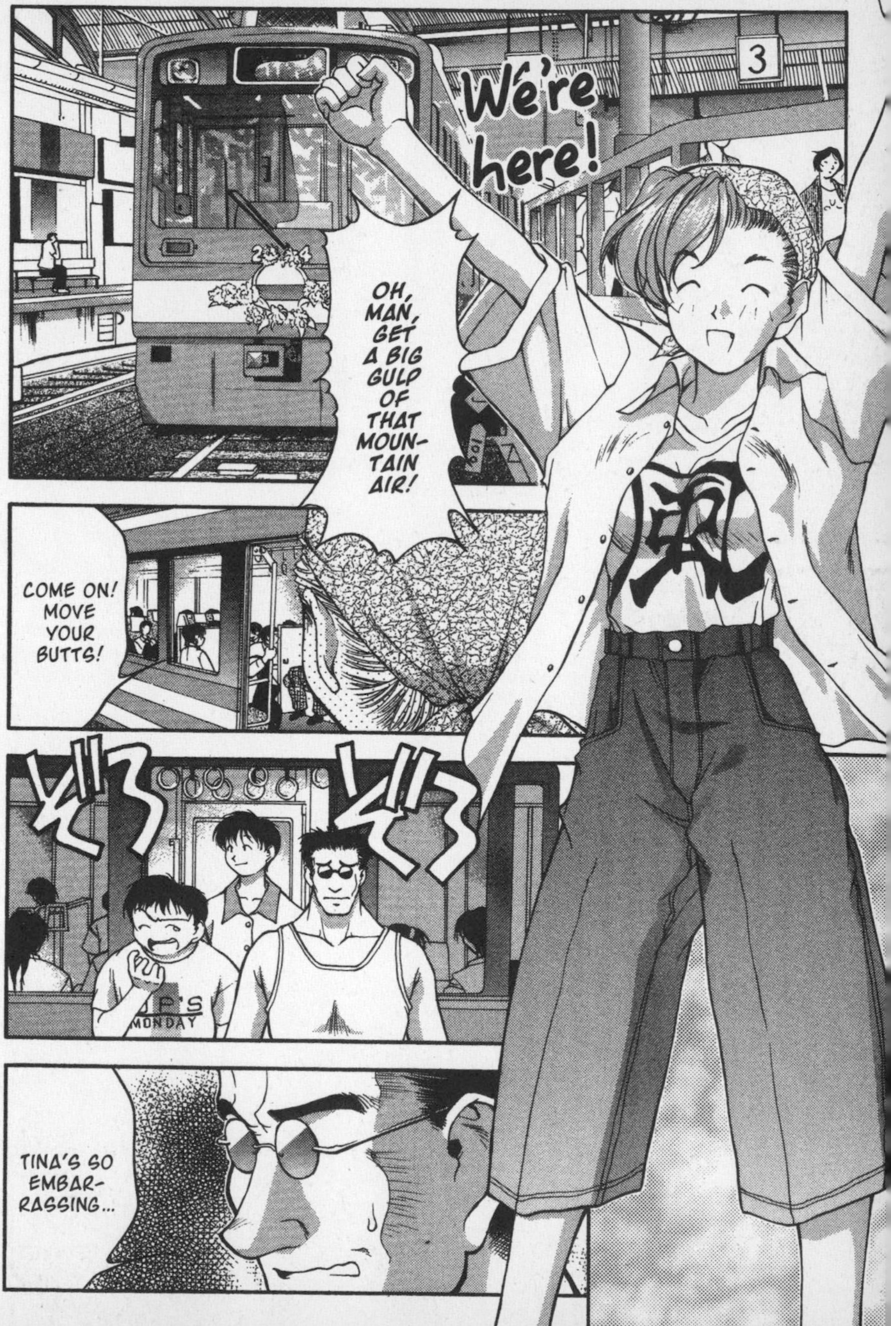
We're here!
OH, MAN, GET A BIG GULP OF THAT MOUNTAIN AIR!
COME ON! MOVE YOUR BUTTS!
ぞろ ぞろ
TINA'S SO EMBARRASSING...

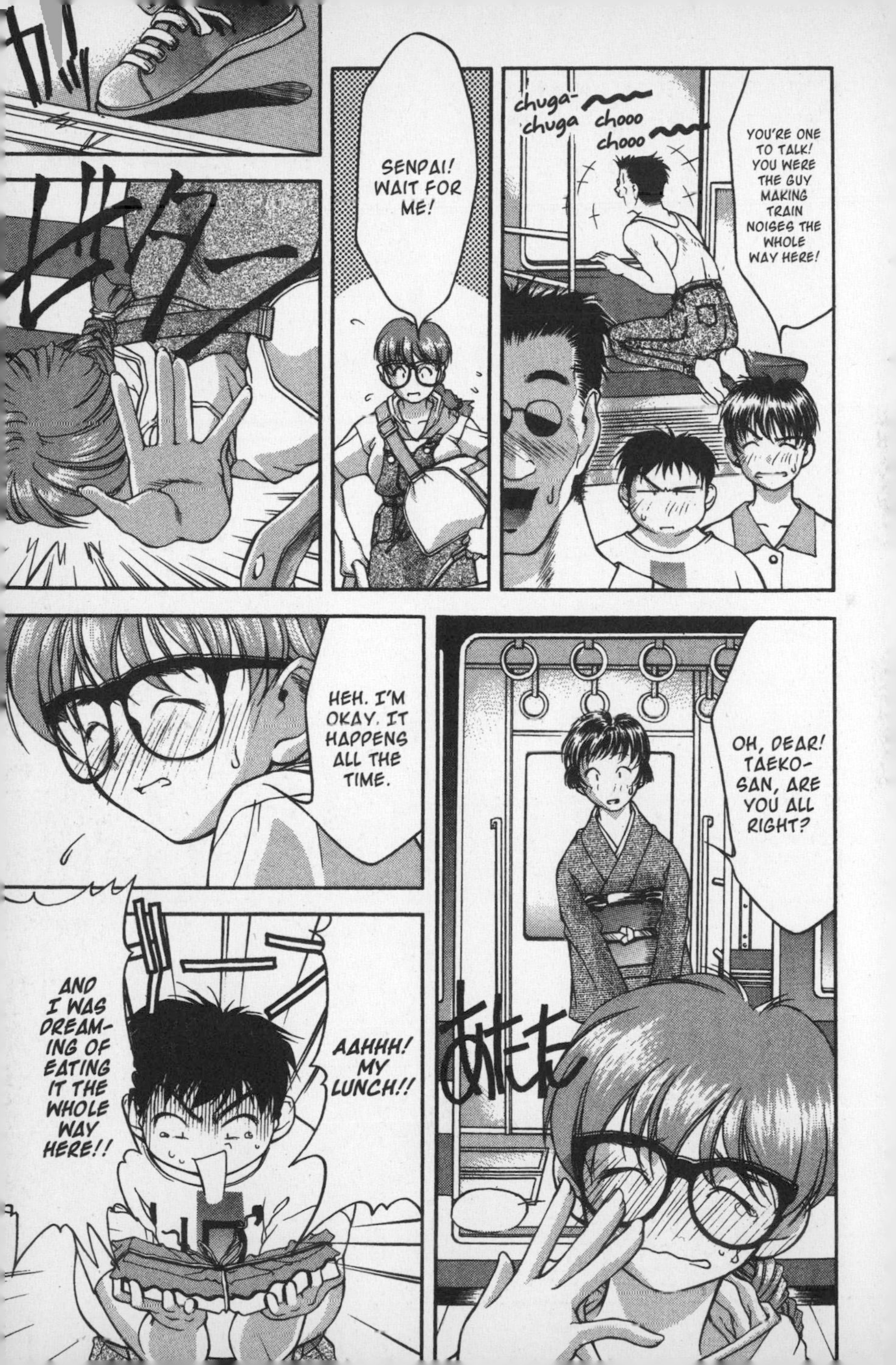
YOU'RE ONE TO TALK! YOU WERE THE GUY MAKING TRAIN NOISES THE WHOLE WAY HERE!
chuga-chuga chooo chooo
SENPAI! WAIT FOR ME!
OH, DEAR! TAEKO-SAN, ARE YOU ALL RIGHT?
HEH. I'M OKAY. IT HAPPENS ALL THE TIME.
AAHHH! MY LUNCH!!
AND I WAS DREAMING OF EATING IT THE WHOLE WAY HERE!!

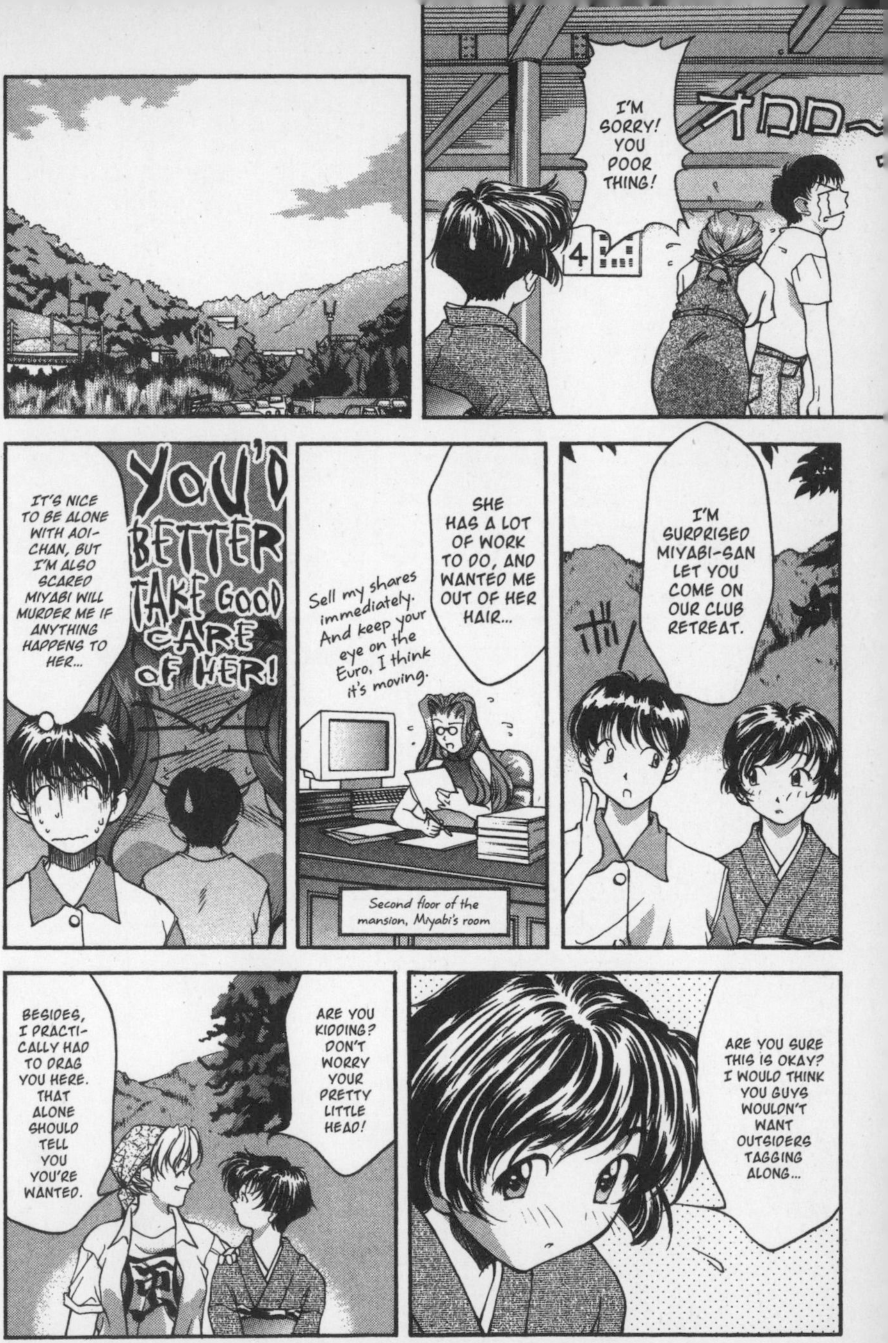

オロロ〜
I'M SORRY! YOU POOR THING!
I'M SURPRISED MIYABI-SAN LET YOU COME ON OUR CLUB RETREAT.
SHE HAS A LOT OF WORK TO DO, AND WANTED ME OUT OF HER HAIR...
Sell my shares immediately. And keep your eye on the Euro, I think it's moving.
Second floor of the mansion, Miyabi's room
YOU'D BETTER TAKE GOOD CARE OF HER!
IT'S NICE TO BE ALONE WITH AOI-CHAN, BUT I'M ALSO SCARED MIYABI WILL MURDER ME IF ANYTHING HAPPENS TO HER...
ARE YOU SURE THIS IS OKAY? I WOULD THINK YOU GUYS WOULDN'T WANT OUTSIDERS TAGGING ALONG...
ARE YOU KIDDING? DON'T WORRY YOUR PRETTY LITTLE HEAD!
BESIDES, I PRACTICALLY HAD TO DRAG YOU HERE. THAT ALONE SHOULD TELL YOU YOU'RE WANTED.

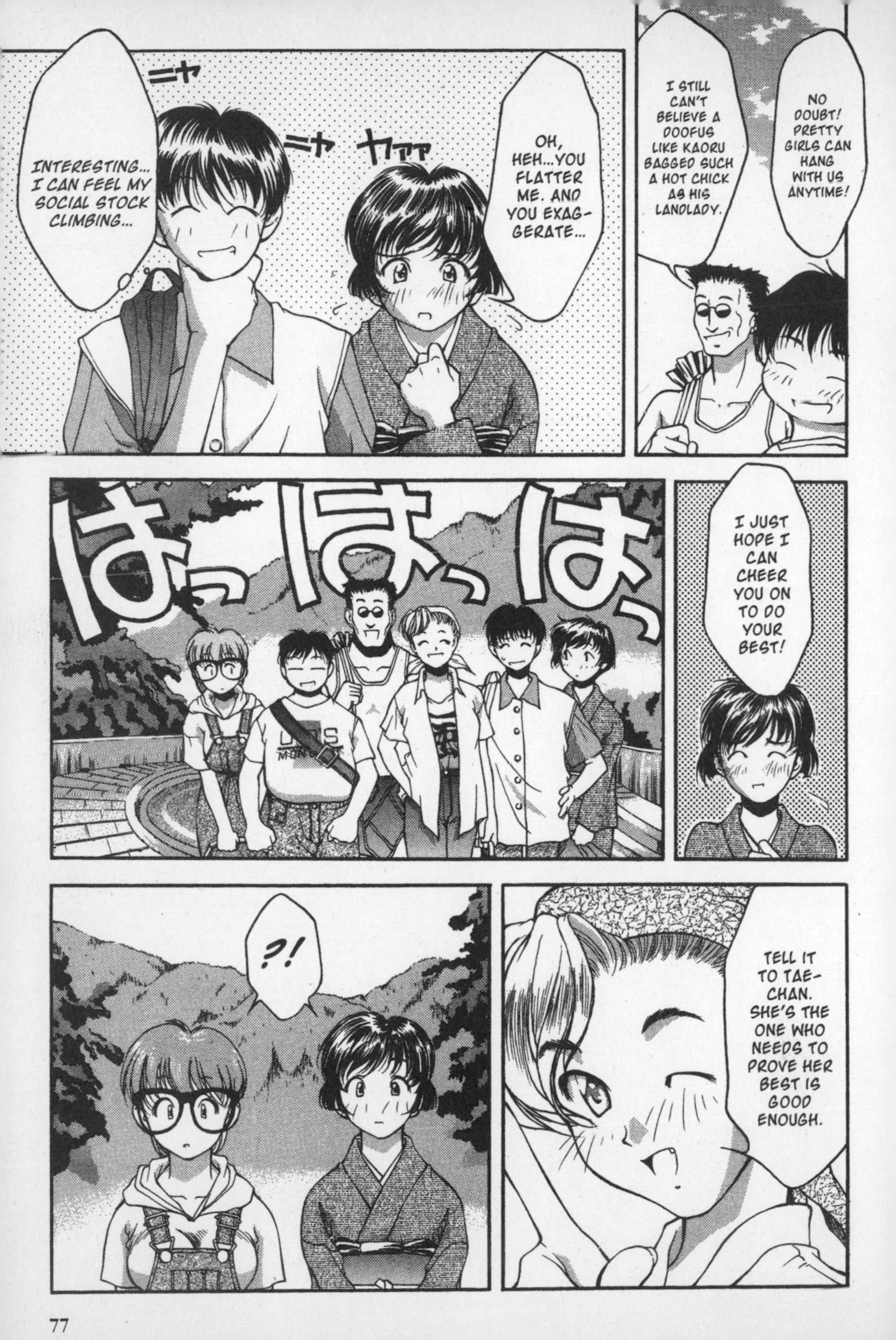
NO DOUBT! PRETTY GIRLS CAN HANG WITH US ANYTIME!
I STILL CAN'T BELIEVE A DOOFUS LIKE KAORU BAGGED SUCH A HOT CHICK AS HIS LANDLADY.
OH, HEH...YOU FLATTER ME. AND YOU EXAG-GERATE...
ニヤ ヤァァ
ニヤ
INTERESTING... I CAN FEEL MY SOCIAL STOCK CLIMBING...
I JUST HOPE I CAN CHEER YOU ON TO DO YOUR BEST!
はっ はっ はっ
TELL IT TO TAE-CHAN. SHE'S THE ONE WHO NEEDS TO PROVE HER BEST IS GOOD ENOUGH.
?!

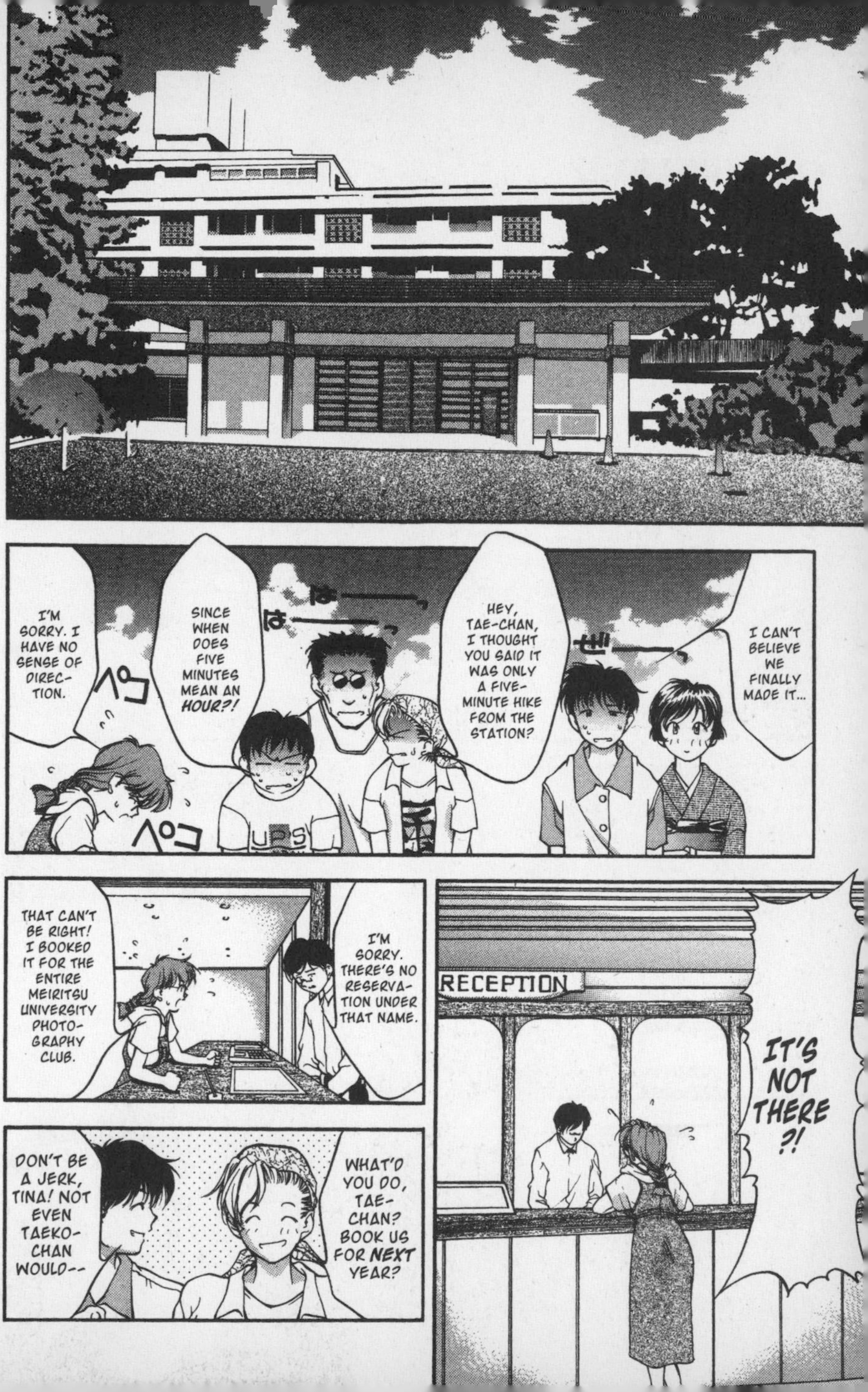
I CAN'T BELIEVE WE FINALLY MADE IT...
ぜー
HEY, TAE-CHAN, I THOUGHT YOU SAID IT WAS ONLY A FIVE-MINUTE HIKE FROM THE STATION?
はー
はー
SINCE WHEN DOES FIVE MINUTES MEAN AN *HOUR?!*
I'M SORRY. I HAVE NO SENSE OF DIREC-TION.
ペコ
ペコ
RECEPTION
IT'S NOT THERE?!
I'M SORRY. THERE'S NO RESERVA-TION UNDER THAT NAME.
THAT CAN'T BE RIGHT! I BOOKED IT FOR THE ENTIRE MEIRITSU UNIVERSITY PHOTO-GRAPHY CLUB.
WHAT'D YOU DO, TAE-CHAN? BOOK US FOR *NEXT* YEAR?
DON'T BE A JERK, TINA! NOT EVEN TAEKO-CHAN WOULD--

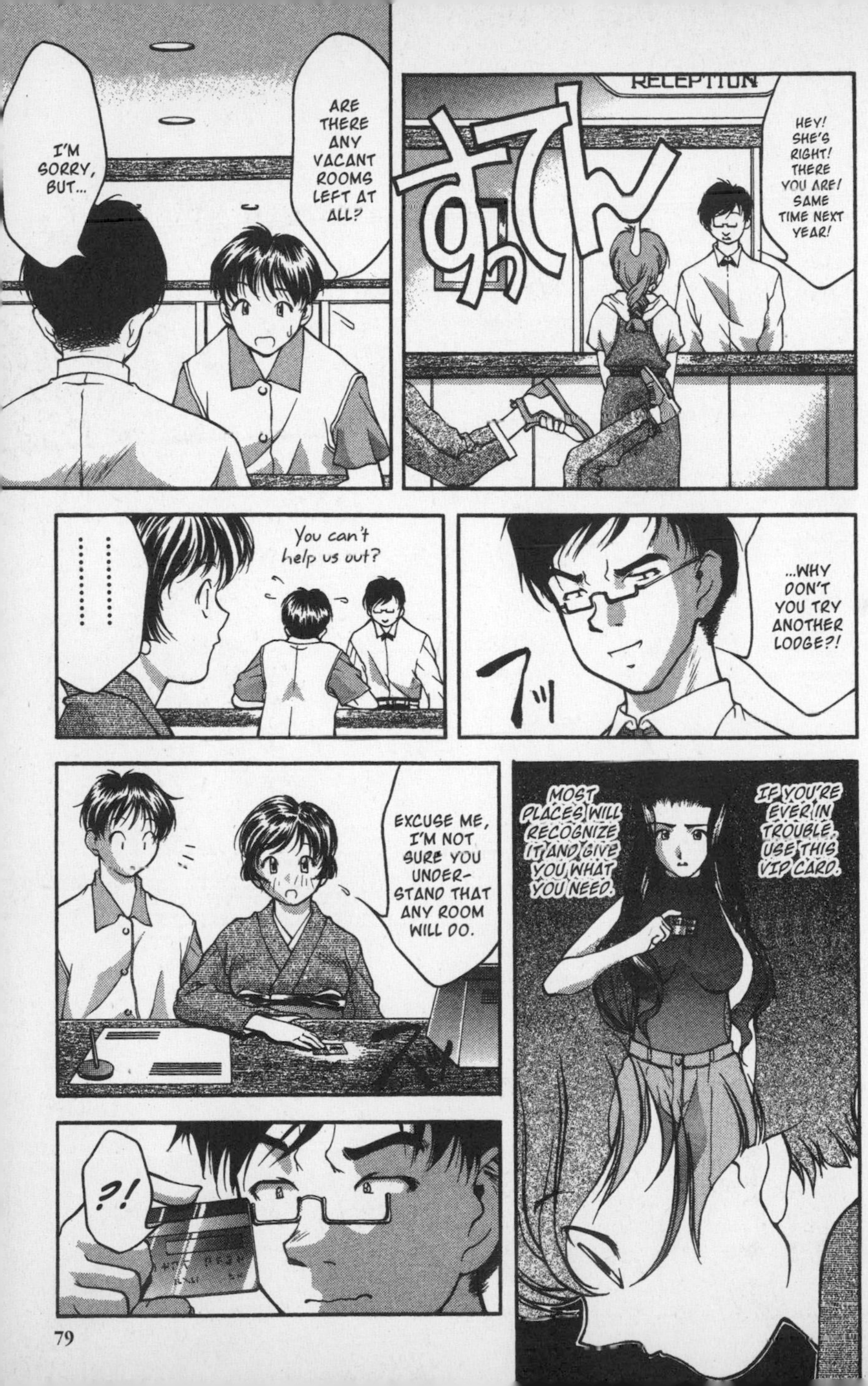
すってん
HEY! SHE'S RIGHT! THERE YOU ARE! SAME TIME NEXT YEAR!
ARE THERE ANY VACANT ROOMS LEFT AT ALL?
I'M SORRY, BUT...
...WHY DON'T YOU TRY ANOTHER LODGE?!
ッ
You can't help us out?
......
IF YOU'RE EVER IN TROUBLE, USE THIS VIP CARD.
MOST PLACES WILL RECOGNIZE IT AND GIVE YOU WHAT YOU NEED.
EXCUSE ME, I'M NOT SURE YOU UNDER-STAND THAT ANY ROOM WILL DO.
?!

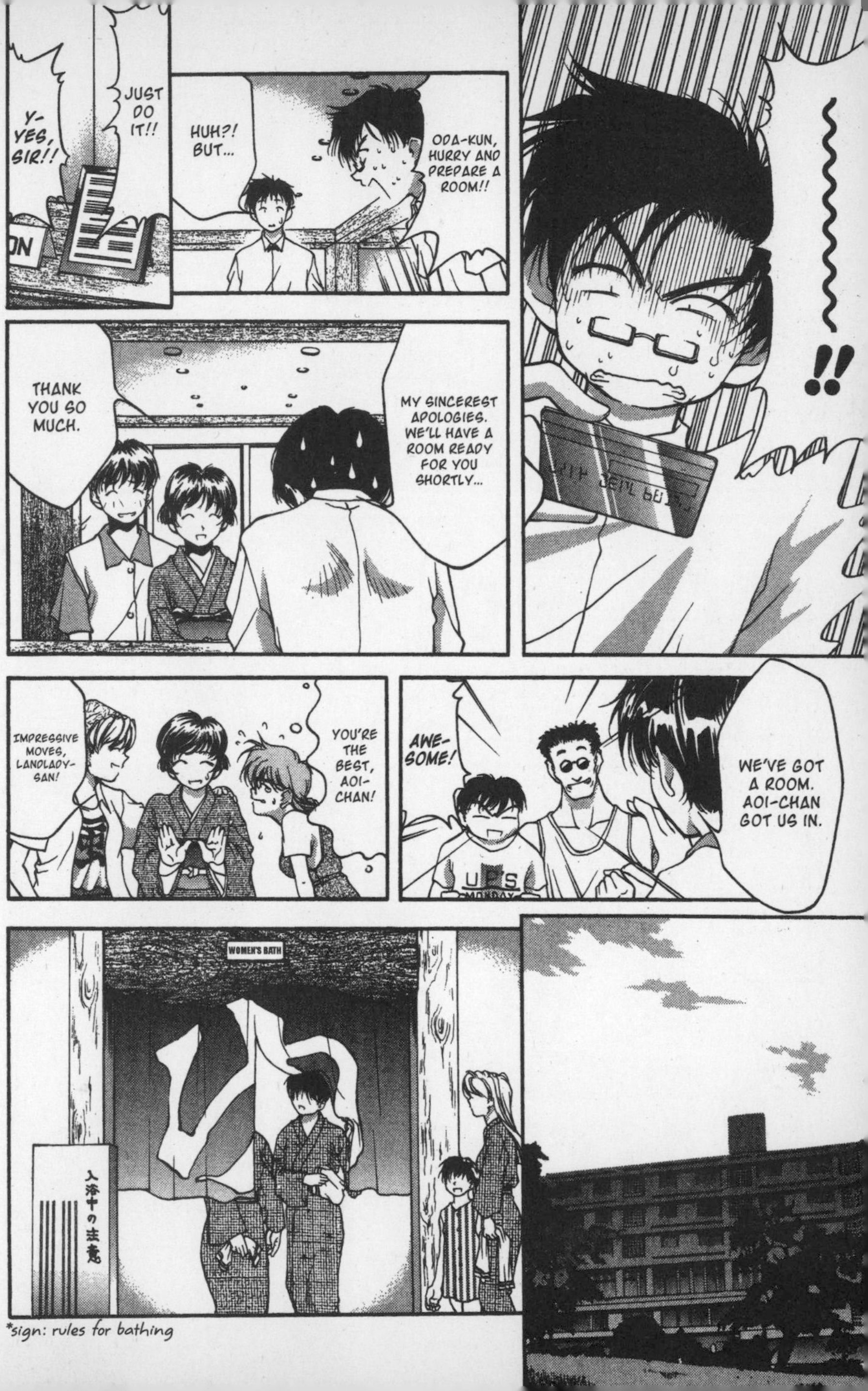
!!
ODA-KUN, HURRY AND PREPARE A ROOM!!
HUH?! BUT...
JUST DO IT!!
Y-YES, SIR!!
MY SINCEREST APOLOGIES. WE'LL HAVE A ROOM READY FOR YOU SHORTLY...
THANK YOU SO MUCH.
WE'VE GOT A ROOM. AOI-CHAN GOT US IN.
AWESOME!
YOU'RE THE BEST, AOI-CHAN!
IMPRESSIVE MOVES, LANDLADY-SAN!
WOMEN'S BATH
入浴中の注意
*sign: rules for bathing

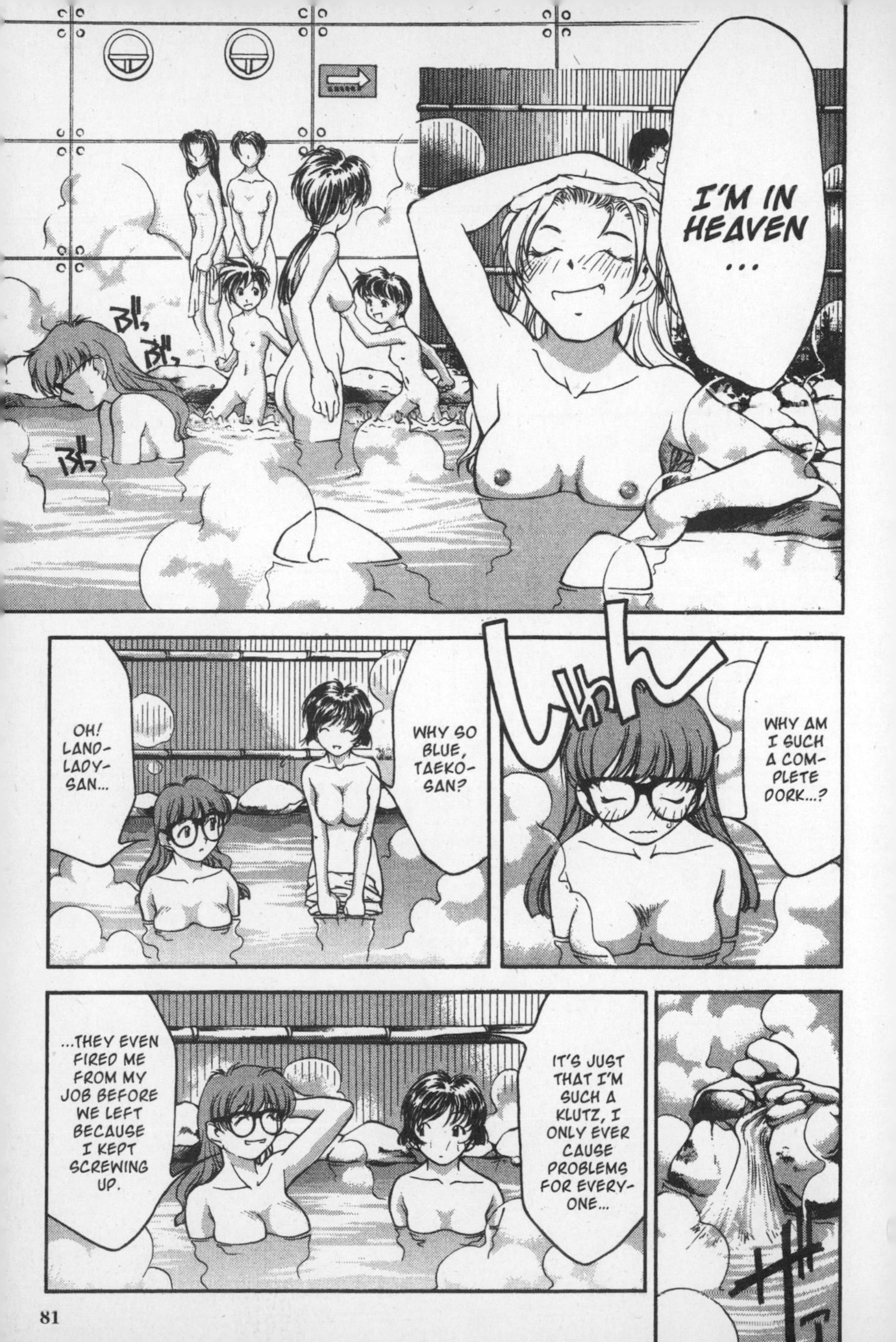
I'M IN HEAVEN ...
しゅん
WHY AM I SUCH A COMPLETE DORK...?
WHY SO BLUE, TAEKO-SAN?
OH! LANDLADY-SAN...
IT'S JUST THAT I'M SUCH A KLUTZ, I ONLY EVER CAUSE PROBLEMS FOR EVERYONE...
...THEY EVEN FIRED ME FROM MY JOB BEFORE WE LEFT BECAUSE I KEPT SCREWING UP.

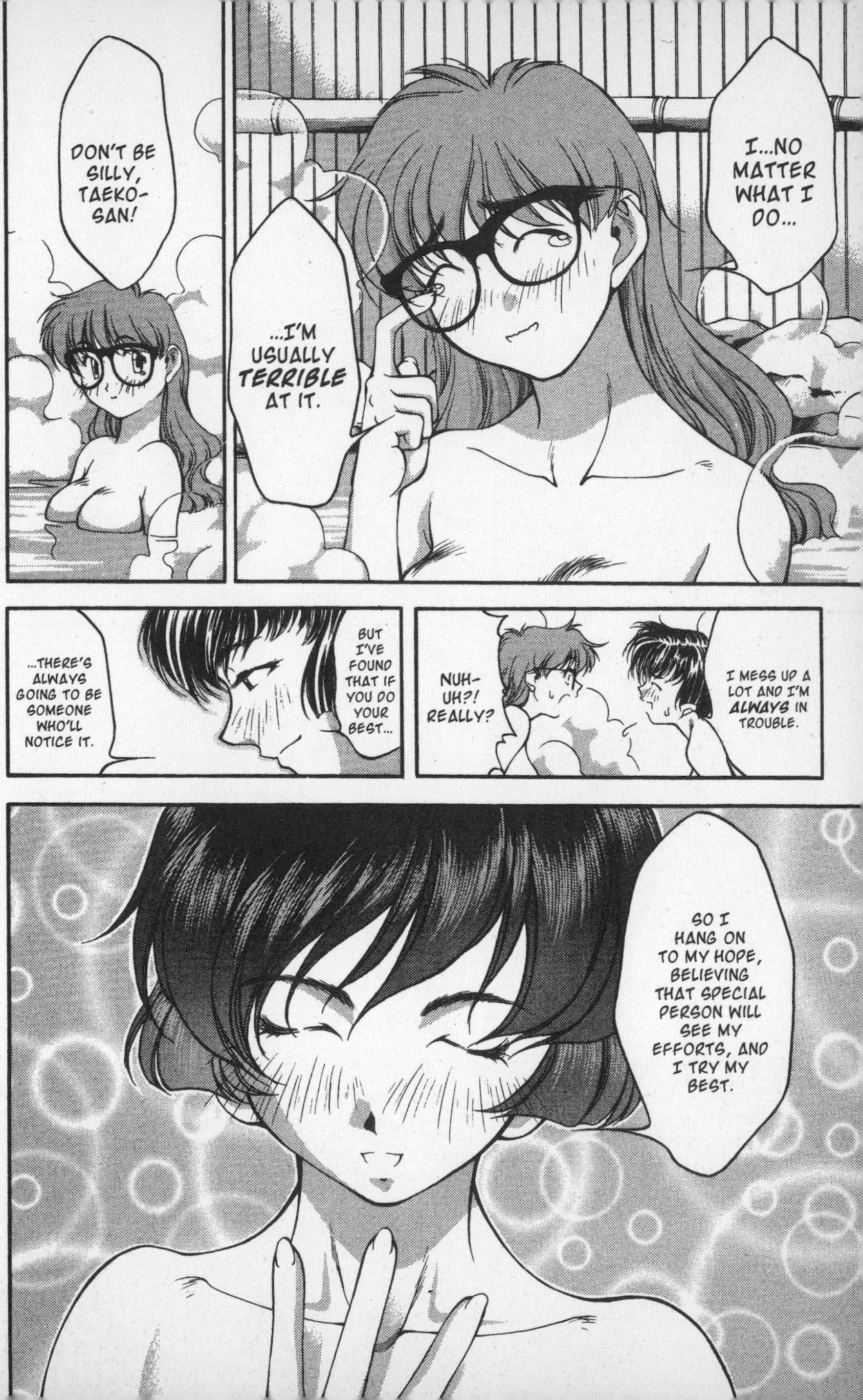
I...NO MATTER WHAT I DO...
...I'M USUALLY TERRIBLE AT IT.
DON'T BE SILLY, TAEKO-SAN!
I MESS UP A LOT AND I'M ALWAYS IN TROUBLE.
NUH-UH?! REALLY?
BUT I'VE FOUND THAT IF YOU DO YOUR BEST...
...THERE'S ALWAYS GOING TO BE SOMEONE WHO'LL NOTICE IT.
SO I HANG ON TO MY HOPE, BELIEVING THAT SPECIAL PERSON WILL SEE MY EFFORTS, AND I TRY MY BEST.

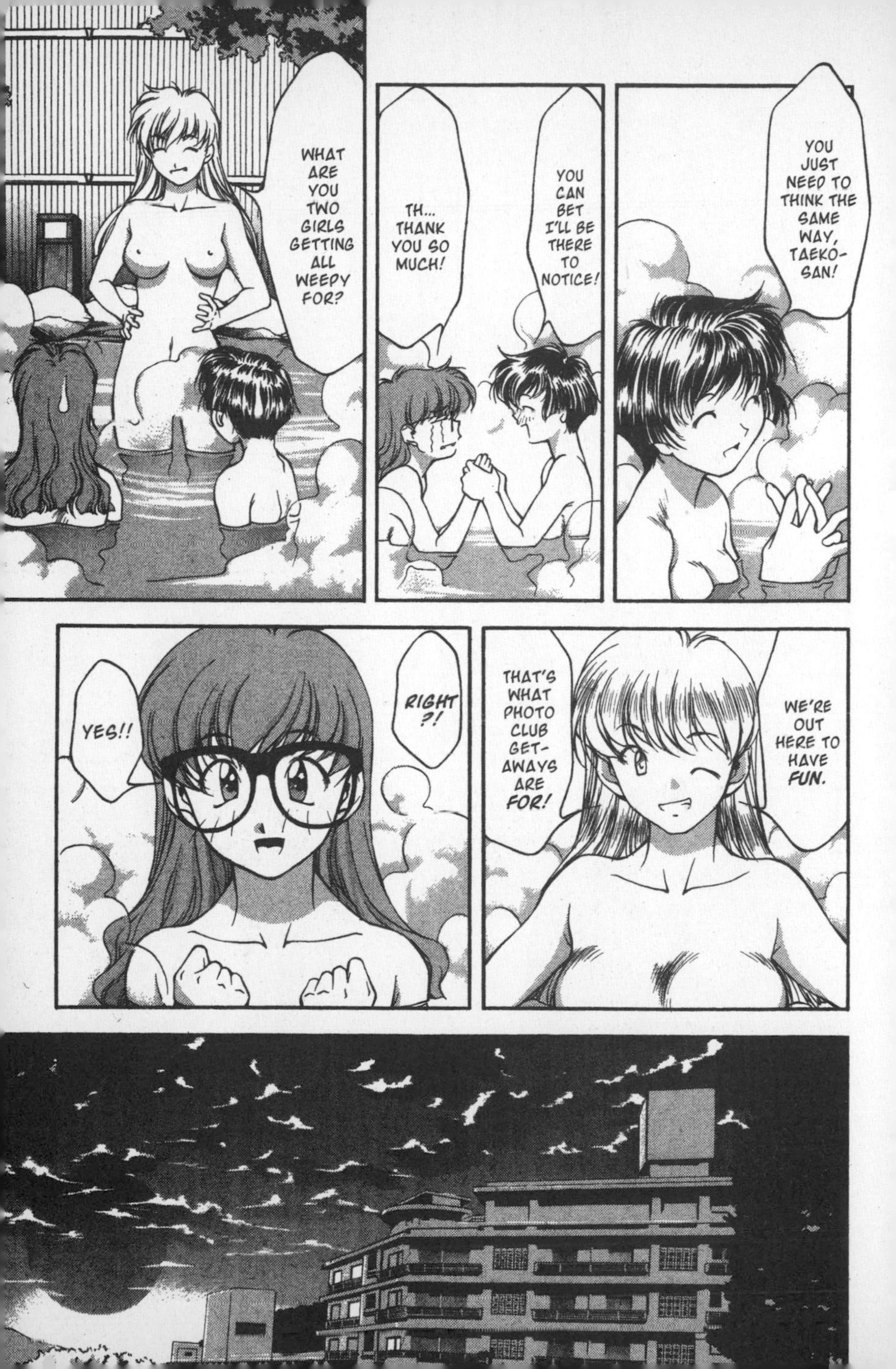
YOU JUST NEED TO THINK THE SAME WAY, TAEKO-SAN!
YOU CAN BET I'LL BE THERE TO NOTICE!
TH... THANK YOU SO MUCH!
WHAT ARE YOU TWO GIRLS GETTING ALL WEEPY FOR?
WE'RE OUT HERE TO HAVE FUN.
THAT'S WHAT PHOTO CLUB GET-AWAYS ARE FOR!
RIGHT?!
YES!!

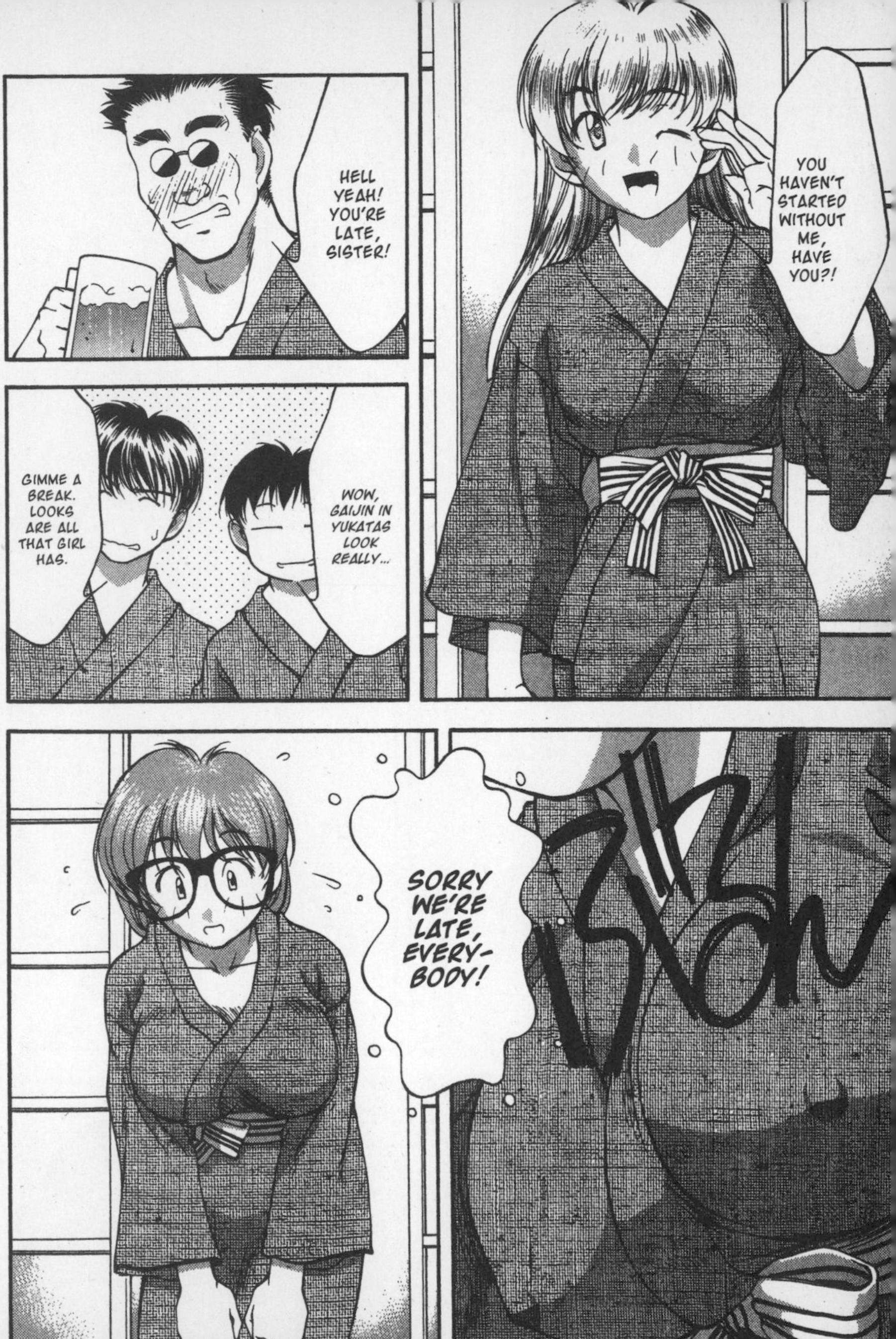
YOU HAVEN'T STARTED WITHOUT ME, HAVE YOU?!
HELL YEAH! YOU'RE LATE, SISTER!
WOW, GAIJIN IN YUKATAS LOOK REALLY...
GIMME A BREAK. LOOKS ARE ALL THAT GIRL HAS.
SORRY WE'RE LATE, EVERY-BODY!

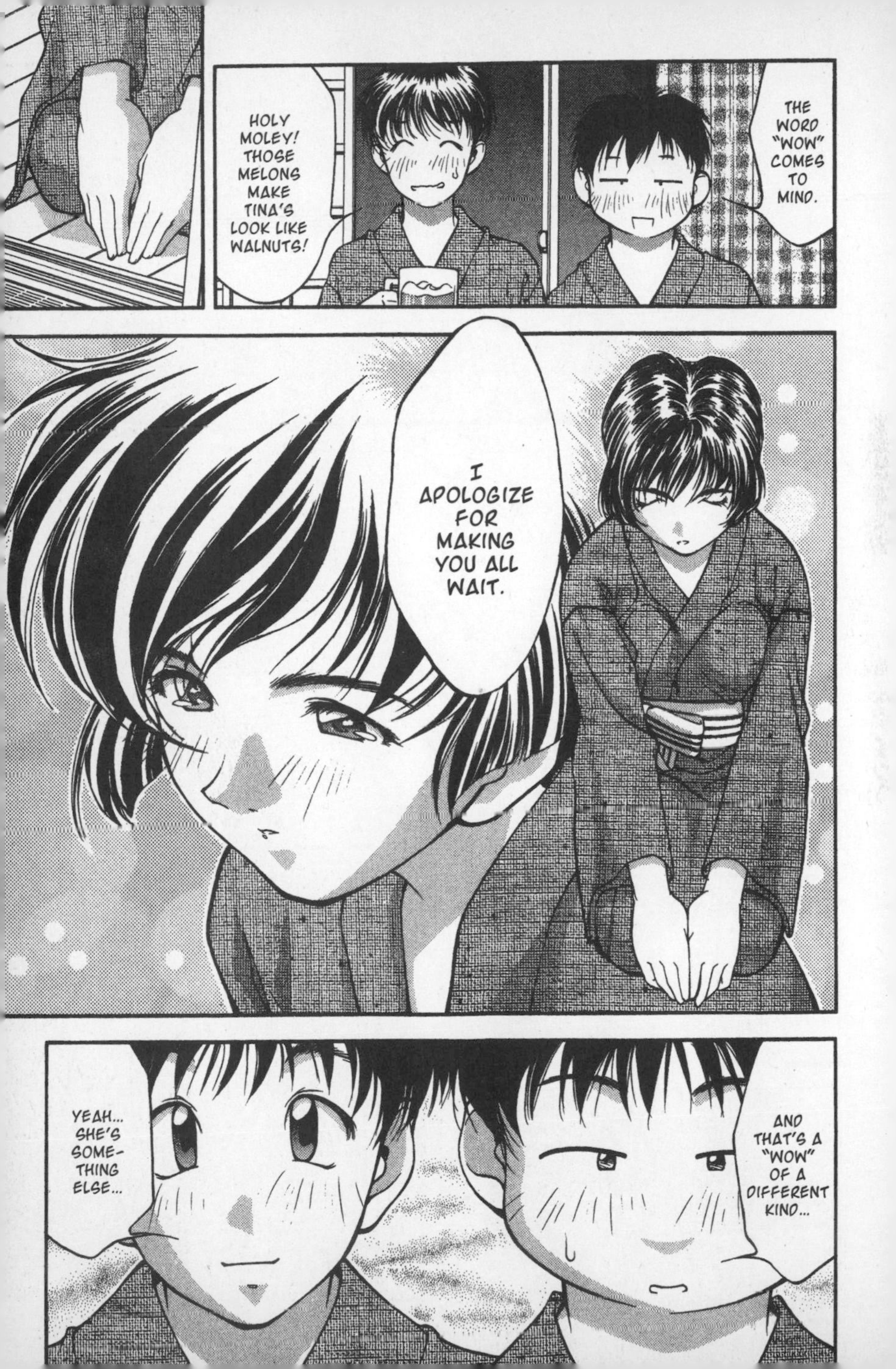
THE WORD "WOW" COMES TO MIND.
HOLY MOLEY! THOSE MELONS MAKE TINA'S LOOK LIKE WALNUTS!
I APOLOGIZE FOR MAKING YOU ALL WAIT.
AND THAT'S A "WOW" OF A DIFFERENT KIND...
YEAH... SHE'S SOME-THING ELSE...

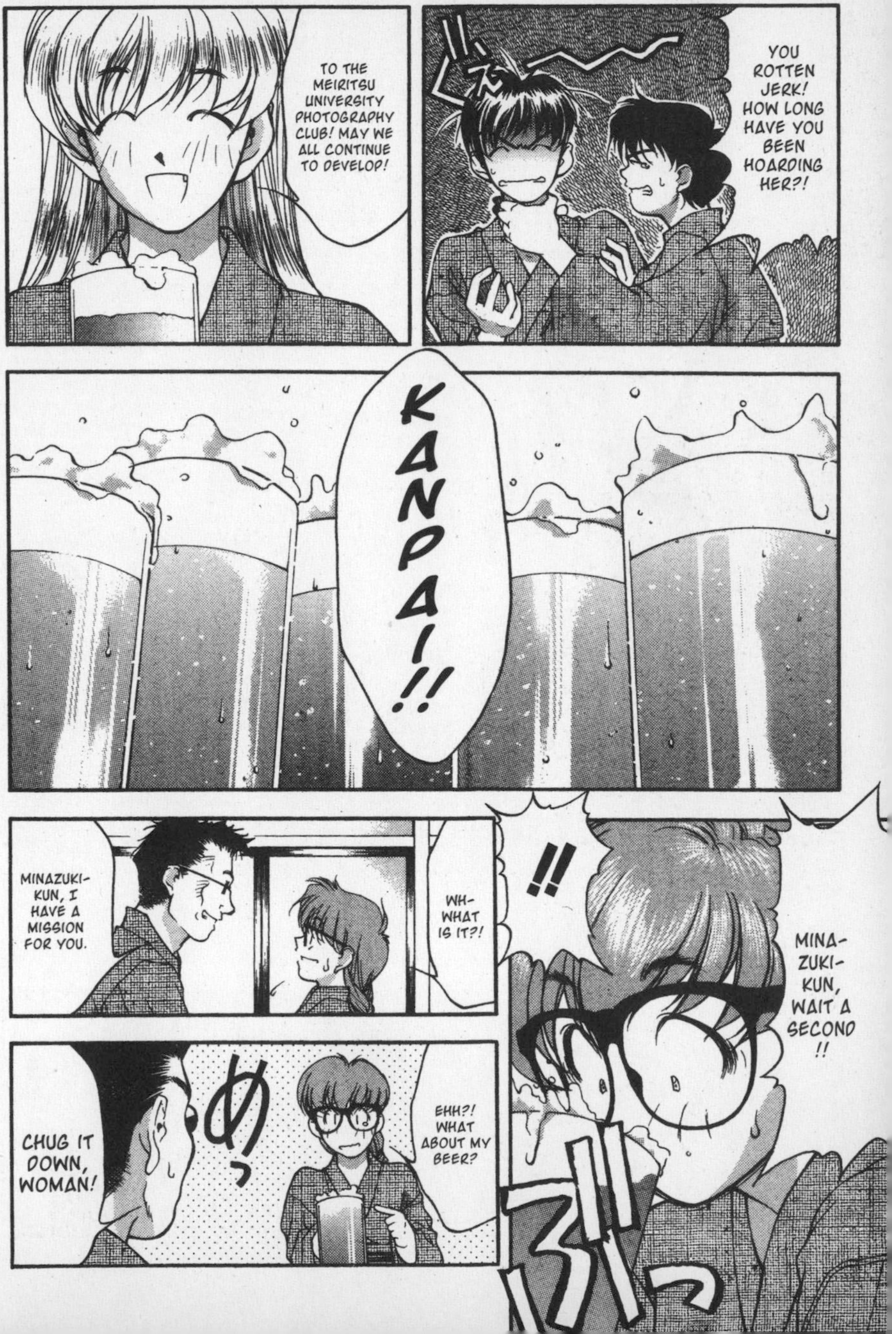
YOU ROTTEN JERK! HOW LONG HAVE YOU BEEN HOARDING HER?!
TO THE MEIRITSU UNIVERSITY PHOTOGRAPHY CLUB! MAY WE ALL CONTINUE TO DEVELOP!
KANPAI!!
!!
MINA-ZUKI-KUN, WAIT A SECOND!!
WH-WHAT IS IT?!
MINAZUKI-KUN, I HAVE A MISSION FOR YOU.
EHH?! WHAT ABOUT MY BEER?
CHUG IT DOWN, WOMAN!

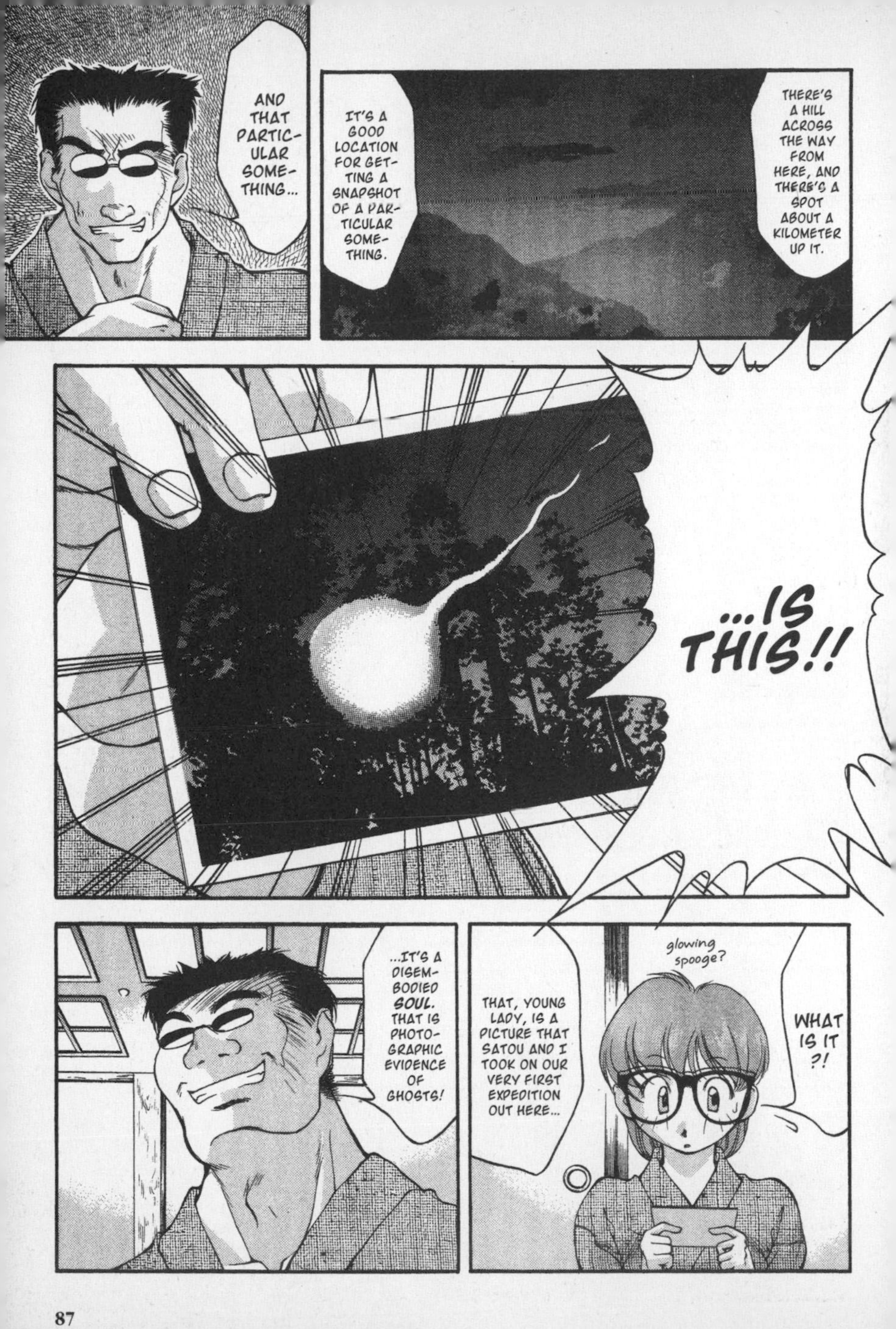
THERE'S A HILL ACROSS THE WAY FROM HERE, AND THERE'S A SPOT ABOUT A KILOMETER UP IT.
IT'S A GOOD LOCATION FOR GETTING A SNAPSHOT OF A PARTICULAR SOMETHING.
AND THAT PARTICULAR SOMETHING...
...IS THIS!!
WHAT IS IT ?!
glowing spooge?
THAT, YOUNG LADY, IS A PICTURE THAT SATOU AND I TOOK ON OUR VERY FIRST EXPEDITION OUT HERE...
...IT'S A DISEMBODIED **SOUL**. THAT IS PHOTOGRAPHIC EVIDENCE OF GHOSTS!

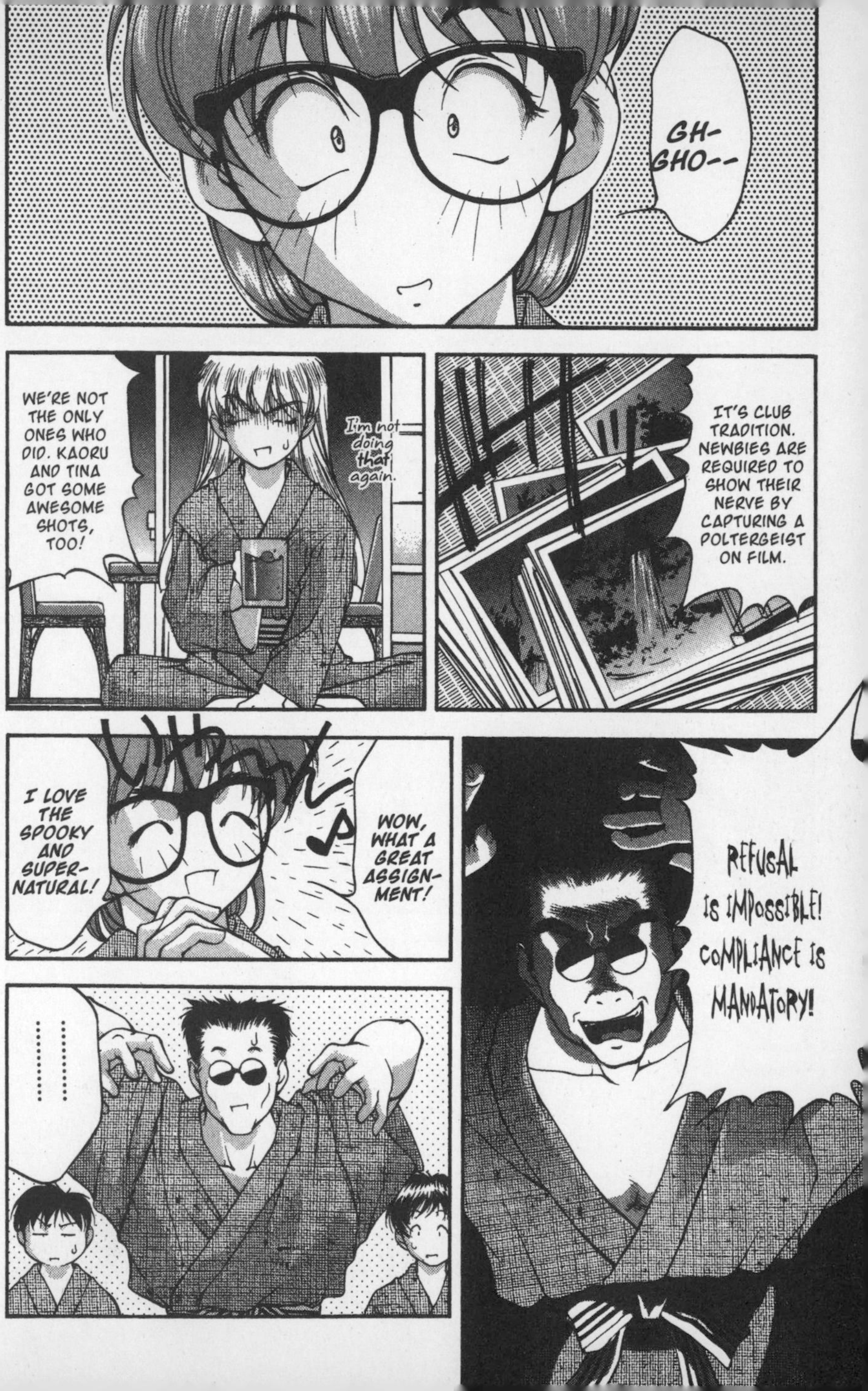
GH- GHO--
IT'S CLUB TRADITION. NEWBIES ARE REQUIRED TO SHOW THEIR NERVE BY CAPTURING A POLTERGEIST ON FILM.
WE'RE NOT THE ONLY ONES WHO DID. KAORU AND TINA GOT SOME AWESOME SHOTS, TOO!
I'm not doing that again.
REFUSAL IS IMPOSSIBLE! COMPLIANCE IS MANDATORY!
WOW, WHAT A GREAT ASSIGNMENT!
I LOVE THE SPOOKY AND SUPER-NATURAL!
......

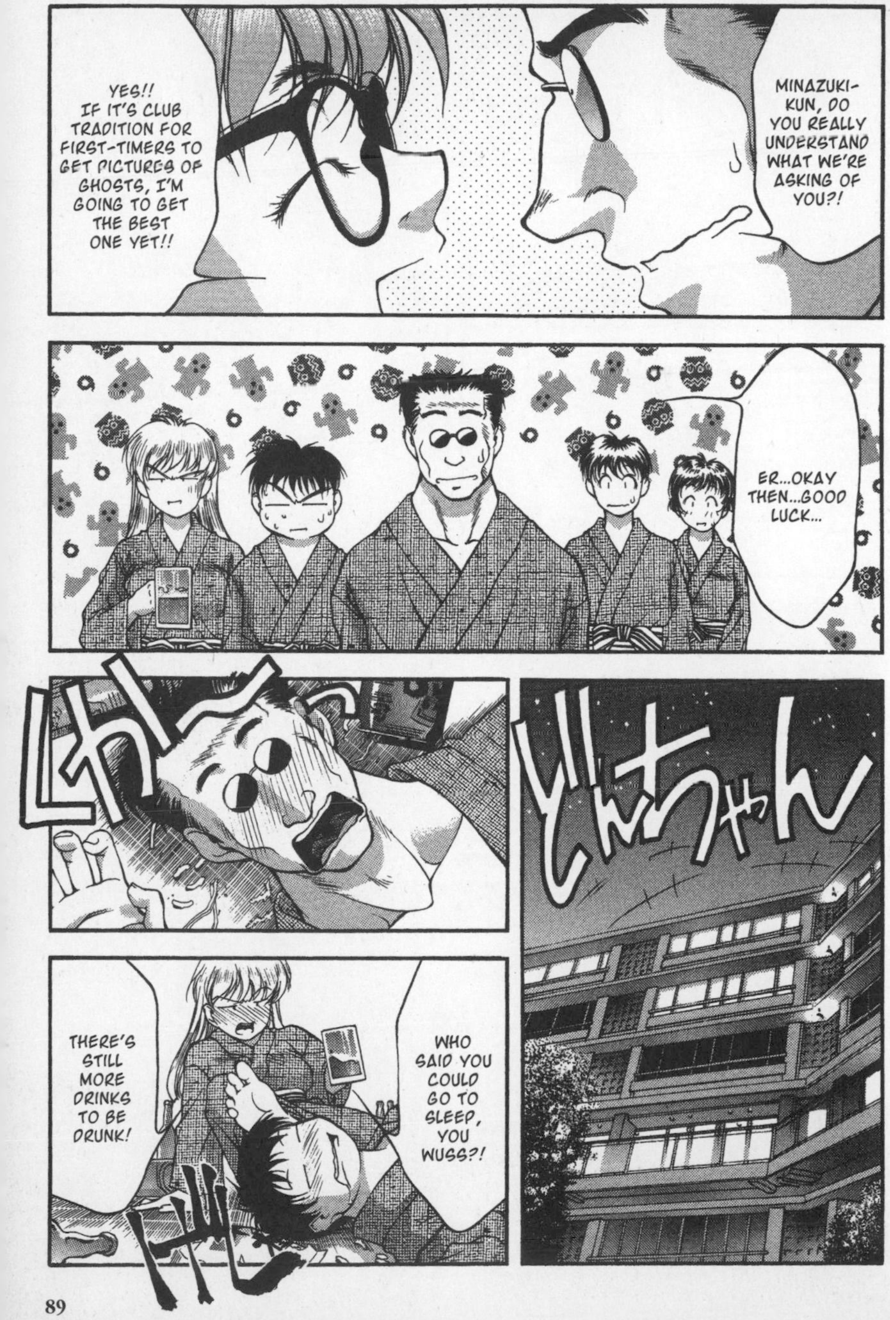
MINAZUKI-KUN, DO YOU REALLY UNDERSTAND WHAT WE'RE ASKING OF YOU?!
YES!! IF IT'S CLUB TRADITION FOR FIRST-TIMERS TO GET PICTURES OF GHOSTS, I'M GOING TO GET THE BEST ONE YET!!
ER...OKAY THEN...GOOD LUCK...
どんちゃん
WHO SAID YOU COULD GO TO SLEEP, YOU WUSS?!
THERE'S STILL MORE DRINKS TO BE DRUNK!

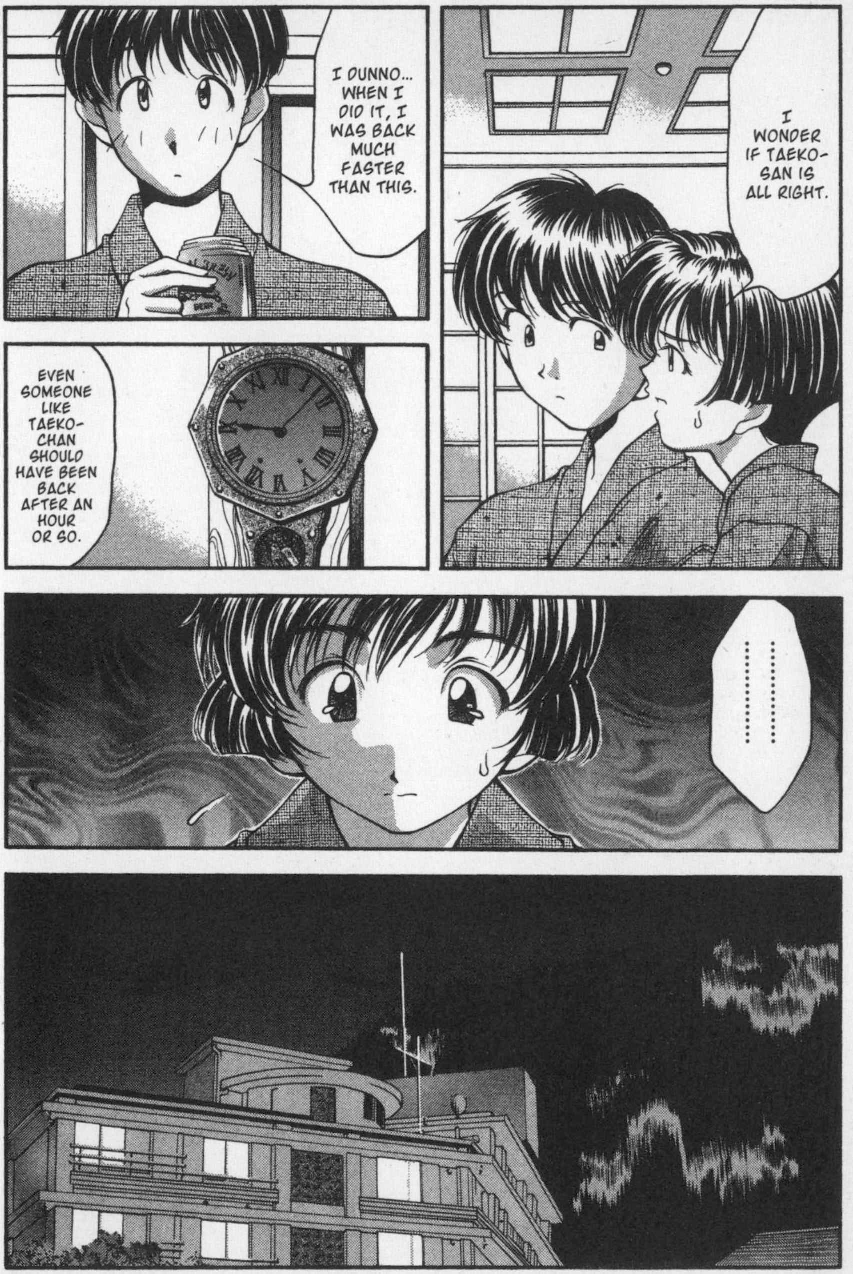
I WONDER IF TAEKO-SAN IS ALL RIGHT.
I DUNNO... WHEN I DID IT, I WAS BACK MUCH FASTER THAN THIS.
EVEN SOMEONE LIKE TAEKO-CHAN SHOULD HAVE BEEN BACK AFTER AN HOUR OR SO.
......

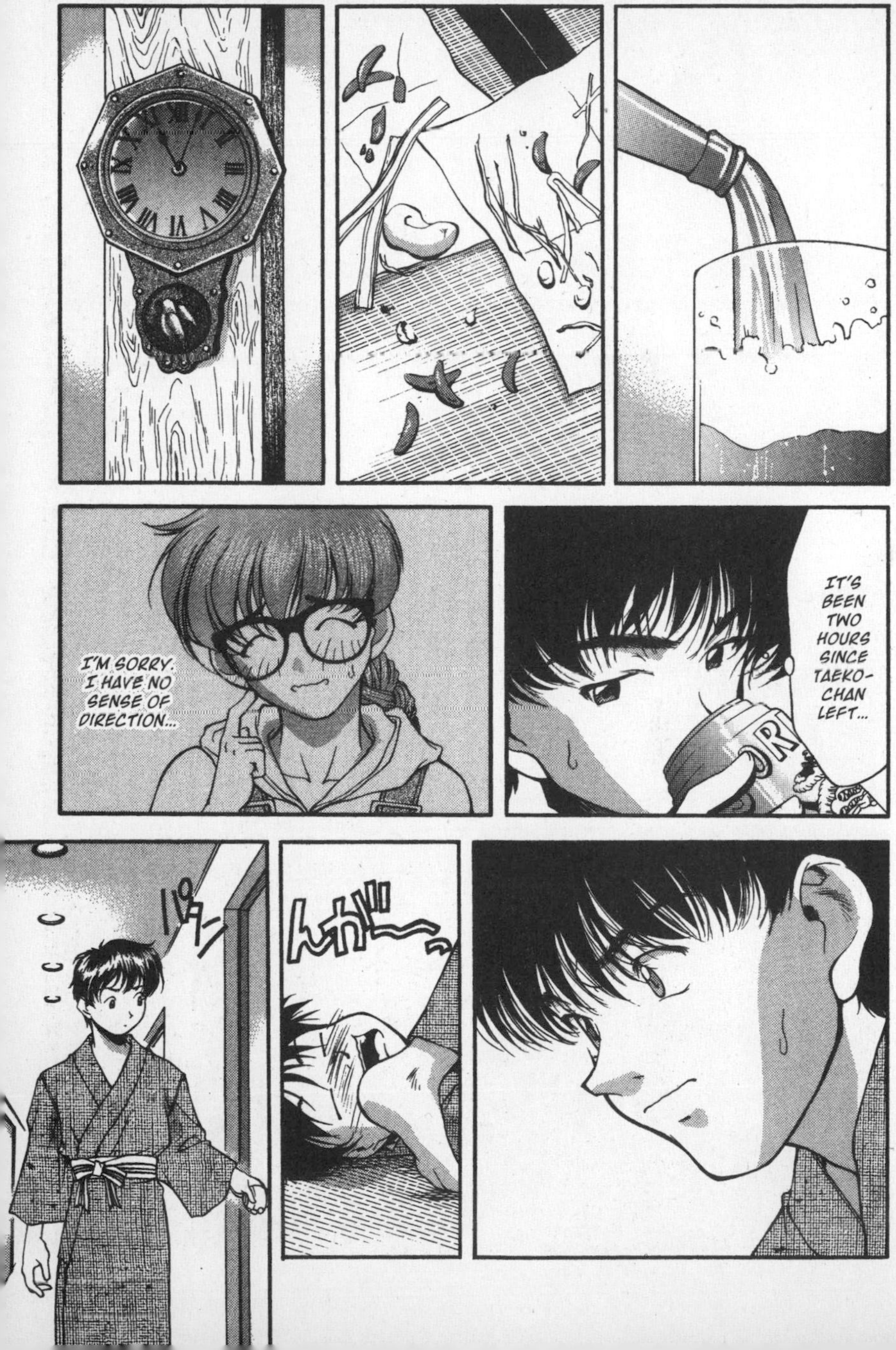
IT'S BEEN TWO HOURS SINCE TAEKO-CHAN LEFT...
I'M SORRY. I HAVE NO SENSE OF DIRECTION...
んガ〜〜
パタン

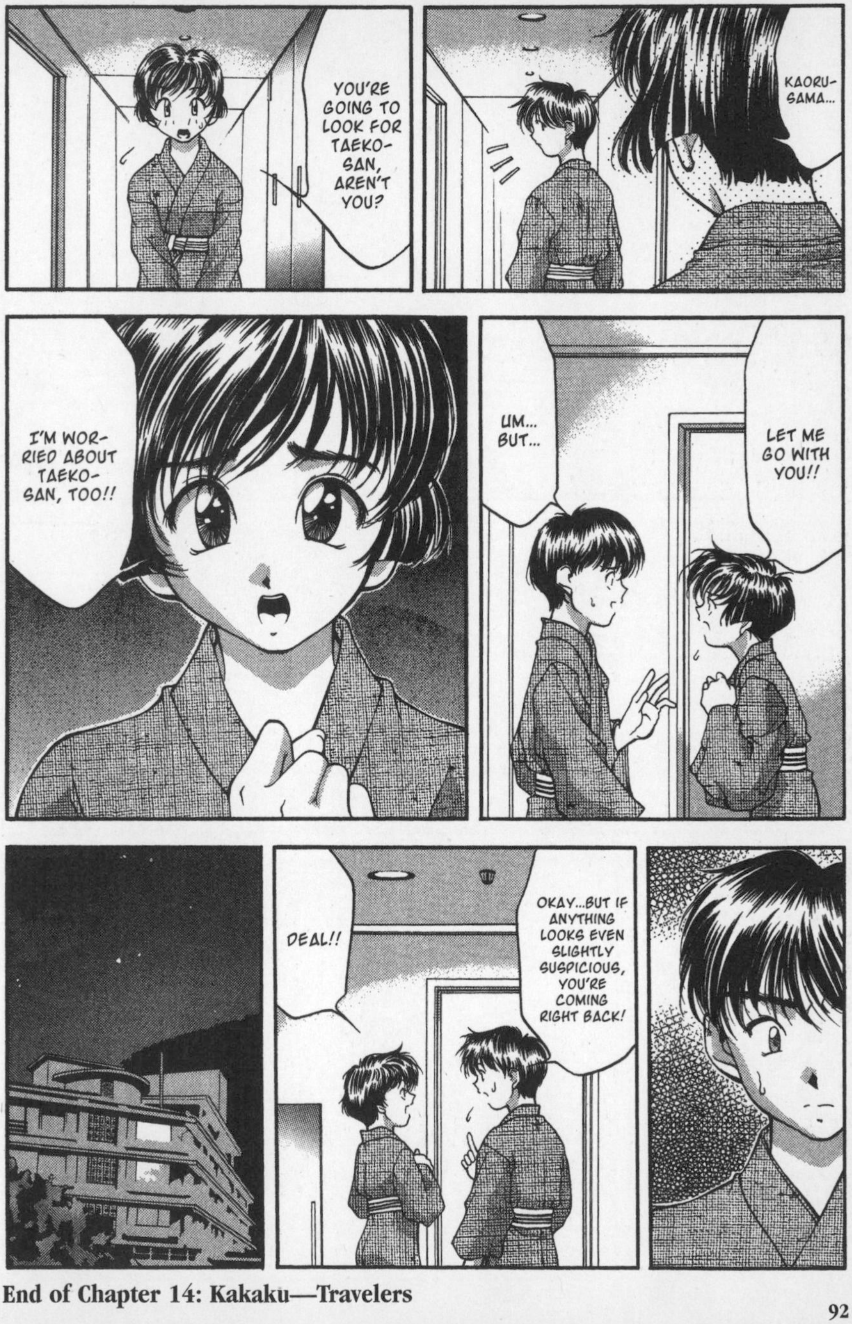
KAORU-SAMA...
YOU'RE GOING TO LOOK FOR TAEKO-SAN, AREN'T YOU?
LET ME GO WITH YOU!!
UM... BUT...
I'M WOR-RIED ABOUT TAEKO-SAN, TOO!!
OKAY...BUT IF ANYTHING LOOKS EVEN SLIGHTLY SUSPICIOUS, YOU'RE COMING RIGHT BACK!
DEAL!!

End of Chapter 14: Kakaku—Travelers

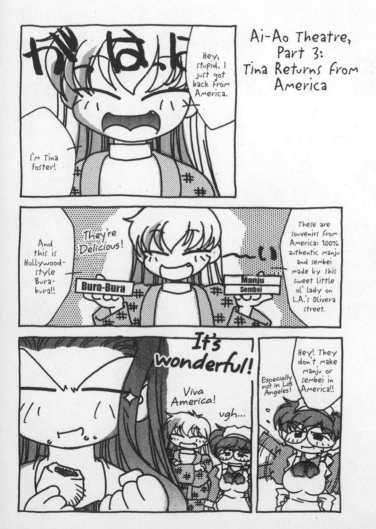

Ai-Ao Theatre, Part 3: Tina Returns from America
Hey, stupid, I just got back from America.
I'm Tina Foster!
These are souvenirs from America: 100% authentic manju and sembei made by this sweet little ol' lady on L.A.'s Olivera street.
Manju
Sembei
They're Delicious!
And this is Hollywood-style Bura-bura!!
Bura-Bura
Hey! They don't make manju or sembei in America!!
Especially not in Los Angeles!
It's wonderful!
Viva America!
ugh...

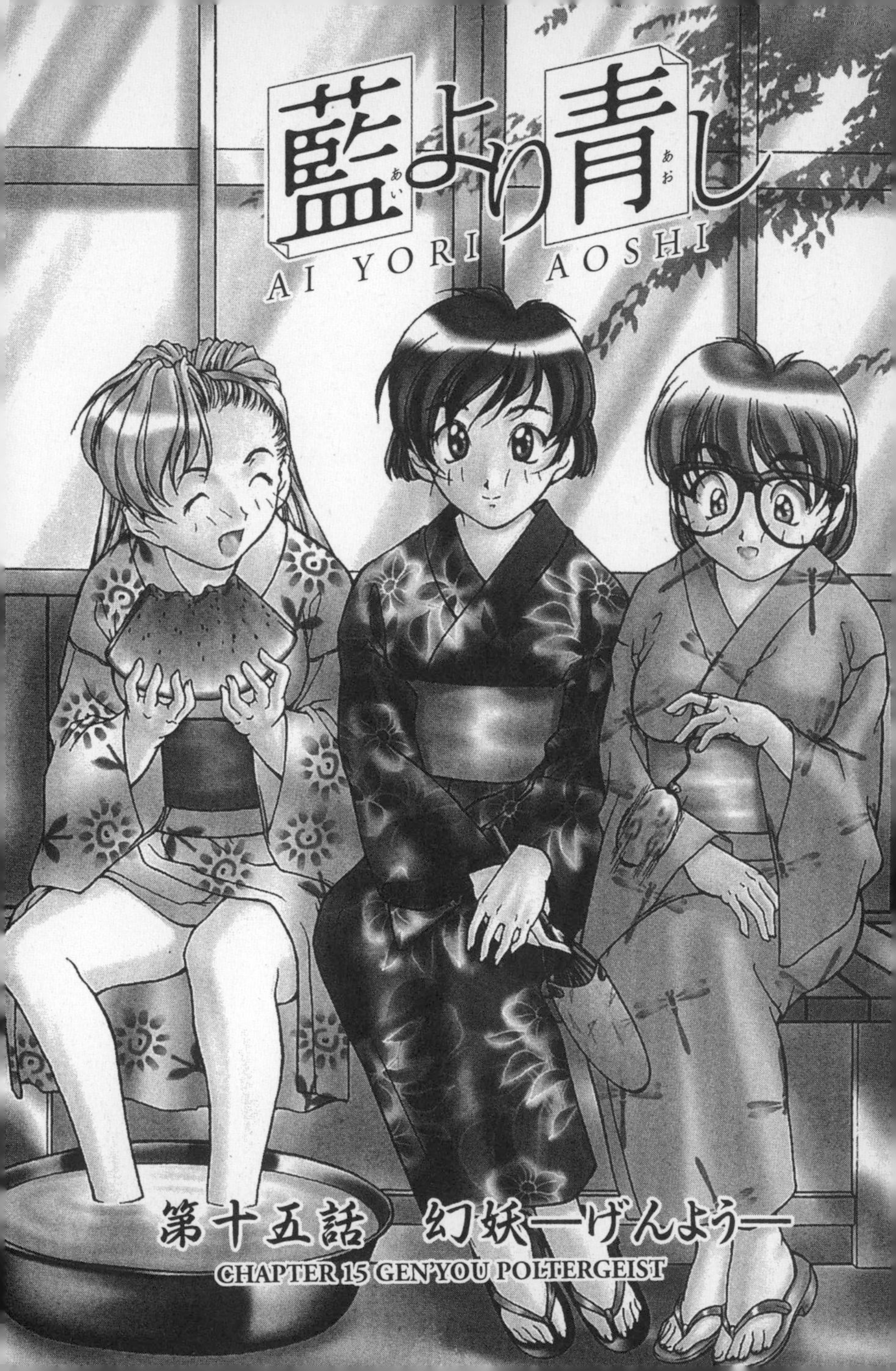
藍より青し
あい
あお
AI YORI AOSHI
第十五話　幻妖―げんよう―
CHAPTER 15 GEN'YOU POLTERGEIST

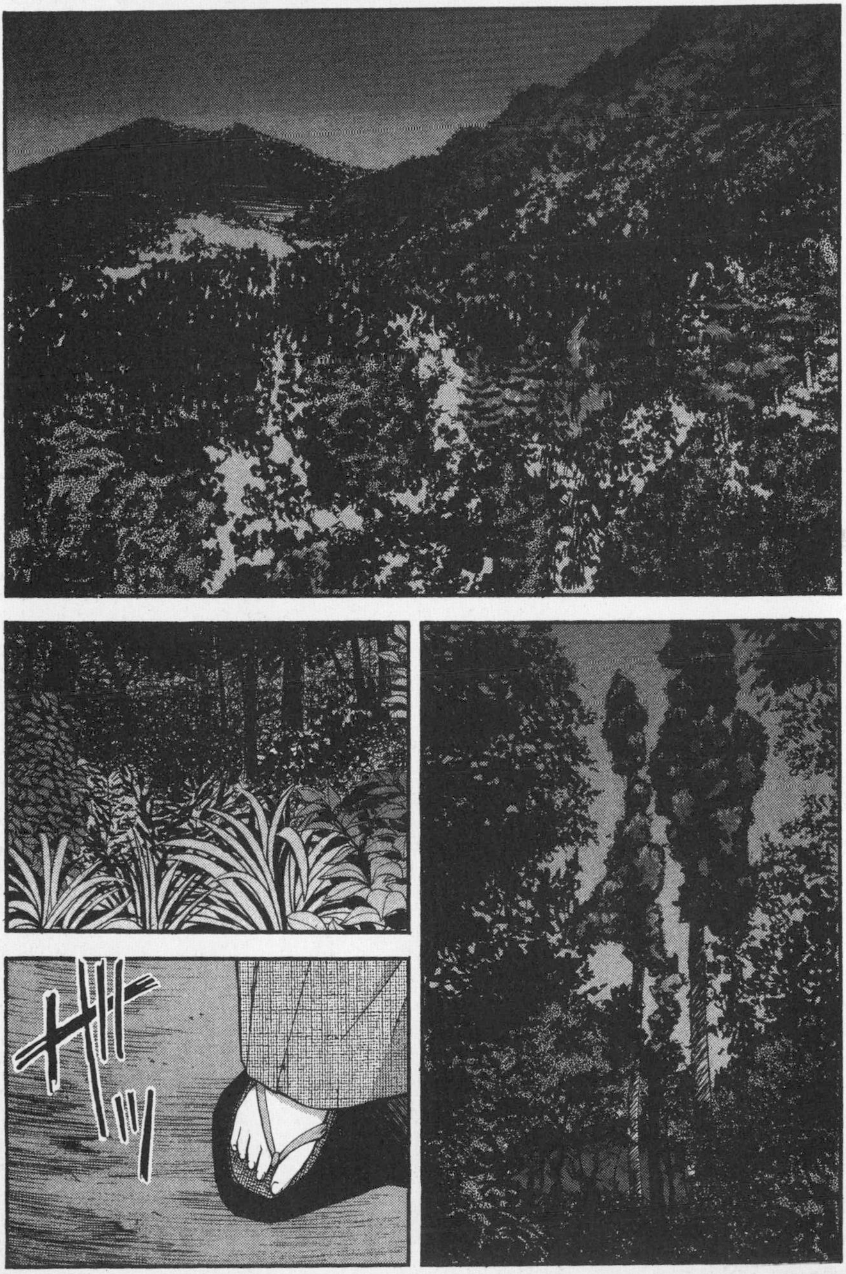
ザッ

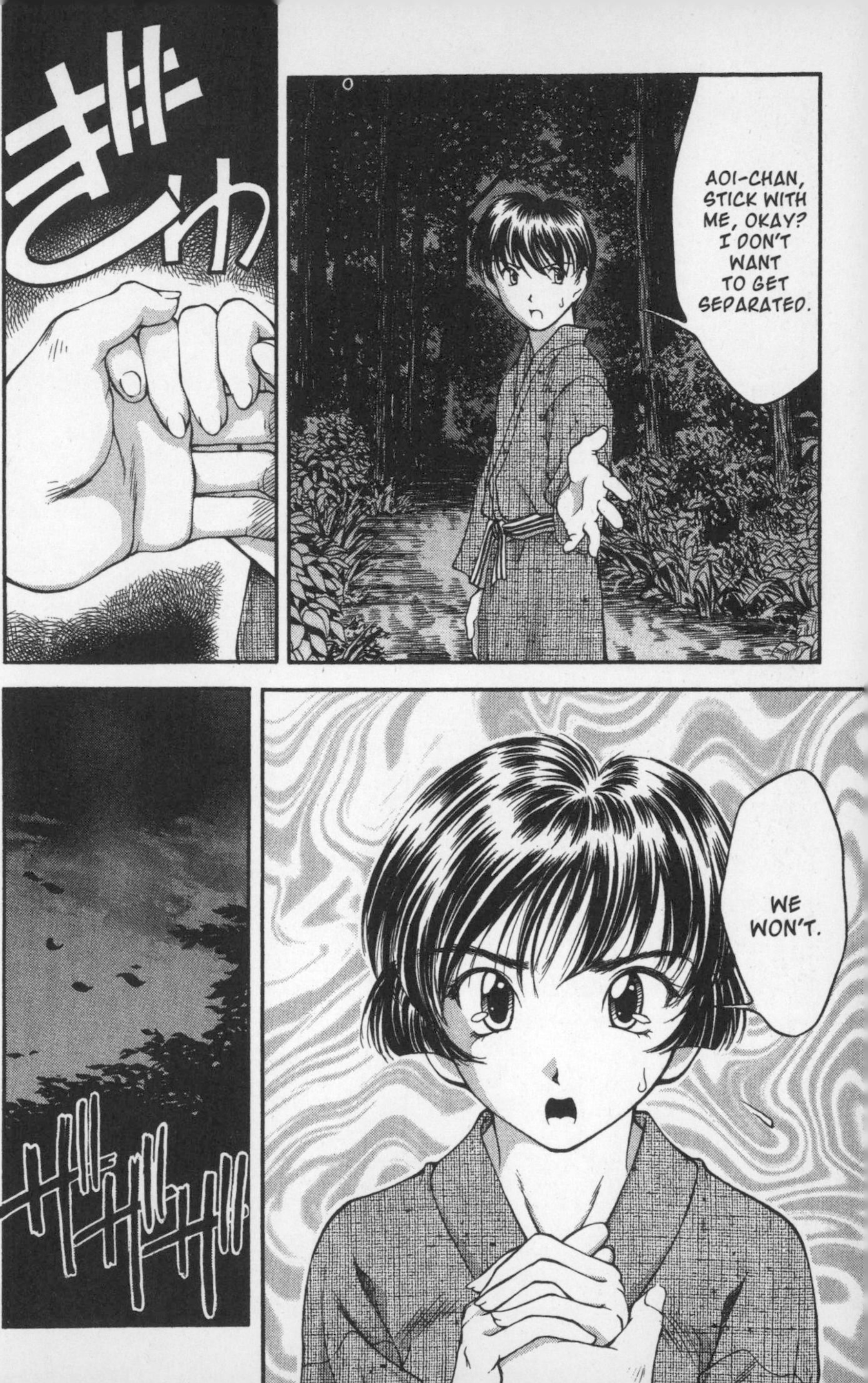
AOI-CHAN, STICK WITH ME, OKAY? I DON'T WANT TO GET SEPARATED.
WE WON'T.

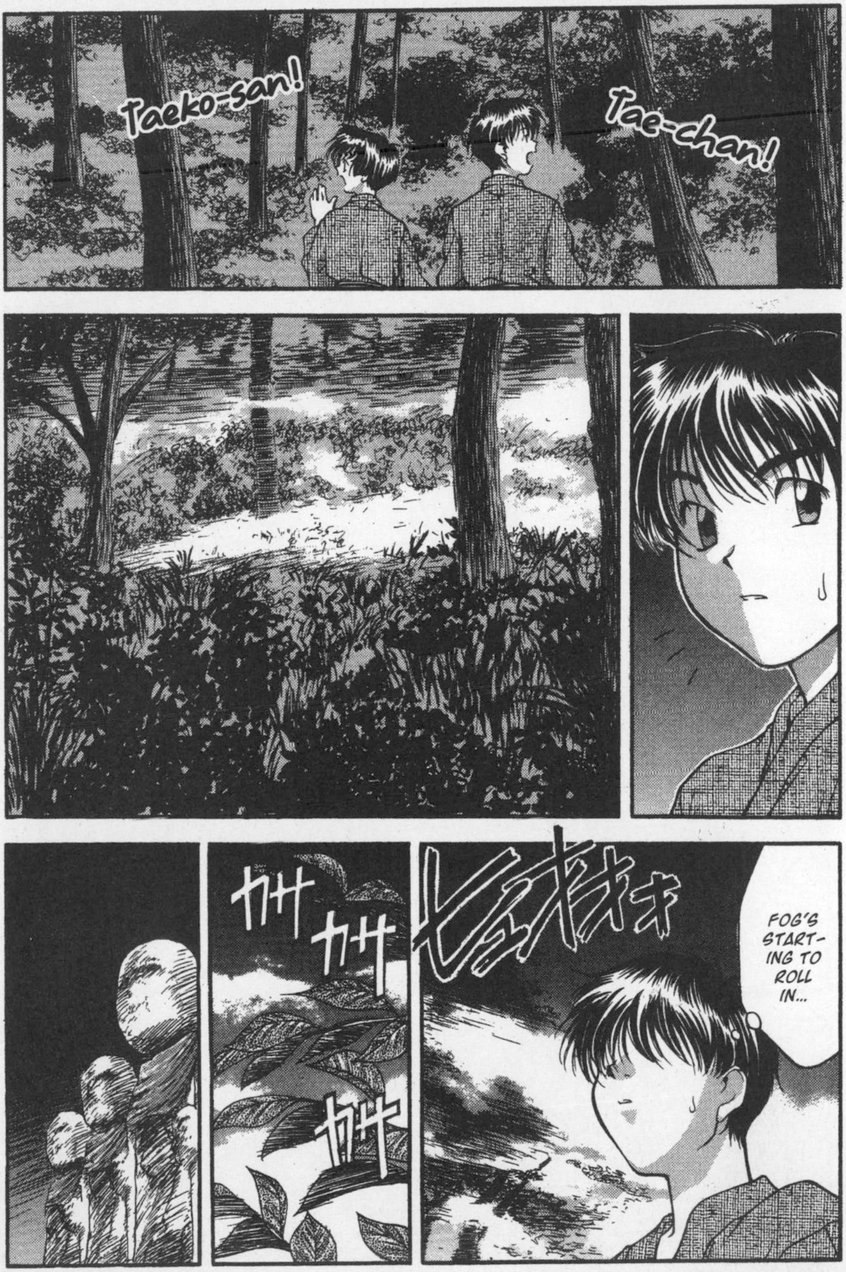
Tae-chan!
Taeko-san!
FOG'S STARTING TO ROLL IN...
ヒュオオォ
カサ
カサ
カサ

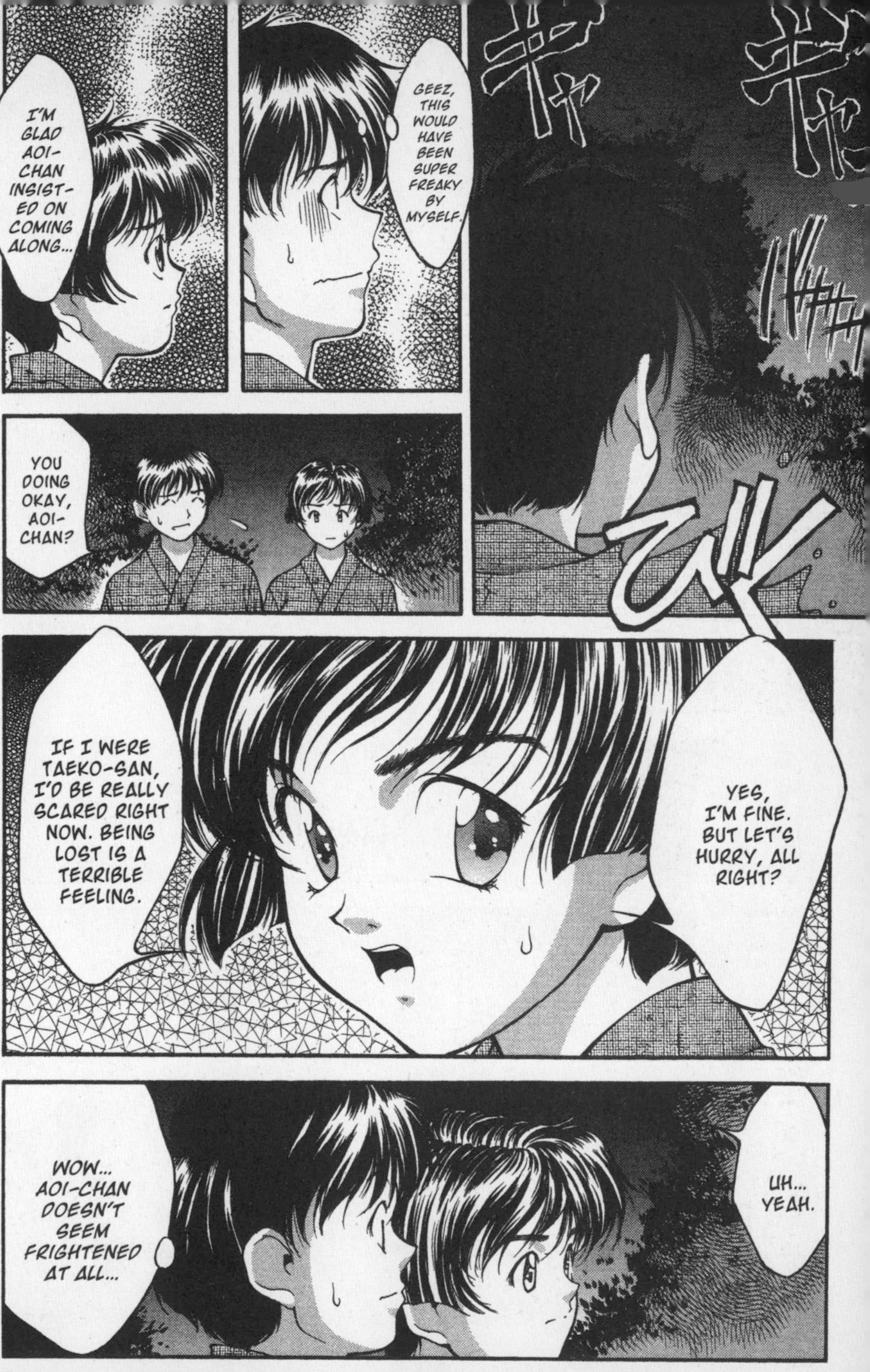
ギャ
ギャ
ひッ
GEEZ, THIS WOULD HAVE BEEN SUPER FREAKY BY MYSELF.
I'M GLAD AOI-CHAN INSISTED ON COMING ALONG...
YOU DOING OKAY, AOI-CHAN?
YES, I'M FINE. BUT LET'S HURRY, ALL RIGHT?
IF I WERE TAEKO-SAN, I'D BE REALLY SCARED RIGHT NOW. BEING LOST IS A TERRIBLE FEELING.
UH... YEAH.
WOW... AOI-CHAN DOESN'T SEEM FRIGHTENED AT ALL...

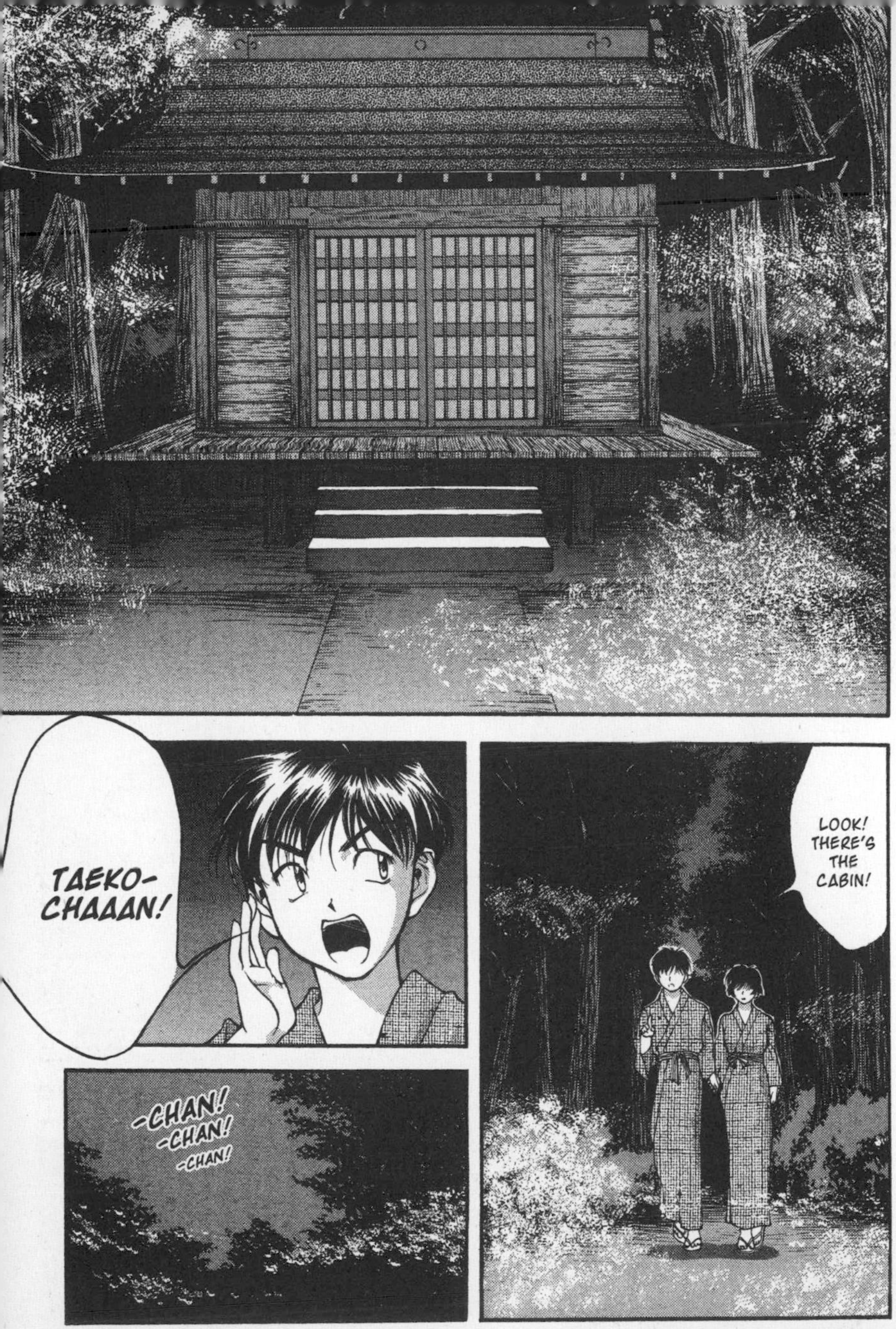
LOOK! THERE'S THE CABIN!
TAEKO-CHAAAN!
-CHAN! -CHAN! -CHAN!

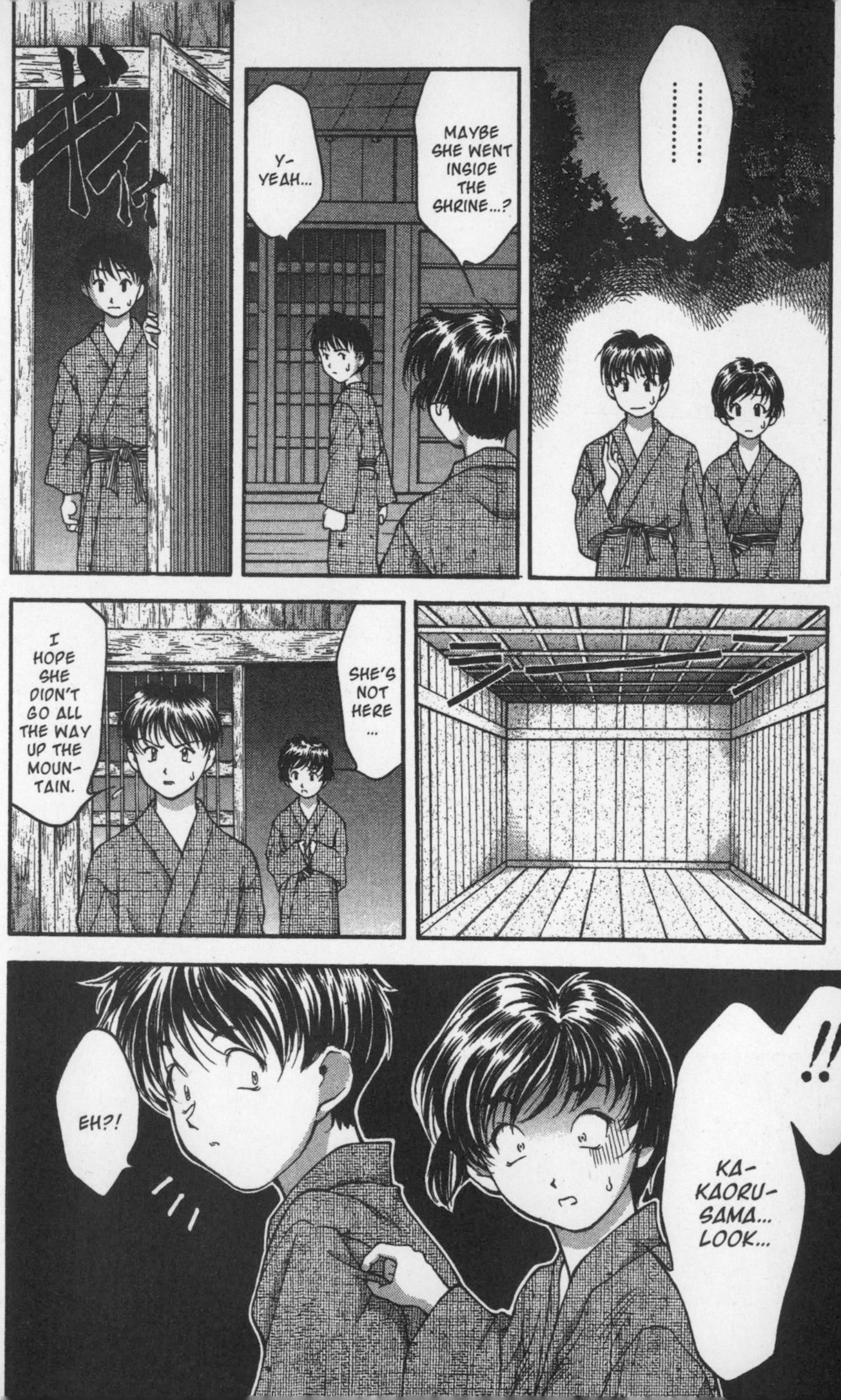
......
MAYBE SHE WENT INSIDE THE SHRINE...?
Y-YEAH...
SHE'S NOT HERE ...
I HOPE SHE DIDN'T GO ALL THE WAY UP THE MOUNTAIN.
!!
KA-KAORU-SAMA... LOOK...
EH?!

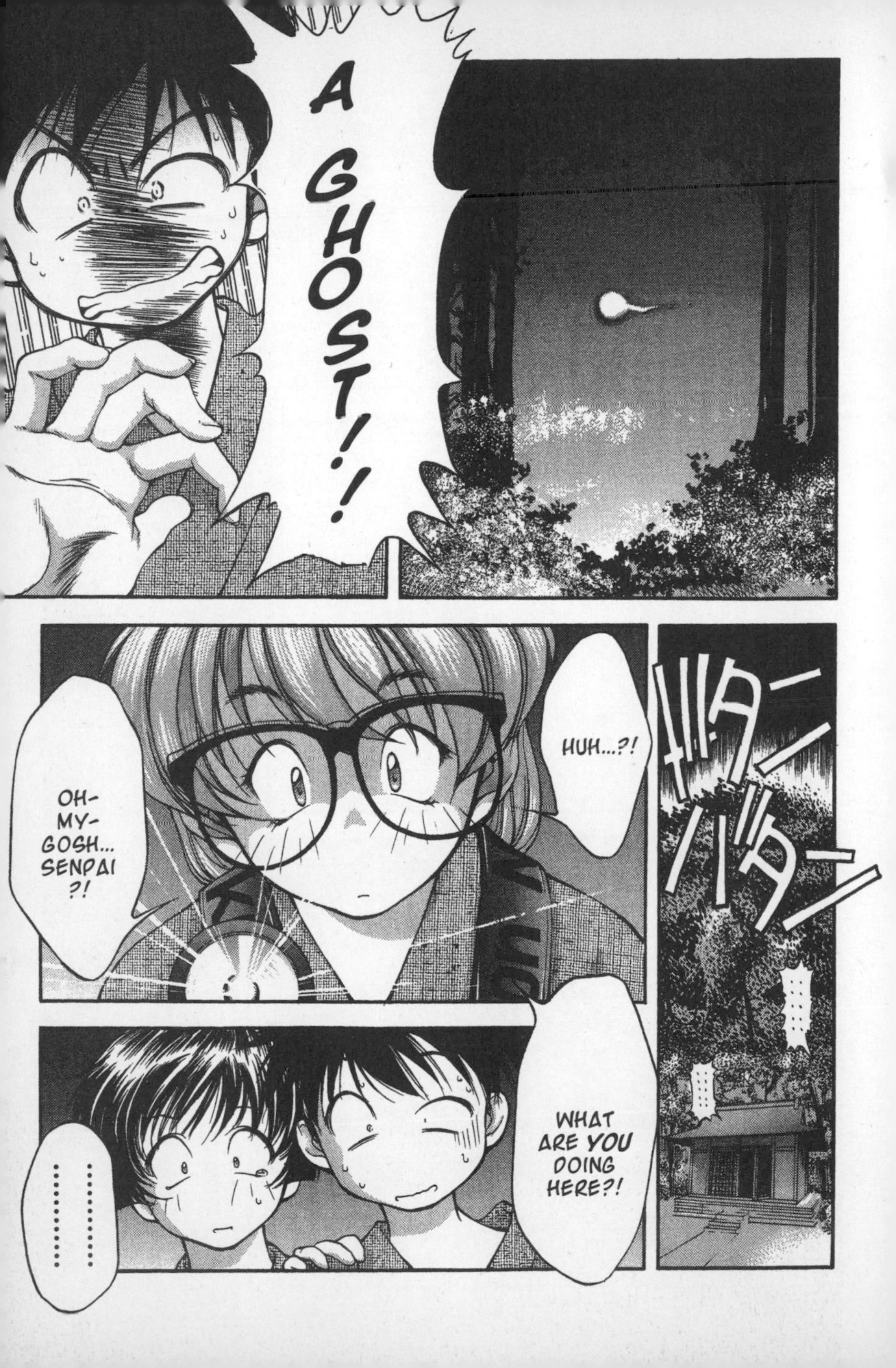
A GHOST!!
HUH...?!
OH-MY-GOSH... SENPAI?!
WHAT ARE YOU DOING HERE?!
......

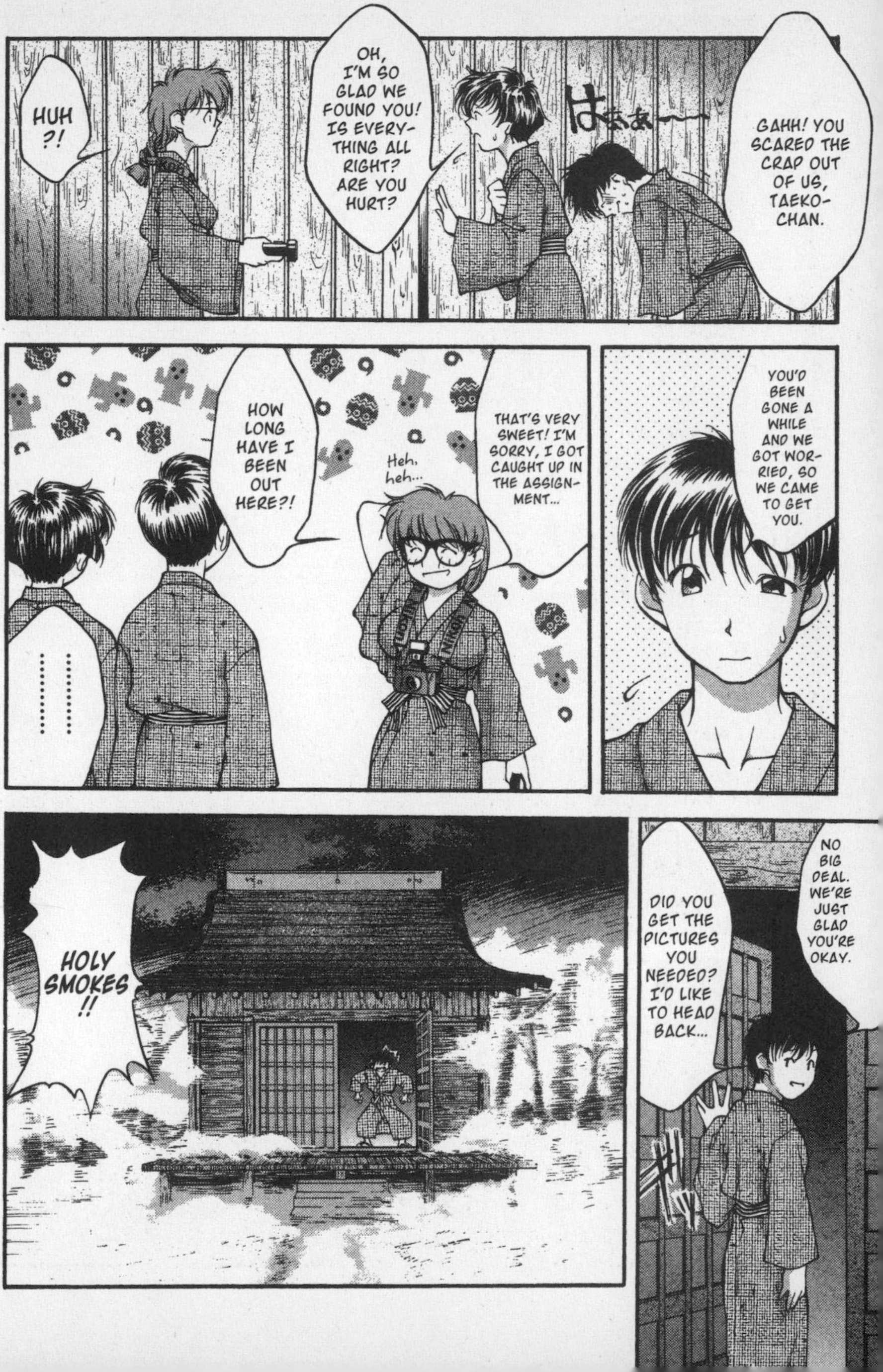
GAHH! YOU SCARED THE CRAP OUT OF US, TAEKO-CHAN.
はぁあー
OH, I'M SO GLAD WE FOUND YOU! IS EVERYTHING ALL RIGHT? ARE YOU HURT?
HUH ?!
YOU'D BEEN GONE A WHILE AND WE GOT WORRIED, SO WE CAME TO GET YOU.
THAT'S VERY SWEET! I'M SORRY, I GOT CAUGHT UP IN THE ASSIGNMENT...
Heh, heh...
HOW LONG HAVE I BEEN OUT HERE?!
......
NO BIG DEAL. WE'RE JUST GLAD YOU'RE OKAY.
DID YOU GET THE PICTURES YOU NEEDED? I'D LIKE TO HEAD BACK...
HOLY SMOKES !!

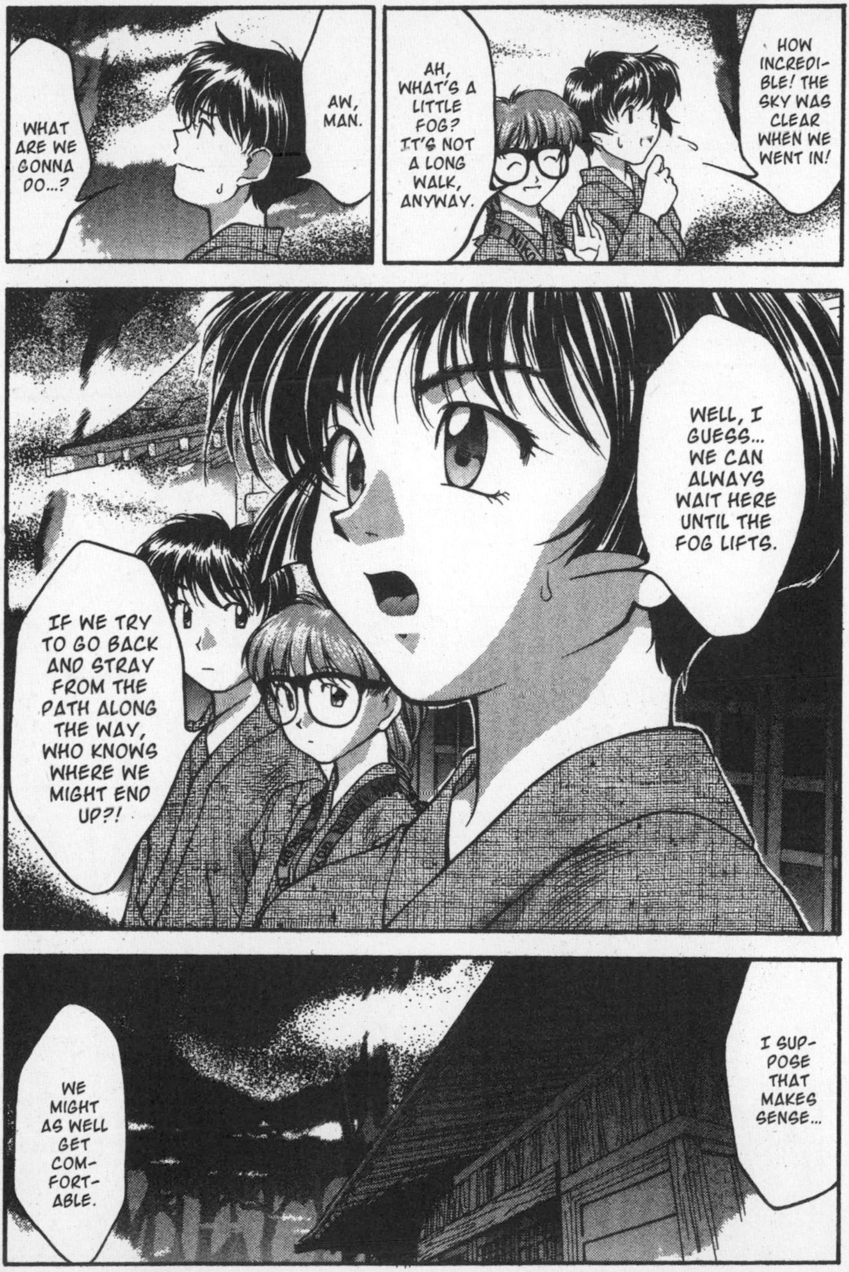
HOW INCREDIBLE! THE SKY WAS CLEAR WHEN WE WENT IN!
AH, WHAT'S A LITTLE FOG? IT'S NOT A LONG WALK, ANYWAY.
AW, MAN.
WHAT ARE WE GONNA DO...?
WELL, I GUESS... WE CAN ALWAYS WAIT HERE UNTIL THE FOG LIFTS.
IF WE TRY TO GO BACK AND STRAY FROM THE PATH ALONG THE WAY, WHO KNOWS WHERE WE MIGHT END UP?!
I SUPPOSE THAT MAKES SENSE...
WE MIGHT AS WELL GET COMFORTABLE.

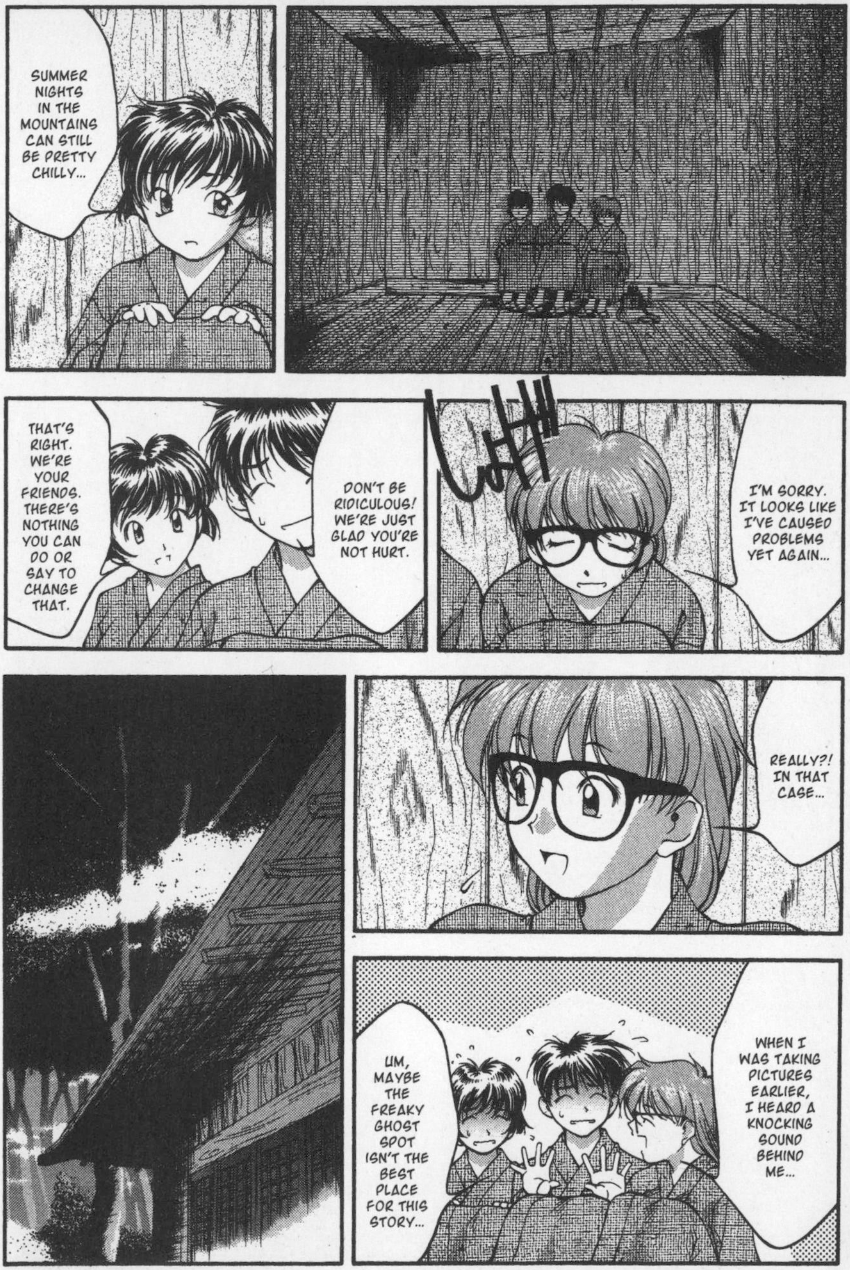
SUMMER NIGHTS IN THE MOUNTAINS CAN STILL BE PRETTY CHILLY...
I'M SORRY. IT LOOKS LIKE I'VE CAUSED PROBLEMS YET AGAIN...
DON'T BE RIDICULOUS! WE'RE JUST GLAD YOU'RE NOT HURT.
THAT'S RIGHT. WE'RE YOUR FRIENDS. THERE'S NOTHING YOU CAN DO OR SAY TO CHANGE THAT.
REALLY?! IN THAT CASE...
WHEN I WAS TAKING PICTURES EARLIER, I HEARD A KNOCKING SOUND BEHIND ME...
UM, MAYBE THE FREAKY GHOST SPOT ISN'T THE BEST PLACE FOR THIS STORY...

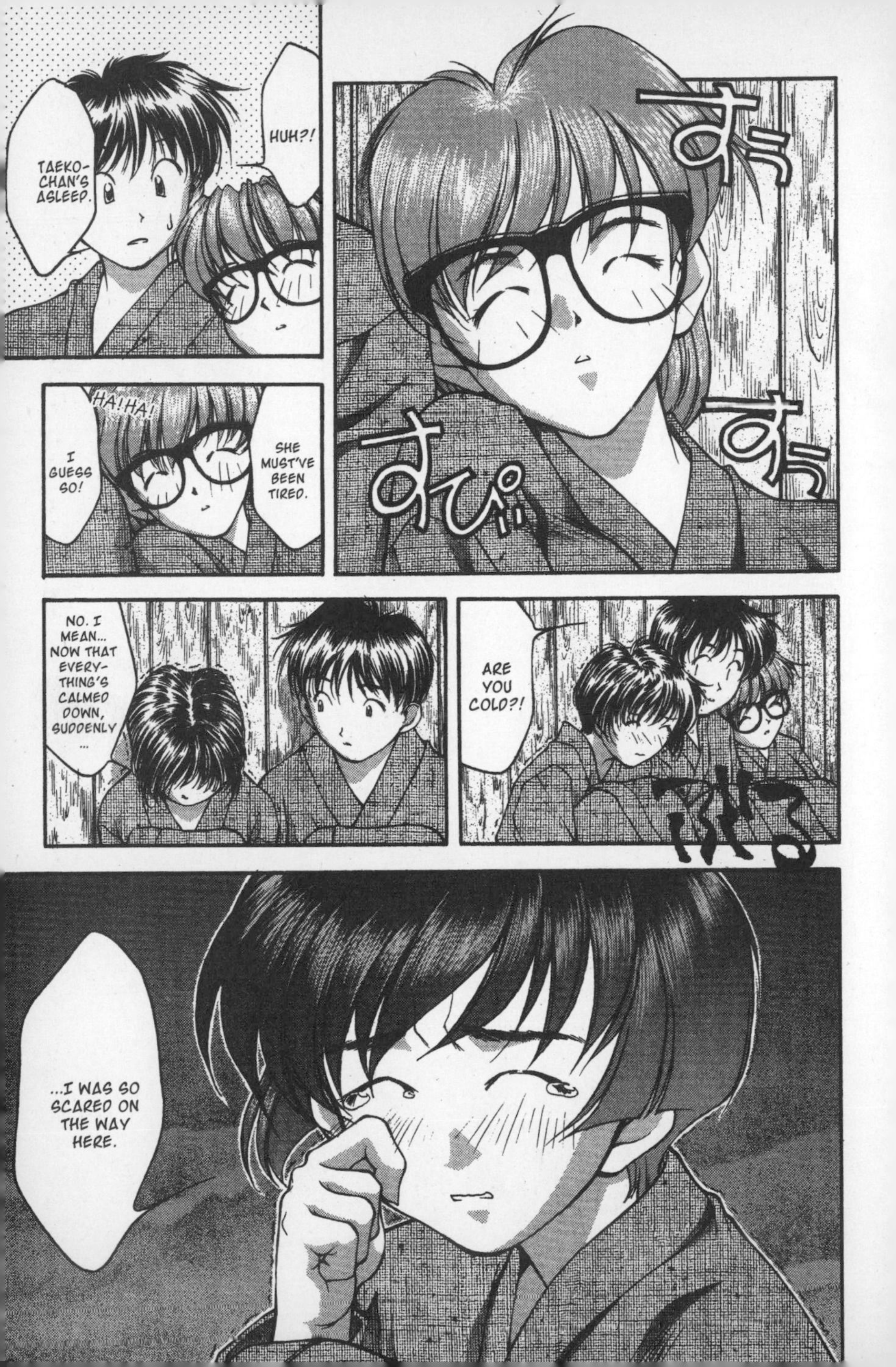
すぅ
すぅ
すぴ
HUH?!
TAEKO-CHAN'S ASLEEP.
SHE MUST'VE BEEN TIRED.
HA! HA!
I GUESS SO!
ARE YOU COLD?!
NO. I MEAN... NOW THAT EVERYTHING'S CALMED DOWN, SUDDENLY ...
...I WAS SO SCARED ON THE WAY HERE.

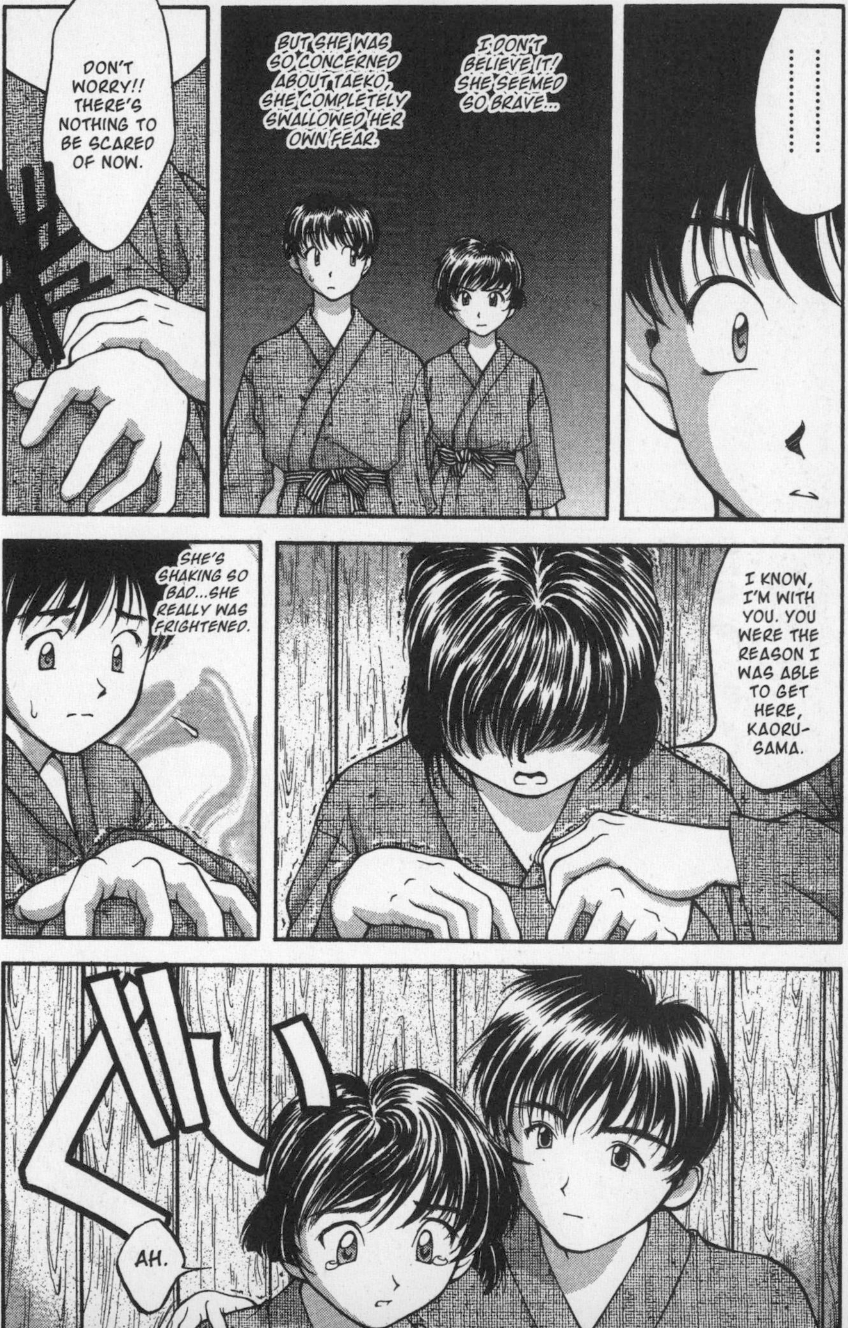
......
I DON'T BELIEVE IT! SHE SEEMED SO BRAVE...
BUT SHE WAS SO CONCERNED ABOUT TAEKO, SHE COMPLETELY SWALLOWED HER OWN FEAR.
DON'T WORRY!! THERE'S NOTHING TO BE SCARED OF NOW.
I KNOW, I'M WITH YOU. YOU WERE THE REASON I WAS ABLE TO GET HERE, KAORU-SAMA.
SHE'S SHAKING SO BAD...SHE REALLY WAS FRIGHTENED.
AH.

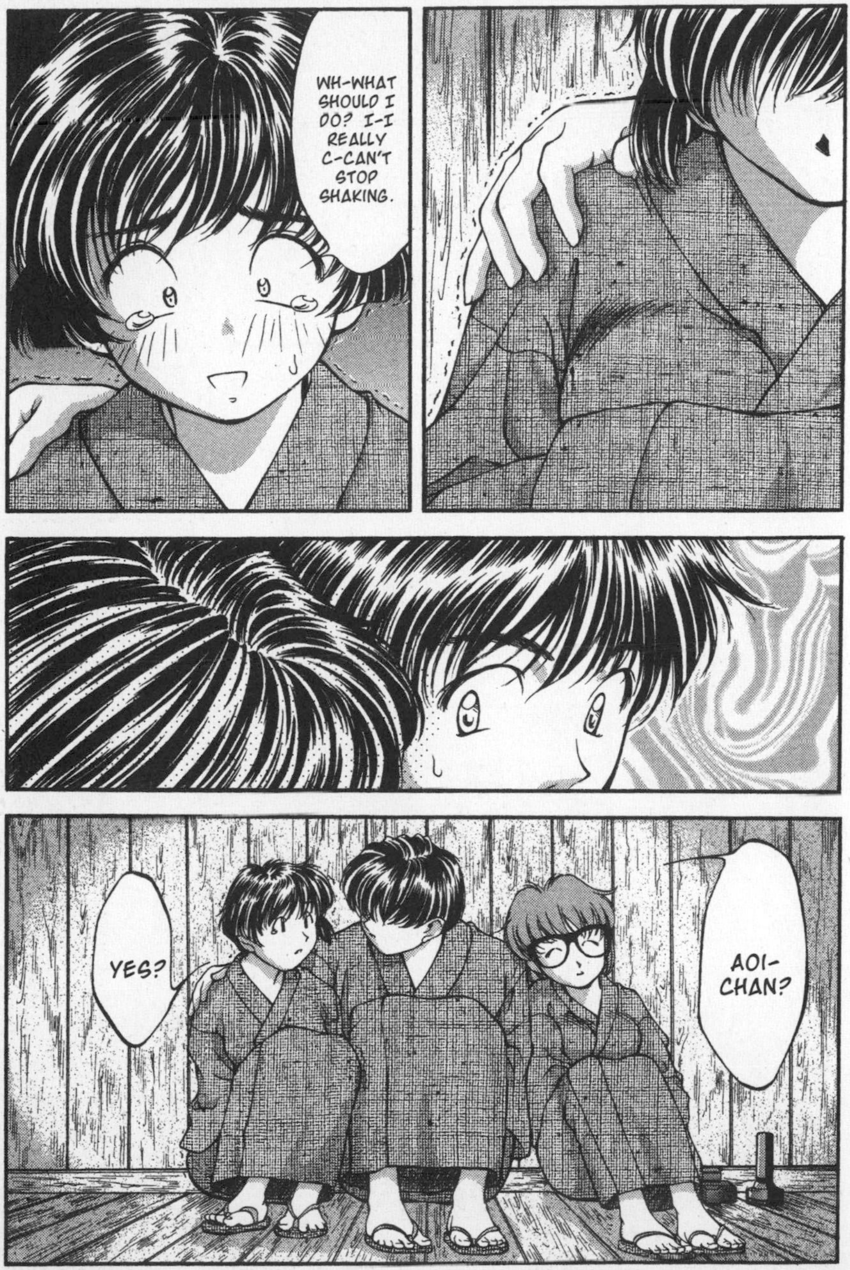
WH-WHAT SHOULD I DO? I-I REALLY C-CAN'T STOP SHAKING.
AOI-CHAN?
YES?

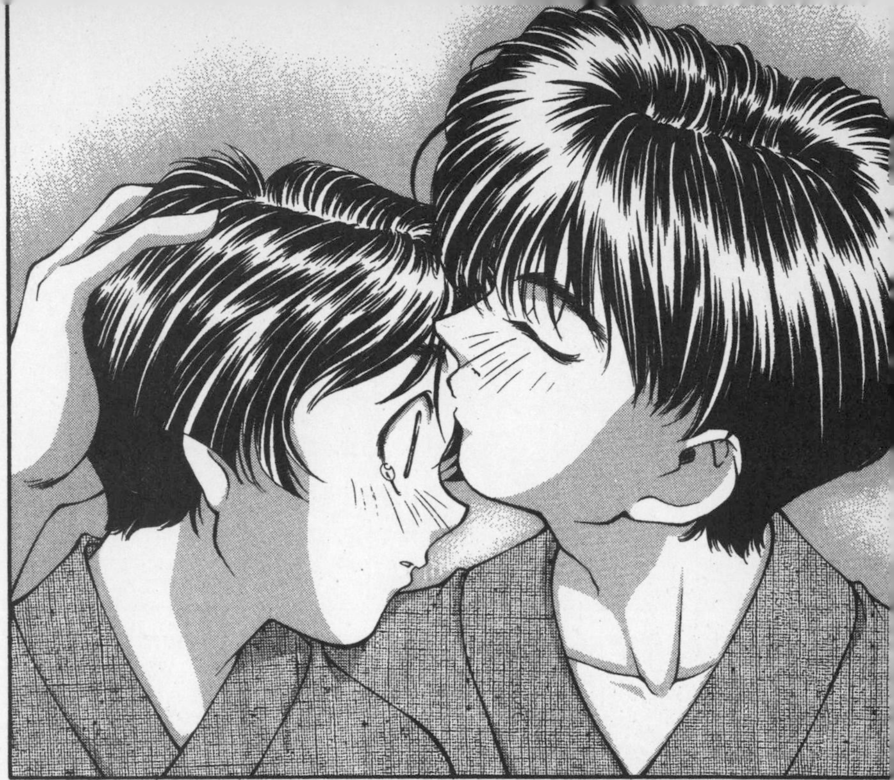

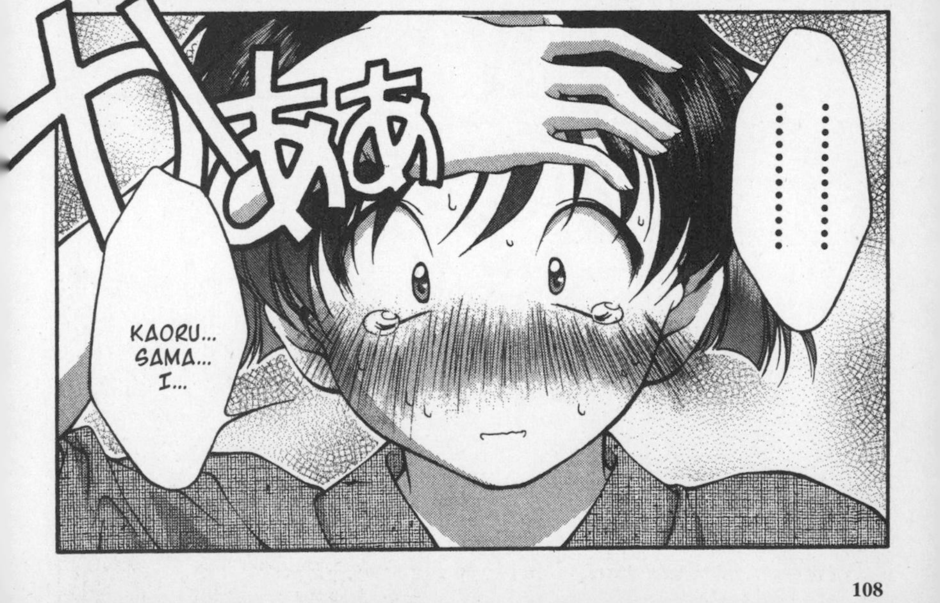
…………
KAORU... SAMA... I...

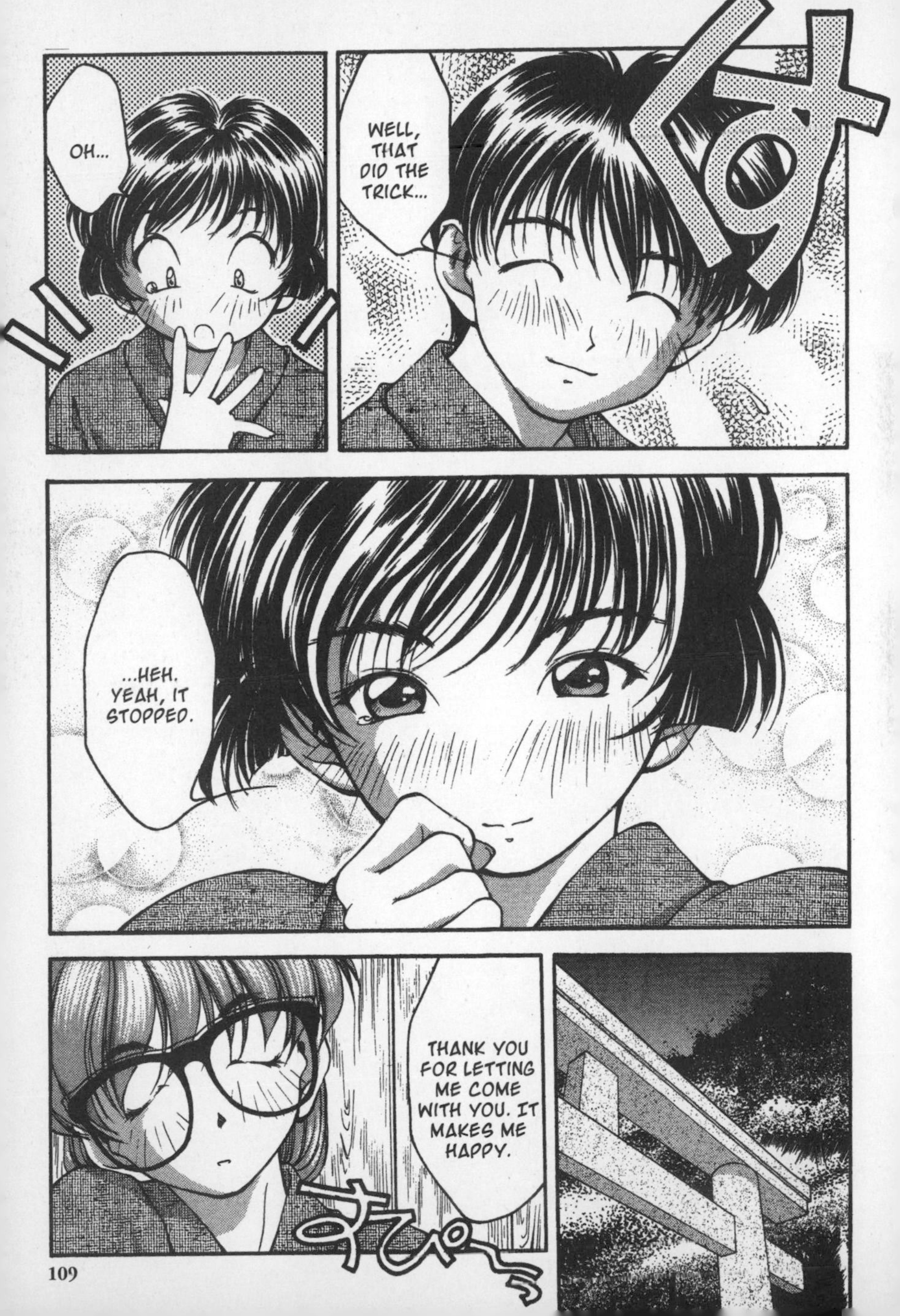
WELL, THAT DID THE TRICK...
OH...
...HEH. YEAH, IT STOPPED.
THANK YOU FOR LETTING ME COME WITH YOU. IT MAKES ME HAPPY.

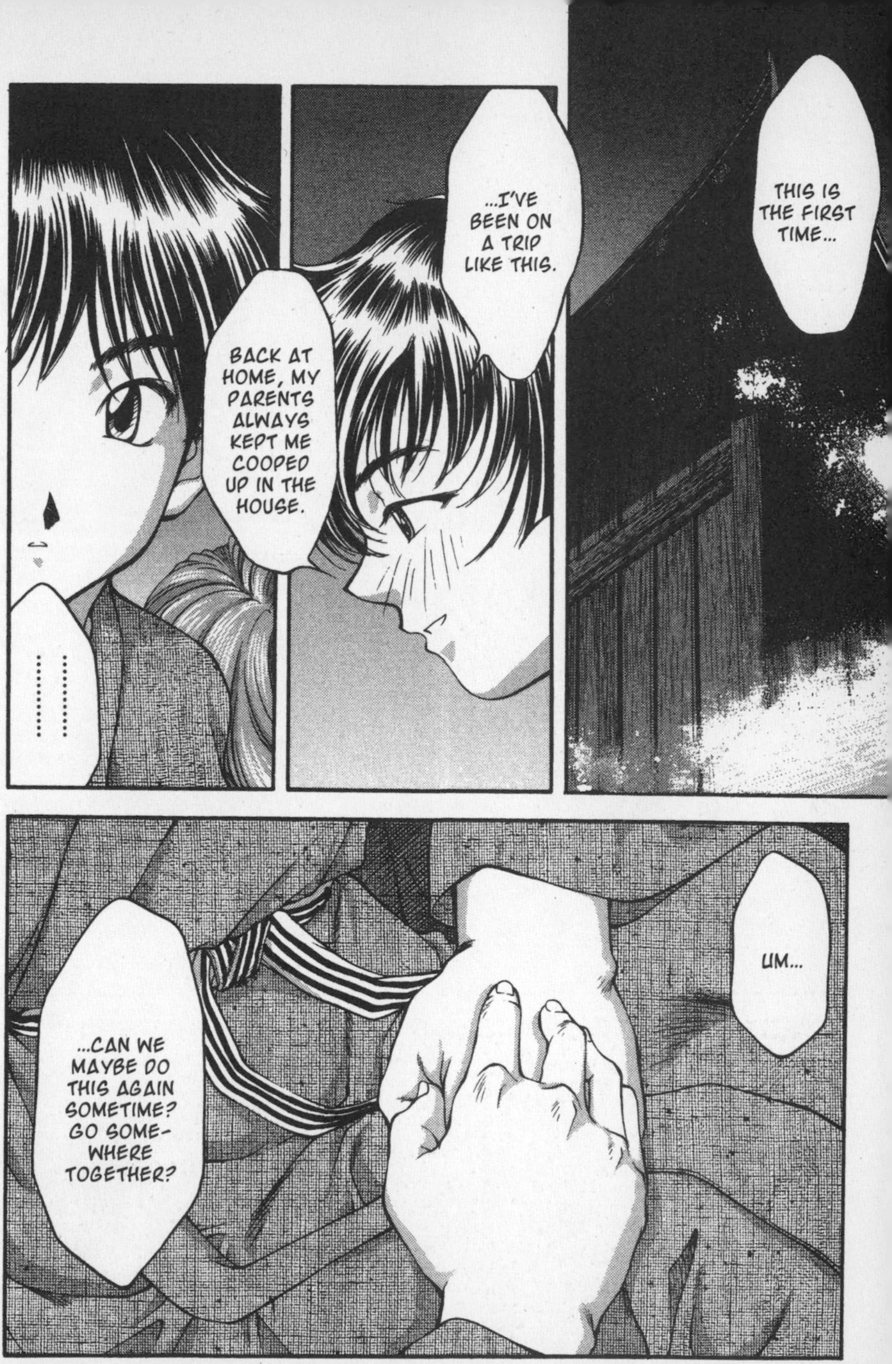
THIS IS THE FIRST TIME...
...I'VE BEEN ON A TRIP LIKE THIS.
BACK AT HOME, MY PARENTS ALWAYS KEPT ME COOPED UP IN THE HOUSE.
......
UM...
...CAN WE MAYBE DO THIS AGAIN SOMETIME? GO SOME-WHERE TOGETHER?

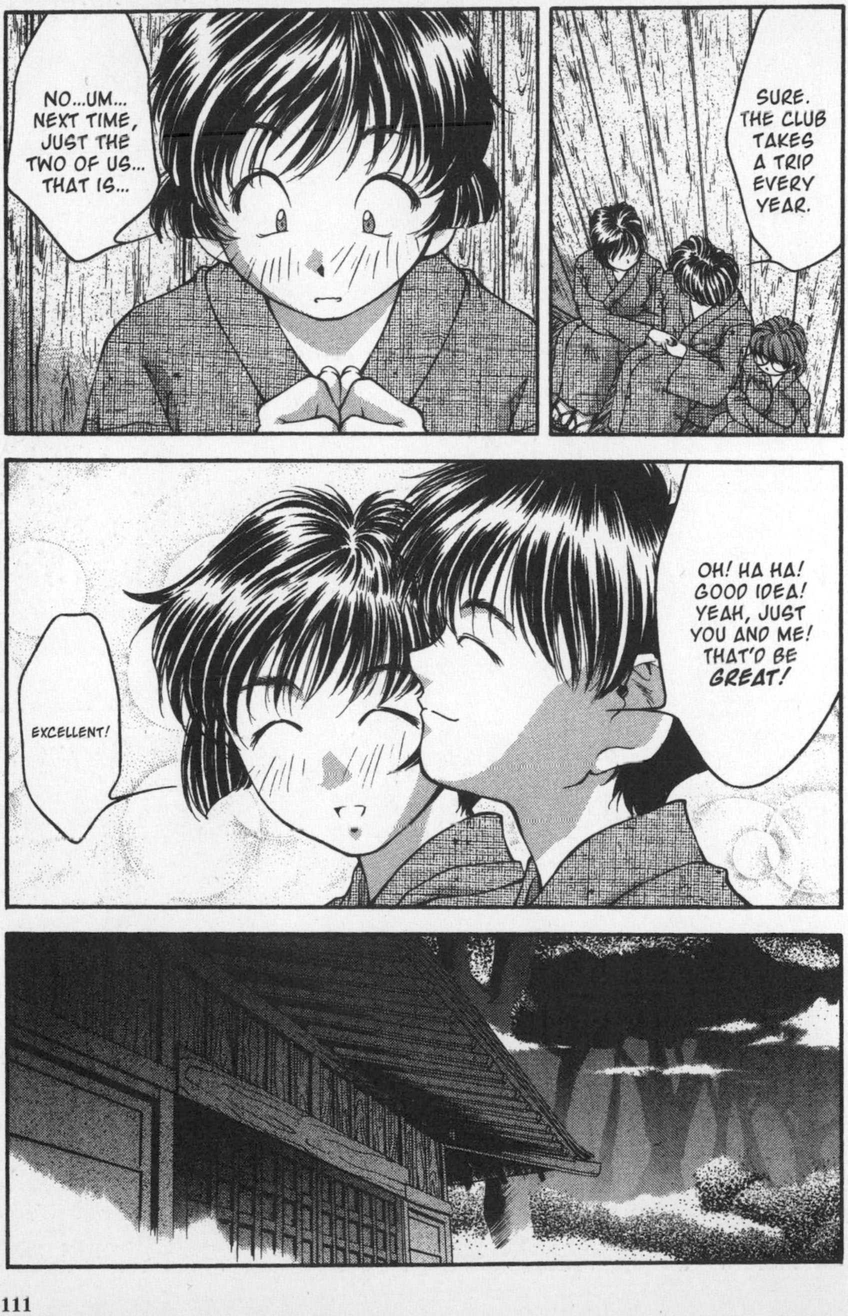
SURE. THE CLUB TAKES A TRIP EVERY YEAR.
NO...UM... NEXT TIME, JUST THE TWO OF US... THAT IS...
OH! HA HA! GOOD IDEA! YEAH, JUST YOU AND ME! THAT'D BE **GREAT**!
EXCELLENT!

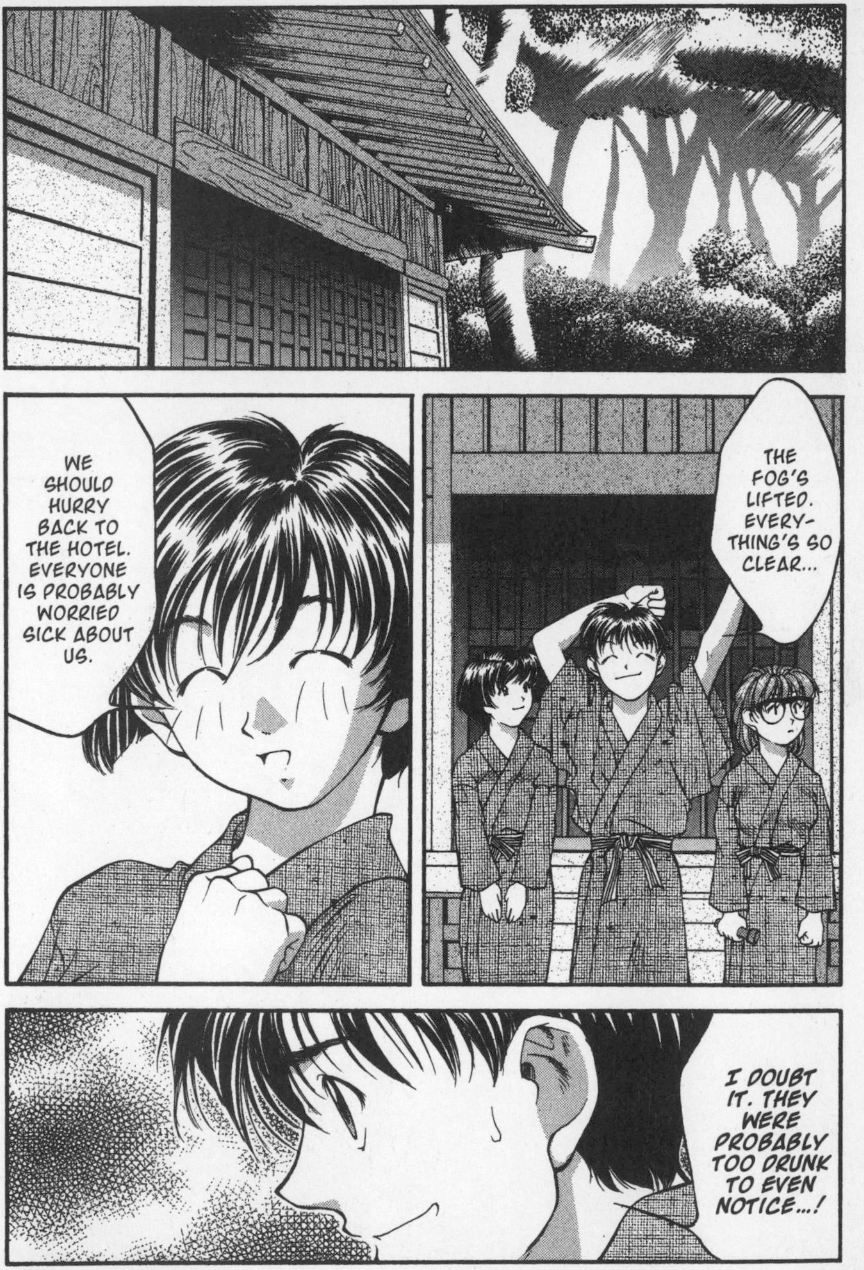
THE FOG'S LIFTED. EVERY-THING'S SO CLEAR...
WE SHOULD HURRY BACK TO THE HOTEL. EVERYONE IS PROBABLY WORRIED SICK ABOUT US.
I DOUBT IT. THEY WERE PROBABLY TOO DRUNK TO EVEN NOTICE...!

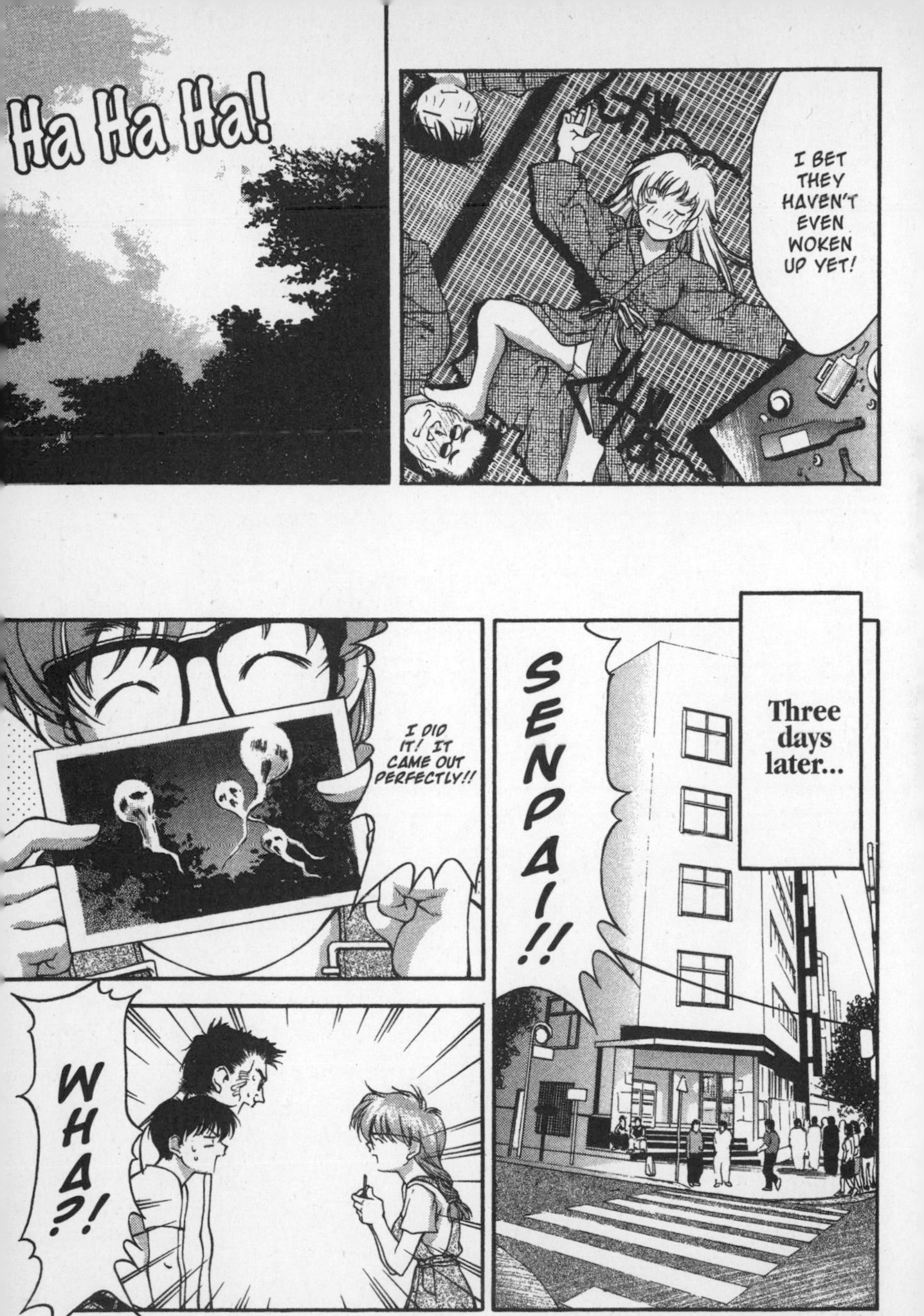
I BET THEY HAVEN'T EVEN WOKEN UP YET!
Ha Ha Ha!
Three days later...
SENPAI!!
I DID IT! IT CAME OUT PERFECTLY!!
WHA?!

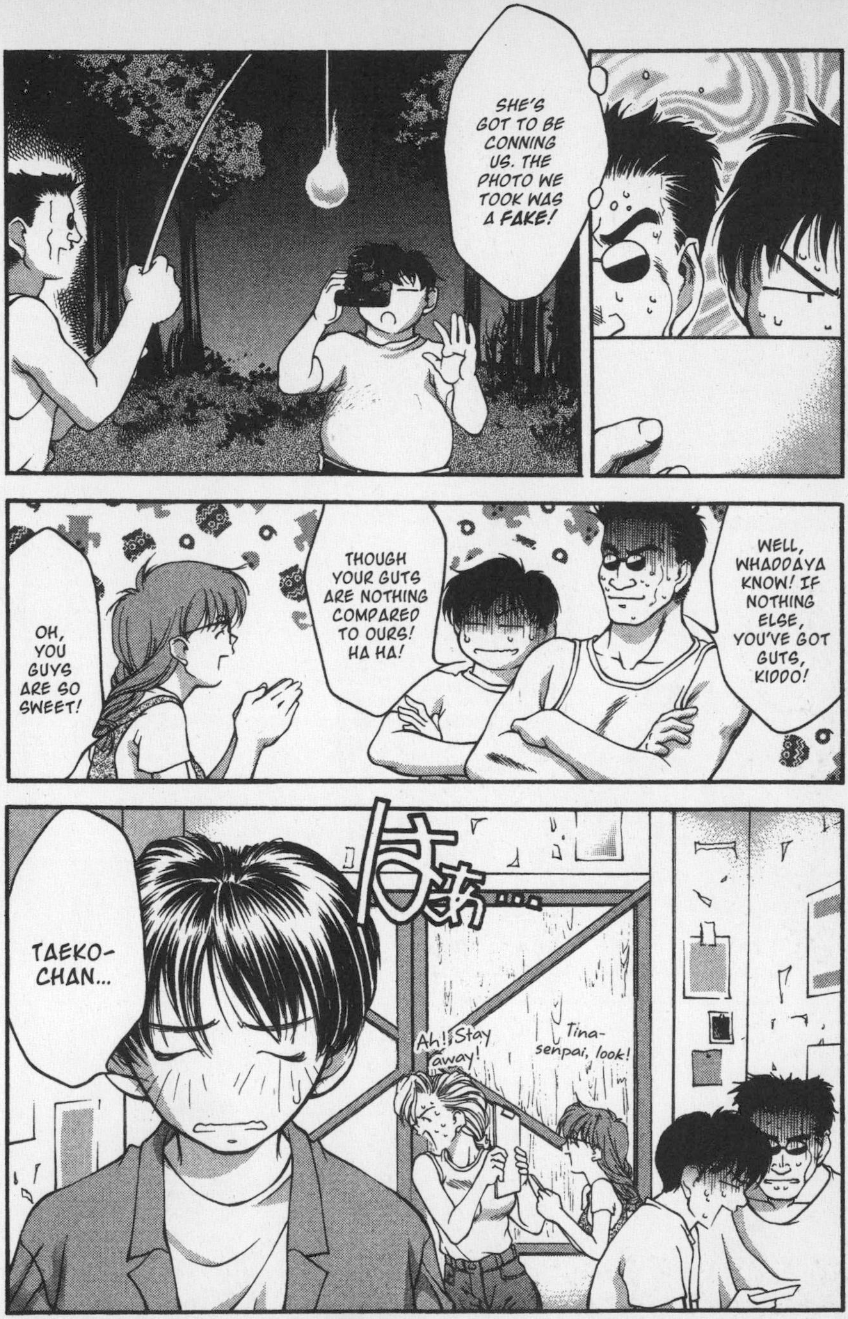
SHE'S GOT TO BE CONNING US. THE PHOTO WE TOOK WAS A FAKE!
WELL, WHADDAYA KNOW! IF NOTHING ELSE, YOU'VE GOT GUTS, KIDDO!
THOUGH YOUR GUTS ARE NOTHING COMPARED TO OURS! HA HA!
OH, YOU GUYS ARE SO SWEET!
はぁ...
TAEKO-CHAN...
Tina-senpai, look!
Ah! Stay away!

End of Chapter 15: Gen'you—Poltergeist

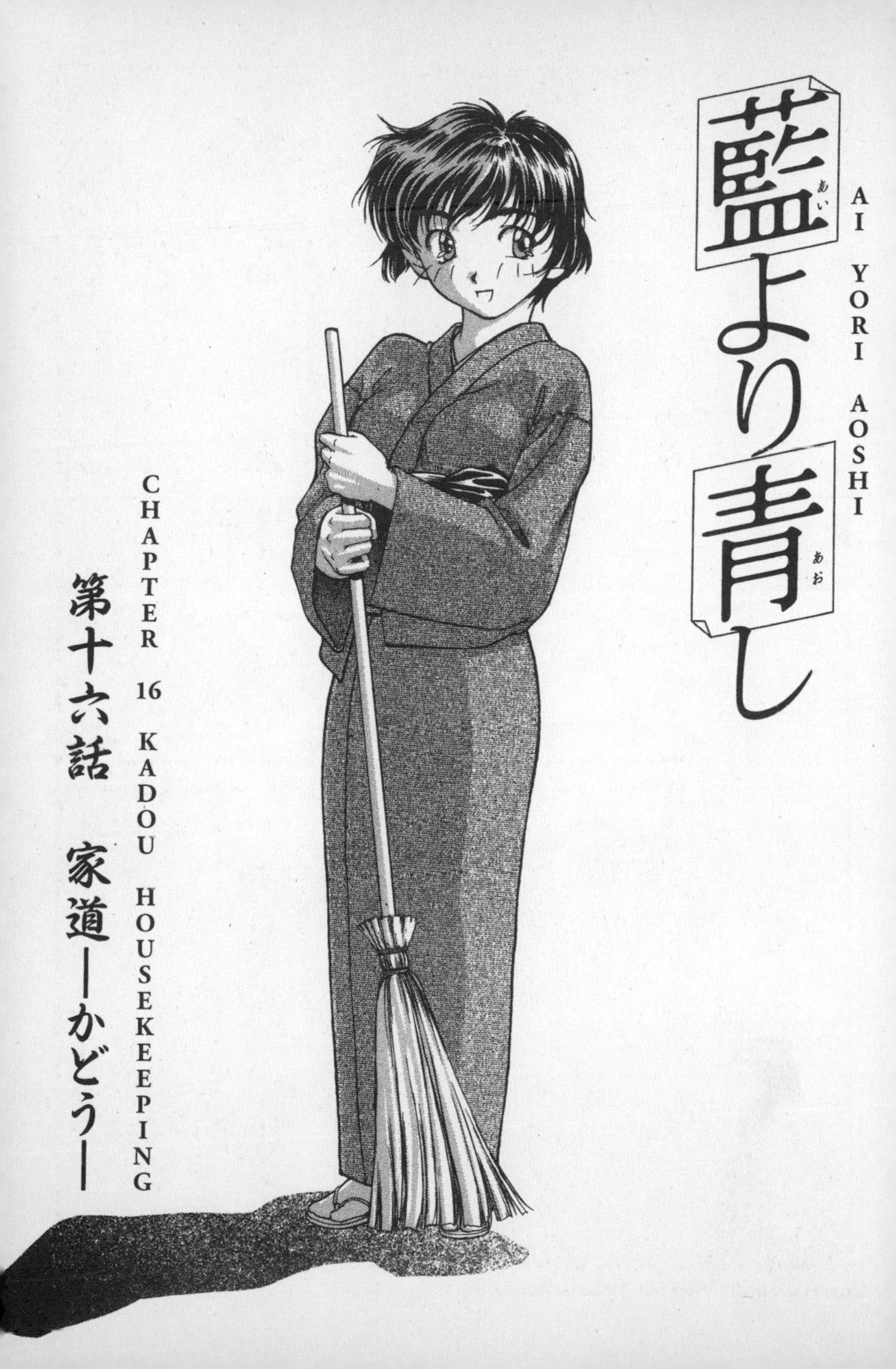
藍より青し
AI YORI AOSHI
CHAPTER 16 KADOU HOUSEKEEPING
第十六話 家道―かどう―

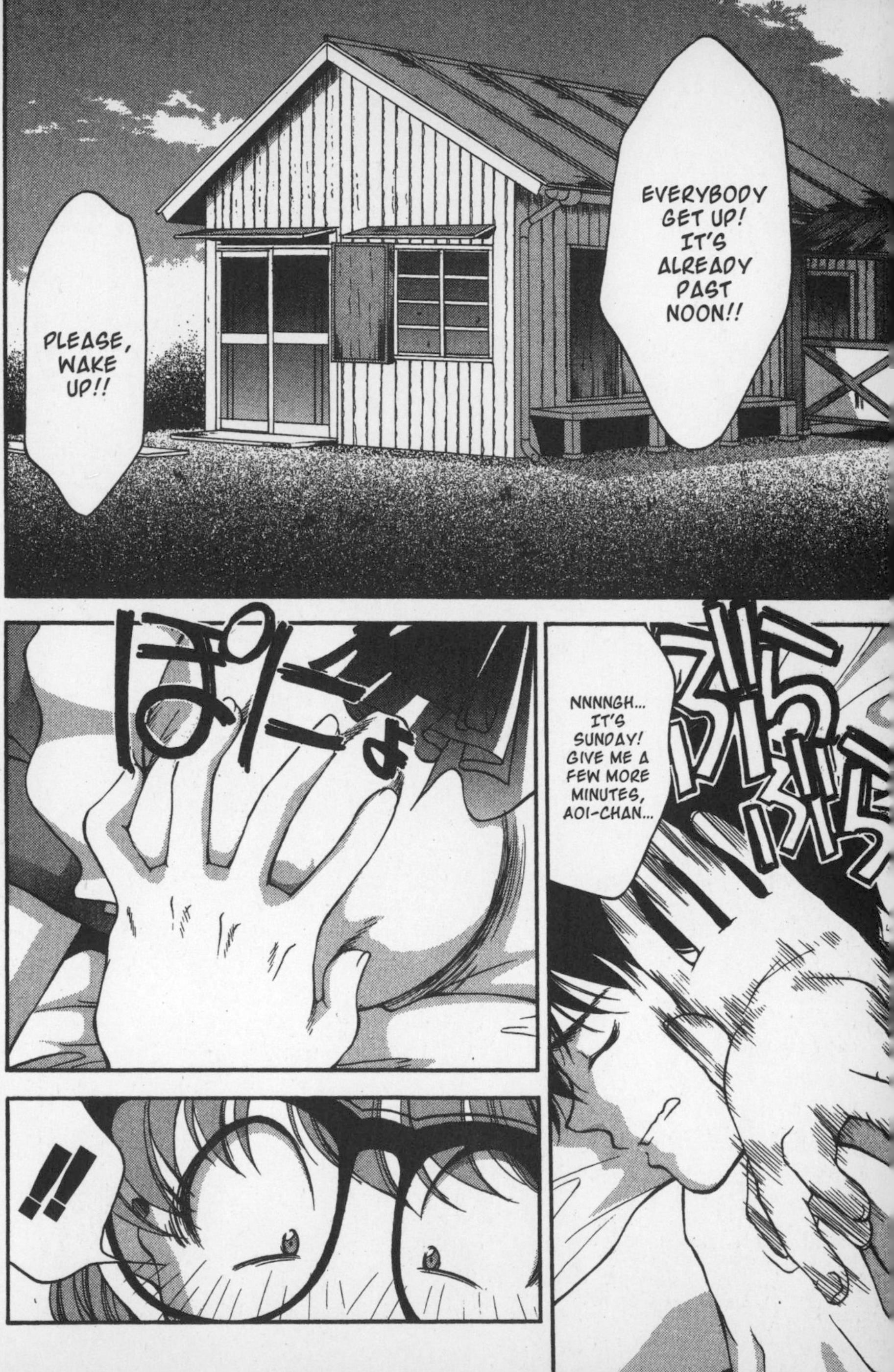
EVERYBODY GET UP! IT'S ALREADY PAST NOON!!
PLEASE, WAKE UP!!
NNNNGH... IT'S SUNDAY! GIVE ME A FEW MORE MINUTES, AOI-CHAN...
ぱにょ
!!

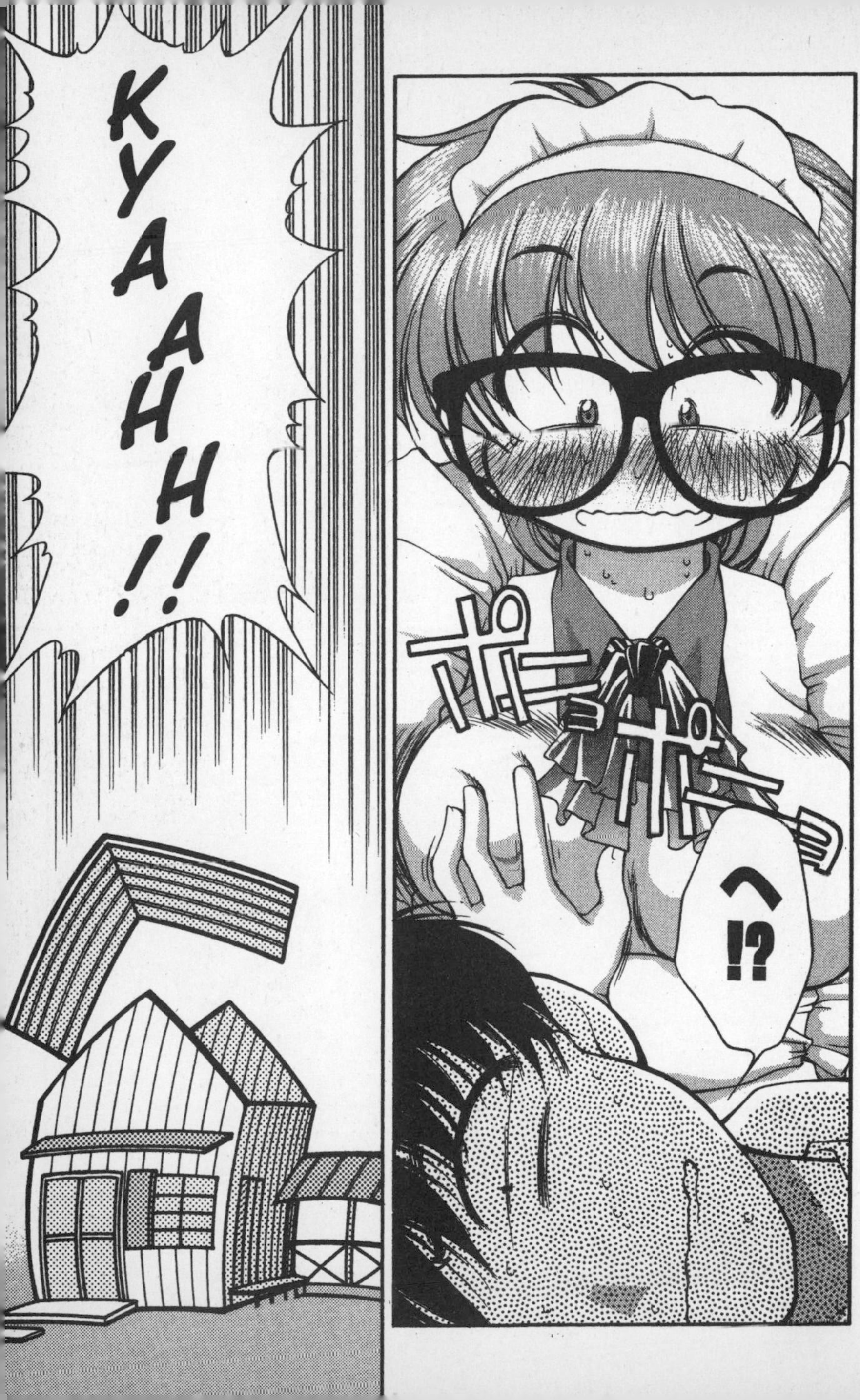
ポニョポニョ
へ!?
KYAAHH!!

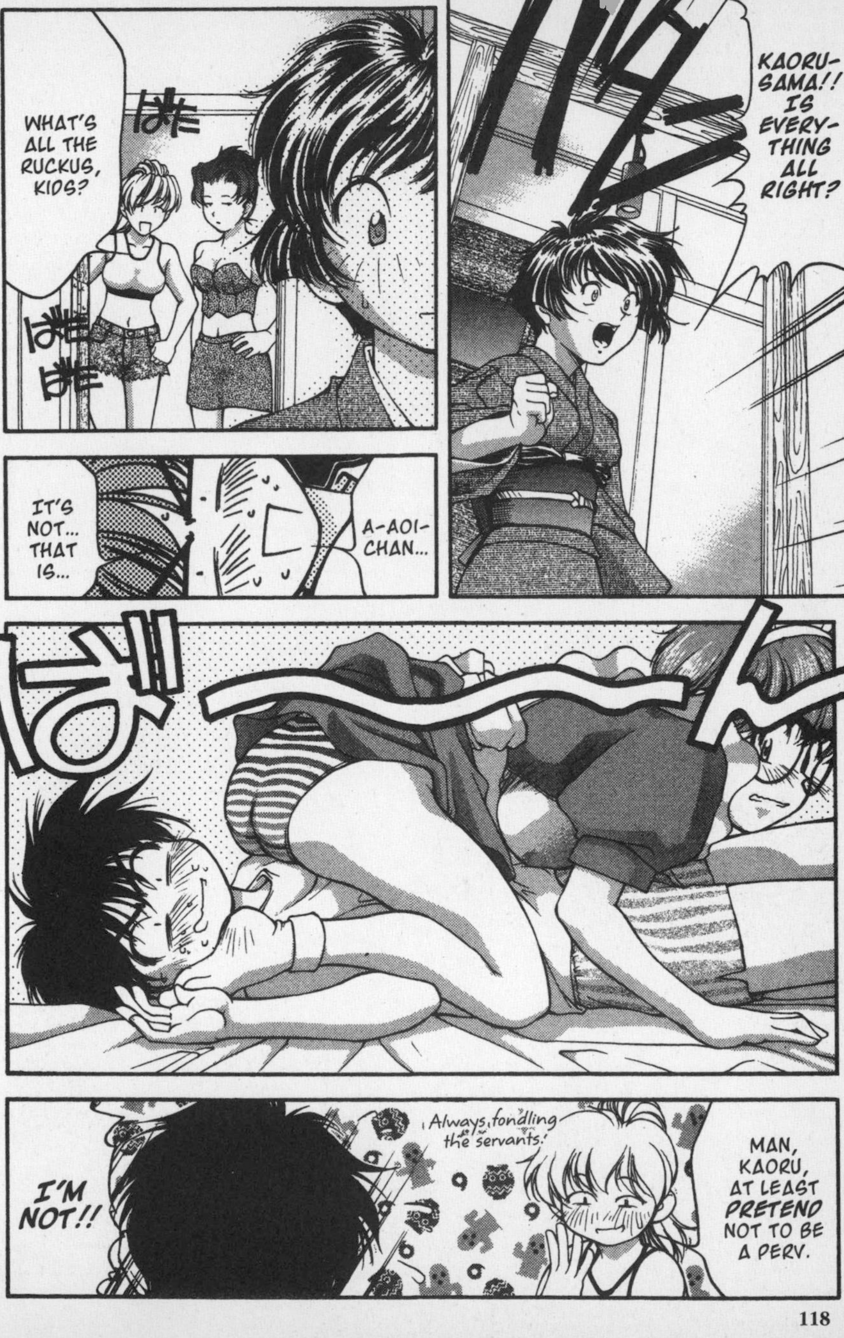
KAORU-SAMA!! IS EVERYTHING ALL RIGHT?
WHAT'S ALL THE RUCKUS, KIDS?
A-AOI-CHAN...
IT'S NOT... THAT IS...
MAN, KAORU, AT LEAST PRETEND NOT TO BE A PERV.
Always fondling the servants.
I'M NOT!!

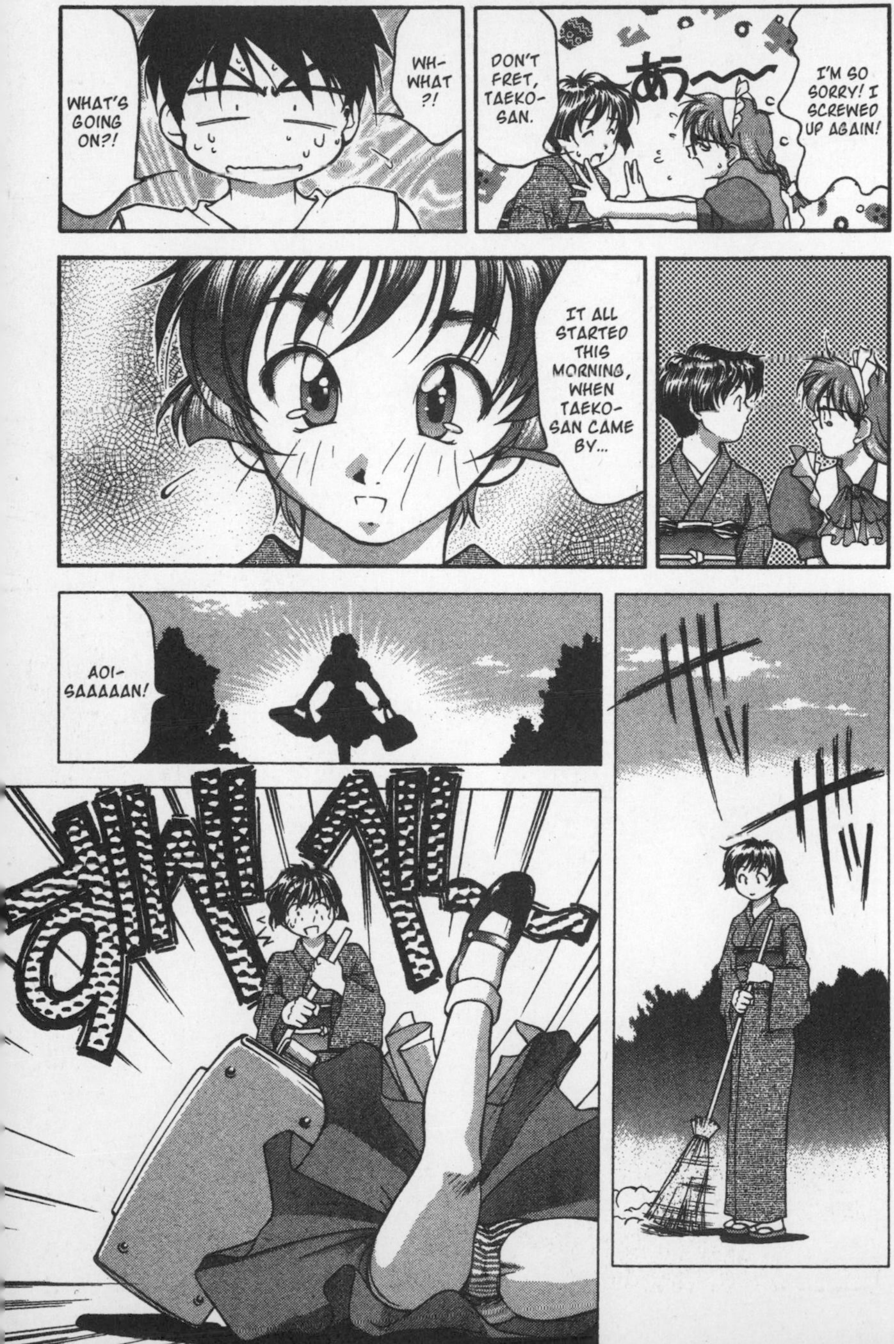
I'M SO SORRY! I SCREWED UP AGAIN!
あ~~~
DON'T FRET, TAEKO-SAN.
WH-WHAT?!
WHAT'S GOING ON?!
IT ALL STARTED THIS MORNING, WHEN TAEKO-SAN CAME BY...
AOI-SAAAAAN!

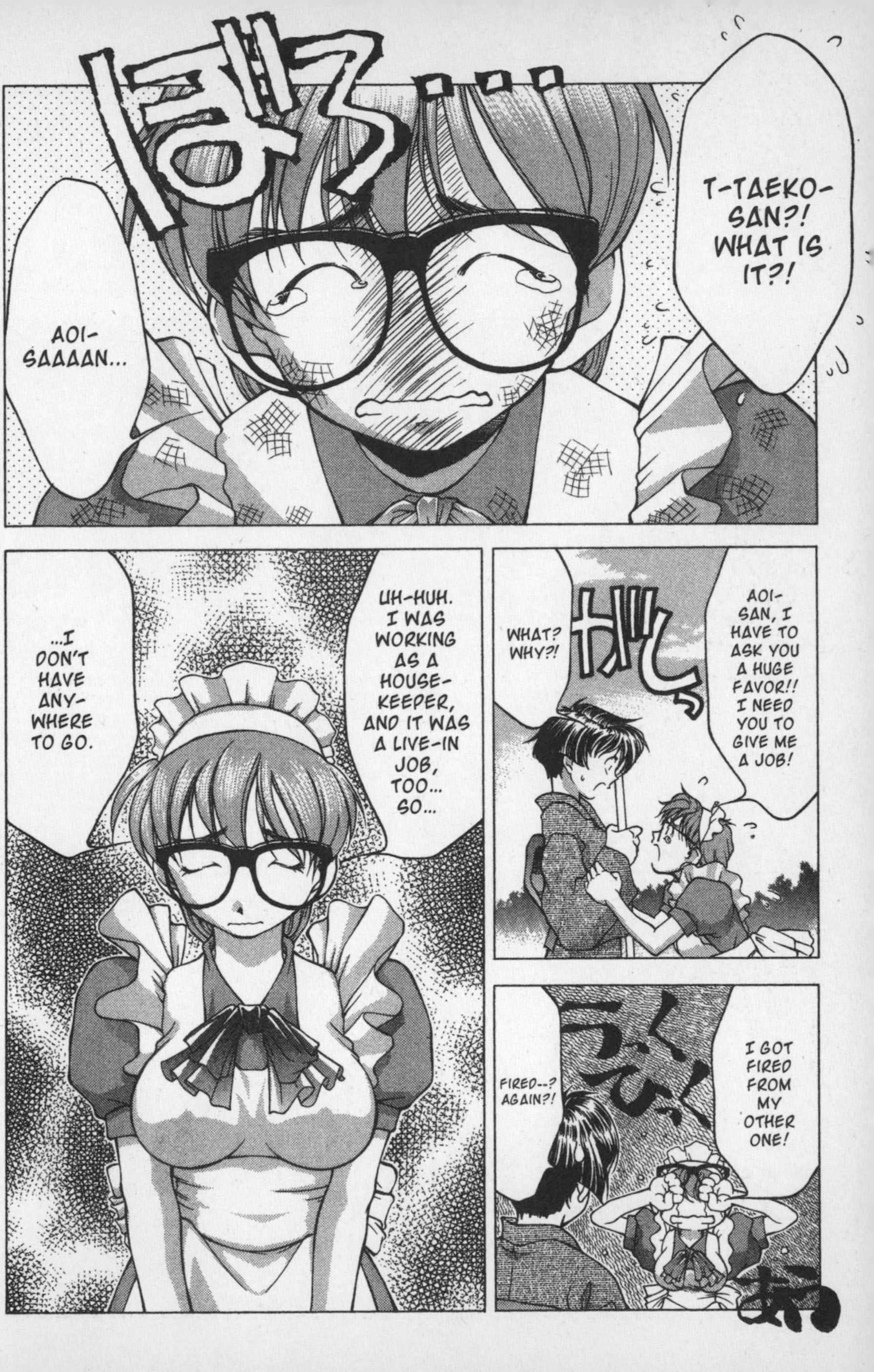
ぼろ...
T-TAEKO-SAN?! WHAT IS IT?!
AOI-SAAAAN...
AOI-SAN, I HAVE TO ASK YOU A HUGE FAVOR!! I NEED YOU TO GIVE ME A JOB!
WHAT? WHY?!
I GOT FIRED FROM MY OTHER ONE!
FIRED--? AGAIN?!
UH-HUH. I WAS WORKING AS A HOUSE-KEEPER, AND IT WAS A LIVE-IN JOB, TOO... SO...
...I DON'T HAVE ANY-WHERE TO GO.

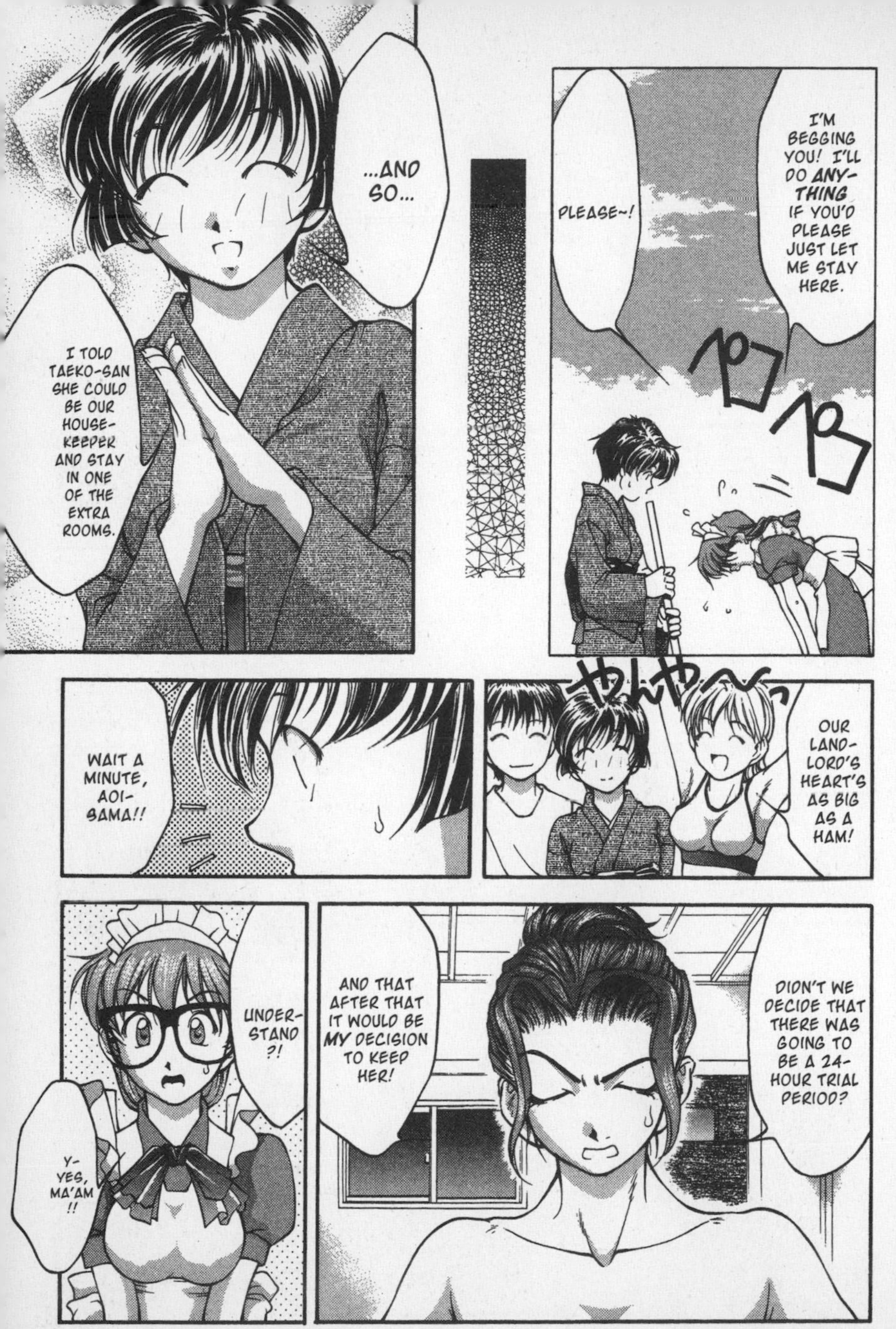
I'M BEGGING YOU! I'LL DO ANY-THING IF YOU'D PLEASE JUST LET ME STAY HERE.
PLEASE~!
ぺコ ぺコ
...AND SO...
I TOLD TAEKO-SAN SHE COULD BE OUR HOUSE-KEEPER AND STAY IN ONE OF THE EXTRA ROOMS.
やんや～っ
OUR LAND-LORD'S HEART'S AS BIG AS A HAM!
WAIT A MINUTE, AOI-SAMA!!
DIDN'T WE DECIDE THAT THERE WAS GOING TO BE A 24-HOUR TRIAL PERIOD?
AND THAT AFTER THAT IT WOULD BE MY DECISION TO KEEP HER!
UNDER-STAND ?!
Y-YES, MA'AM !!

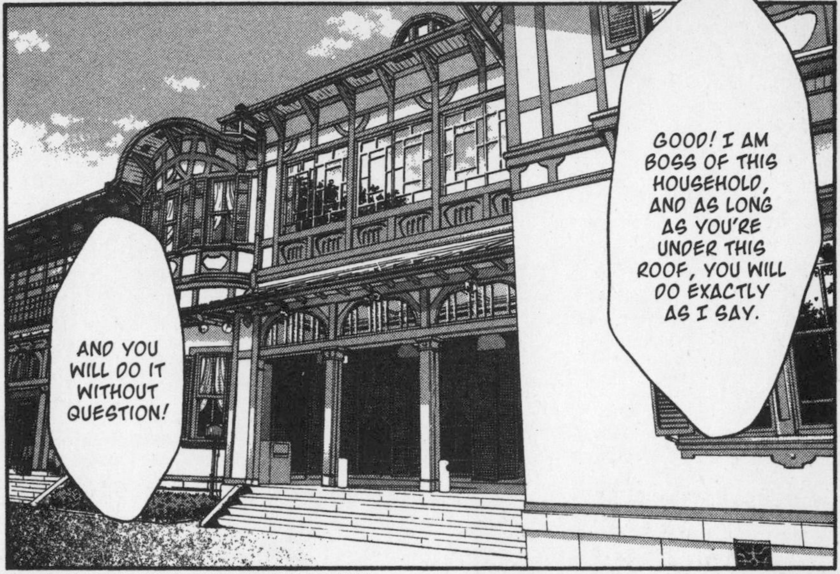
GOOD! I AM BOSS OF THIS HOUSEHOLD, AND AS LONG AS YOU'RE UNDER THIS ROOF, YOU WILL DO EXACTLY AS I SAY.
AND YOU WILL DO IT WITHOUT QUESTION!
THE SIDE VIEW OF AOI'S MANSION FOR THE FIRST TIME ANYWHERE!

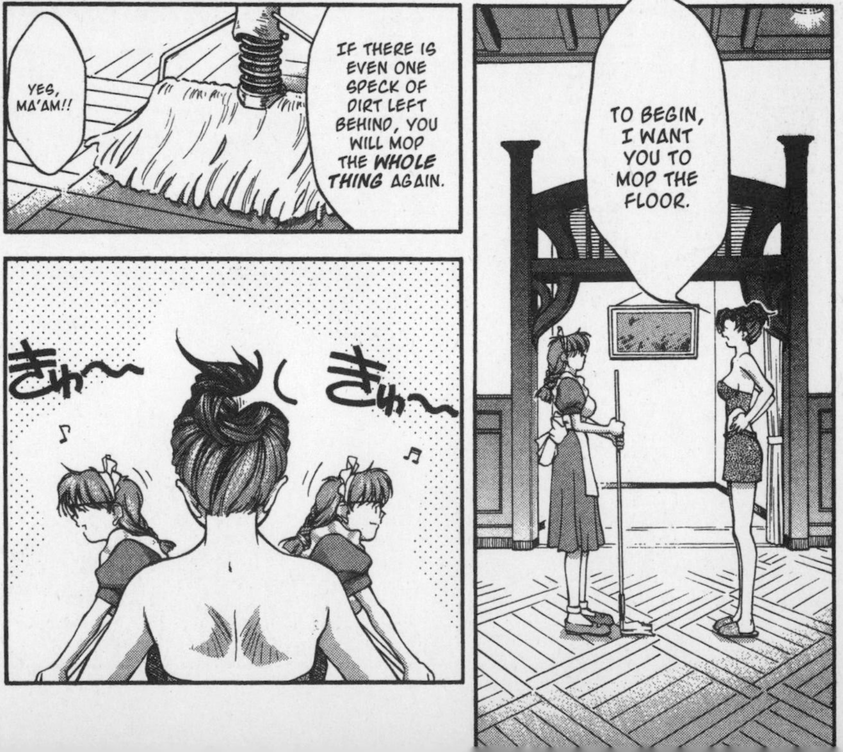
TO BEGIN, I WANT YOU TO MOP THE FLOOR.
IF THERE IS EVEN ONE SPECK OF DIRT LEFT BEHIND, YOU WILL MOP THE **WHOLE THING** AGAIN.
YES, MA'AM!!
きゅ〜
きゅ〜

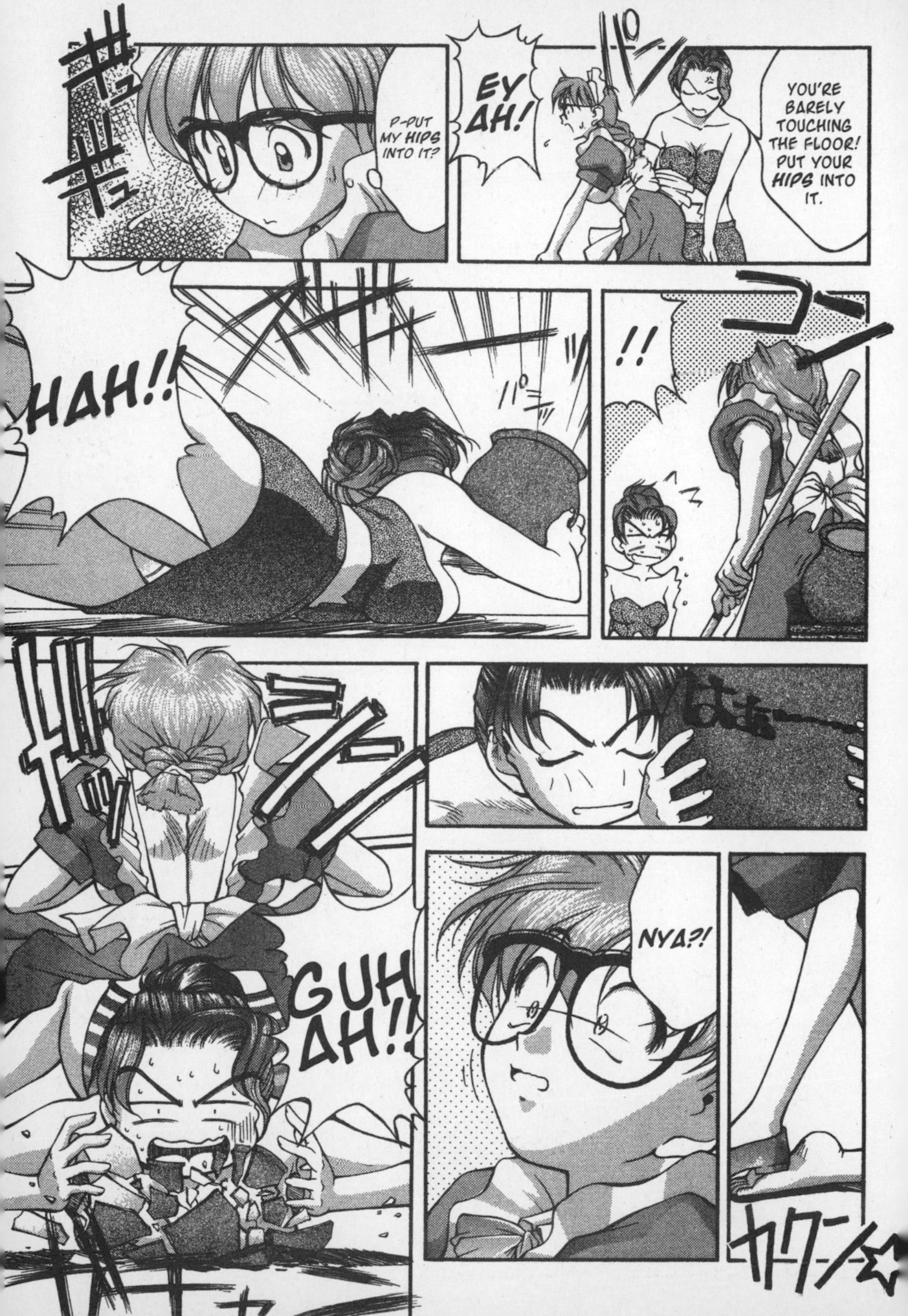
YOU'RE BARELY TOUCHING THE FLOOR! PUT YOUR HIPS INTO IT.
EY AH!
P-PUT MY HIPS INTO IT?
!!
HAH!!
GUH AH!!
NYA?!

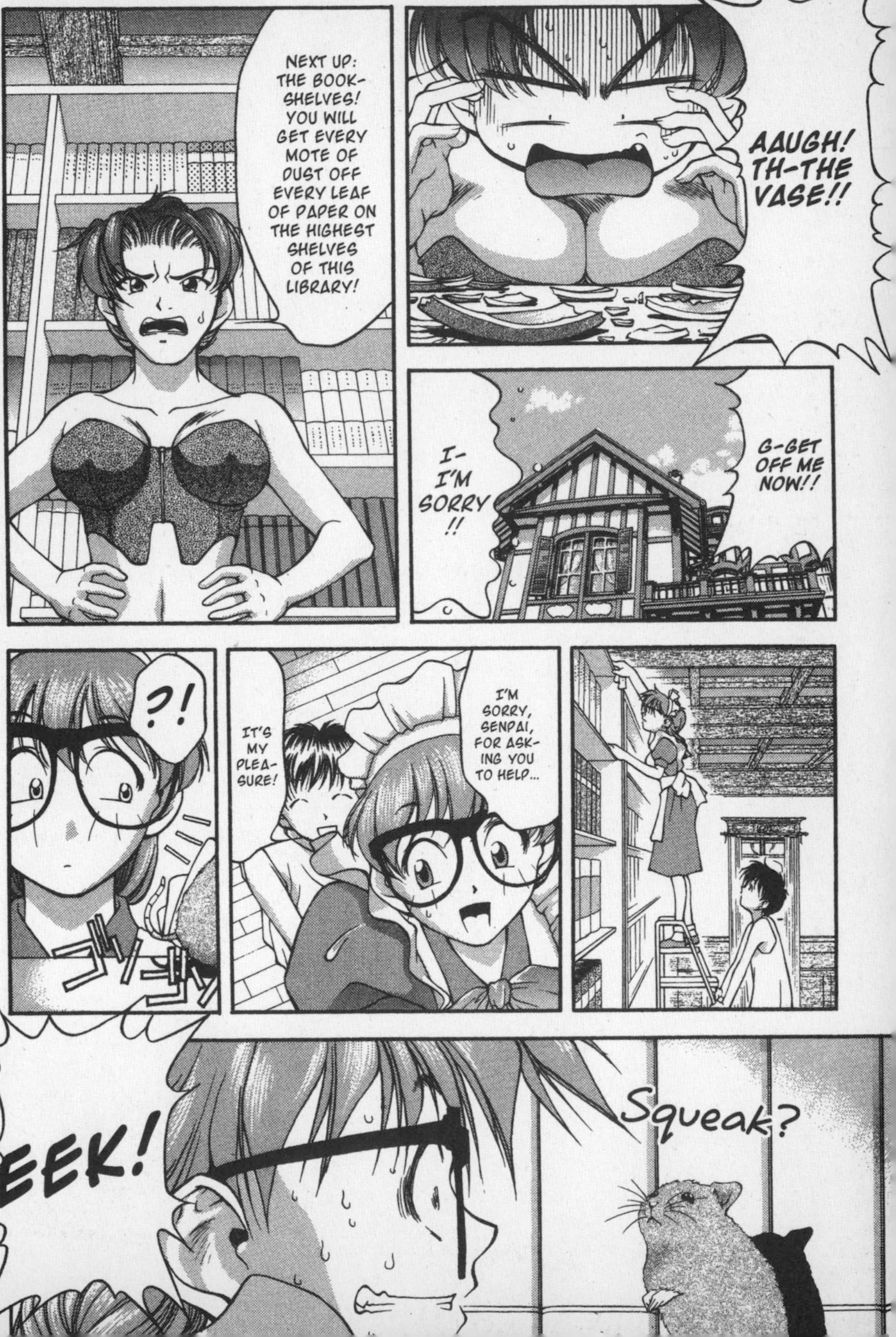
AAUGH! TH-THE VASE!!
G-GET OFF ME NOW!!
I- I'M SORRY!!
NEXT UP: THE BOOK-SHELVES! YOU WILL GET EVERY MOTE OF DUST OFF EVERY LEAF OF PAPER ON THE HIGHEST SHELVES OF THIS LIBRARY!
I'M SORRY, SENPAI, FOR ASKING YOU TO HELP...
IT'S MY PLEASURE!
?!
Squeak?
EEK!

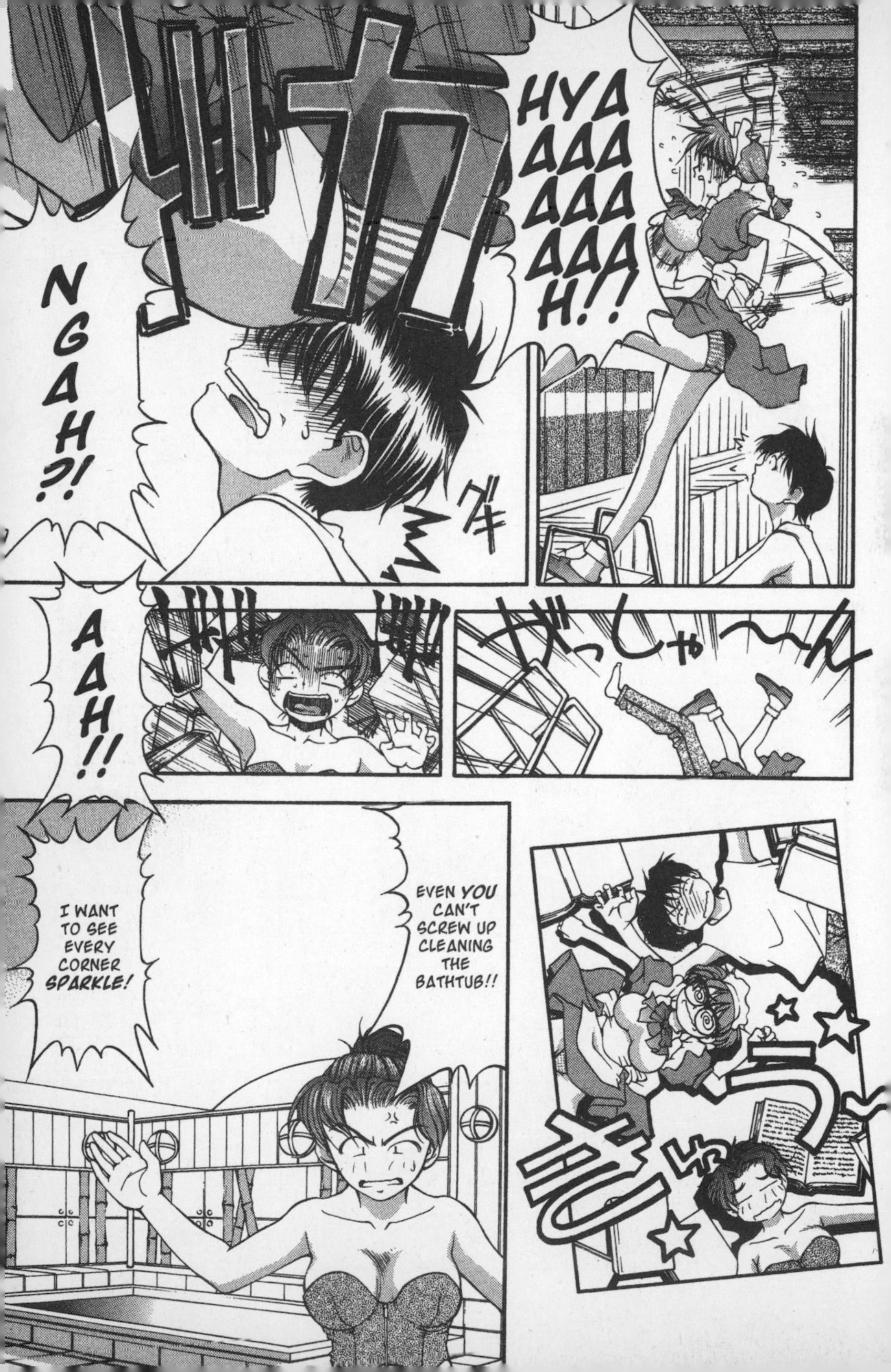
HYAAAAAAAAAAAAAH!!
NGAH?!
ゴキ
がっしゃ〜〜ん
AAAH!!
EVEN *YOU* CAN'T SCREW UP CLEANING THE BATHTUB!!
I WANT TO SEE EVERY CORNER *SPARKLE!*

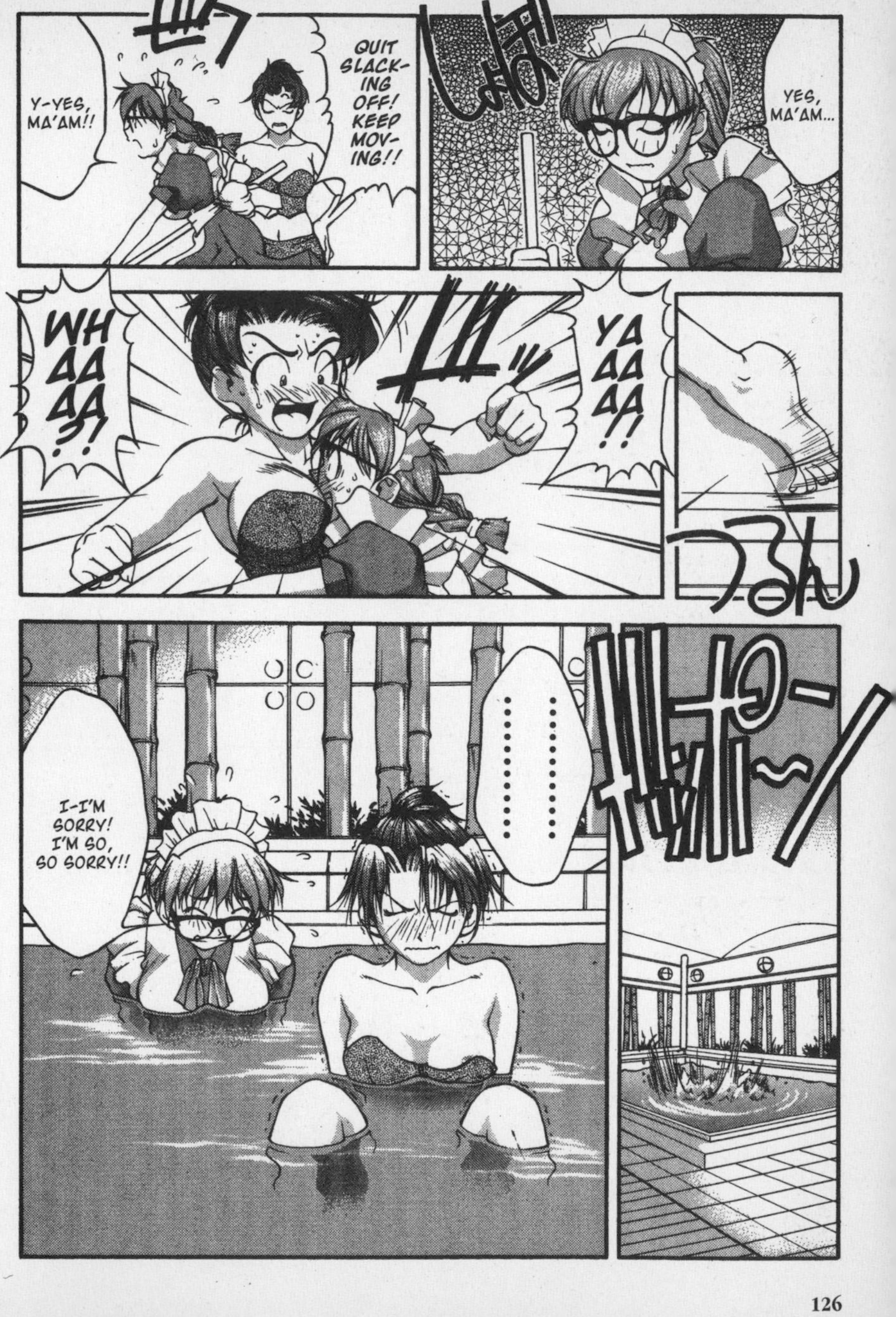
YES, MA'AM...
QUIT SLACKING OFF! KEEP MOVING!!
Y-YES, MA'AM!!
つるん
YAAAAA!!
WHAAAA?!
......
I-I'M SORRY! I'M SO, SO SORRY!!

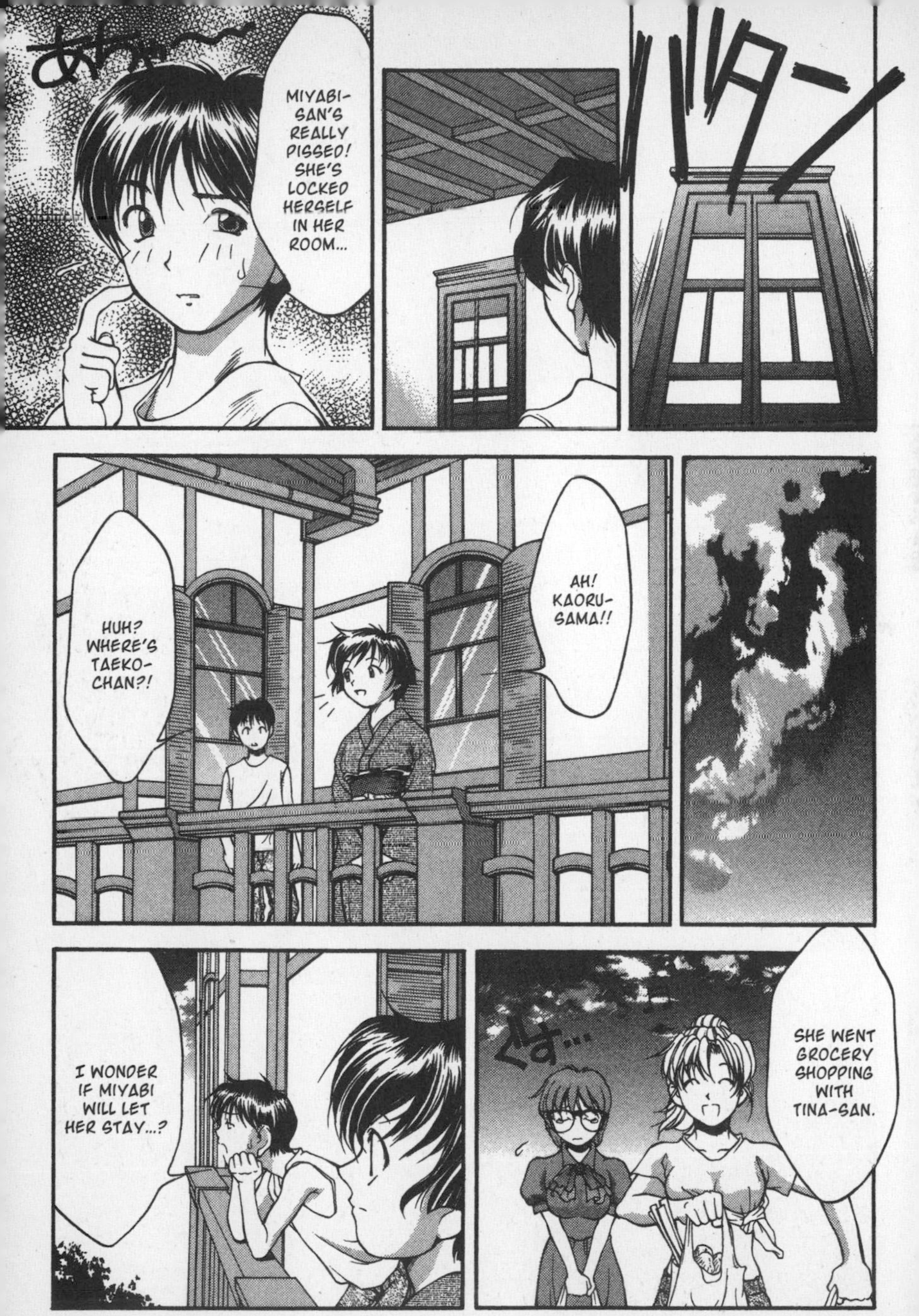
バターン
MIYABI-SAN'S REALLY PISSED! SHE'S LOCKED HERSELF IN HER ROOM...
AH! KAORU-SAMA!!
HUH? WHERE'S TAEKO-CHAN?!
SHE WENT GROCERY SHOPPING WITH TINA-SAN.
くす...
I WONDER IF MIYABI WILL LET HER STAY...?

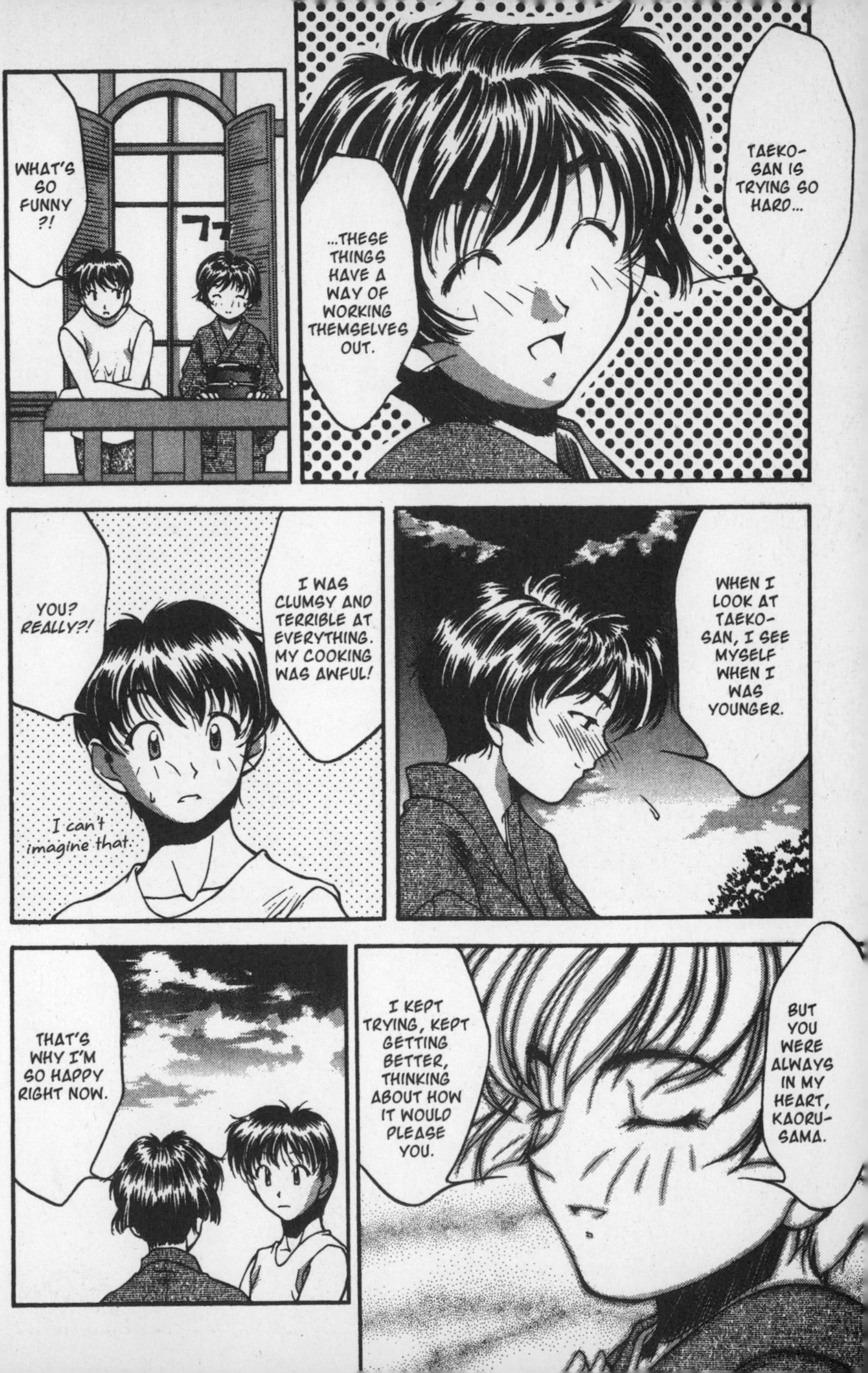
TAEKO-SAN IS TRYING SO HARD...
...THESE THINGS HAVE A WAY OF WORKING THEMSELVES OUT.
WHAT'S SO FUNNY ?!
WHEN I LOOK AT TAEKO-SAN, I SEE MYSELF WHEN I WAS YOUNGER.
I WAS CLUMSY AND TERRIBLE AT EVERYTHING. MY COOKING WAS AWFUL!
YOU? REALLY?!
I can't imagine that.
BUT YOU WERE ALWAYS IN MY HEART, KAORU-SAMA.
I KEPT TRYING, KEPT GETTING BETTER, THINKING ABOUT HOW IT WOULD PLEASE YOU.
THAT'S WHY I'M SO HAPPY RIGHT NOW.

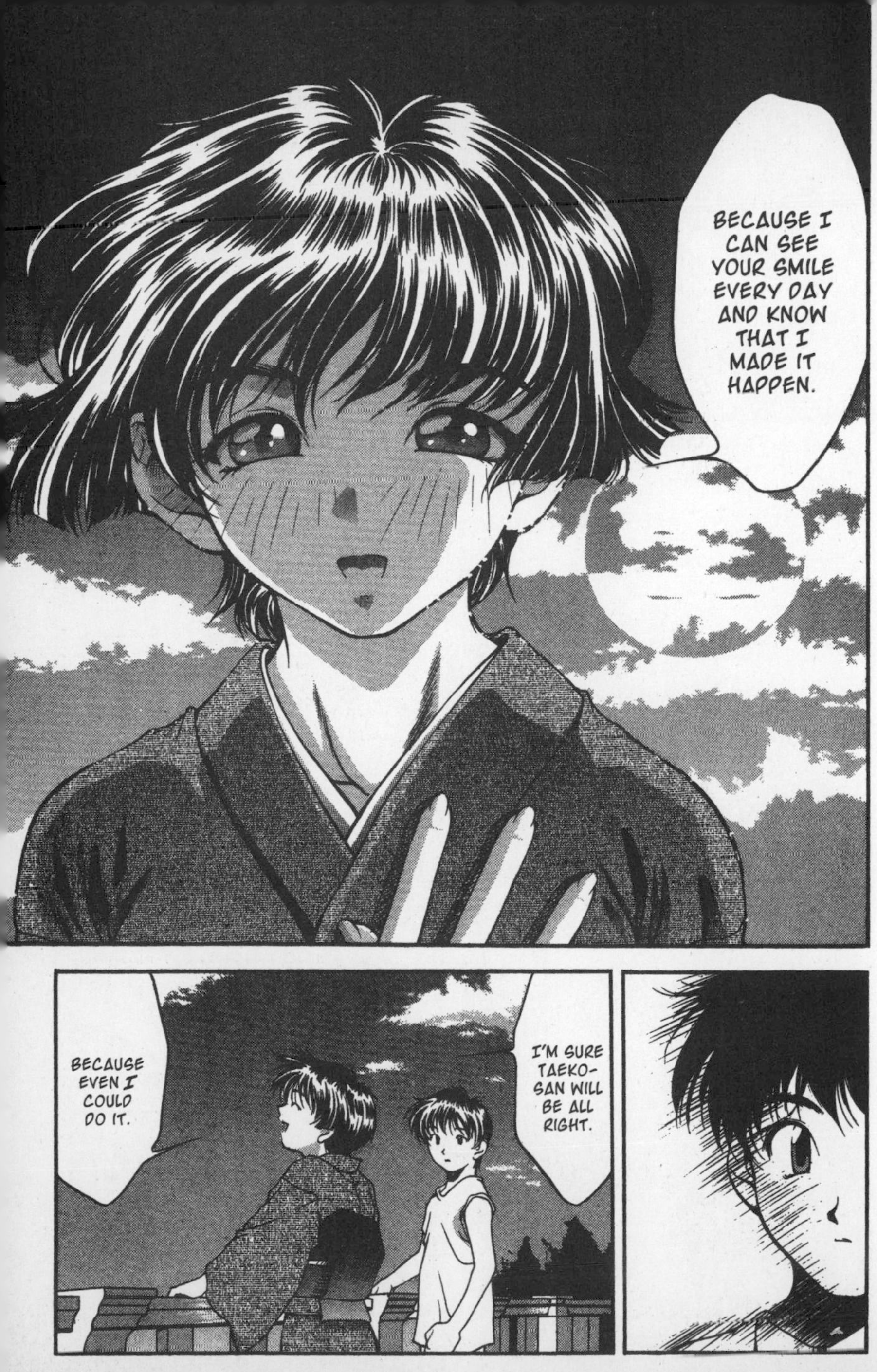
BECAUSE I CAN SEE YOUR SMILE EVERY DAY AND KNOW THAT I MADE IT HAPPEN.
I'M SURE TAEKO-SAN WILL BE ALL RIGHT.
BECAUSE EVEN I COULD DO IT.

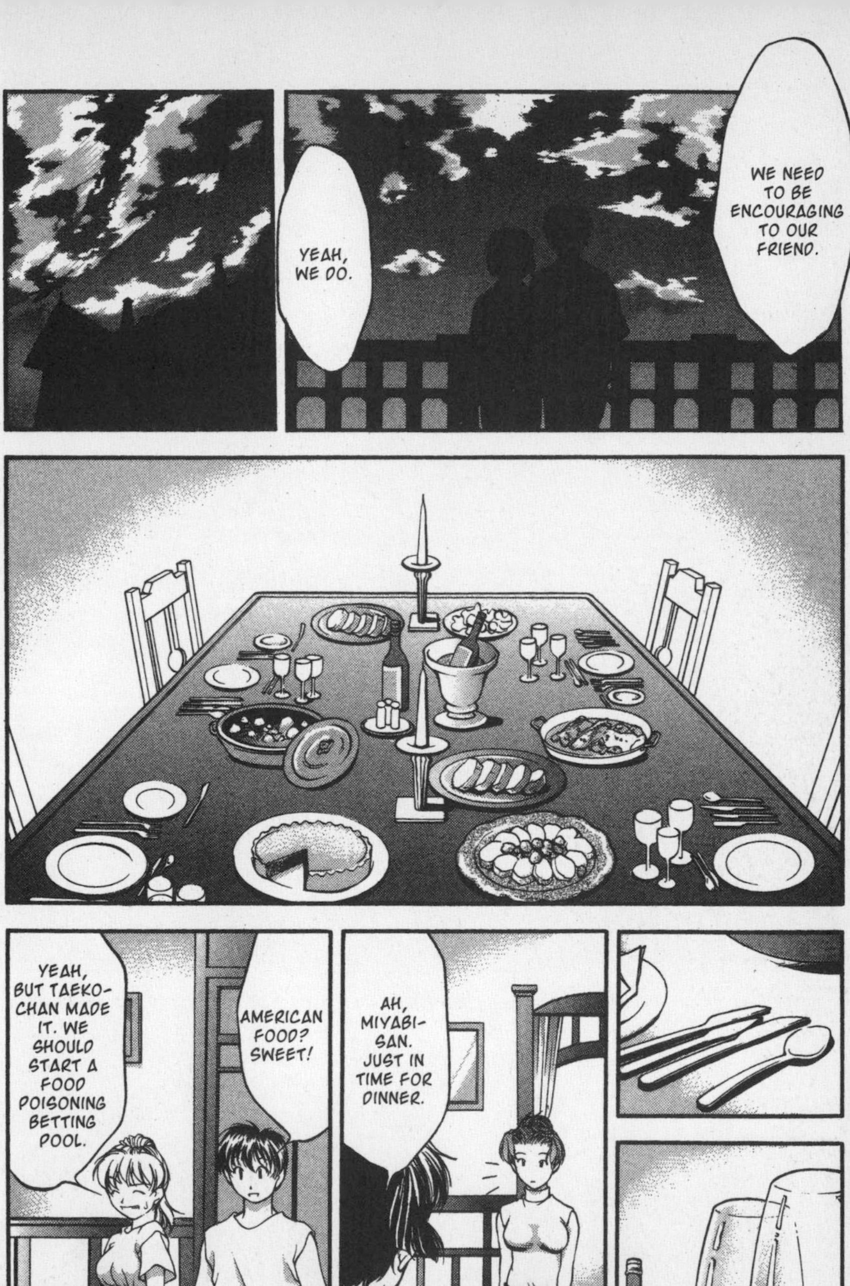
WE NEED TO BE ENCOURAGING TO OUR FRIEND.
YEAH, WE DO.
AH, MIYABI-SAN. JUST IN TIME FOR DINNER.
AMERICAN FOOD? SWEET!
YEAH, BUT TAEKO-CHAN MADE IT. WE SHOULD START A FOOD POISONING BETTING POOL.

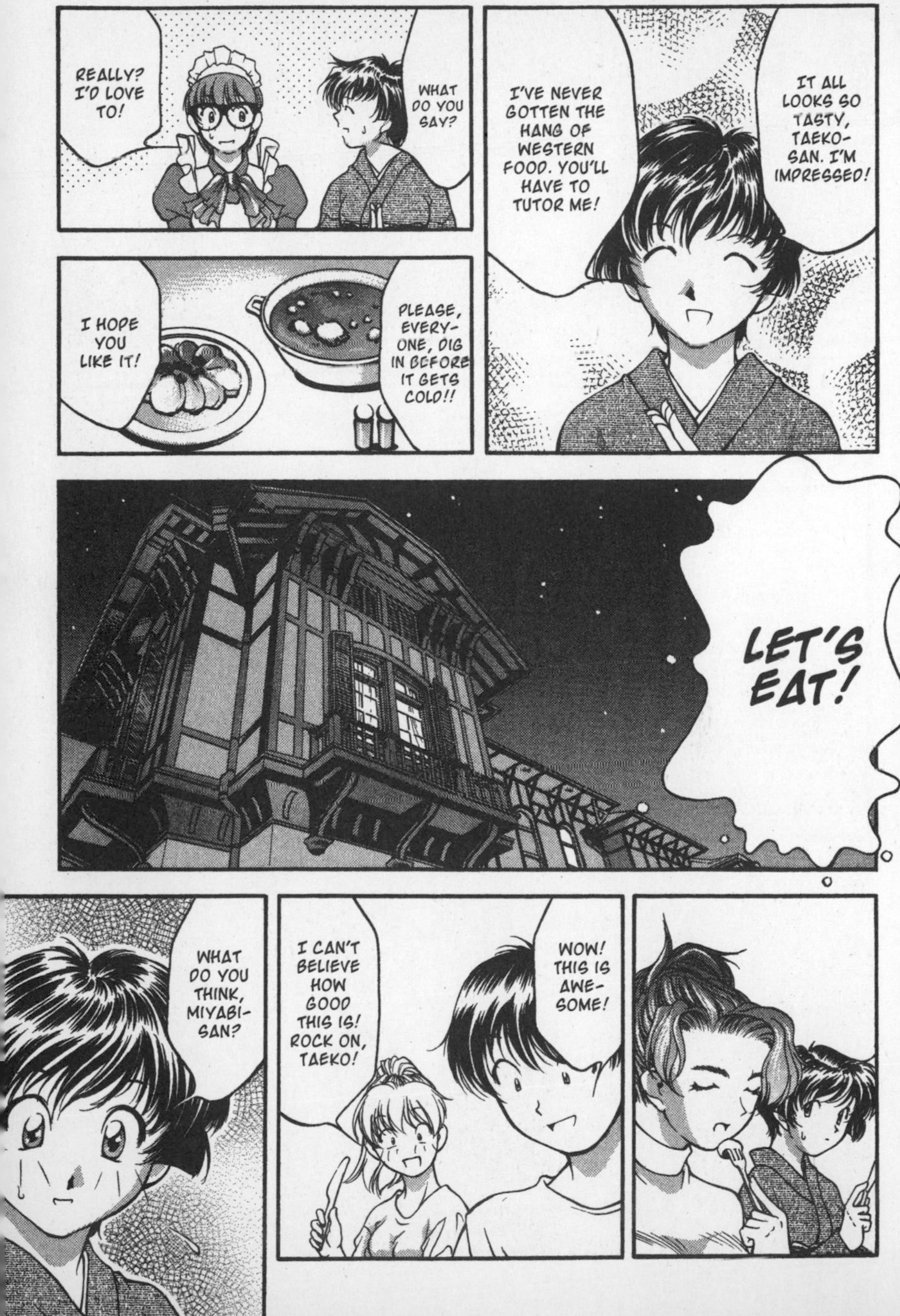
IT ALL LOOKS SO TASTY, TAEKO-SAN. I'M IMPRESSED!
I'VE NEVER GOTTEN THE HANG OF WESTERN FOOD. YOU'LL HAVE TO TUTOR ME!
WHAT DO YOU SAY?
REALLY? I'D LOVE TO!
PLEASE, EVERYONE, DIG IN BEFORE IT GETS COLD!!
I HOPE YOU LIKE IT!
LET'S EAT!
WOW! THIS IS AWESOME!
I CAN'T BELIEVE HOW GOOD THIS IS! ROCK ON, TAEKO!
WHAT DO YOU THINK, MIYABI-SAN?

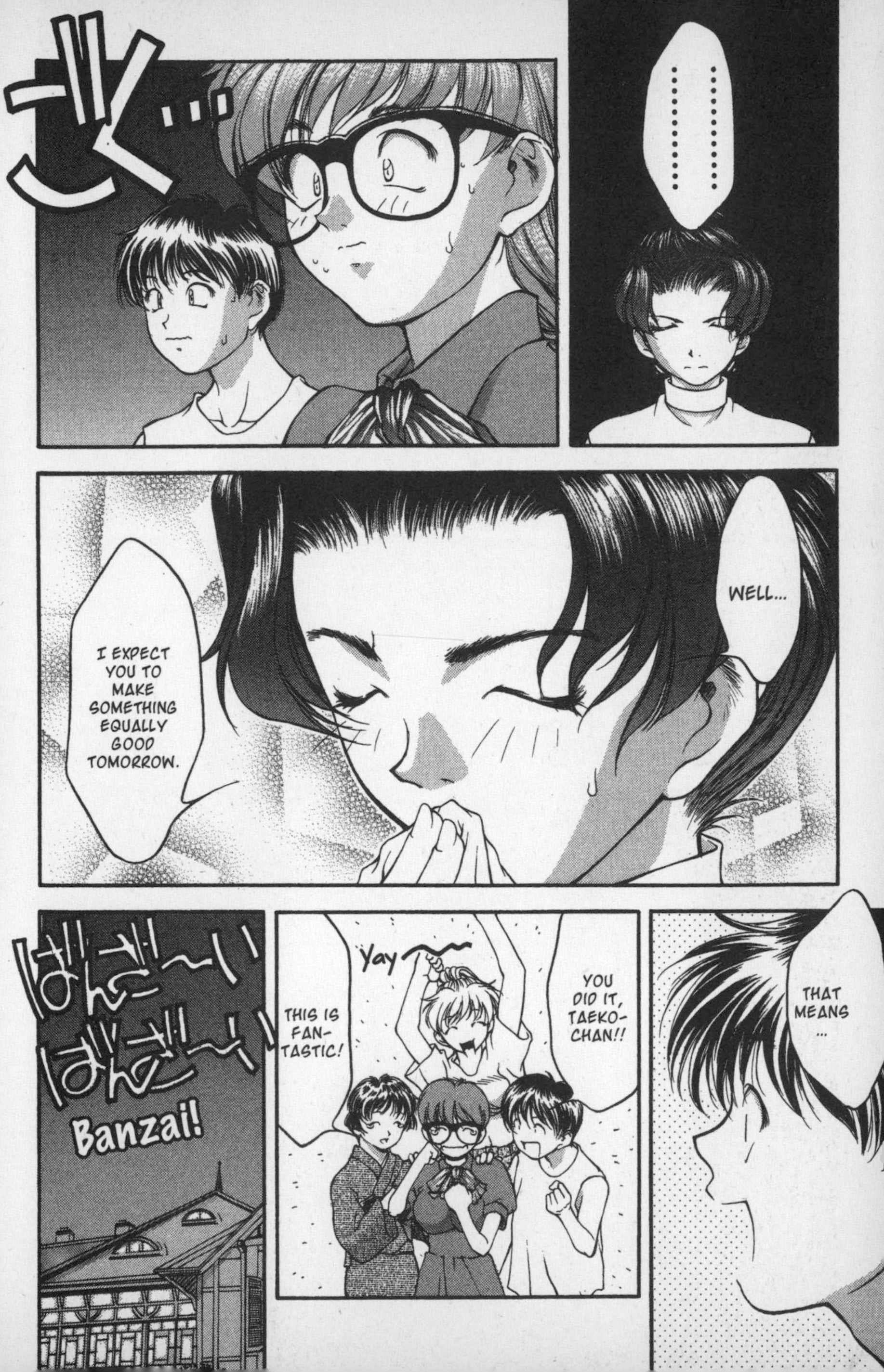

……
ごく…
WELL...
I EXPECT YOU TO MAKE SOMETHING EQUALLY GOOD TOMORROW.
THAT MEANS ...
YOU DID IT, TAEKO-CHAN!!
Yay~
THIS IS FAN-TASTIC!
ばんざ〜い
ばんざ〜い
Banzai!

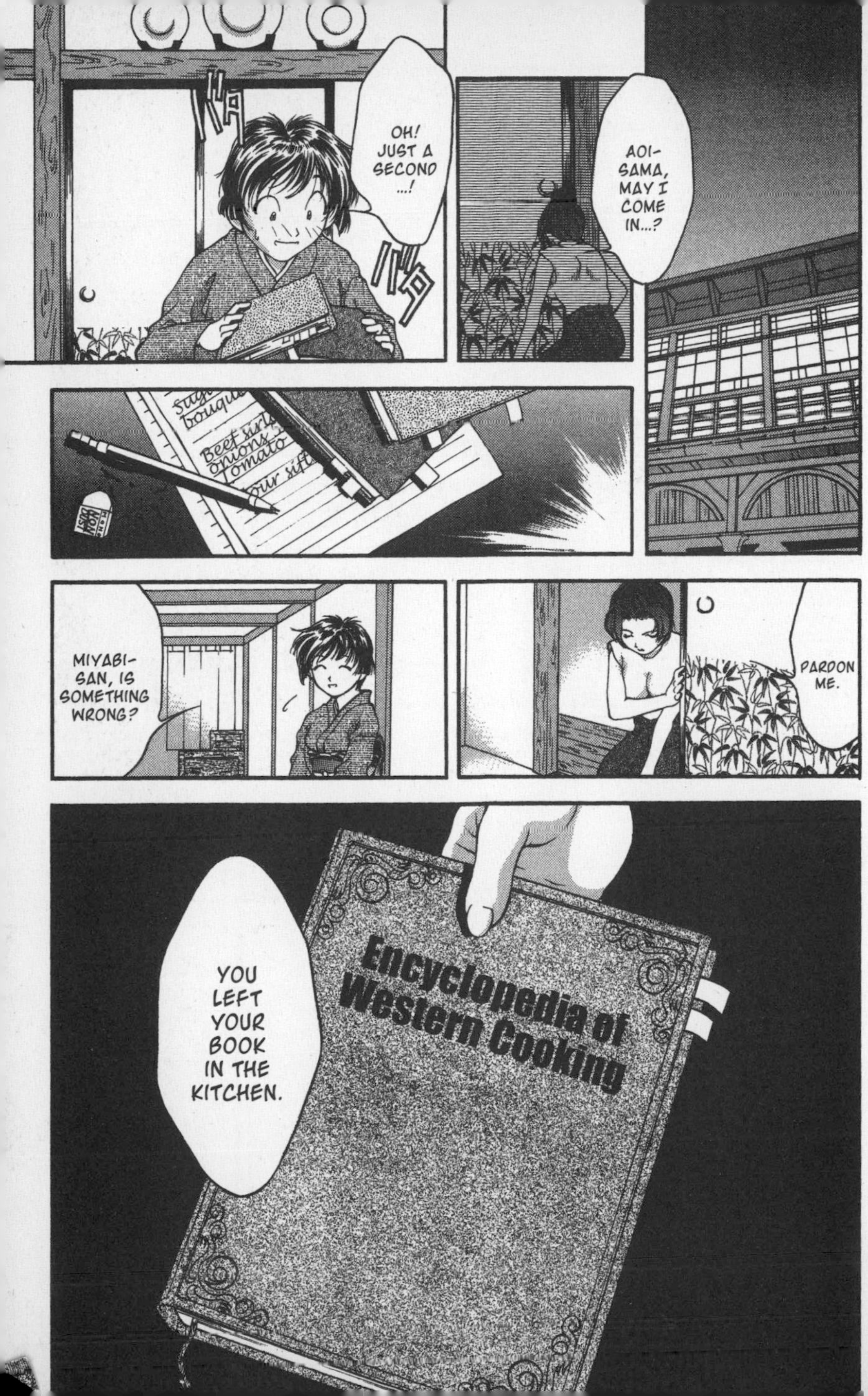
AOI-SAMA, MAY I COME IN...?
OH! JUST A SECOND ...!
PARDON ME.
MIYABI-SAN, IS SOMETHING WRONG?
YOU LEFT YOUR BOOK IN THE KITCHEN.
Encyclopedia of Western Cooking

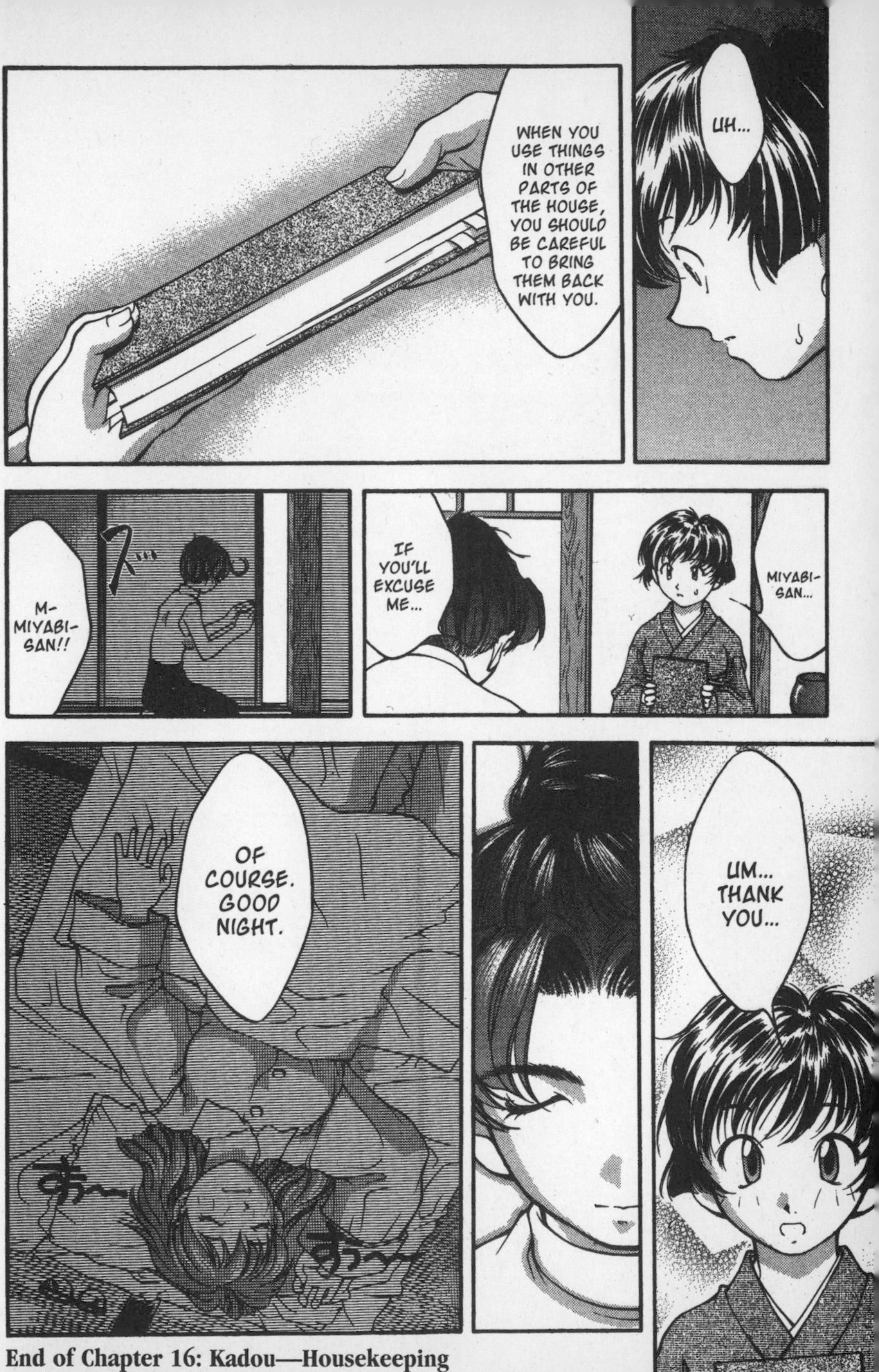
UH...
WHEN YOU USE THINGS IN OTHER PARTS OF THE HOUSE, YOU SHOULD BE CAREFUL TO BRING THEM BACK WITH YOU.
MIYABI-SAN...
IF YOU'LL EXCUSE ME...
M-MIYABI-SAN!!
UM... THANK YOU...
OF COURSE. GOOD NIGHT.

End of Chapter 16: Kadou—Housekeeping

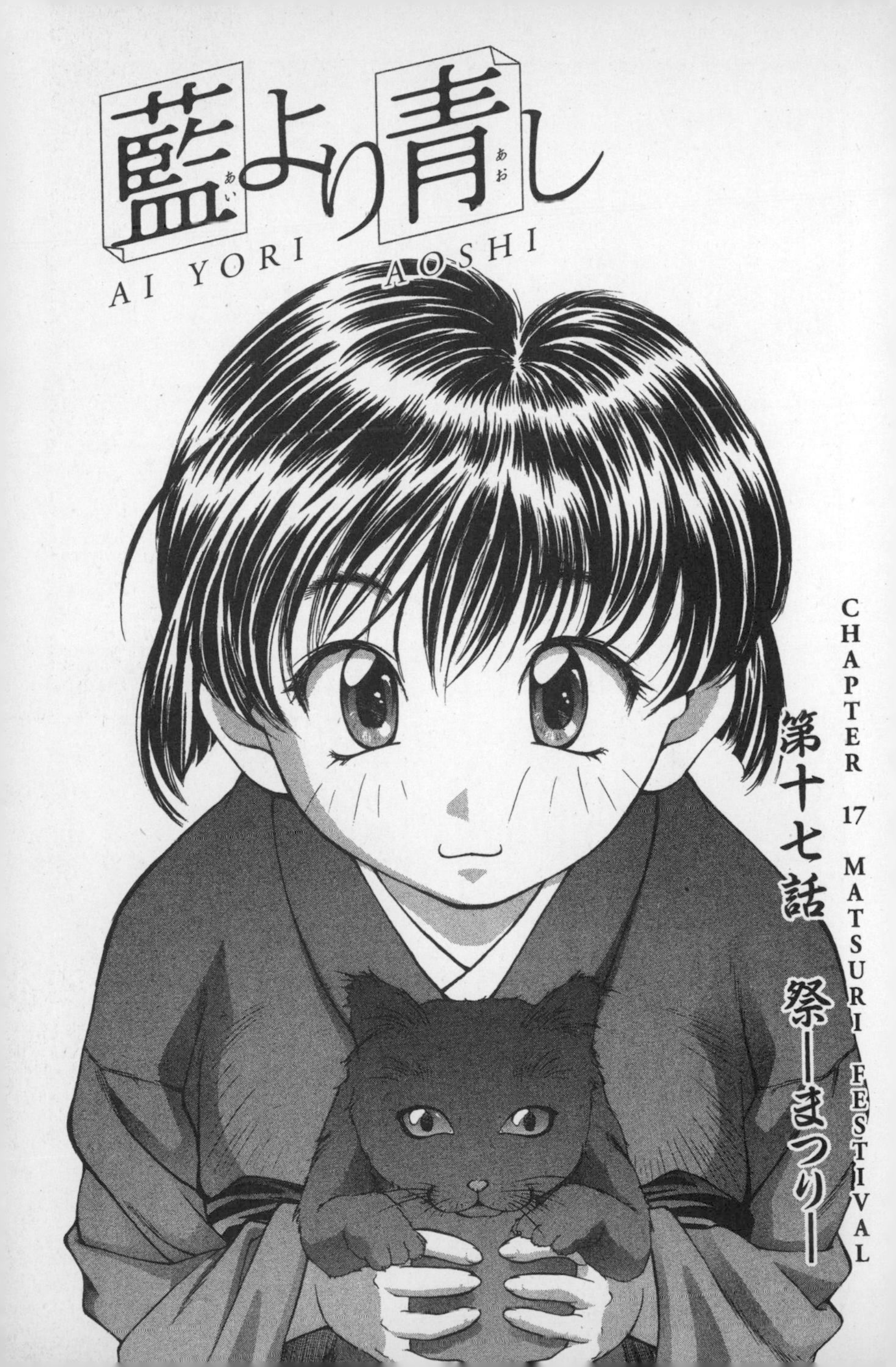
藍(あい)より青(あお)し
AI YORI AOSHI
第十七話 祭ーまつりー
CHAPTER 17 MATSURI FESTIVAL

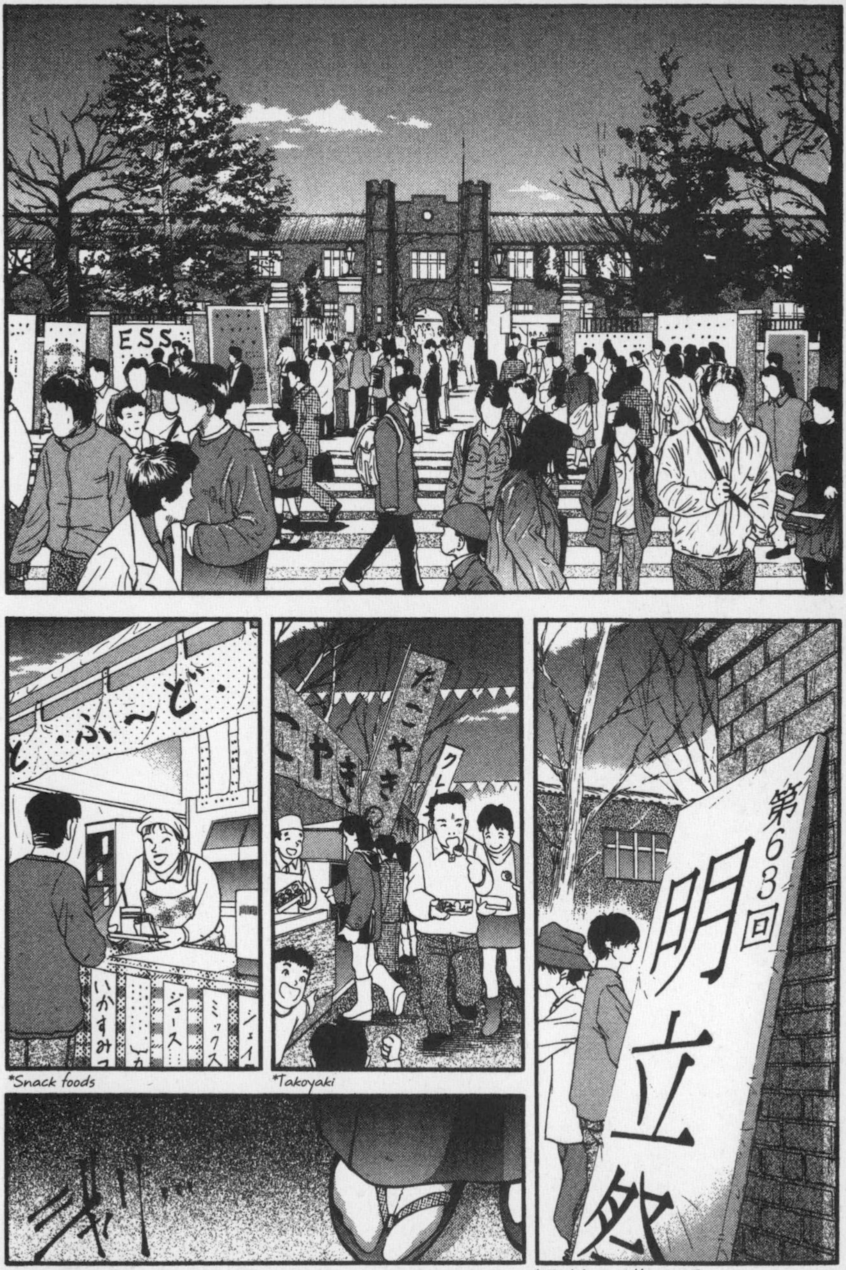
ESS
第63回
明立祭
たこやき
こやき
ふ〜ど
ジュース
ミックス
いかすみ

*63rd Annual Meiritsu Festival

*Takoyaki

*Snack foods

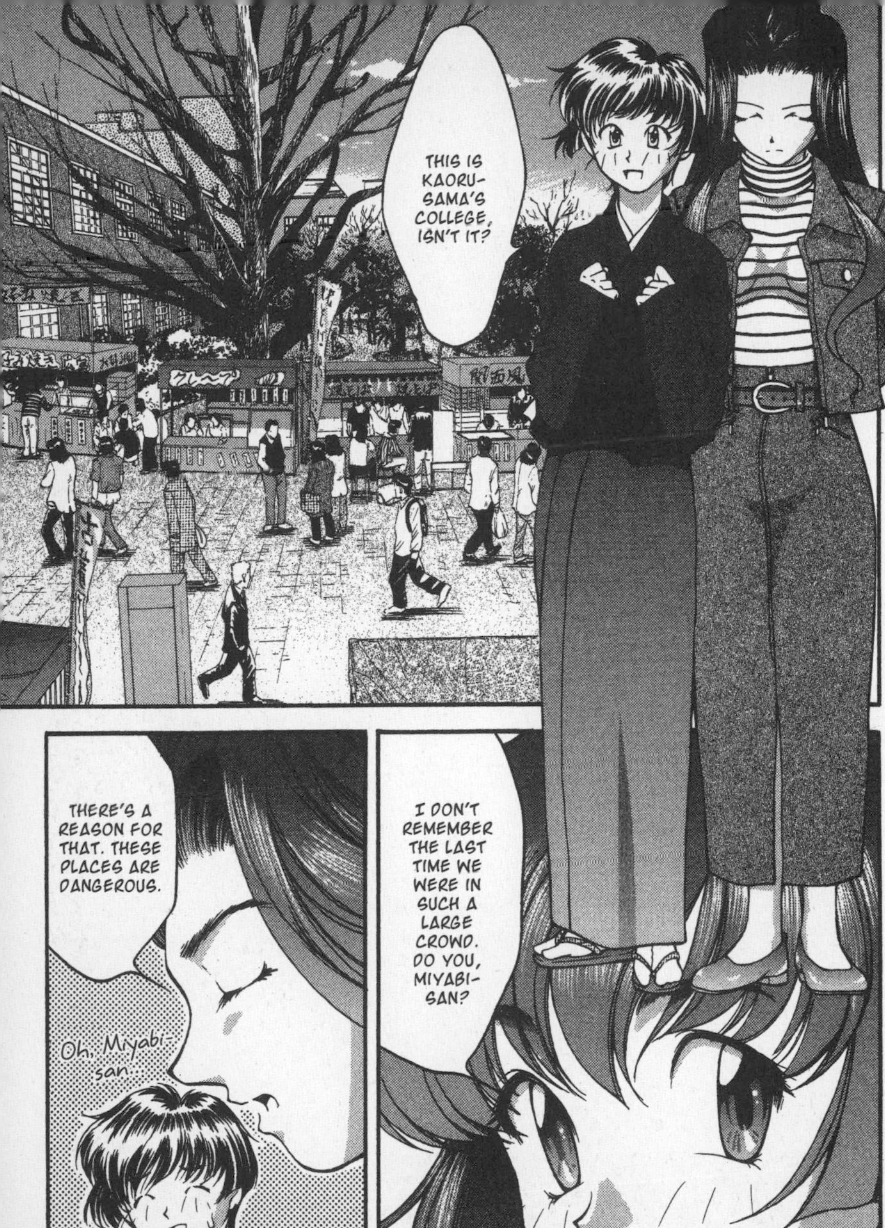
THIS IS KAORU-SAMA'S COLLEGE, ISN'T IT?
I DON'T REMEMBER THE LAST TIME WE WERE IN SUCH A LARGE CROWD. DO YOU, MIYABI-SAN?
THERE'S A REASON FOR THAT. THESE PLACES ARE DANGEROUS.
Oh, Miyabi-san...

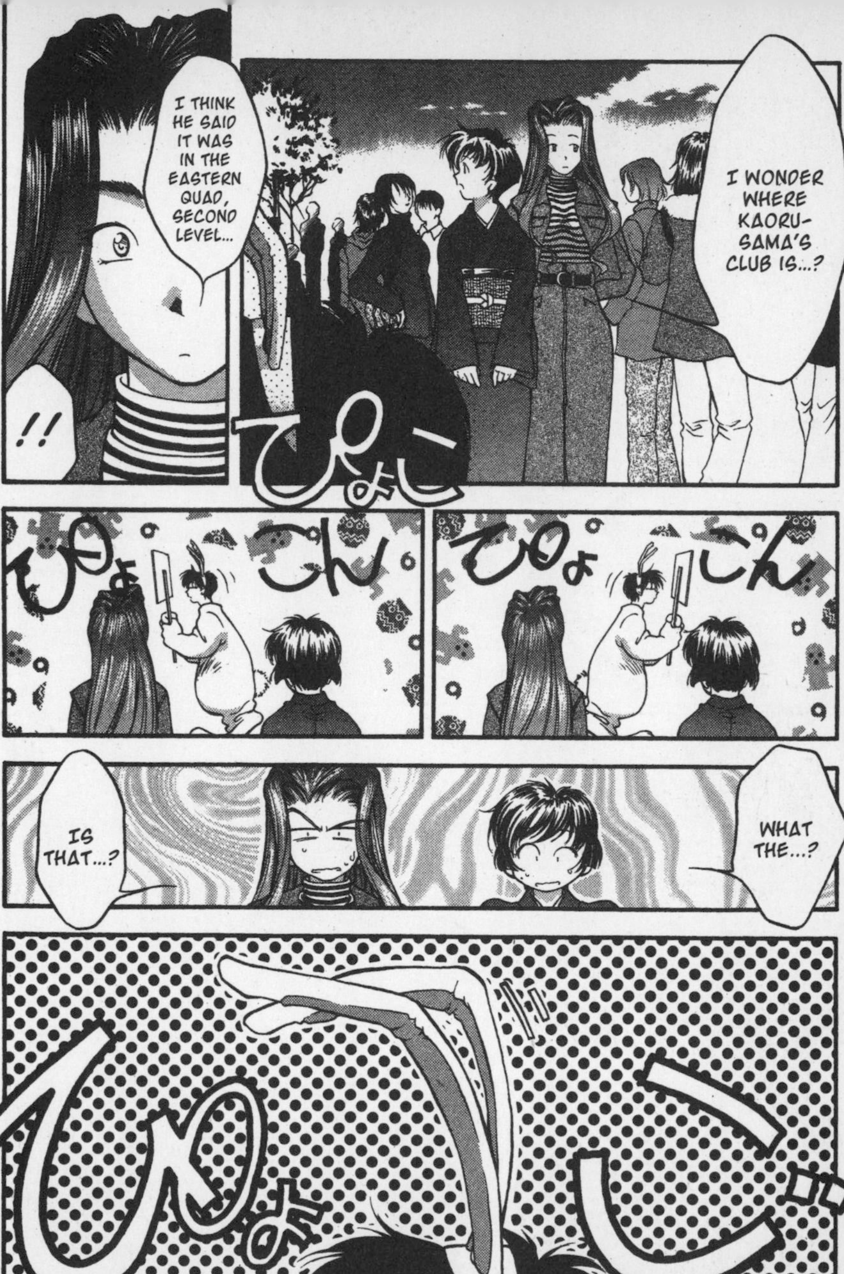
I WONDER WHERE KAORU-SAMA'S CLUB IS...?
I THINK HE SAID IT WAS IN THE EASTERN QUAD, SECOND LEVEL...
!!
ぴょこん
ぴょこん
WHAT THE...?
IS THAT...?

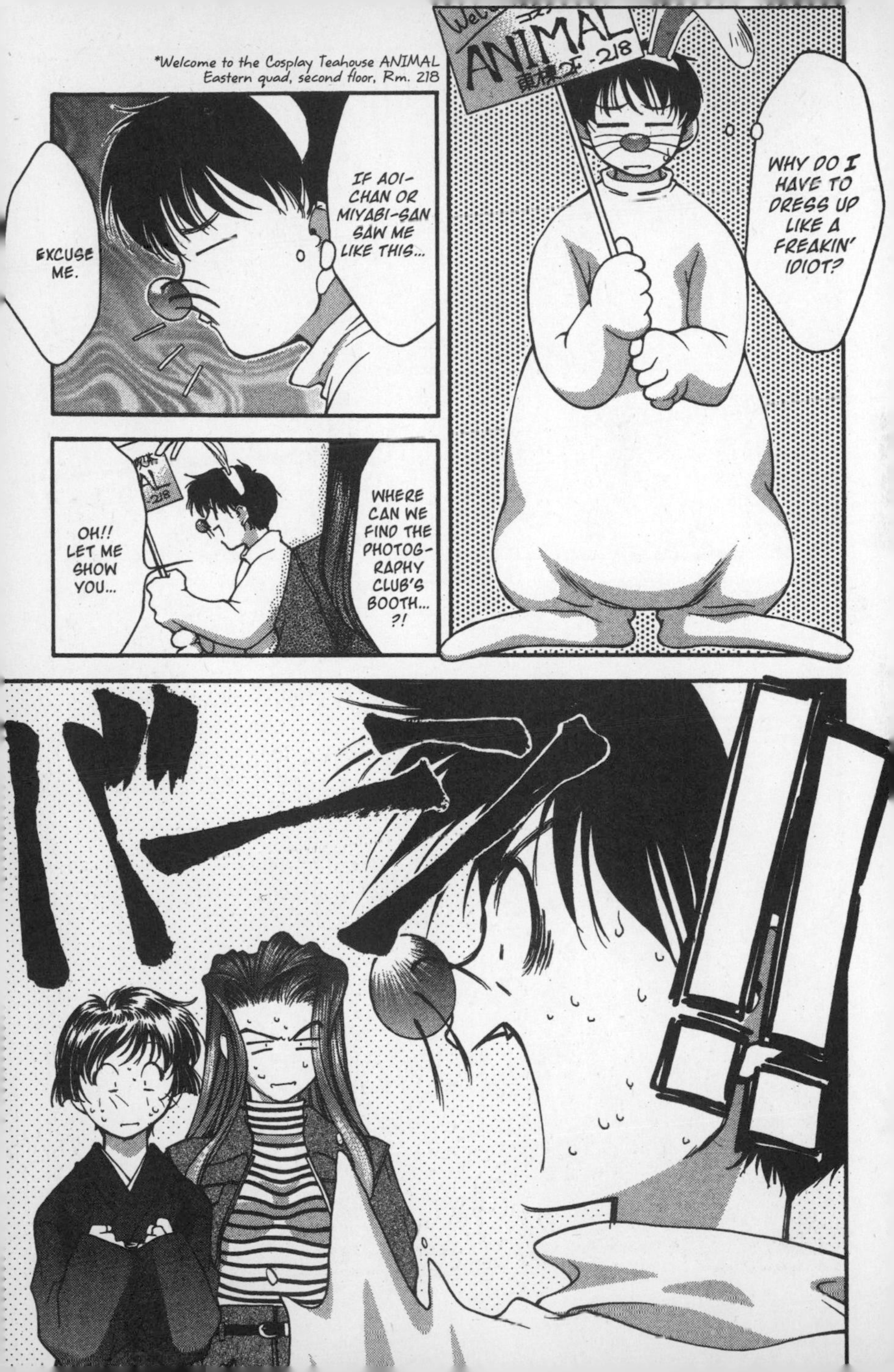
*Welcome to the Cosplay Teahouse ANIMAL
Eastern quad, second floor, Rm. 218
ANIMAL
WHY DO I HAVE TO DRESS UP LIKE A FREAKIN' IDIOT?
IF AOI-CHAN OR MIYABI-SAN SAW ME LIKE THIS...
EXCUSE ME.
WHERE CAN WE FIND THE PHOTOG-RAPHY CLUB'S BOOTH...?!
OH!! LET ME SHOW YOU...

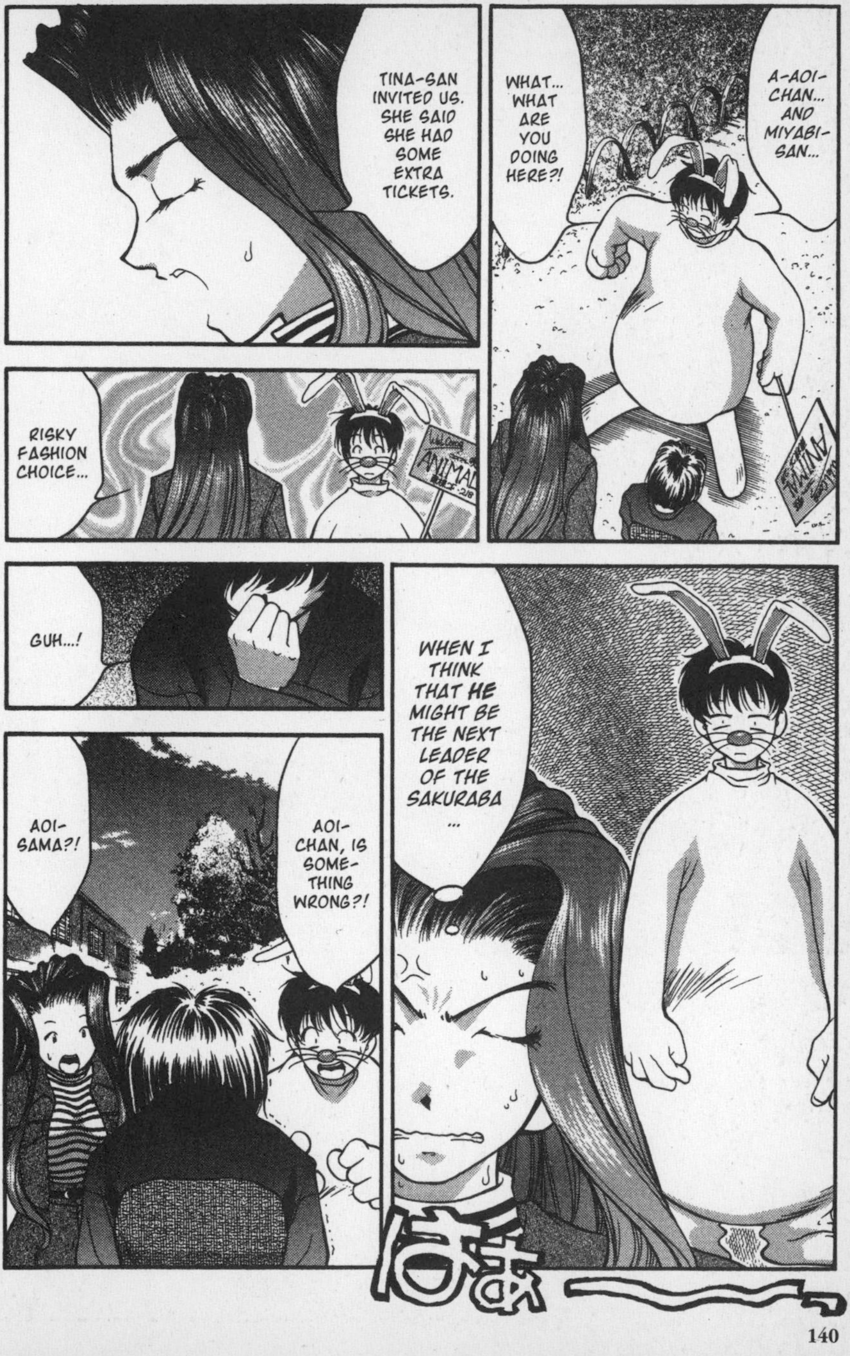
A-AOI-CHAN... AND MIYABI-SAN...
WHAT... WHAT ARE YOU DOING HERE?!
TINA-SAN INVITED US. SHE SAID SHE HAD SOME EXTRA TICKETS.
RISKY FASHION CHOICE...
WHEN I THINK THAT HE MIGHT BE THE NEXT LEADER OF THE SAKURABA ...
GUH...!
AOI-CHAN, IS SOME-THING WRONG?!
AOI-SAMA?!
はぁーーっ

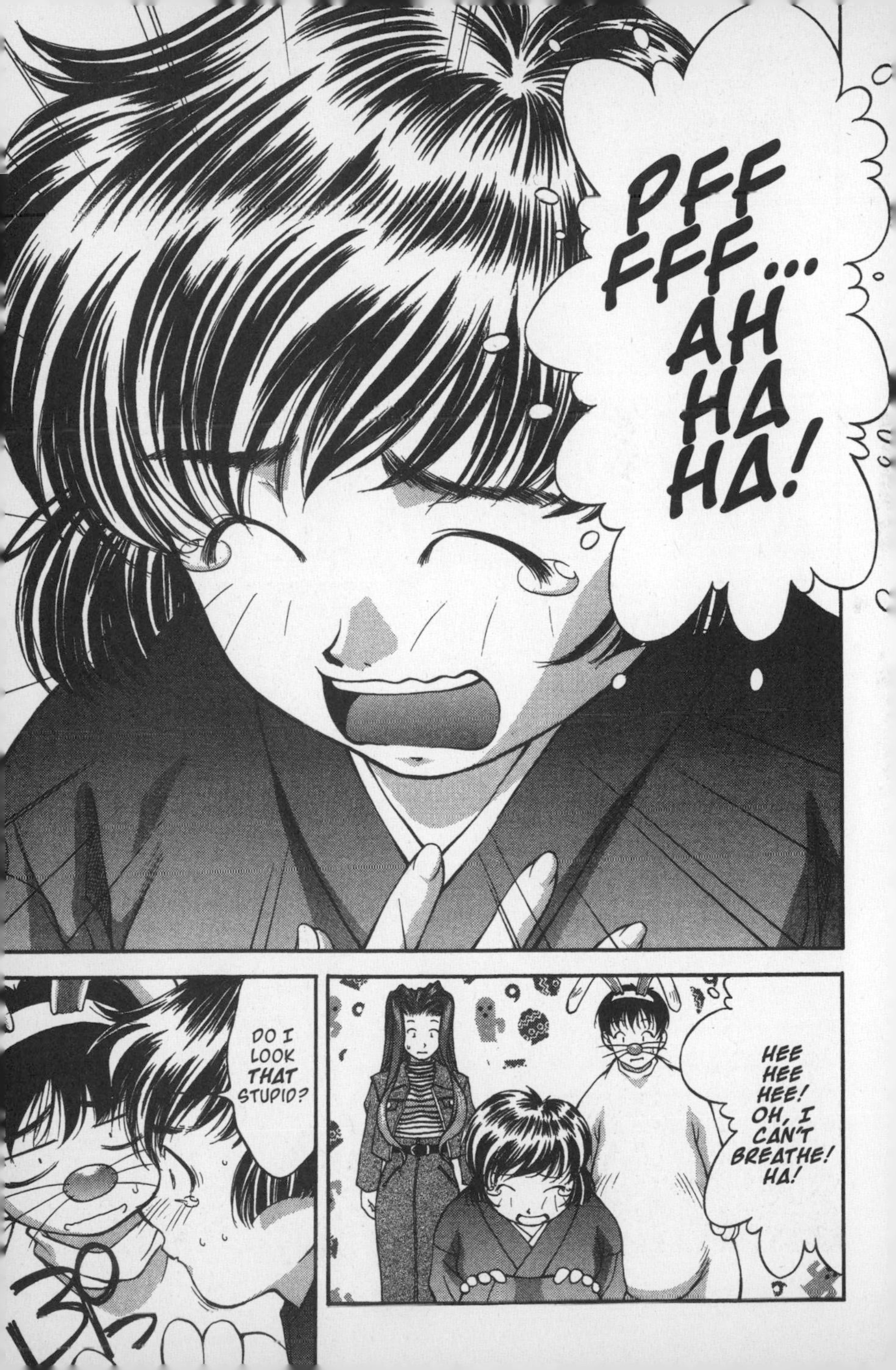
PFF FFF... AH HA HA HA!
HEE HEE HEE! OH, I CAN'T BREATHE! HA!
DO I LOOK THAT STUPID?

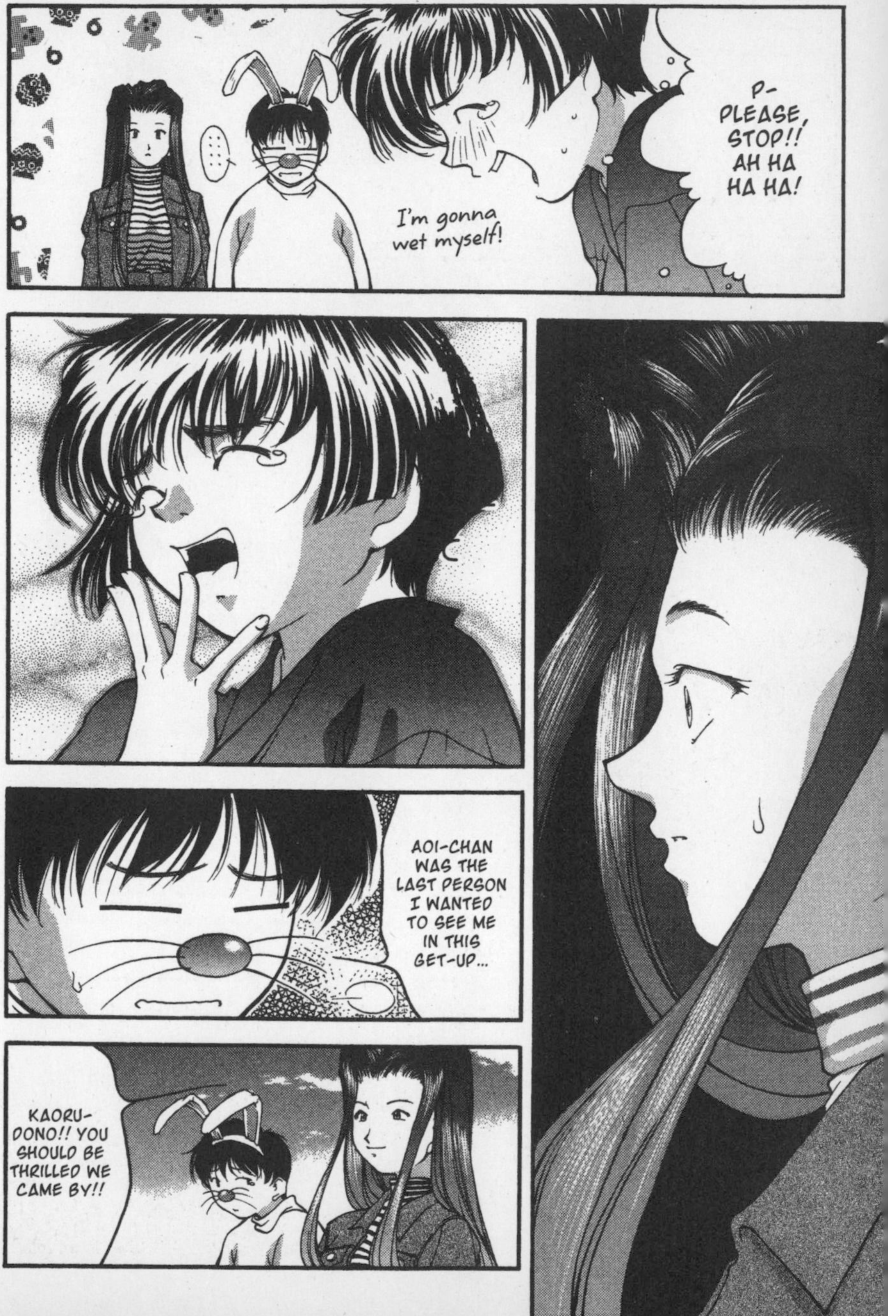
P-PLEASE, STOP!! AH HA HA HA!
I'm gonna wet myself!
AOI-CHAN WAS THE LAST PERSON I WANTED TO SEE ME IN THIS GET-UP...
KAORU-DONO!! YOU SHOULD BE THRILLED WE CAME BY!!

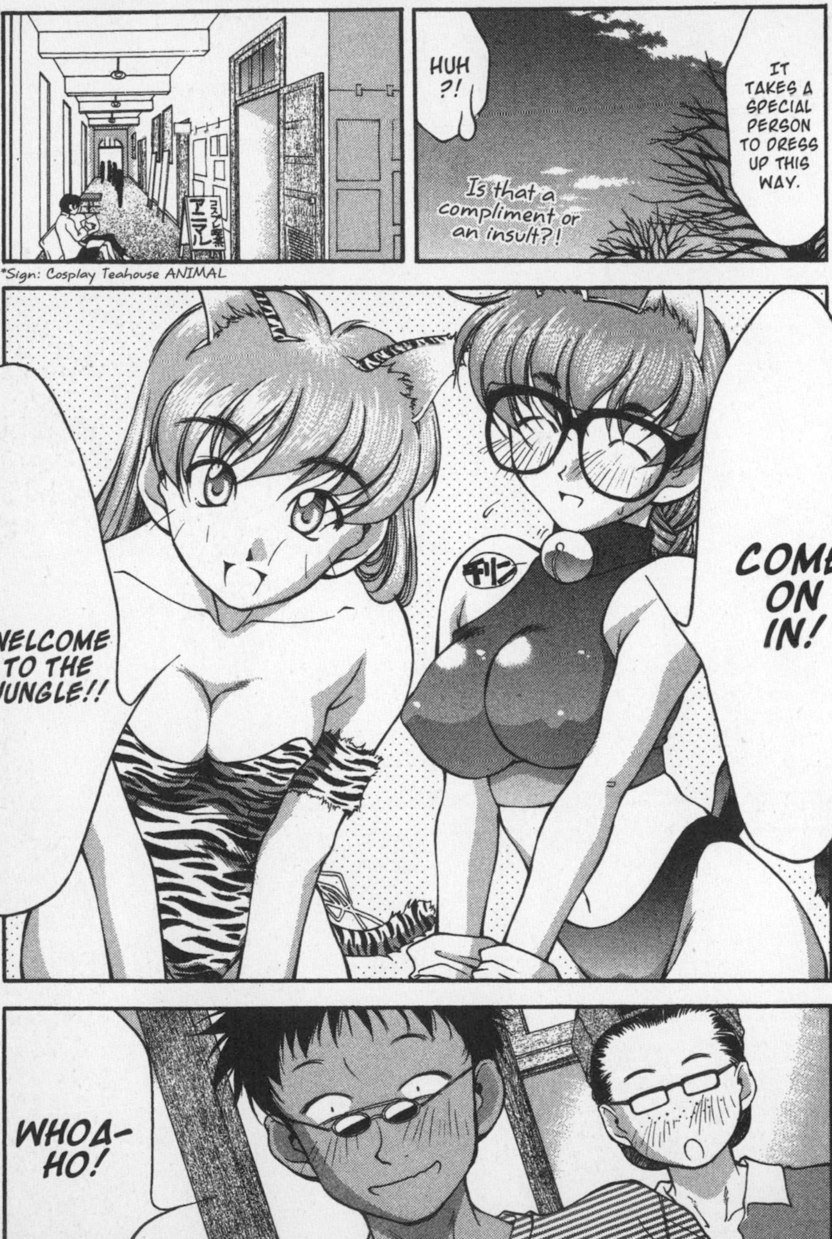
IT TAKES A SPECIAL PERSON TO DRESS UP THIS WAY.
HUH ?!
Is that a compliment or an insult?!
COME ON IN!
WELCOME TO THE JUNGLE!!
WHOA-HO!
*Sign: Cosplay Teahouse ANIMAL

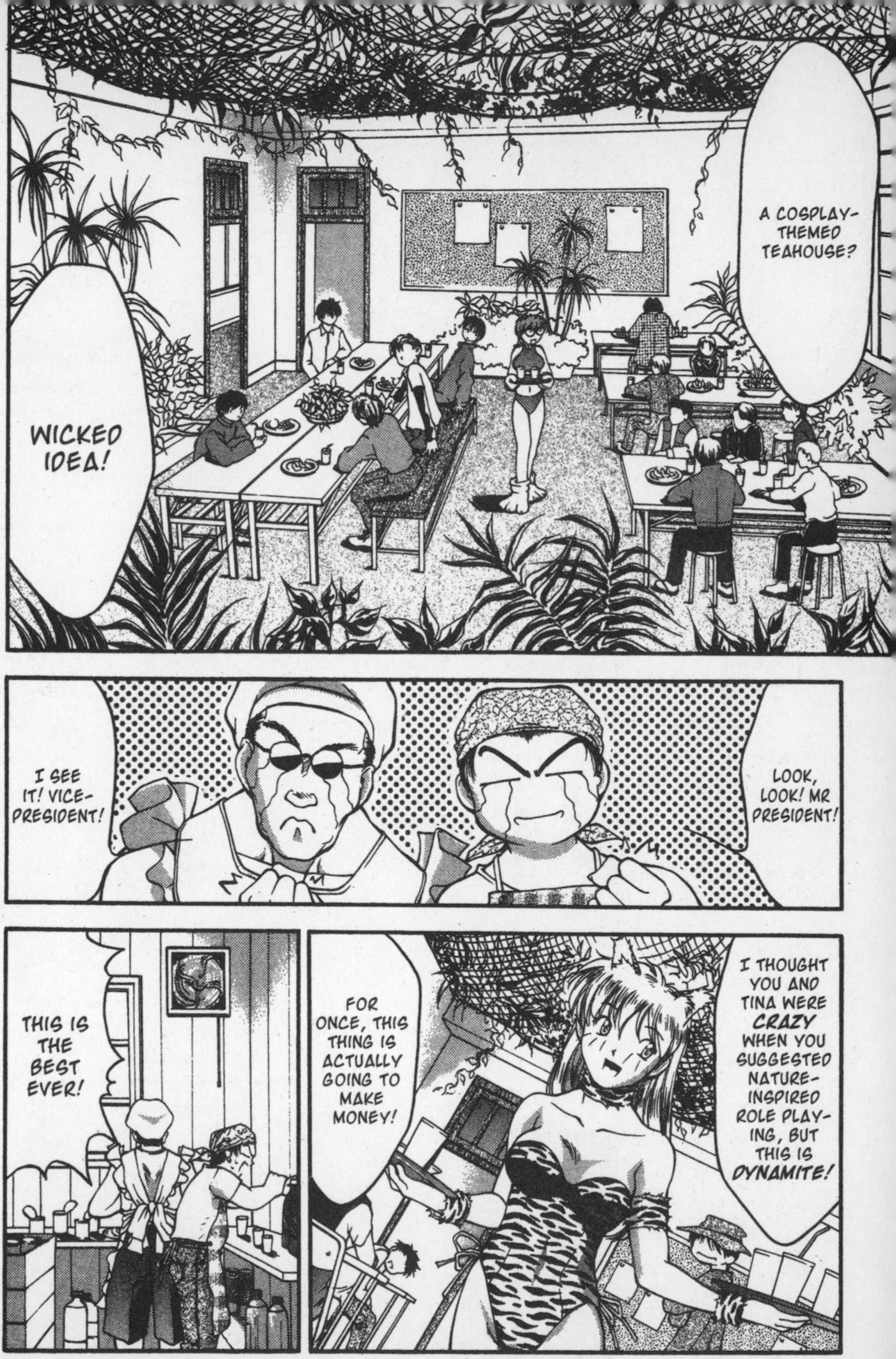
A COSPLAY-THEMED TEAHOUSE?
WICKED IDEA!
LOOK, LOOK! MR PRESIDENT!
I SEE IT! VICE-PRESIDENT!
I THOUGHT YOU AND TINA WERE CRAZY WHEN YOU SUGGESTED NATURE-INSPIRED ROLE PLAYING, BUT THIS IS DYNAMITE!
FOR ONCE, THIS THING IS ACTUALLY GOING TO MAKE MONEY!
THIS IS THE BEST EVER!

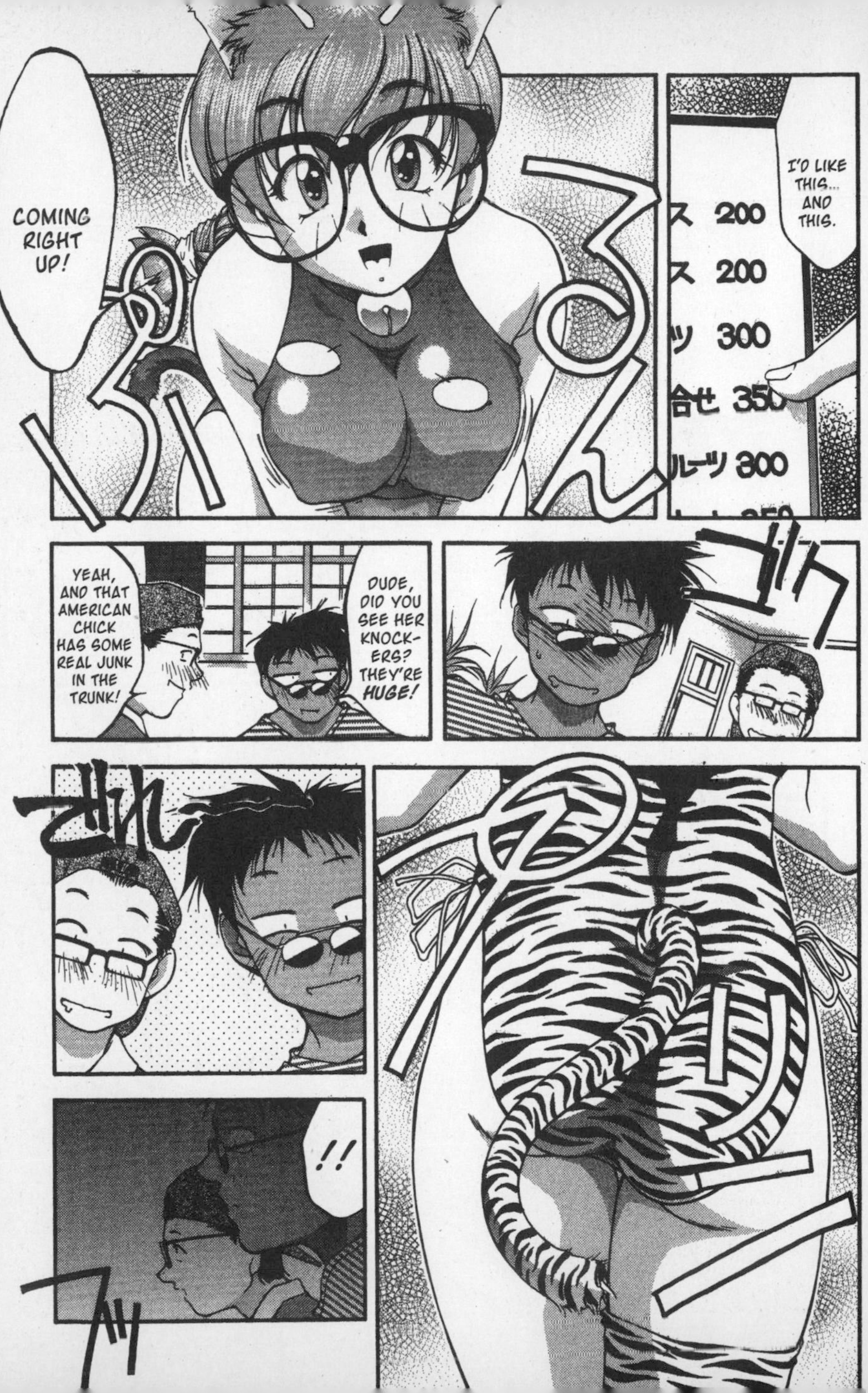
I'D LIKE THIS... AND THIS.
ス 200
ス 200
ツ 300
合せ 350
ルーツ 300
COMING RIGHT UP!
DUDE, DID YOU SEE HER KNOCKERS? THEY'RE HUGE!
YEAH, AND THAT AMERICAN CHICK HAS SOME REAL JUNK IN THE TRUNK!
!!

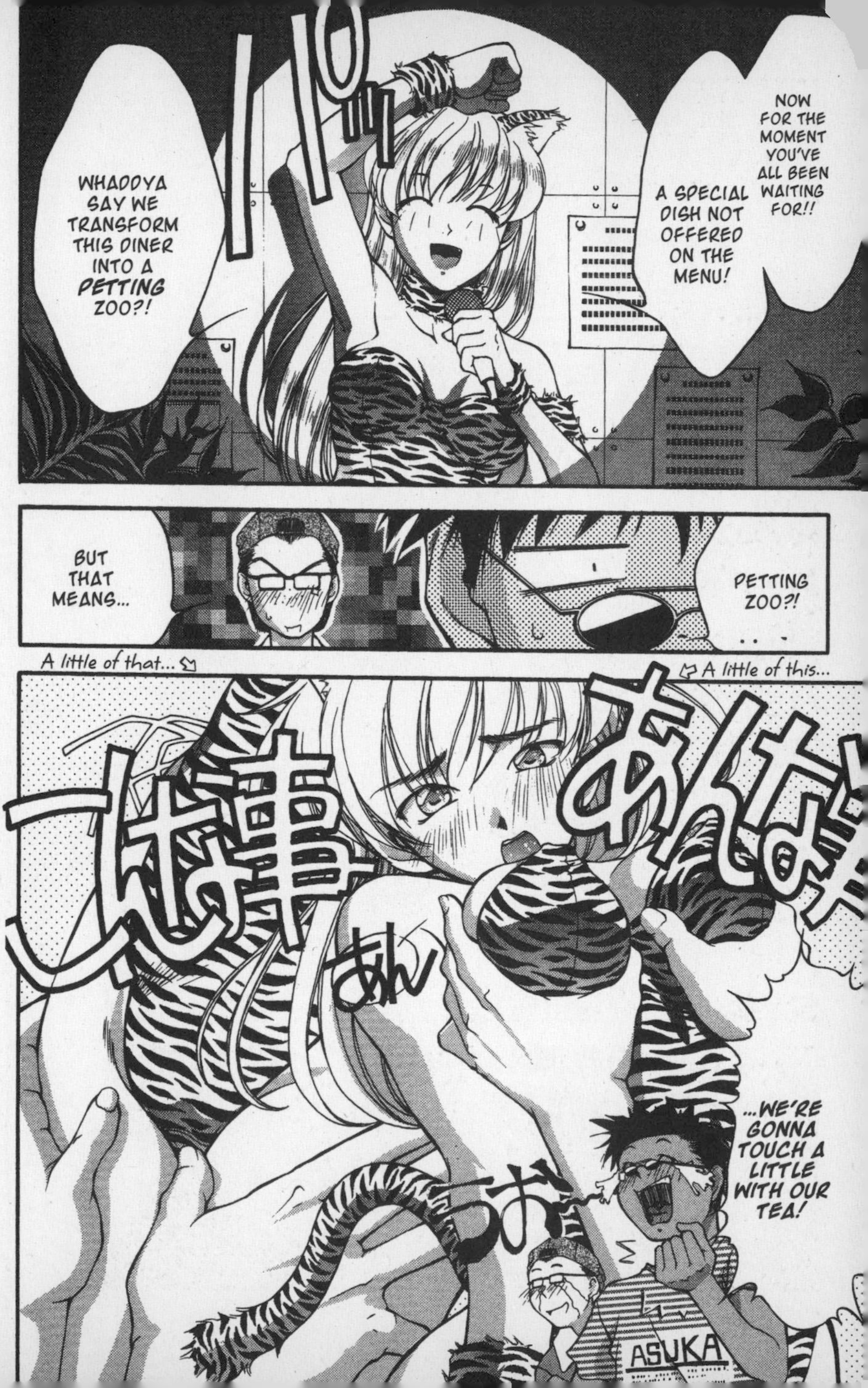
NOW FOR THE MOMENT YOU'VE ALL BEEN WAITING FOR!!
A SPECIAL DISH NOT OFFERED ON THE MENU!
WHADDOYA SAY WE TRANSFORM THIS DINER INTO A *PETTING* ZOO?!
PETTING ZOO?!
BUT THAT MEANS...
A little of this...
A little of that...
あん
...WE'RE GONNA TOUCH A LITTLE WITH OUR TEA!
ASUKA

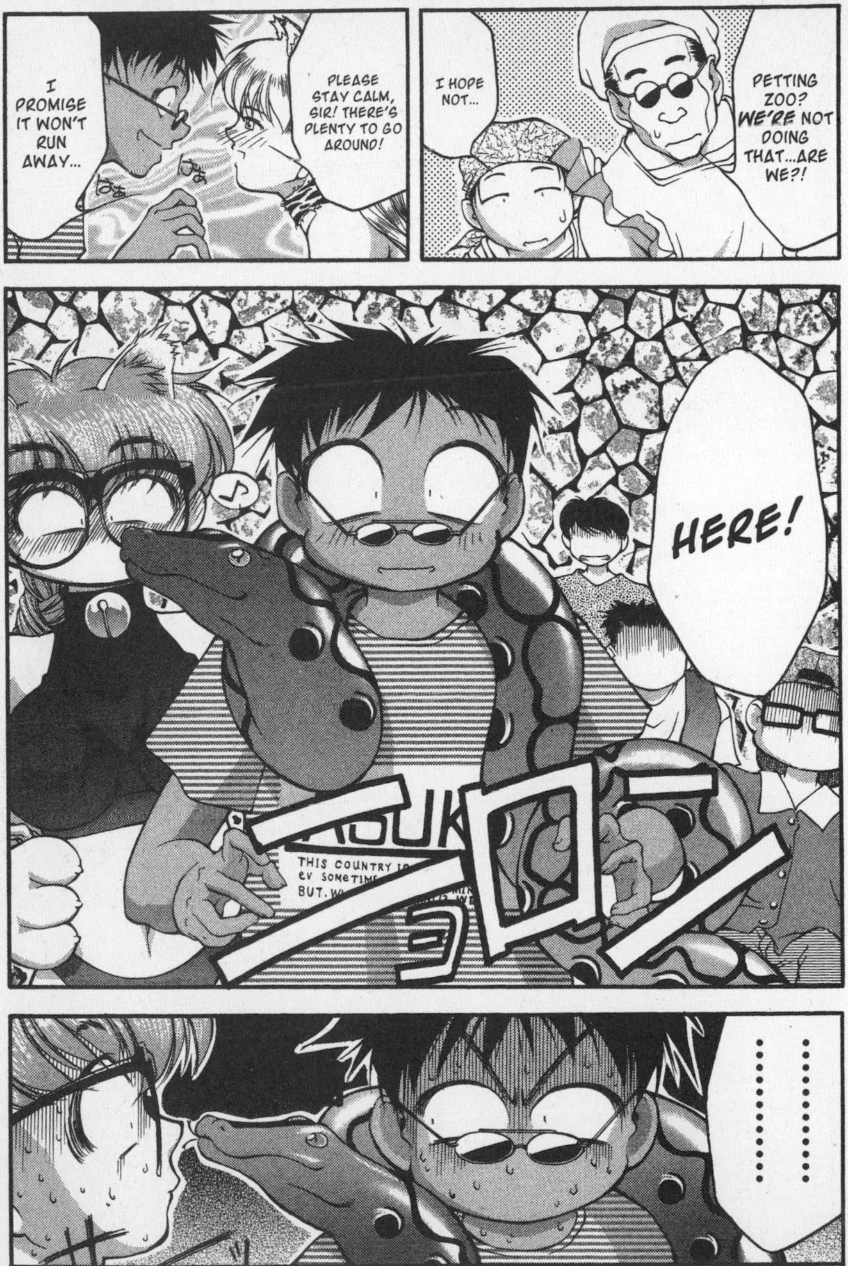
PETTING ZOO? WE'RE NOT DOING THAT...ARE WE?!
I HOPE NOT...
PLEASE STAY CALM, SIR! THERE'S PLENTY TO GO AROUND!
I PROMISE IT WON'T RUN AWAY...
HERE!
......
......

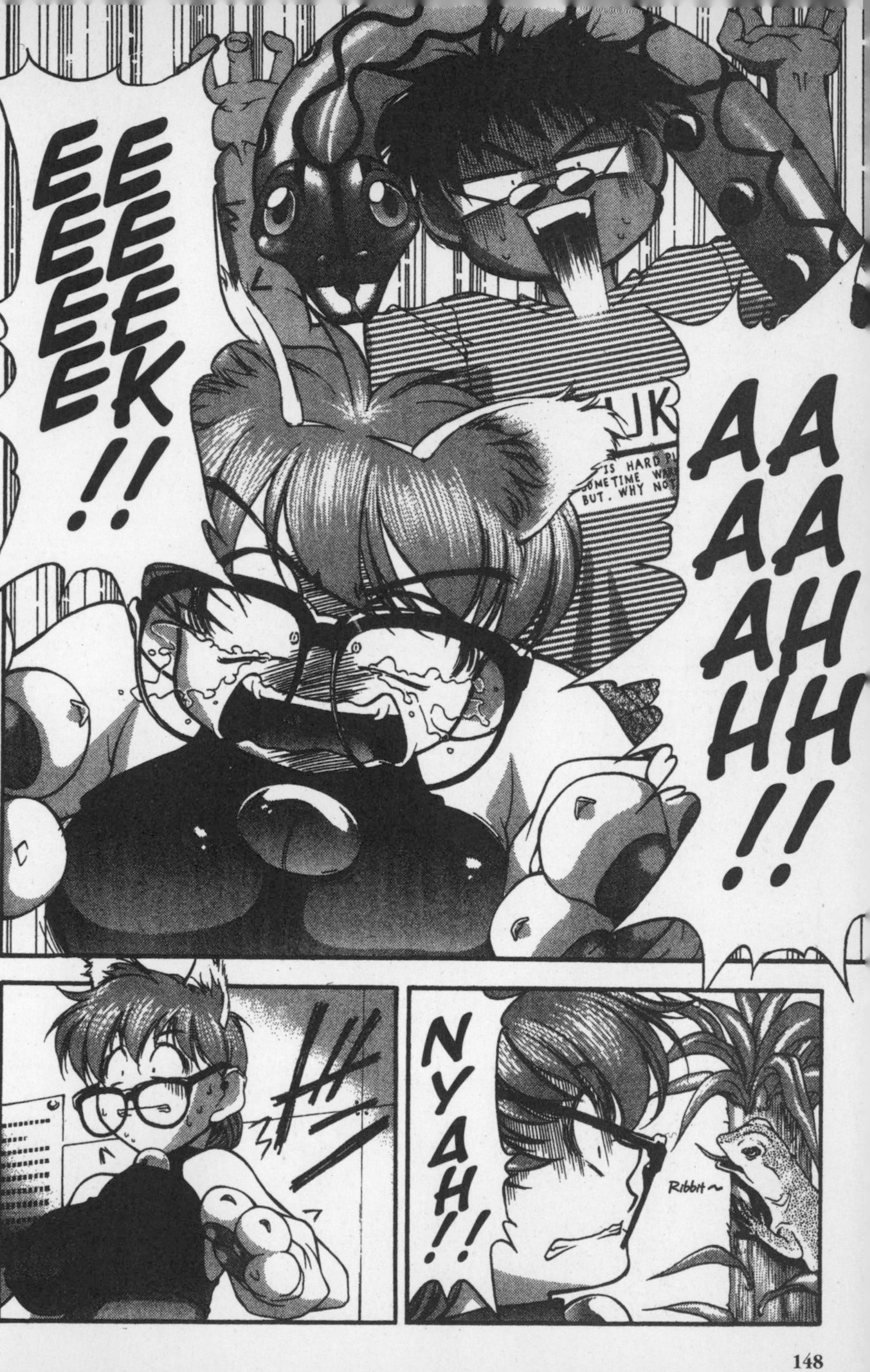
AAAAAHHH!!
EEEEEEEEEK!!
NYAH!!
Ribbit~

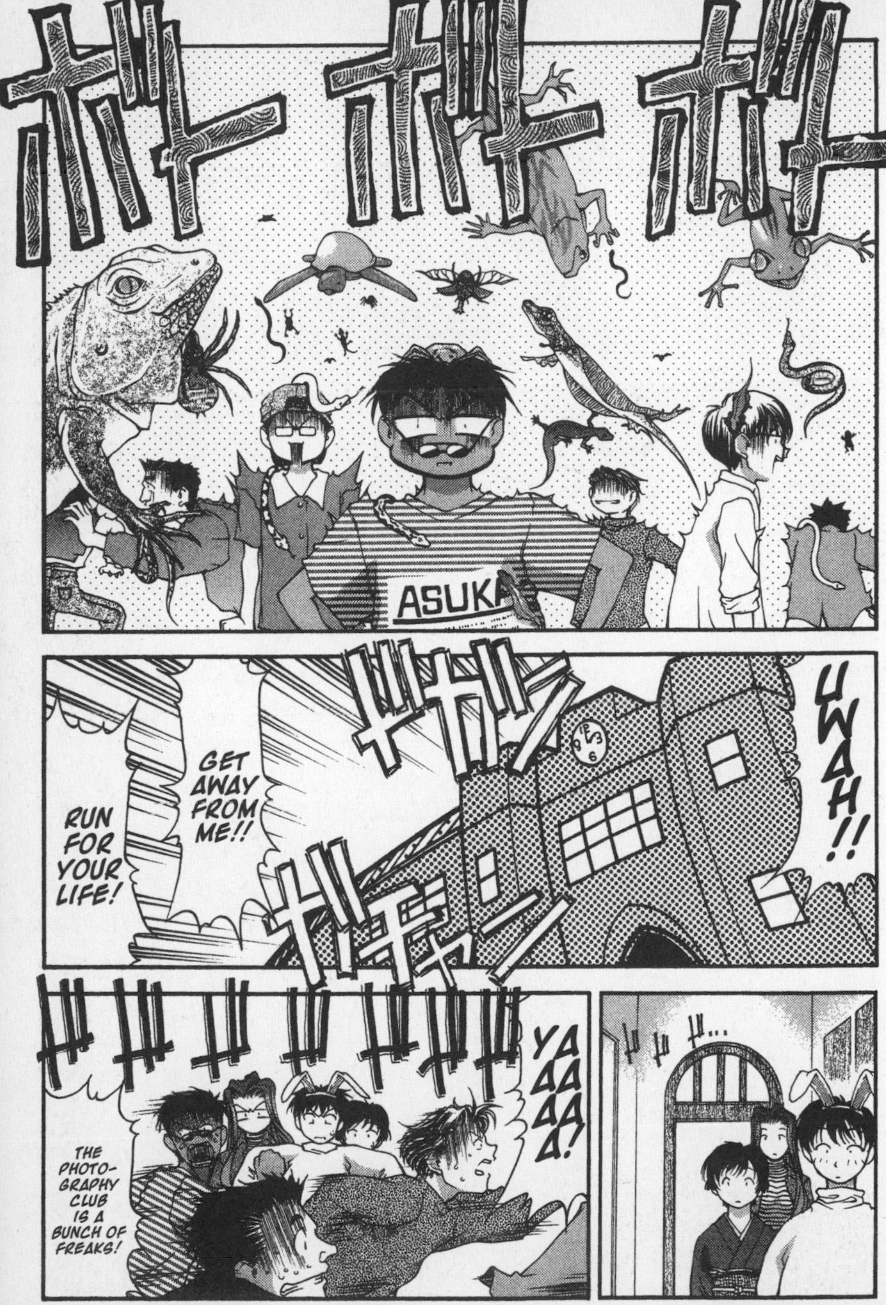
ASUKA
UWAH!!
GET AWAY FROM ME!!
RUN FOR YOUR LIFE!
YAAAAAA!
THE PHOTOGRAPHY CLUB IS A BUNCH OF FREAKS!

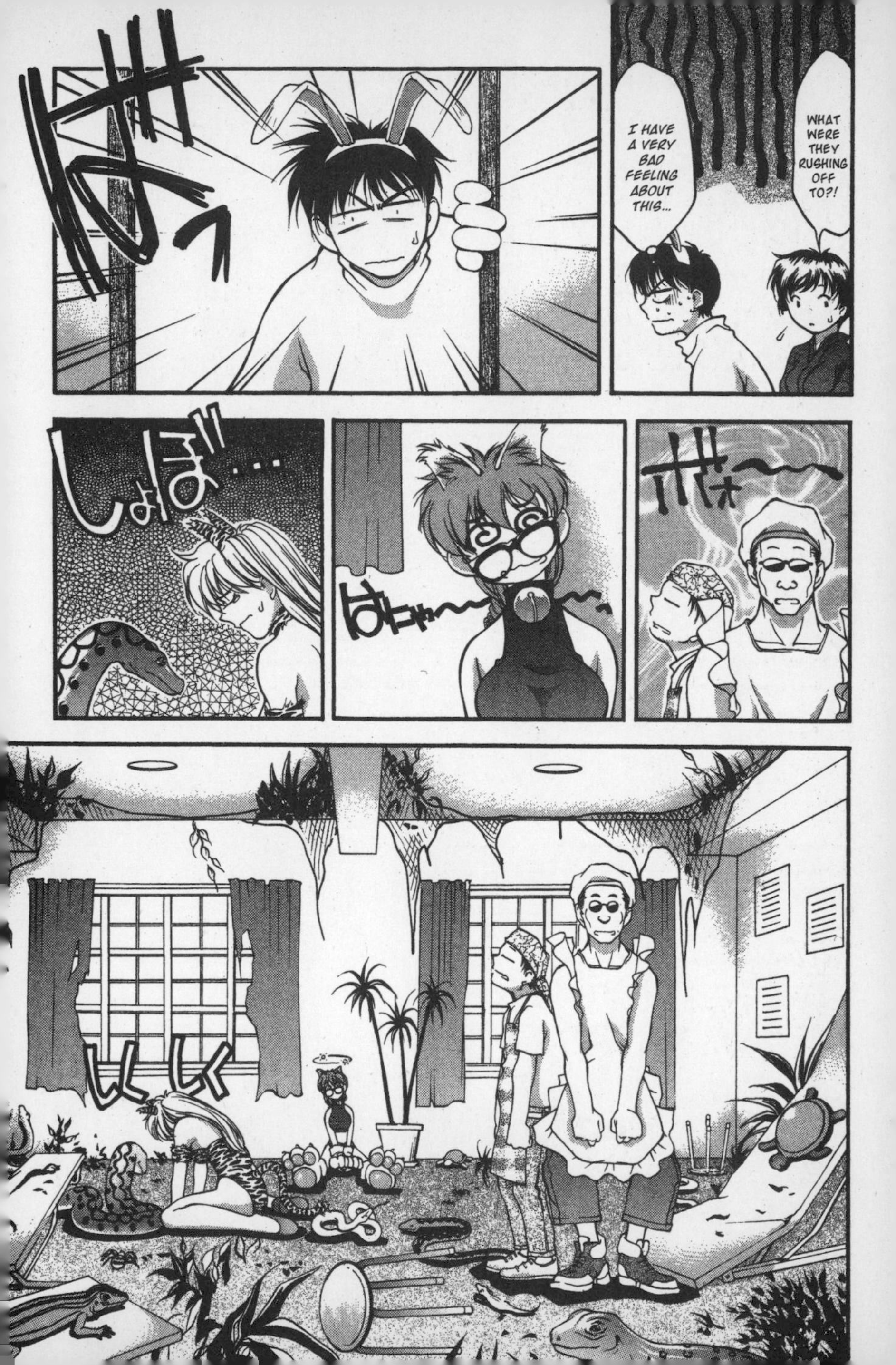
WHAT WERE THEY RUSHING OFF TO?!
I HAVE A VERY BAD FEELING ABOUT THIS...
しょぼ…

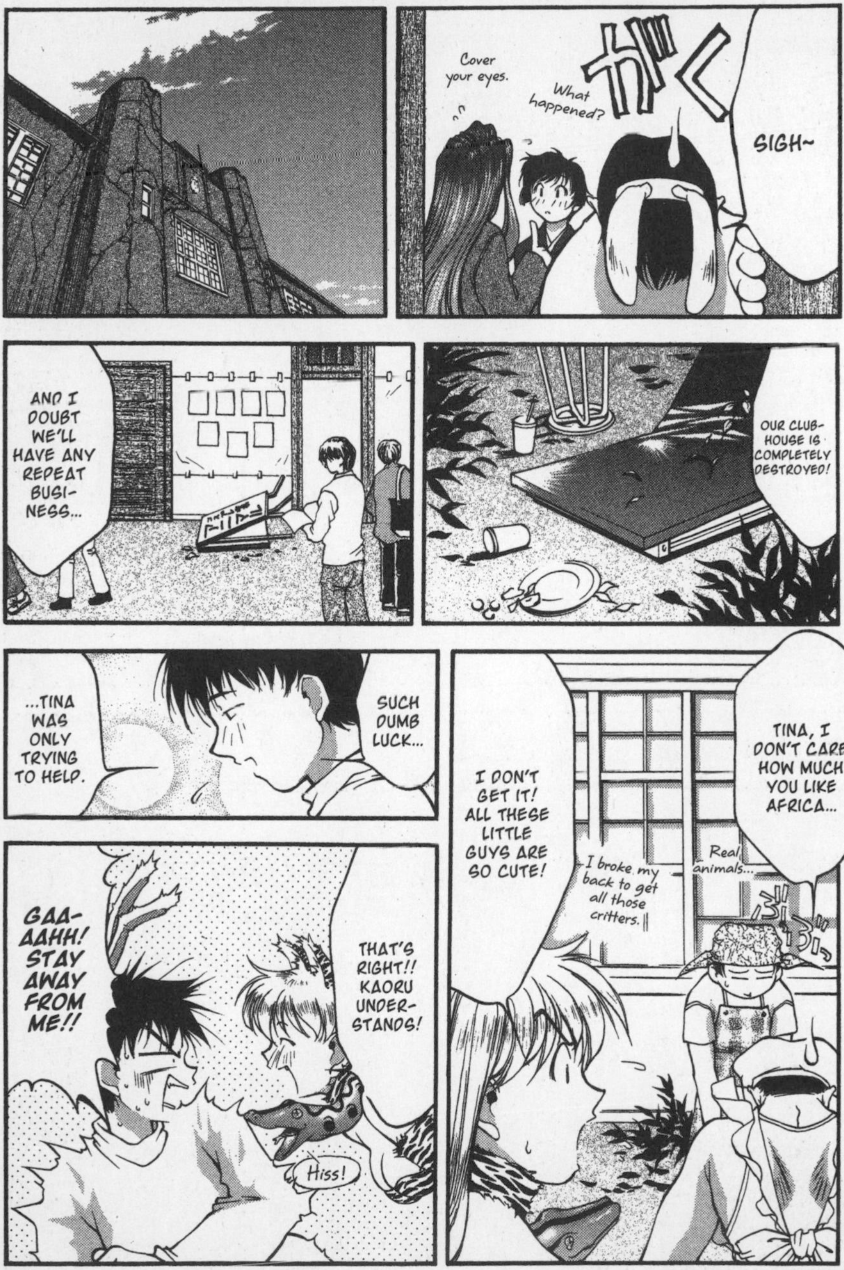

Cover your eyes.
What happened?
がく
SIGH~
OUR CLUBHOUSE IS COMPLETELY DESTROYED!
AND I DOUBT WE'LL HAVE ANY REPEAT BUSINESS...
TINA, I DON'T CARE HOW MUCH YOU LIKE AFRICA...
Real animals...
I broke my back to get all those critters.
I DON'T GET IT! ALL THESE LITTLE GUYS ARE SO CUTE!
SUCH DUMB LUCK...
...TINA WAS ONLY TRYING TO HELP.
THAT'S RIGHT!! KAORU UNDERSTANDS!
Hiss!
GAA-AAHH! STAY AWAY FROM ME!!

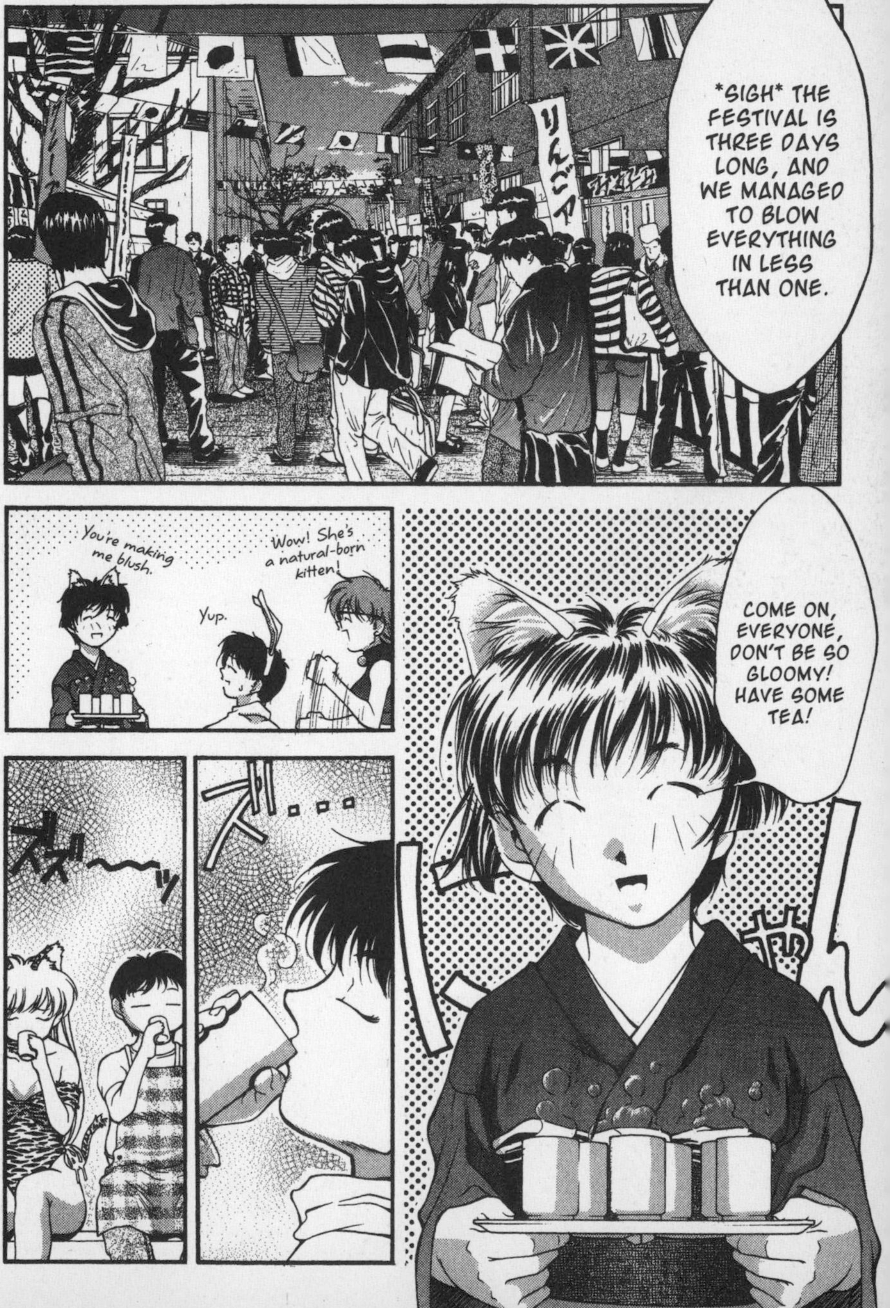
SIGH THE FESTIVAL IS THREE DAYS LONG, AND WE MANAGED TO BLOW EVERYTHING IN LESS THAN ONE.
COME ON, EVERYONE, DON'T BE SO GLOOMY! HAVE SOME TEA!
Wow! She's a natural-born kitten!
Yup.
You're making me blush.
ズ...
ズズ〜〜ッ

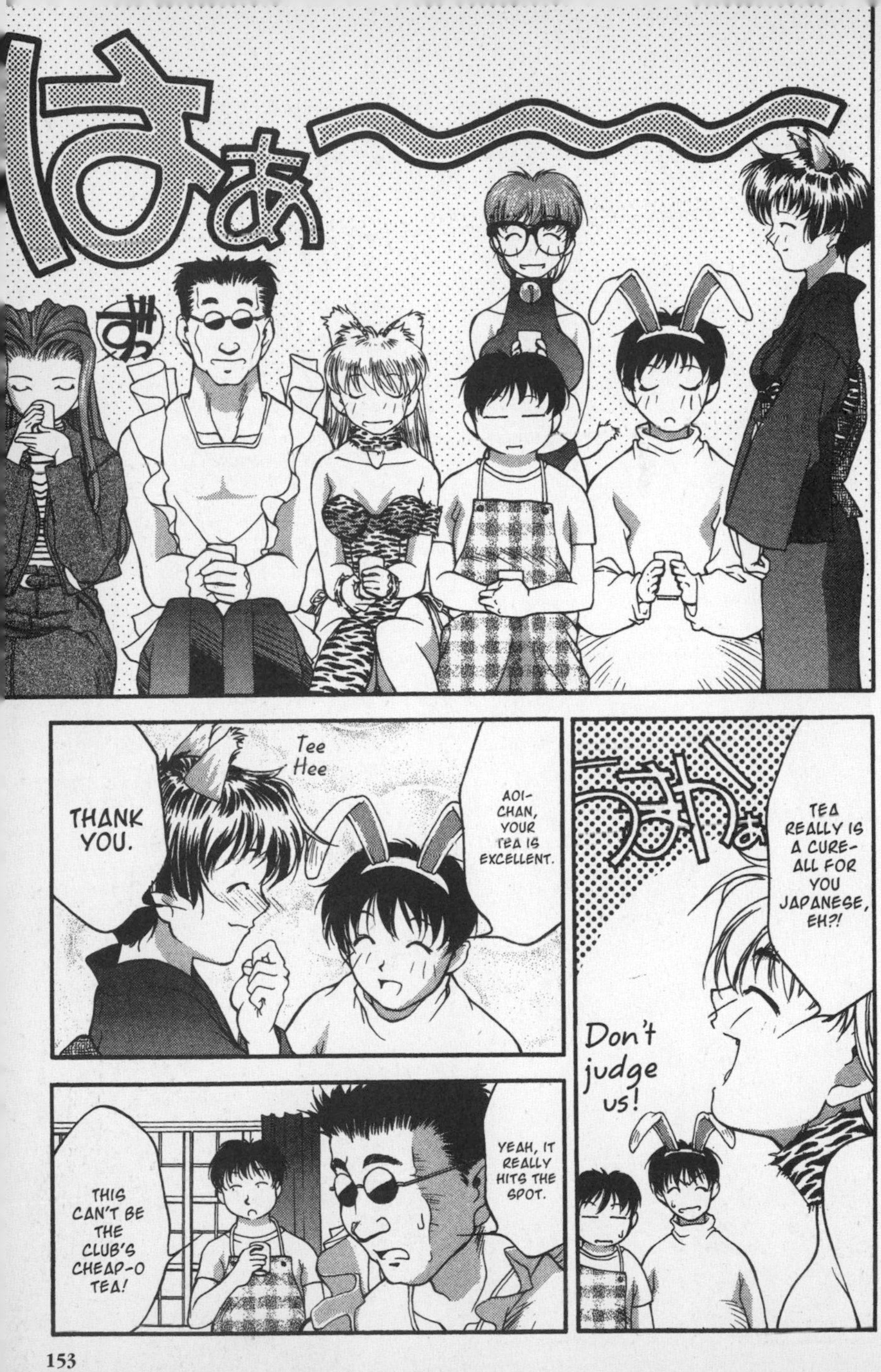
はぁ〜〜〜
ずっ
TEA REALLY IS A CURE-ALL FOR YOU JAPANESE, EH?!
Don't judge us!
AOI-CHAN, YOUR TEA IS EXCELLENT.
Tee Hee
THANK YOU.
YEAH, IT REALLY HITS THE SPOT.
THIS CAN'T BE THE CLUB'S CHEAP-O TEA!

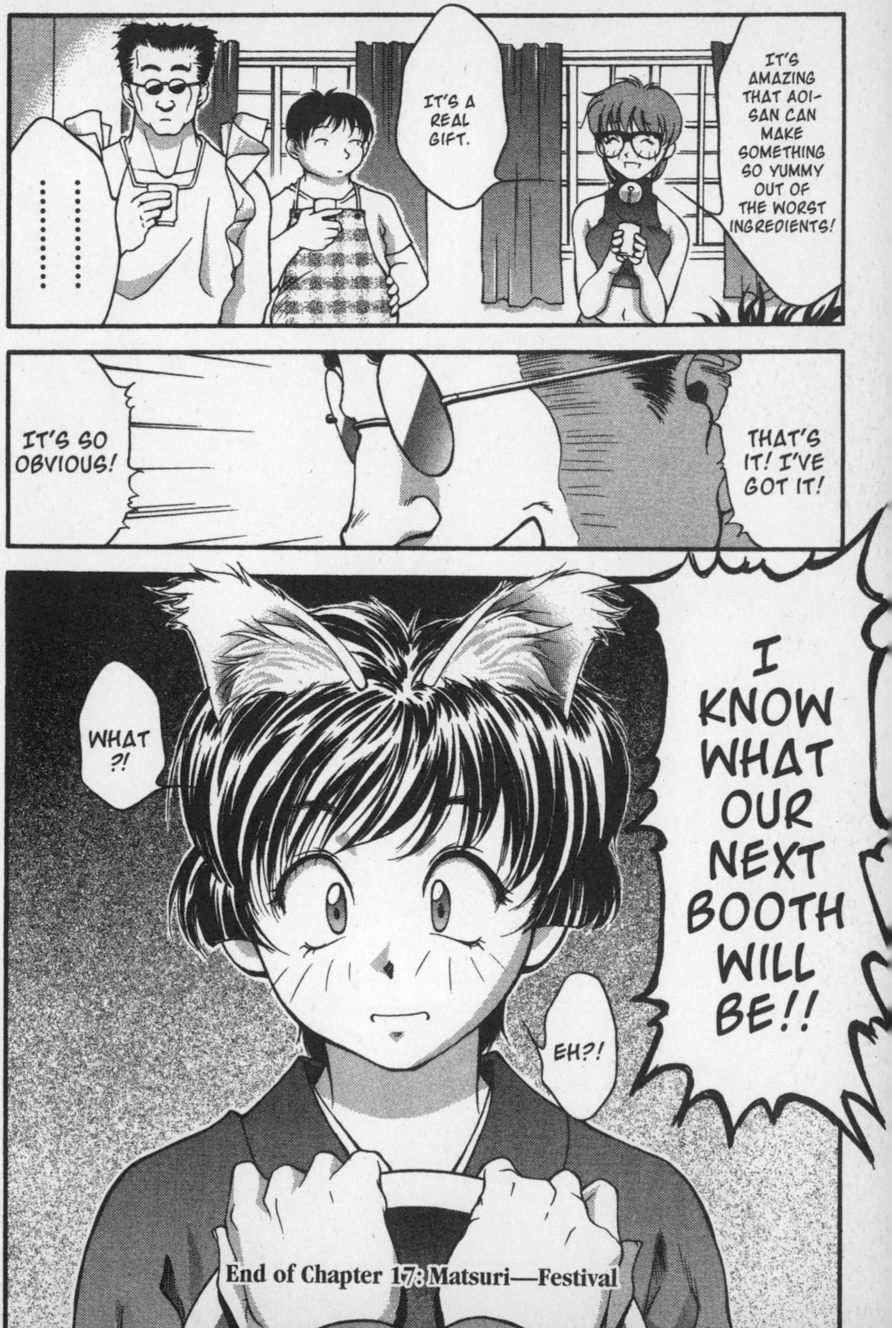
IT'S AMAZING THAT AOI-SAN CAN MAKE SOMETHING SO YUMMY OUT OF THE WORST INGREDIENTS!
IT'S A REAL GIFT.
......
THAT'S IT! I'VE GOT IT!
IT'S SO OBVIOUS!
I KNOW WHAT OUR NEXT BOOTH WILL BE!!
WHAT ?!
EH?!
End of Chapter 17: Matsuri—Festival

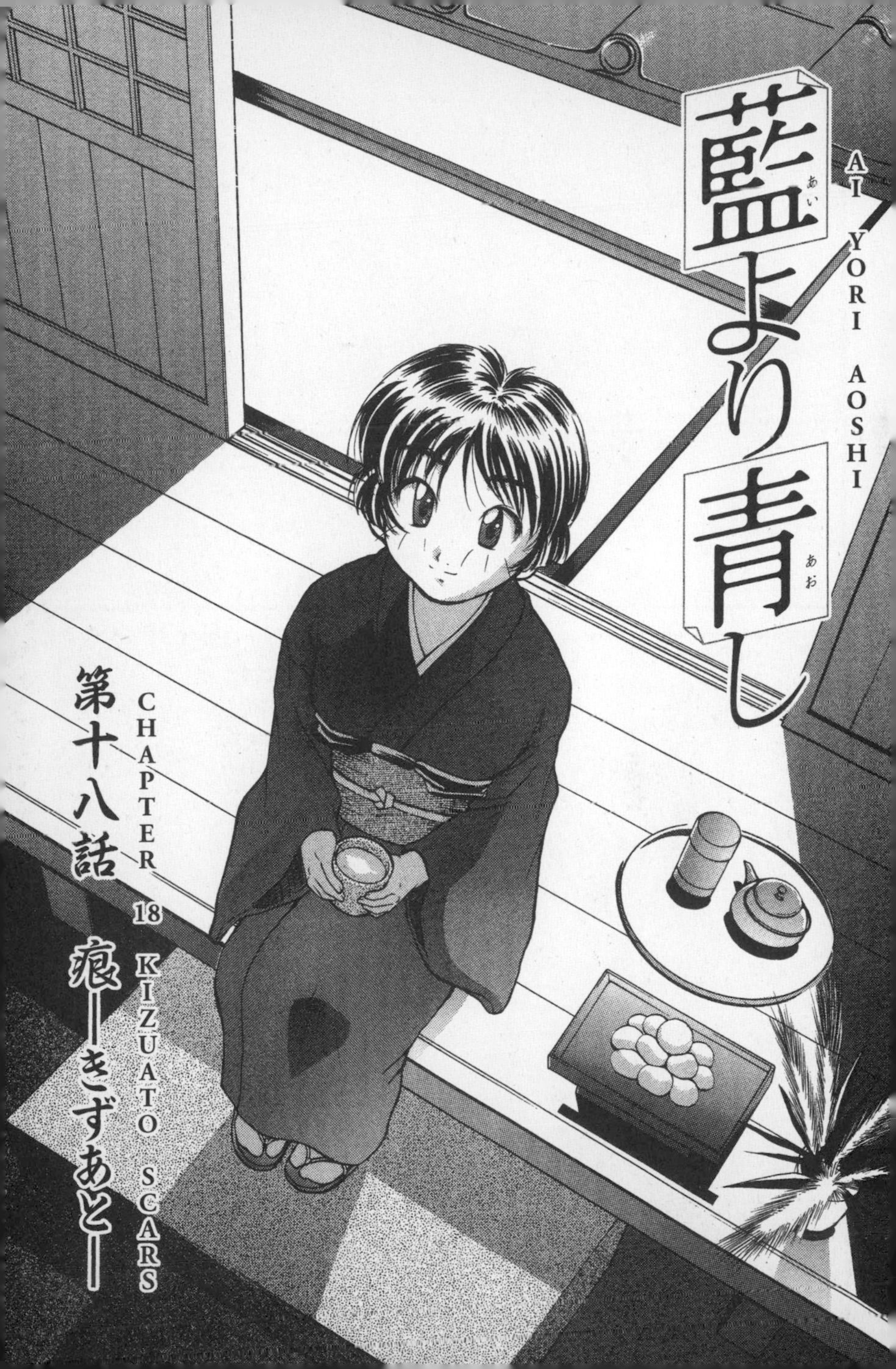
藍より青し
あい
あお
AI YORI AOSHI
第十八話
CHAPTER 18
痕—きずあと—
KIZUATO SCARS

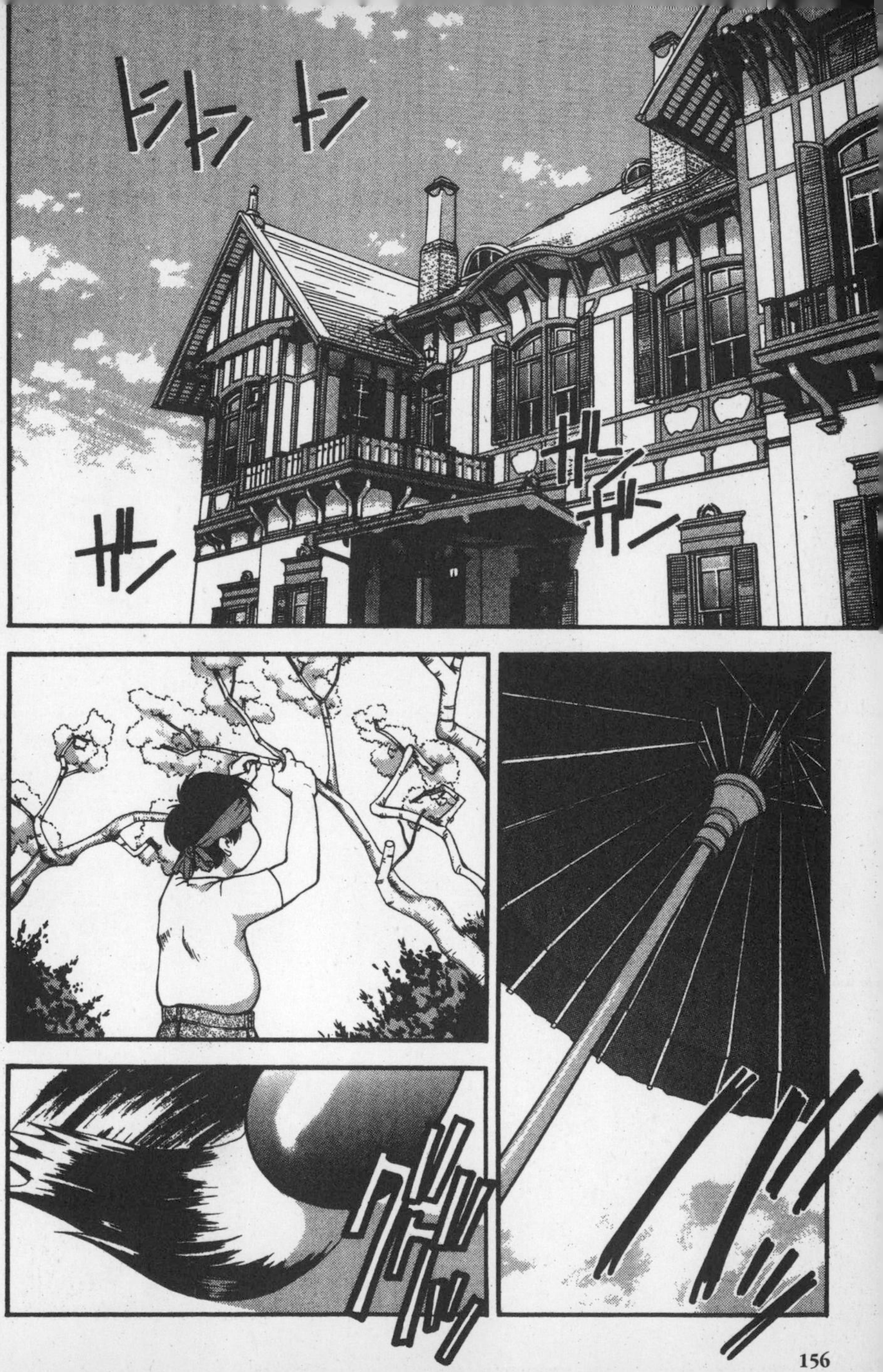
トントン トン
ガン
ガン
ガン

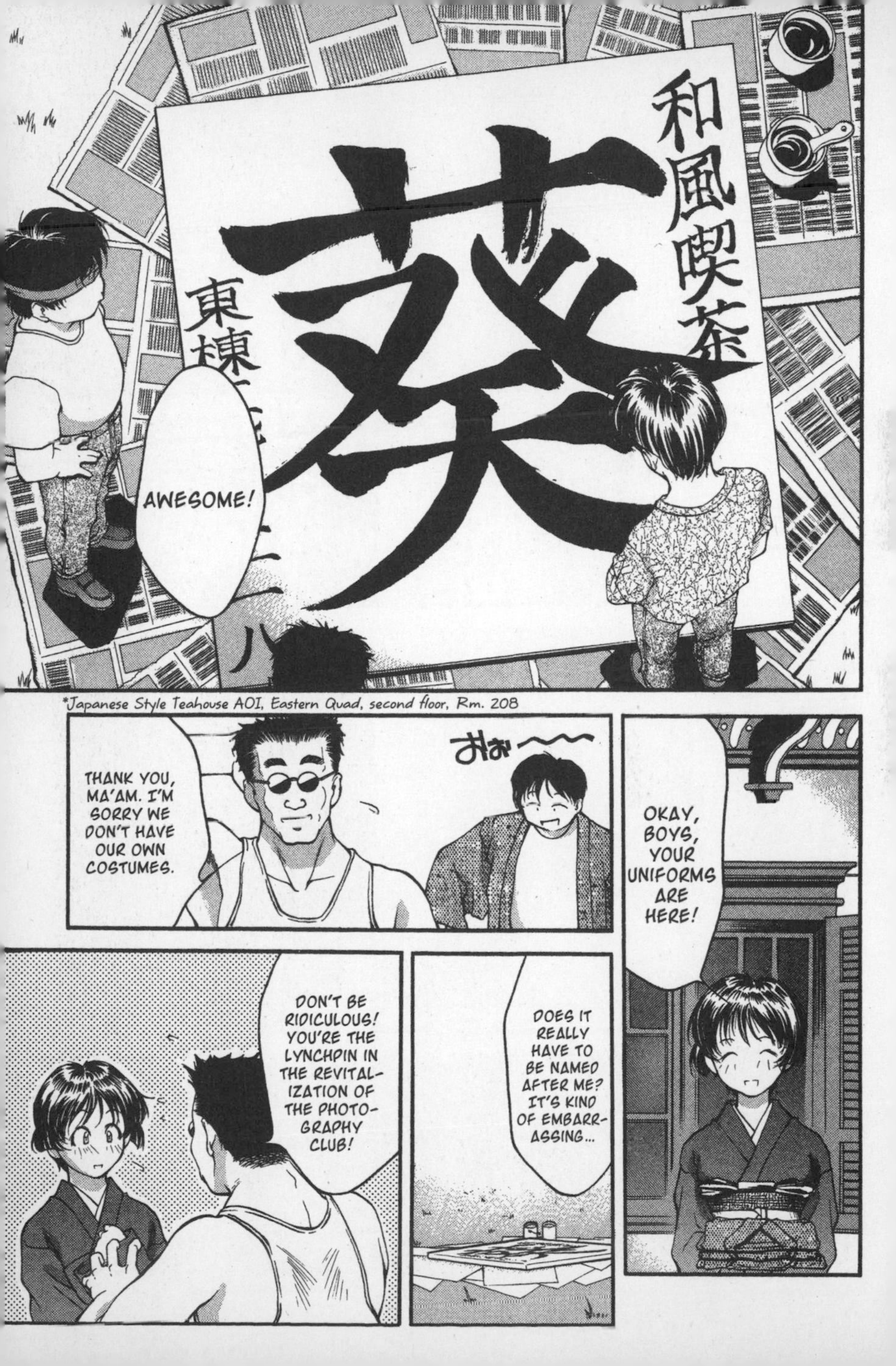
和風喫茶
葵
AWESOME!
OKAY, BOYS, YOUR UNIFORMS ARE HERE!
おぉ〜〜
THANK YOU, MA'AM. I'M SORRY WE DON'T HAVE OUR OWN COSTUMES.
DOES IT REALLY HAVE TO BE NAMED AFTER ME? IT'S KIND OF EMBARRASSING...
DON'T BE RIDICULOUS! YOU'RE THE LYNCHPIN IN THE REVITALIZATION OF THE PHOTOGRAPHY CLUB!
*Japanese Style Teahouse AOI, Eastern Quad, second floor, Rm. 208

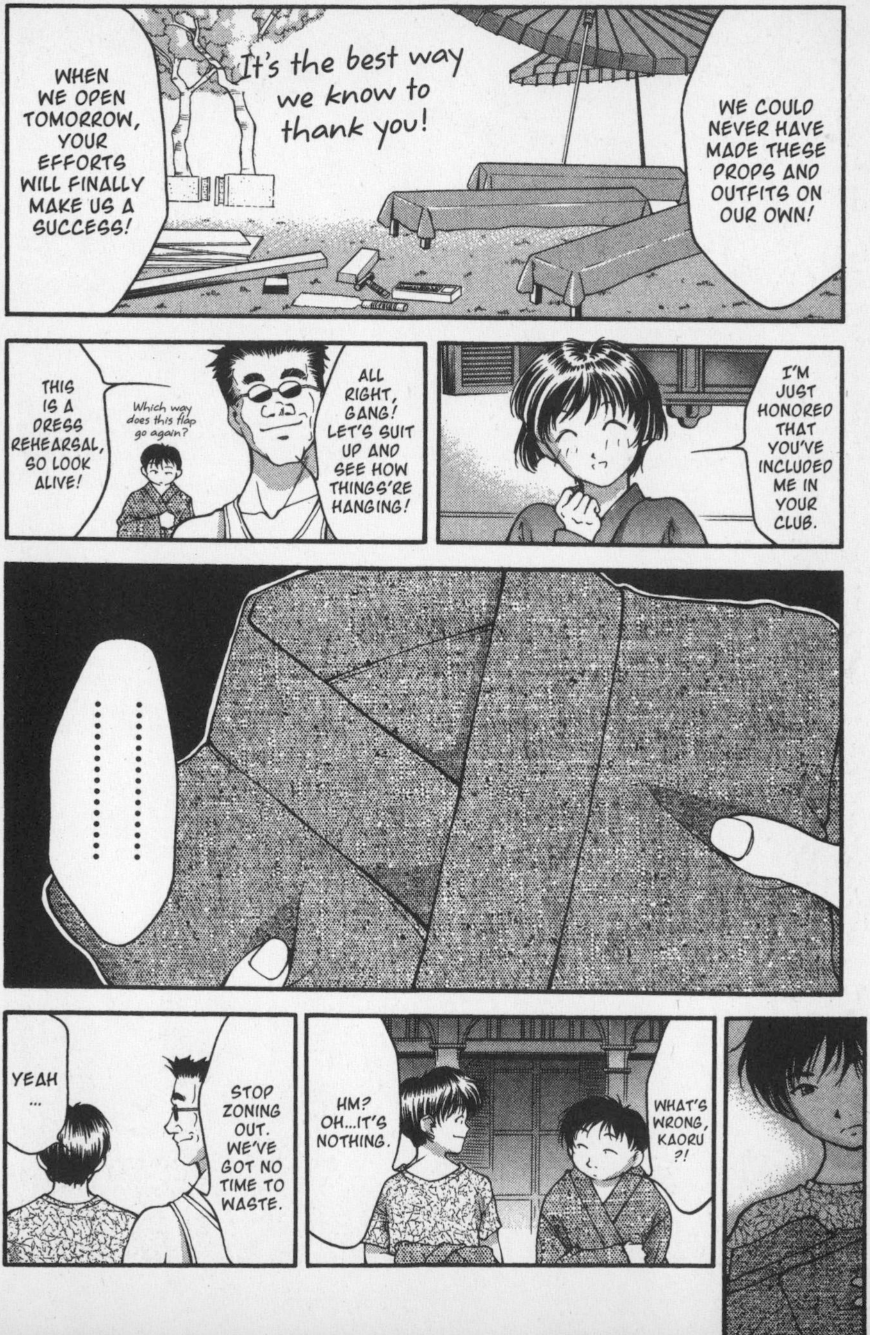
WE COULD NEVER HAVE MADE THESE PROPS AND OUTFITS ON OUR OWN!
It's the best way we know to thank you!
WHEN WE OPEN TOMORROW, YOUR EFFORTS WILL FINALLY MAKE US A SUCCESS!
I'M JUST HONORED THAT YOU'VE INCLUDED ME IN YOUR CLUB.
ALL RIGHT, GANG! LET'S SUIT UP AND SEE HOW THINGS'RE HANGING!
THIS IS A DRESS REHEARSAL, SO LOOK ALIVE!
Which way does this flap go again?
......
WHAT'S WRONG, KAORU?!
HM? OH...IT'S NOTHING.
STOP ZONING OUT. WE'VE GOT NO TIME TO WASTE.
YEAH ...

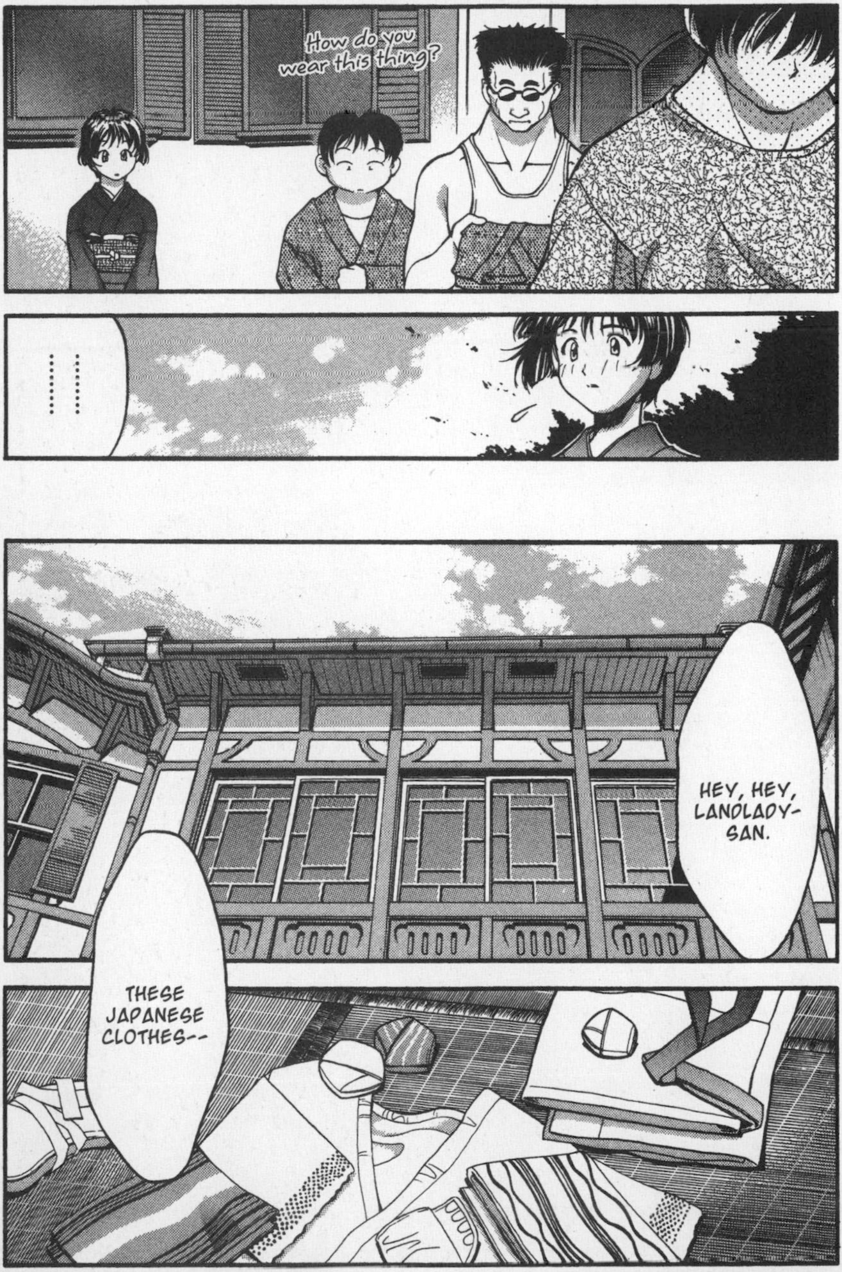
How do you wear this thing?
......
HEY, HEY, LANDLADY-SAN.
THESE JAPANESE CLOTHES--

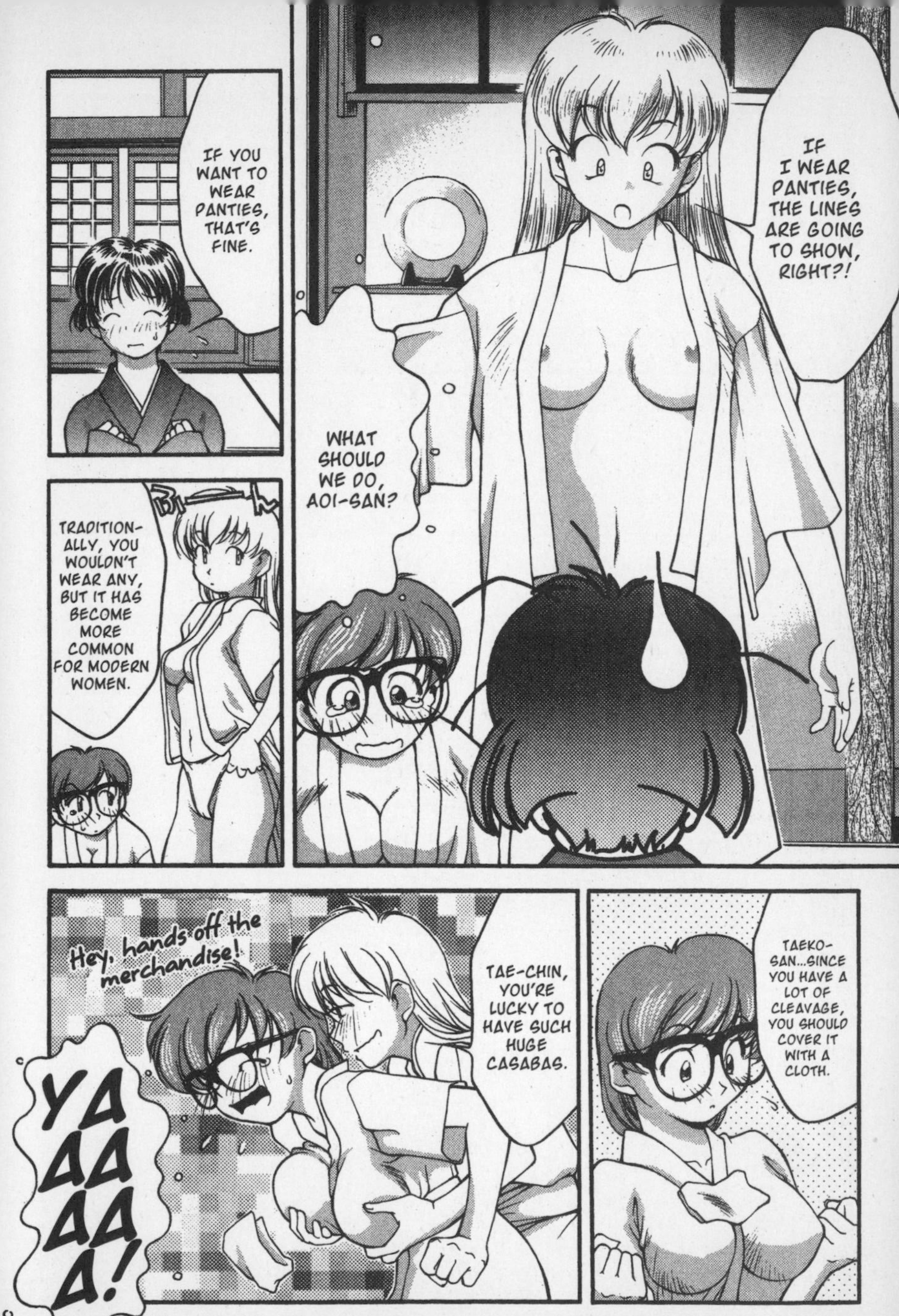
IF I WEAR PANTIES, THE LINES ARE GOING TO SHOW, RIGHT?!
WHAT SHOULD WE DO, AOI-SAN?
IF YOU WANT TO WEAR PANTIES, THAT'S FINE.
TRADITION-ALLY, YOU WOULDN'T WEAR ANY, BUT IT HAS BECOME MORE COMMON FOR MODERN WOMEN.
TAEKO-SAN...SINCE YOU HAVE A LOT OF CLEAVAGE, YOU SHOULD COVER IT WITH A CLOTH.
TAE-CHIN, YOU'RE LUCKY TO HAVE SUCH HUGE CASABAS.
Hey, hands off the merchandise!
YAAAAAA!

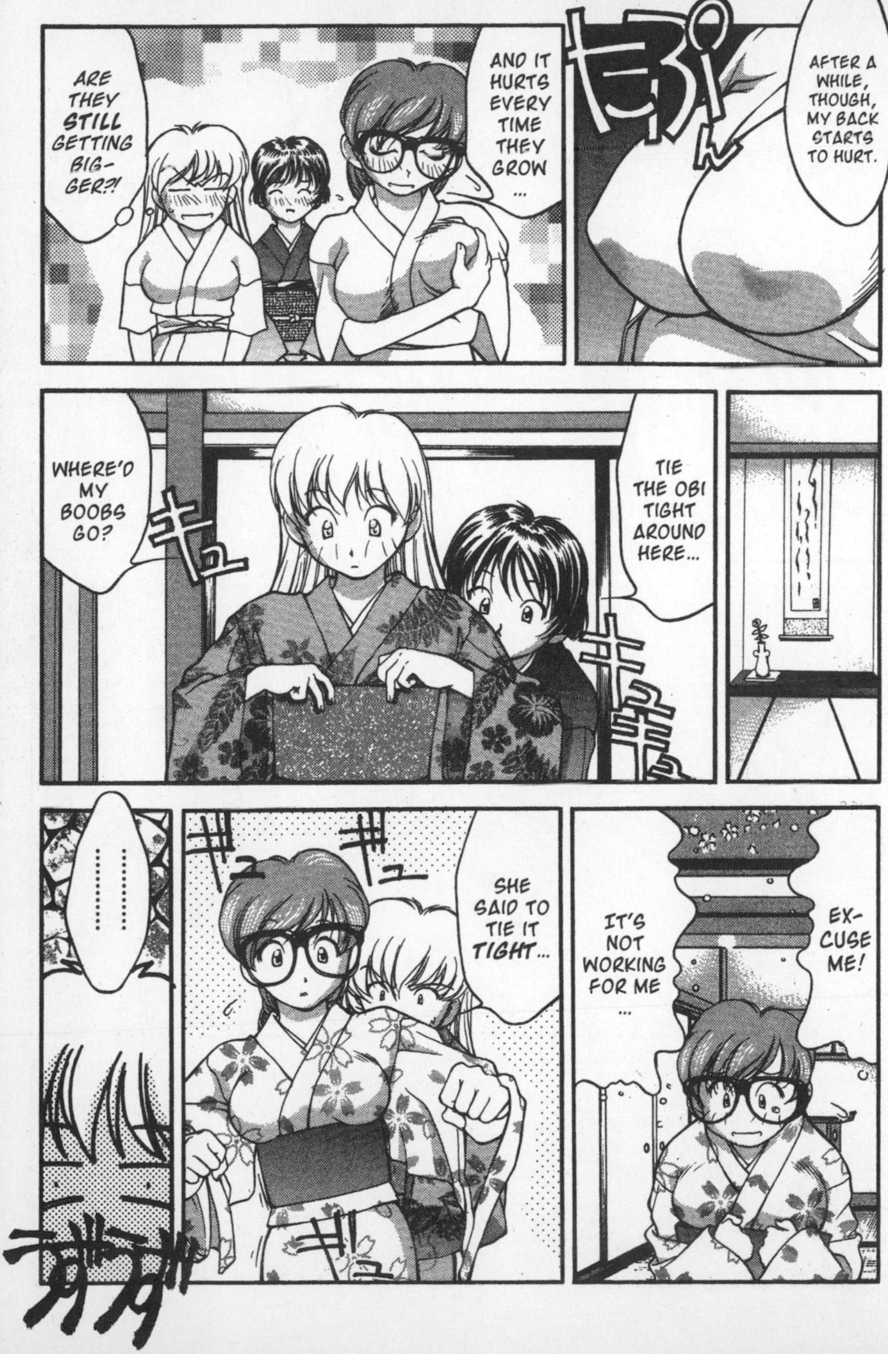
AFTER A WHILE, THOUGH, MY BACK STARTS TO HURT.
たぷん
AND IT HURTS EVERY TIME THEY GROW ...
ARE THEY **STILL** GETTING BIG-GER?!
TIE THE OBI TIGHT AROUND HERE...
キュ
キュ
キュ
WHERE'D MY BOOBS GO?
キュ
EX-CUSE ME!
IT'S NOT WORKING FOR ME ...
SHE SAID TO TIE IT ***TIGHT***...
ギュ
ギュ
ギュ
......

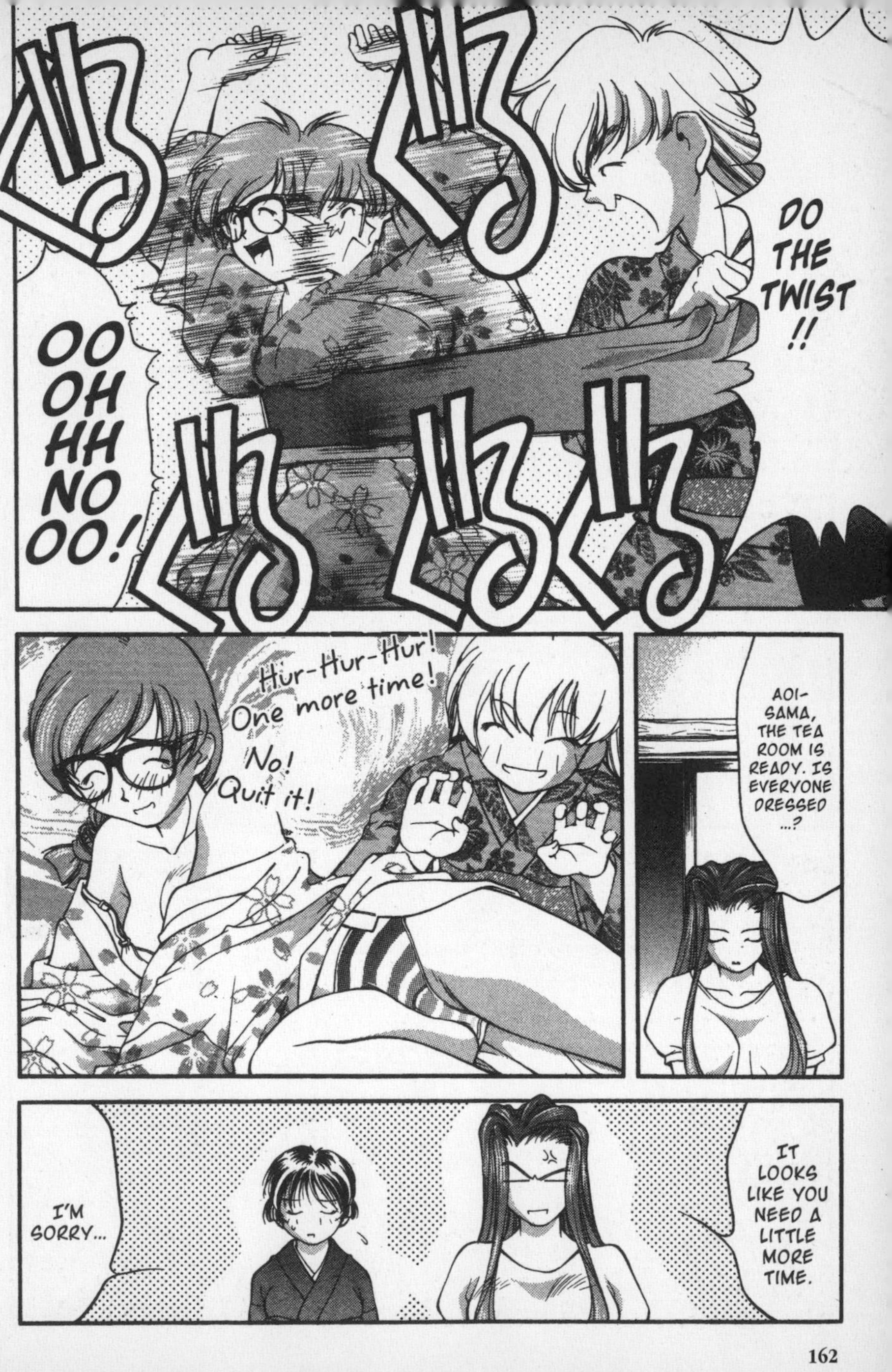
DO THE TWIST!!
OOOHHHNOOO!
AOI-SAMA, THE TEA ROOM IS READY. IS EVERYONE DRESSED ...?
Hur-Hur-Hur! One more time!
No! Quit it!
IT LOOKS LIKE YOU NEED A LITTLE MORE TIME.
I'M SORRY...

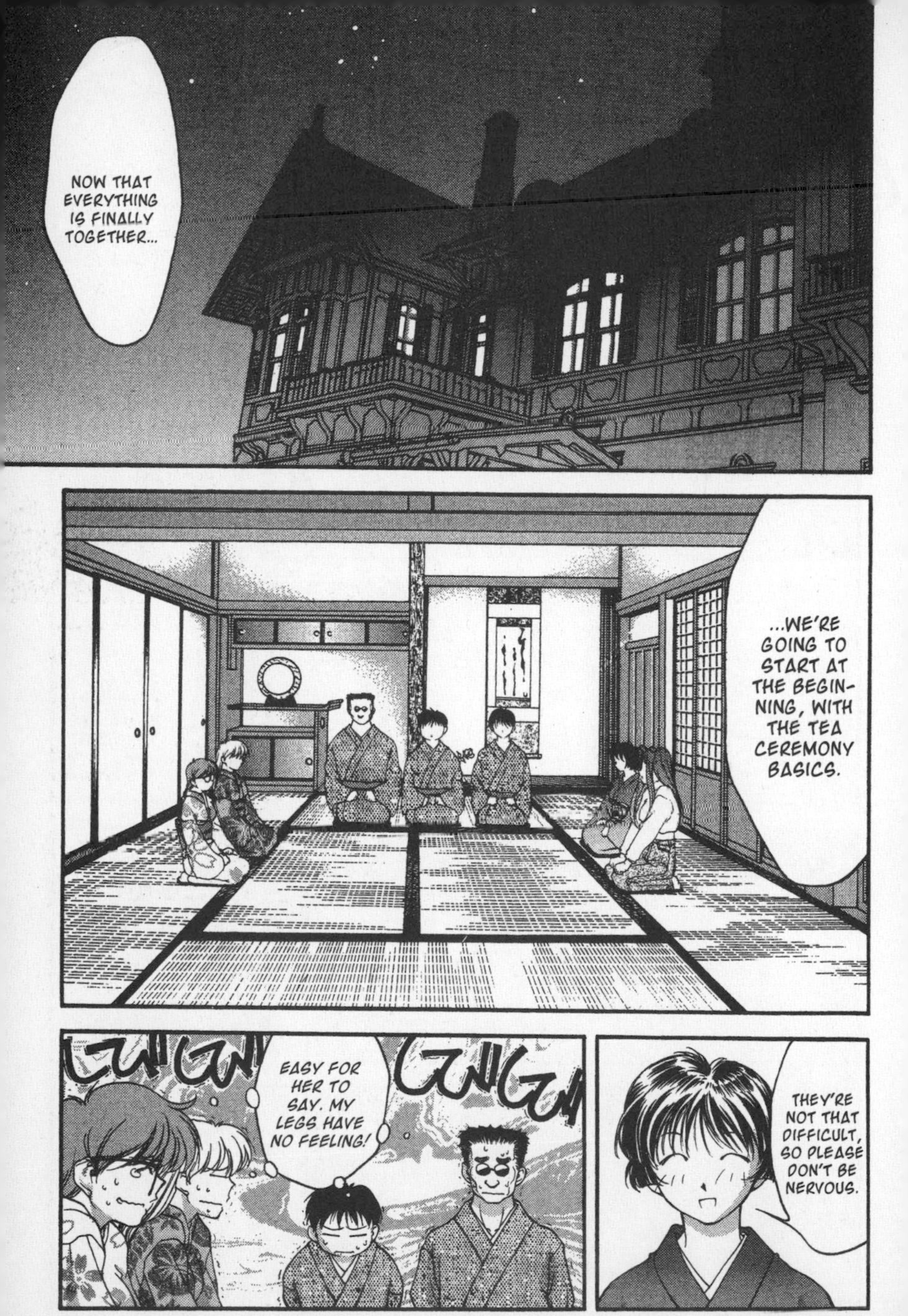

NOW THAT EVERYTHING IS FINALLY TOGETHER...
...WE'RE GOING TO START AT THE BEGINNING, WITH THE TEA CEREMONY BASICS.
THEY'RE NOT THAT DIFFICULT, SO PLEASE DON'T BE NERVOUS.
EASY FOR HER TO SAY. MY LEGS HAVE NO FEELING!

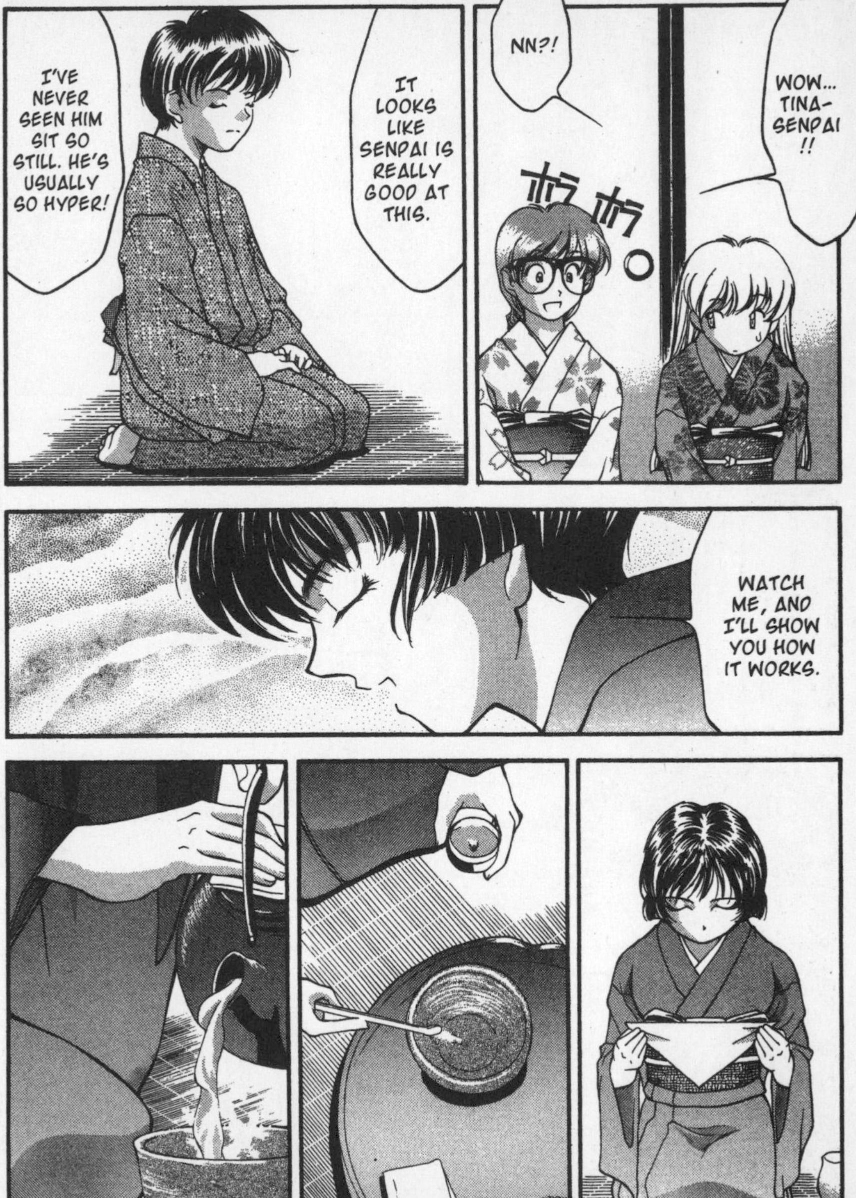
WOW... TINA-SENPAI !!
NN?!
ホラ ホラ
IT LOOKS LIKE SENPAI IS REALLY GOOD AT THIS.
I'VE NEVER SEEN HIM SIT SO STILL. HE'S USUALLY SO HYPER!
WATCH ME, AND I'LL SHOW YOU HOW IT WORKS.

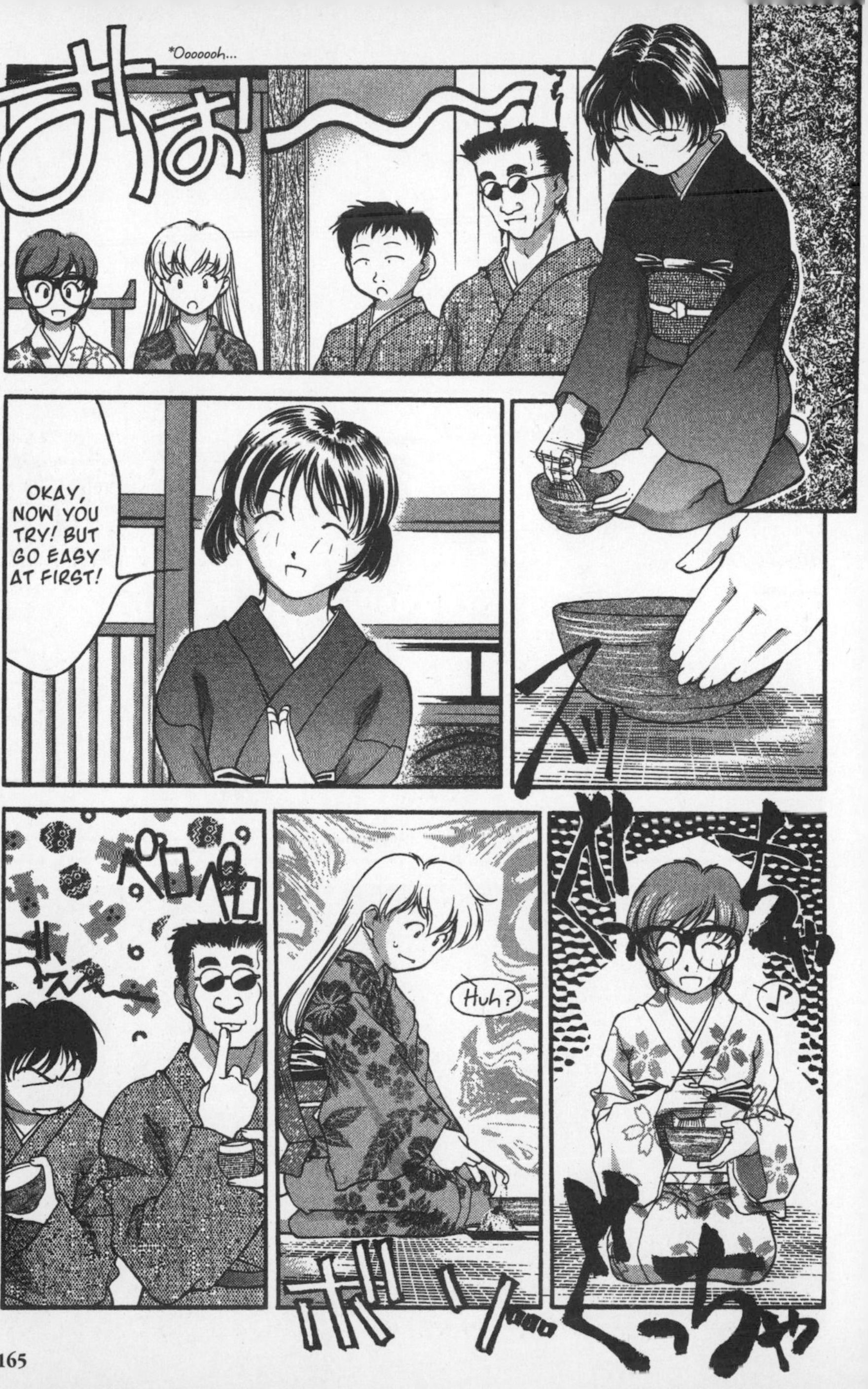
おぉ～～
*Oooooh...
OKAY, NOW YOU TRY! BUT GO EASY AT FIRST!
Huh?
ペロペロ

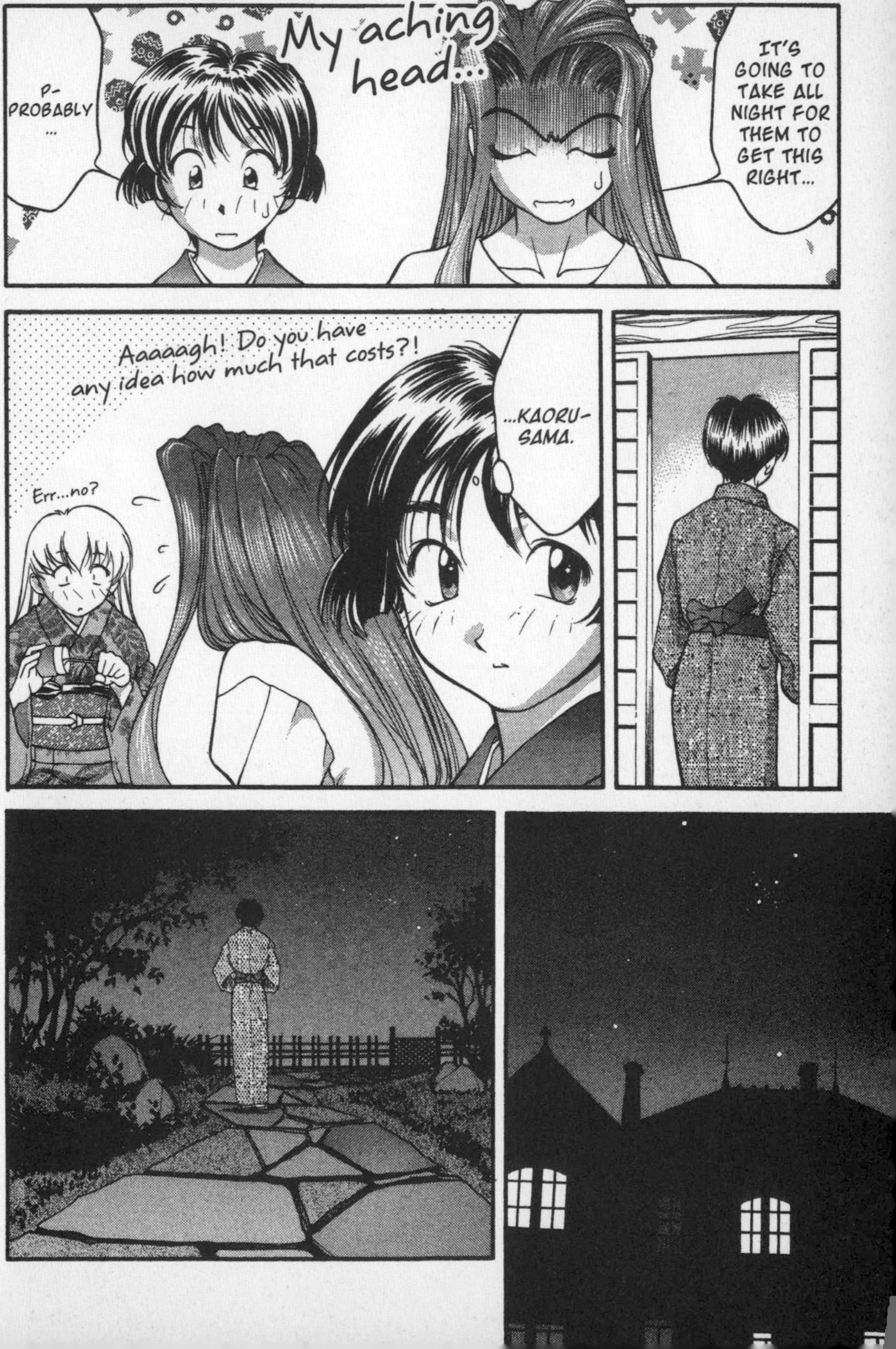
IT'S GOING TO TAKE ALL NIGHT FOR THEM TO GET THIS RIGHT...
My aching head...
P-PROBABLY...
...KAORU-SAMA.
Aaaaagh! Do you have any idea how much that costs?!
Err...no?

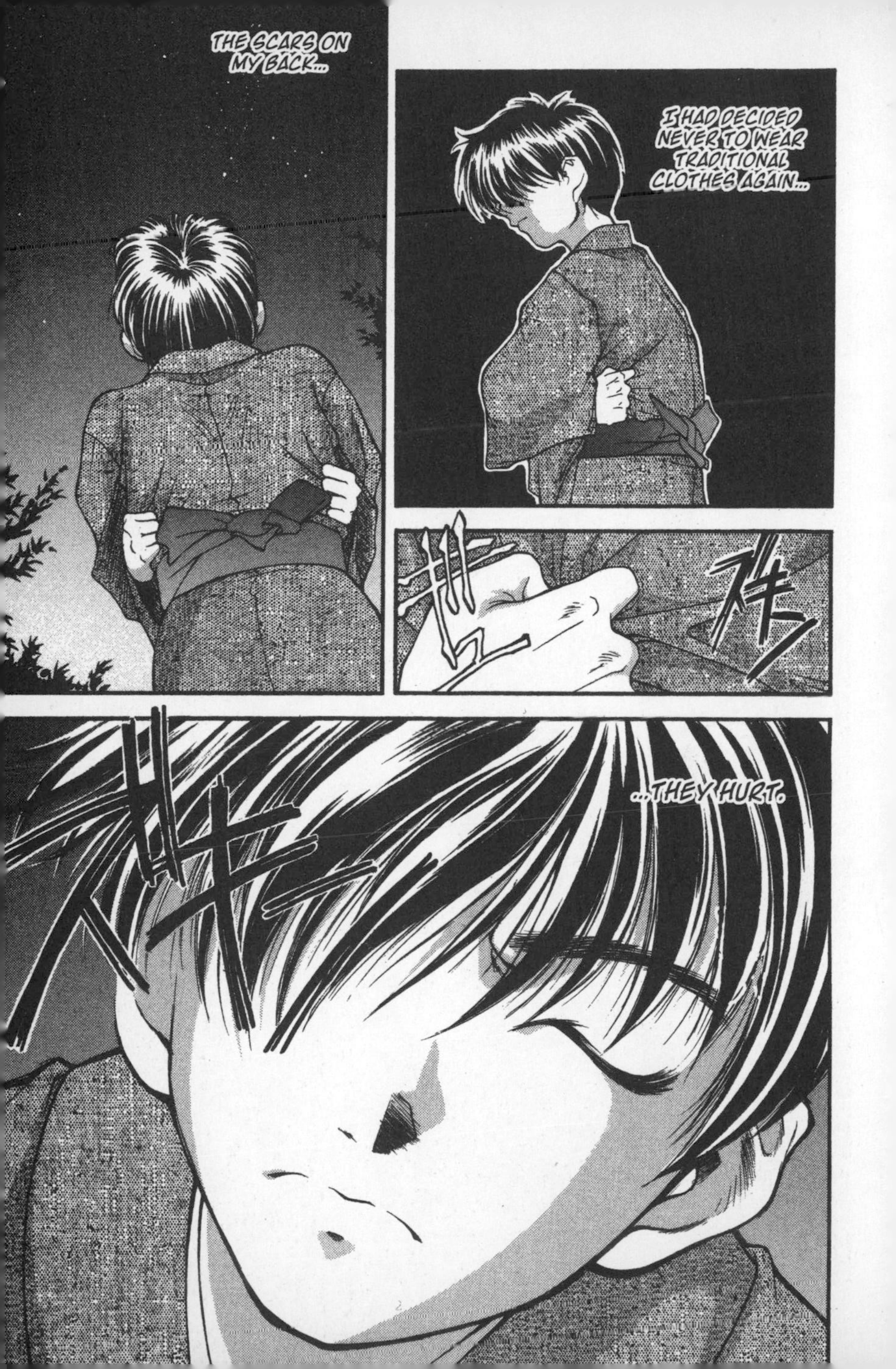
I HAD DECIDED NEVER TO WEAR TRADITIONAL CLOTHES AGAIN...
THE SCARS ON MY BACK...
...THEY HURT.

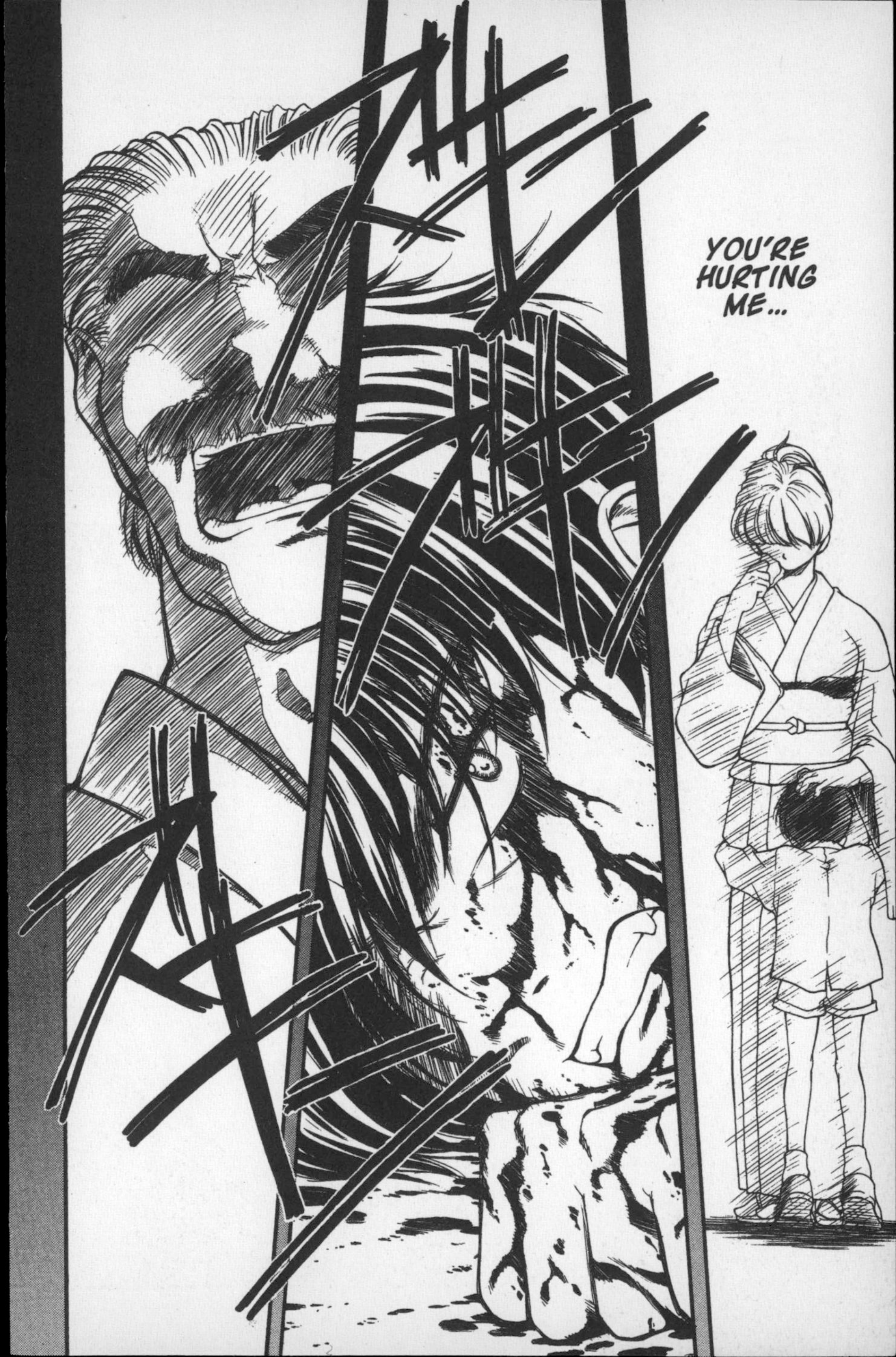
YOU'RE HURTING ME...

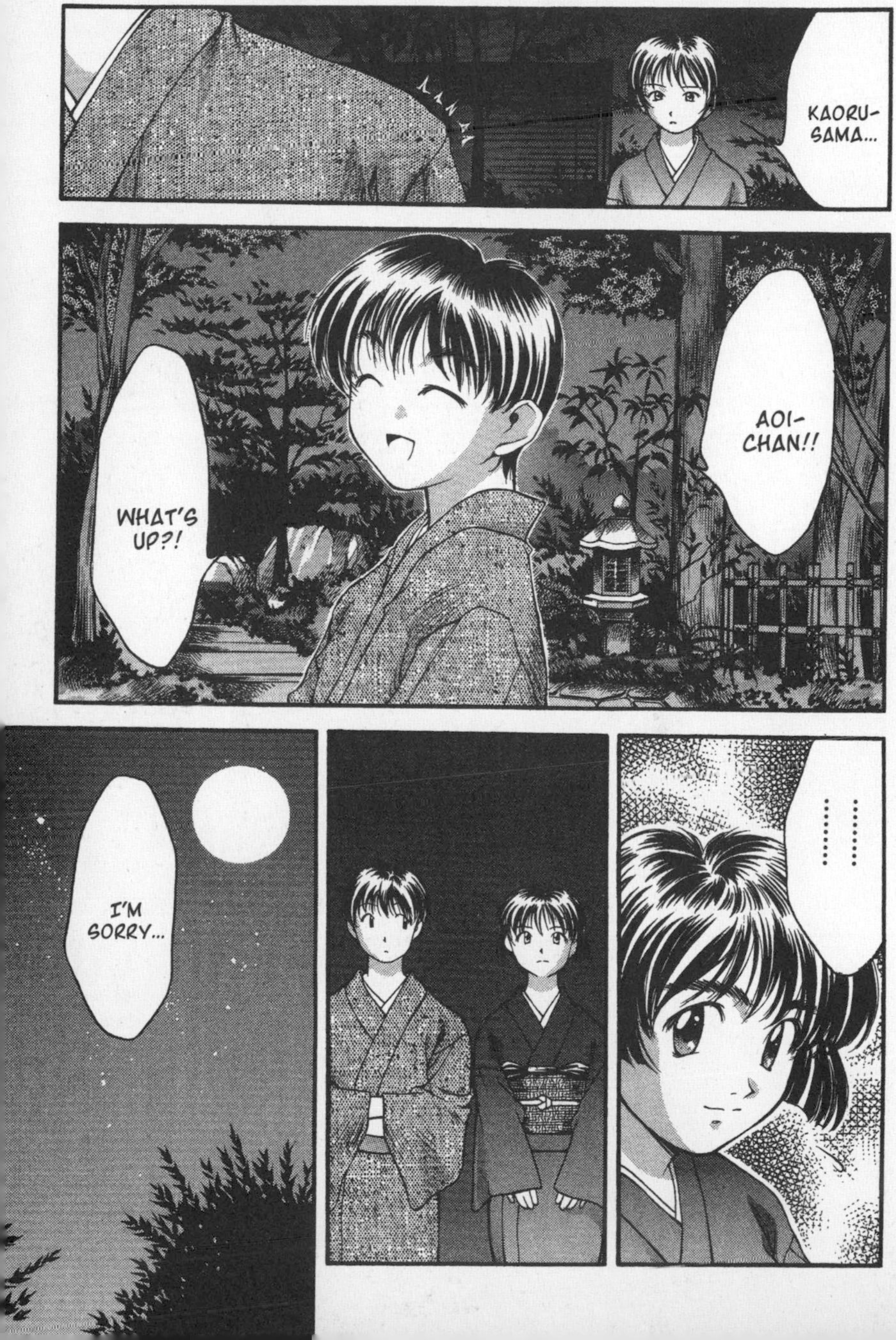
KAORU-SAMA...
AOI-CHAN!!
WHAT'S UP?!
......
I'M SORRY...

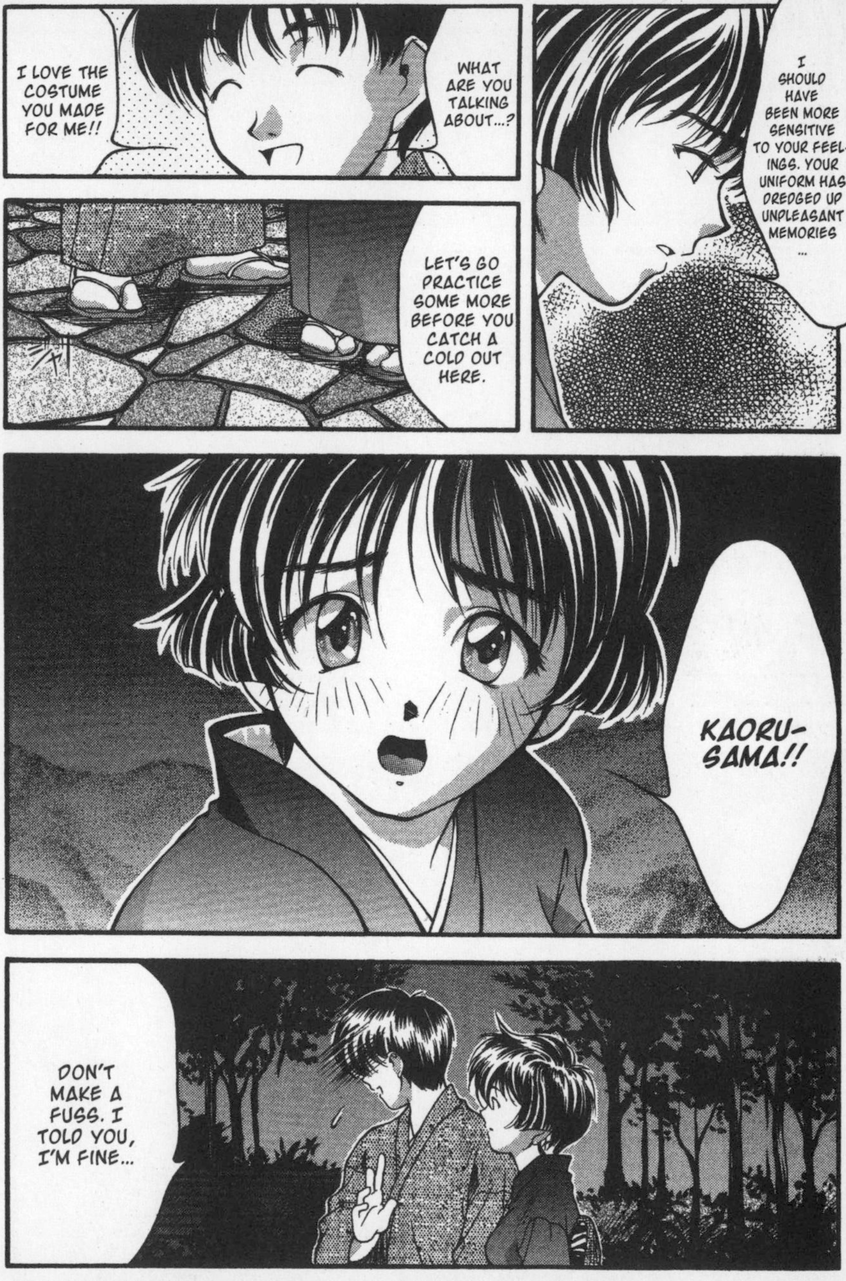
I SHOULD HAVE BEEN MORE SENSITIVE TO YOUR FEEL-INGS. YOUR UNIFORM HAS DREDGED UP UNPLEASANT MEMORIES ...
WHAT ARE YOU TALKING ABOUT...?
I LOVE THE COSTUME YOU MADE FOR ME!!
LET'S GO PRACTICE SOME MORE BEFORE YOU CATCH A COLD OUT HERE.
KAORU-SAMA!!
DON'T MAKE A FUSS. I TOLD YOU, I'M FINE...

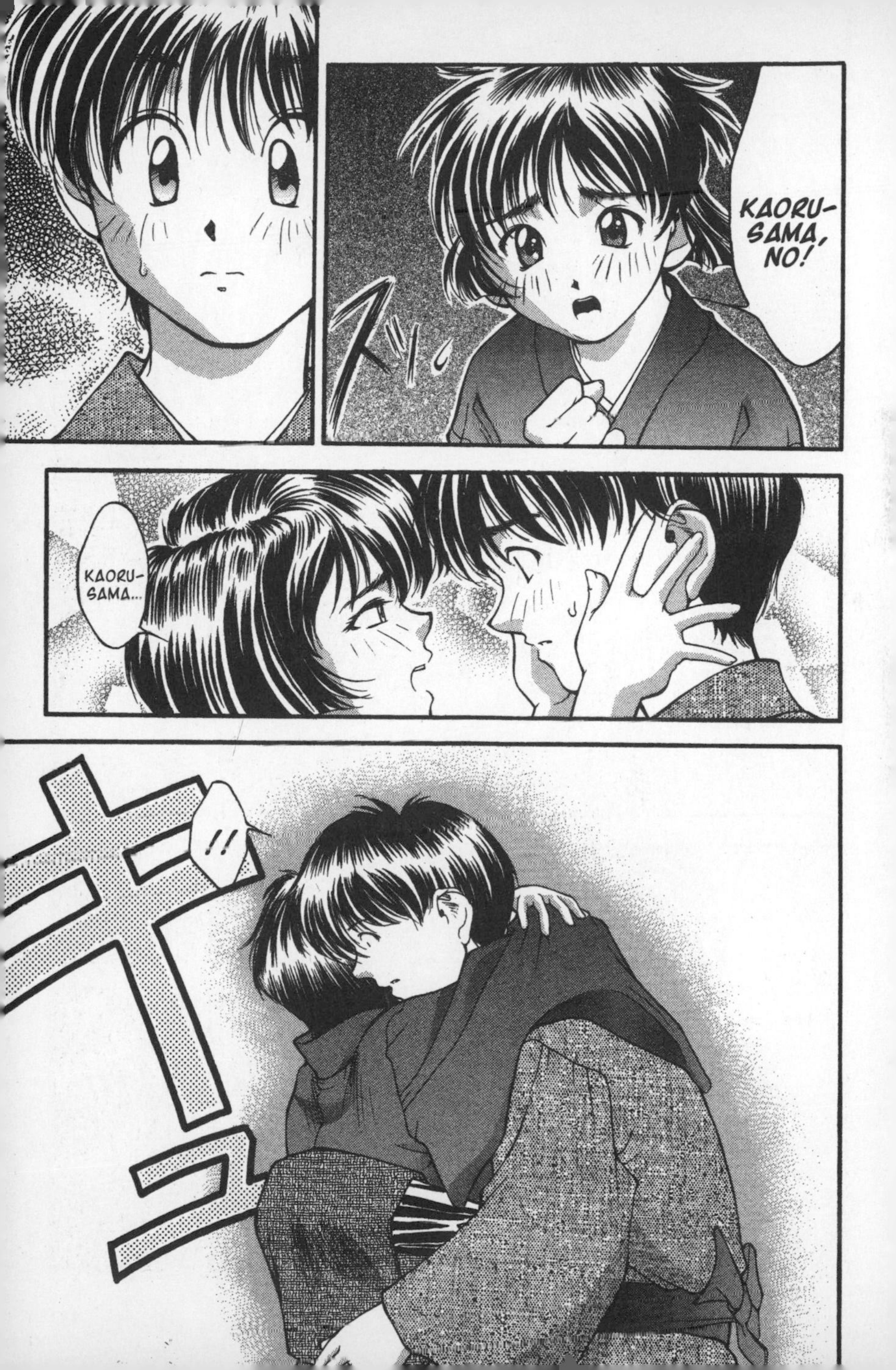
KAORU-SAMA, NO!
KAORU-SAMA...
!!

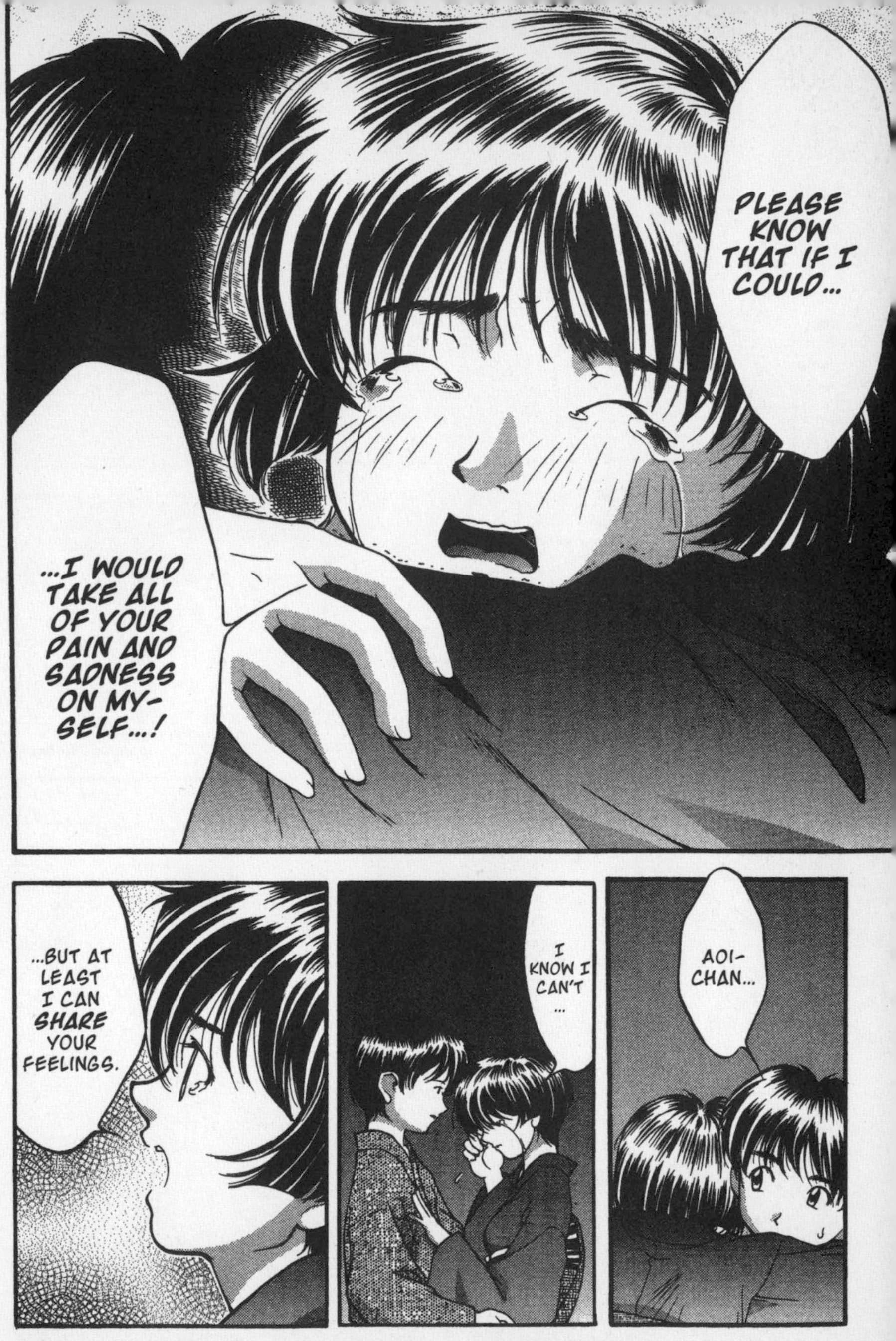
PLEASE KNOW THAT IF I COULD...
...I WOULD TAKE ALL OF YOUR PAIN AND SADNESS ON MY-SELF...!
AOI-CHAN...
I KNOW I CAN'T ...
...BUT AT LEAST I CAN SHARE YOUR FEELINGS.

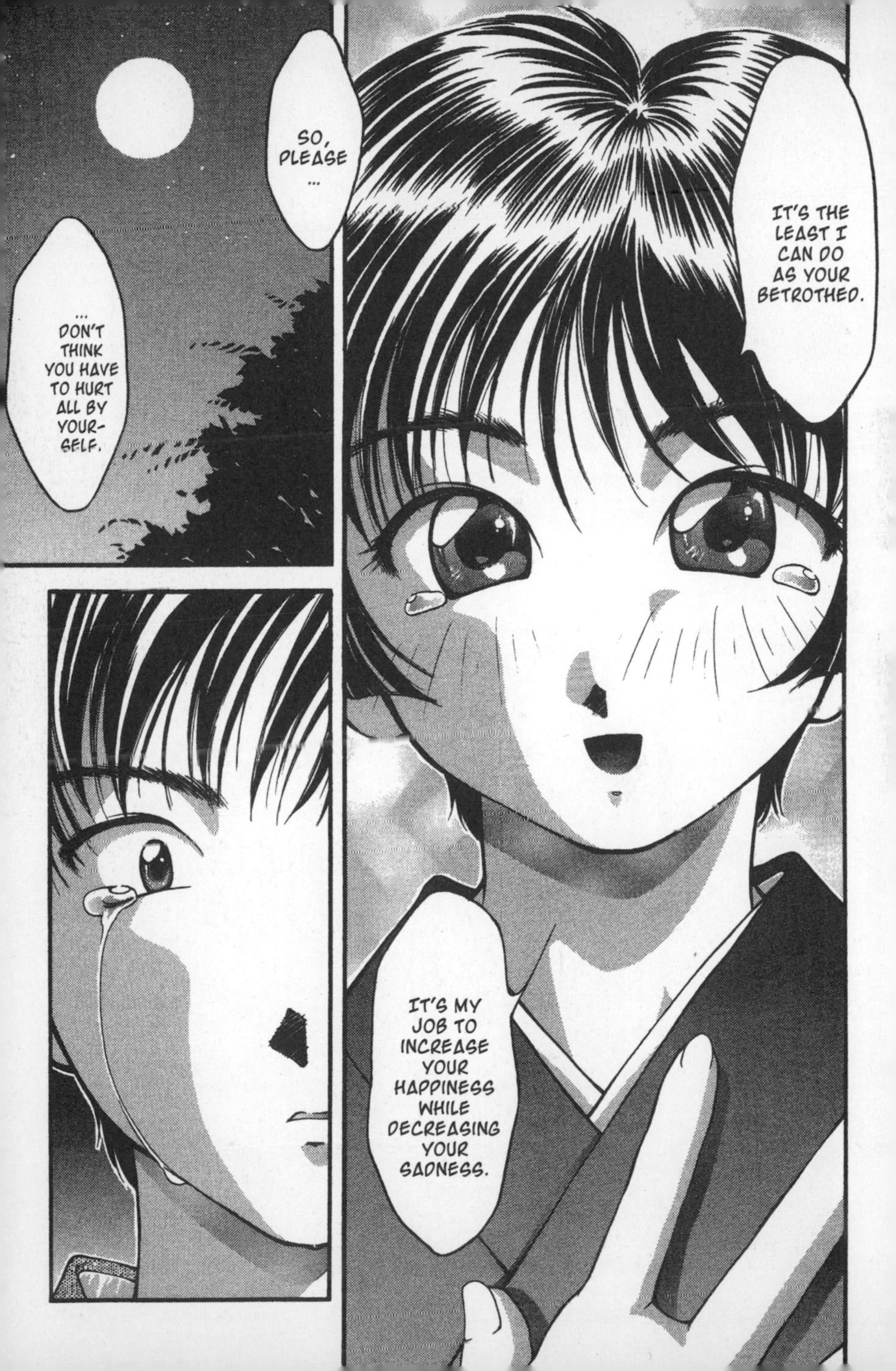
IT'S THE LEAST I CAN DO AS YOUR BETROTHED.
IT'S MY JOB TO INCREASE YOUR HAPPINESS WHILE DECREASING YOUR SADNESS.
SO, PLEASE ...
... DON'T THINK YOU HAVE TO HURT ALL BY YOUR-SELF.

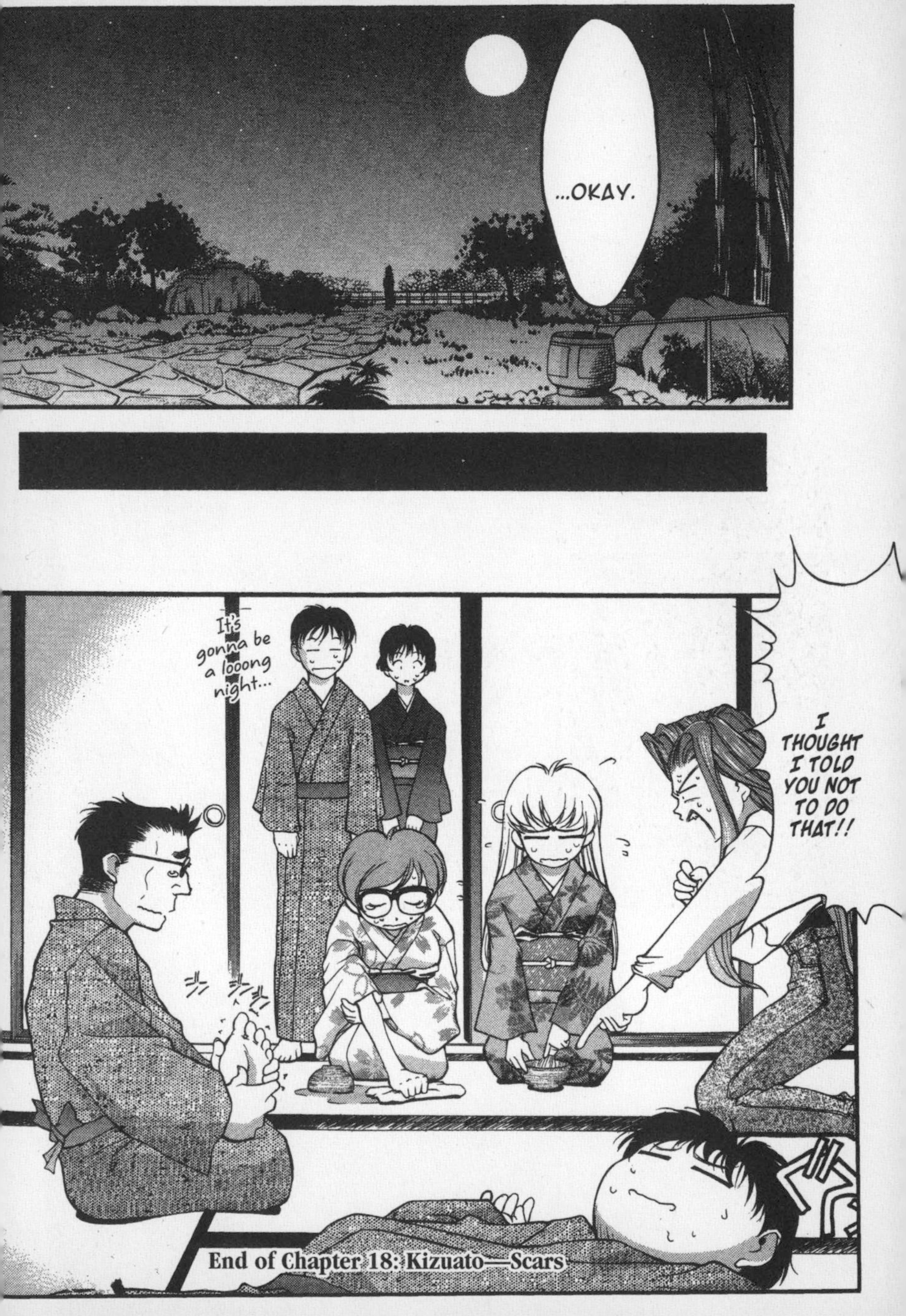
...OKAY.
I THOUGHT I TOLD YOU NOT TO DO THAT!!
It's gonna be a looong night...
End of Chapter 18: Kizuato—Scars

藍より青し

AI YORI AOSHI

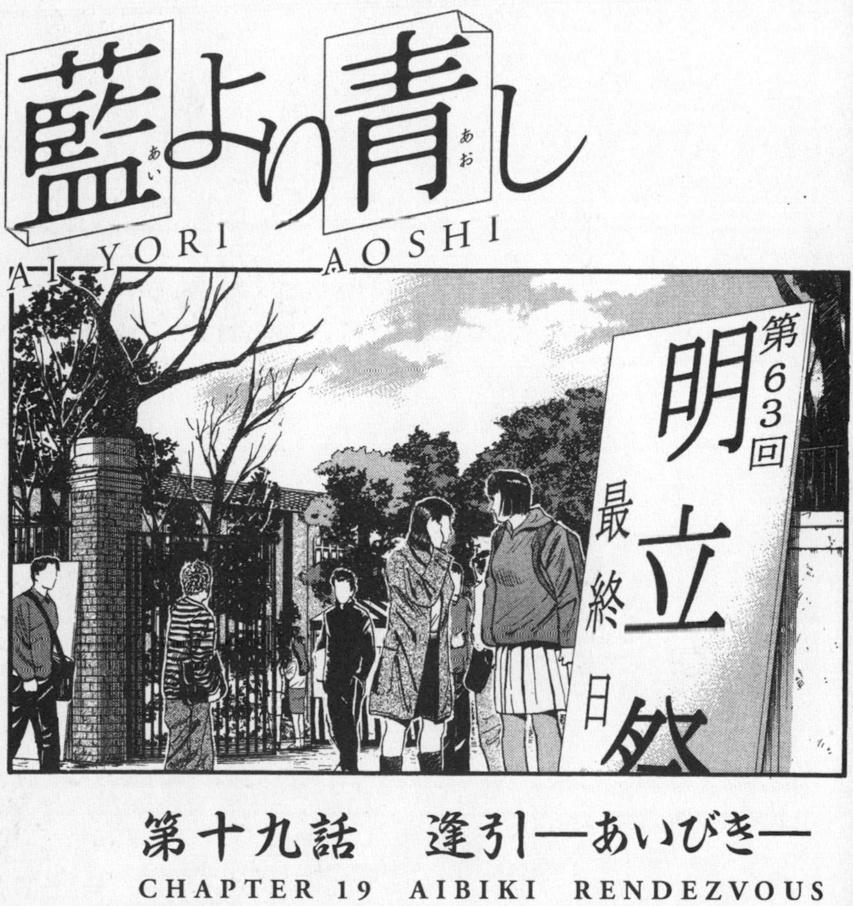
第63回
明立
最終日

第十九話　逢引―あいびき―

CHAPTER 19　AIBIKI　RENDEZVOUS

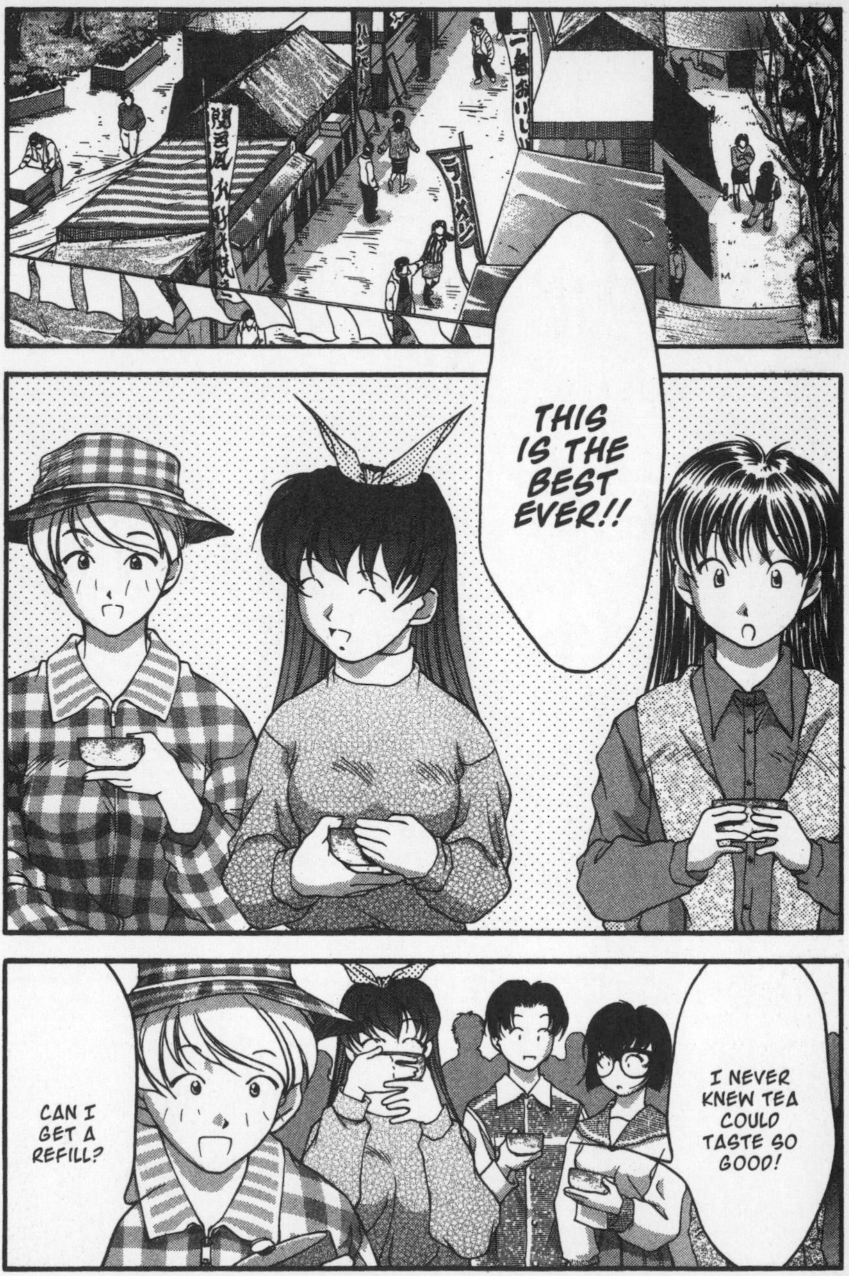
THIS IS THE BEST EVER!!
I NEVER KNEW TEA COULD TASTE SO GOOD!
CAN I GET A REFILL?

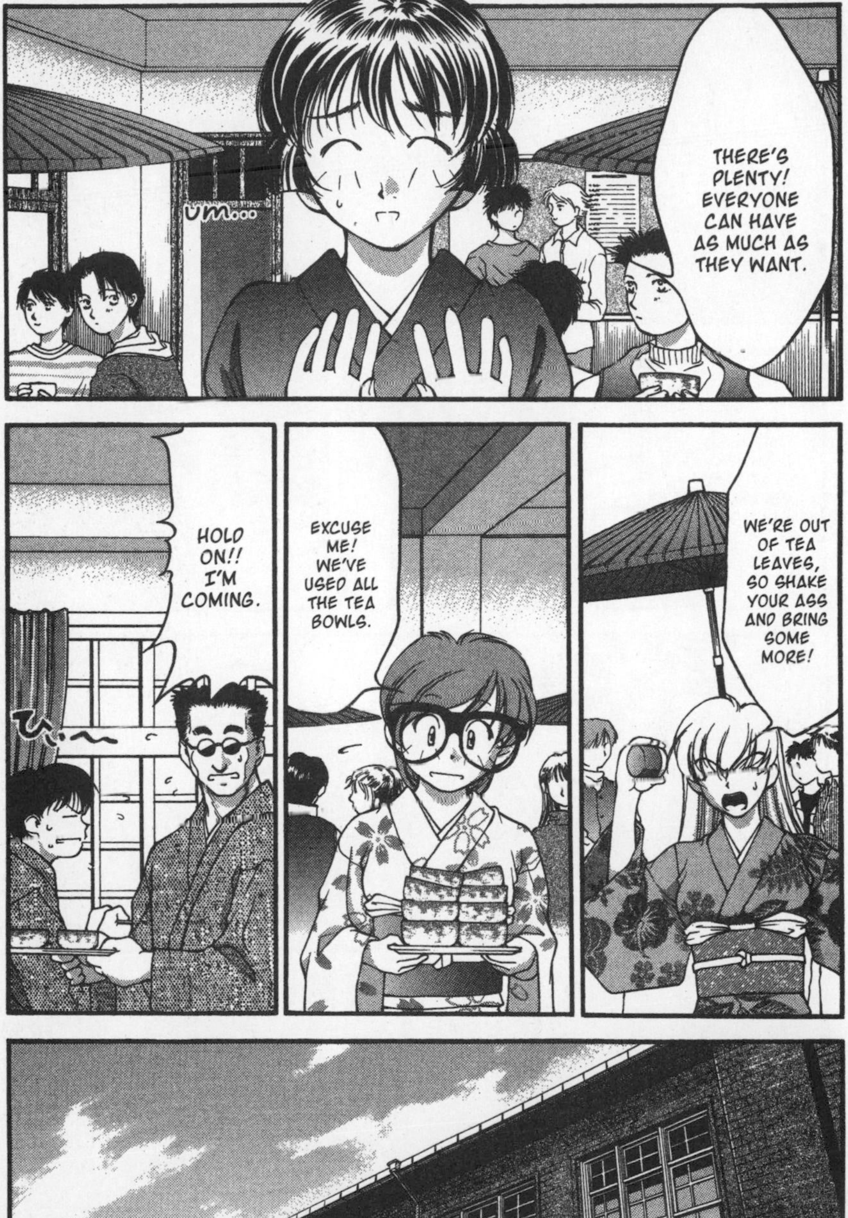
THERE'S PLENTY! EVERYONE CAN HAVE AS MUCH AS THEY WANT.
UM...
WE'RE OUT OF TEA LEAVES, SO SHAKE YOUR ASS AND BRING SOME MORE!
EXCUSE ME! WE'VE USED ALL THE TEA BOWLS.
HOLD ON!! I'M COMING.

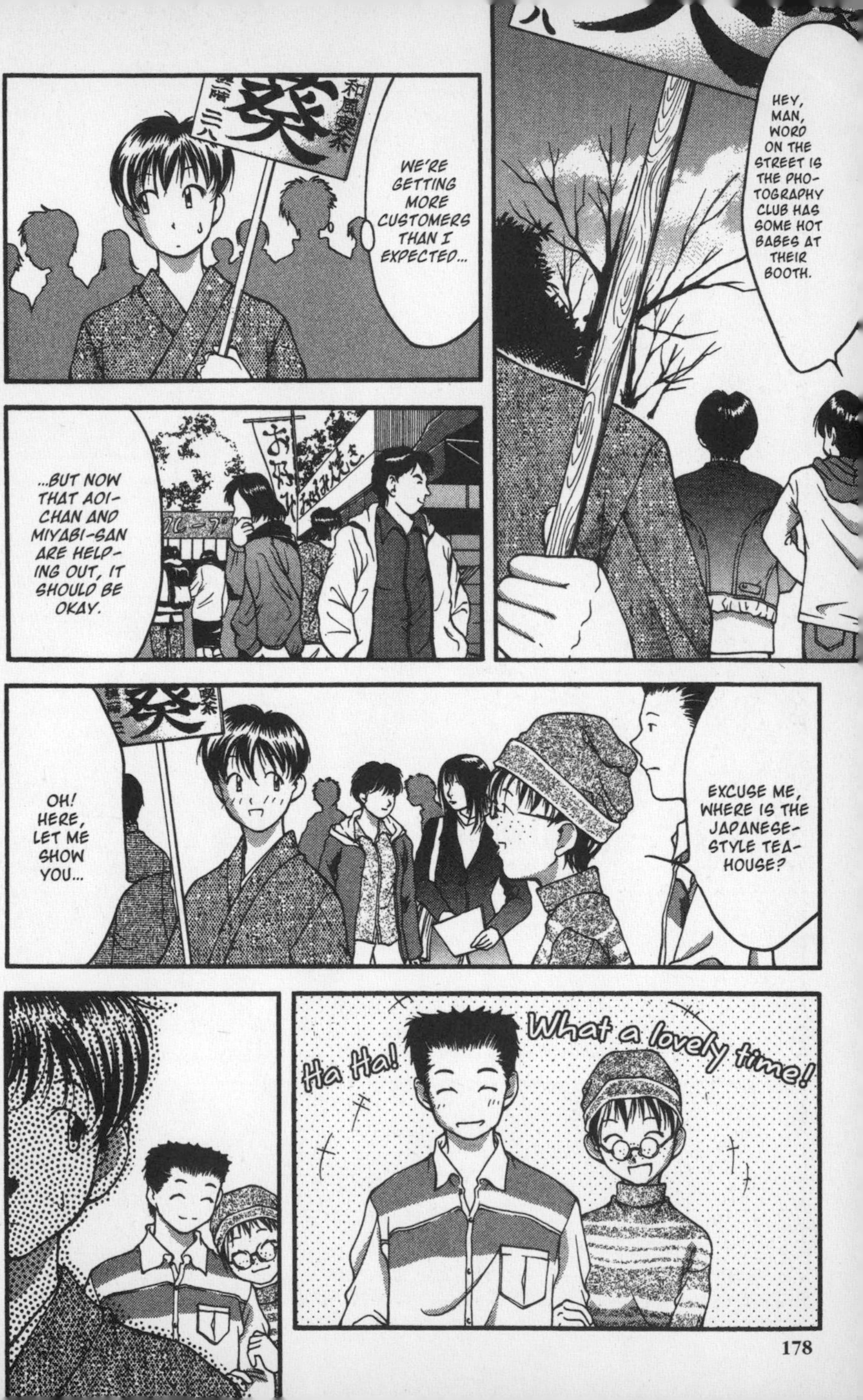
HEY, MAN, WORD ON THE STREET IS THE PHOTOGRAPHY CLUB HAS SOME HOT BABES AT THEIR BOOTH.
WE'RE GETTING MORE CUSTOMERS THAN I EXPECTED...
...BUT NOW THAT AOI-CHAN AND MIYABI-SAN ARE HELPING OUT, IT SHOULD BE OKAY.
EXCUSE ME, WHERE IS THE JAPANESE-STYLE TEA-HOUSE?
OH! HERE, LET ME SHOW YOU...
What a lovely time!
Ha Ha!

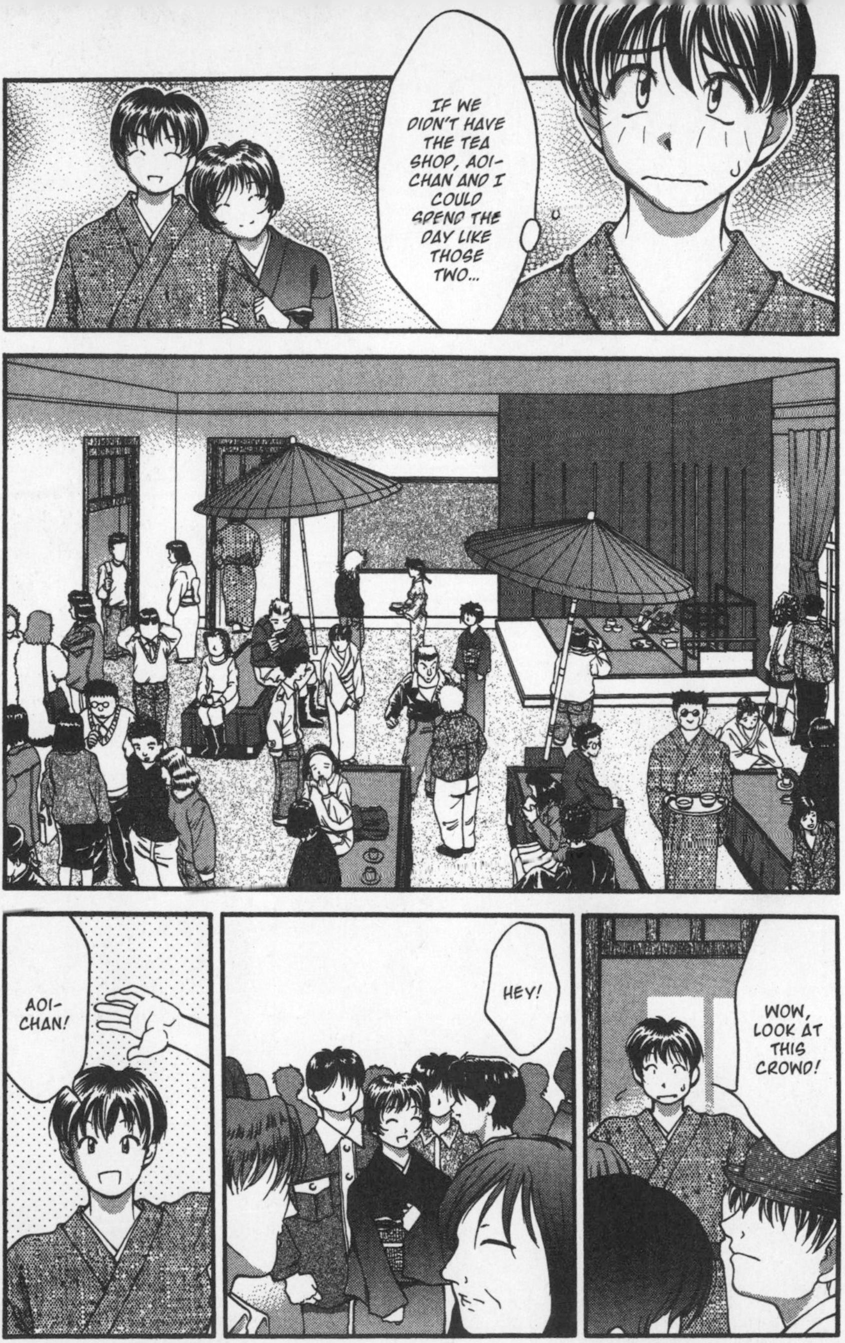
IF WE DIDN'T HAVE THE TEA SHOP, AOI-CHAN AND I COULD SPEND THE DAY LIKE THOSE TWO...
WOW, LOOK AT THIS CROWD!
HEY!
AOI-CHAN!

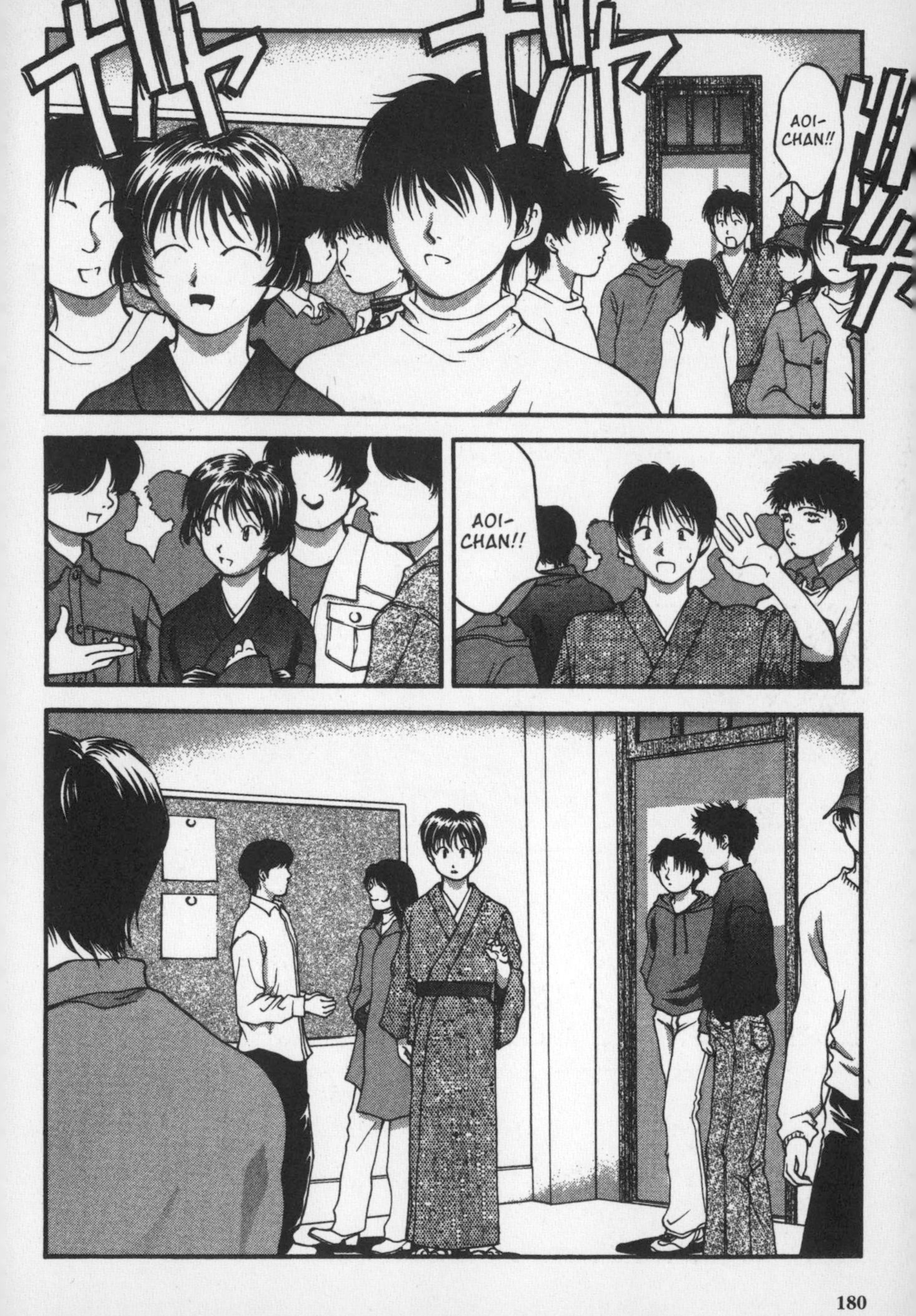
AOI-CHAN!!
AOI-CHAN!!

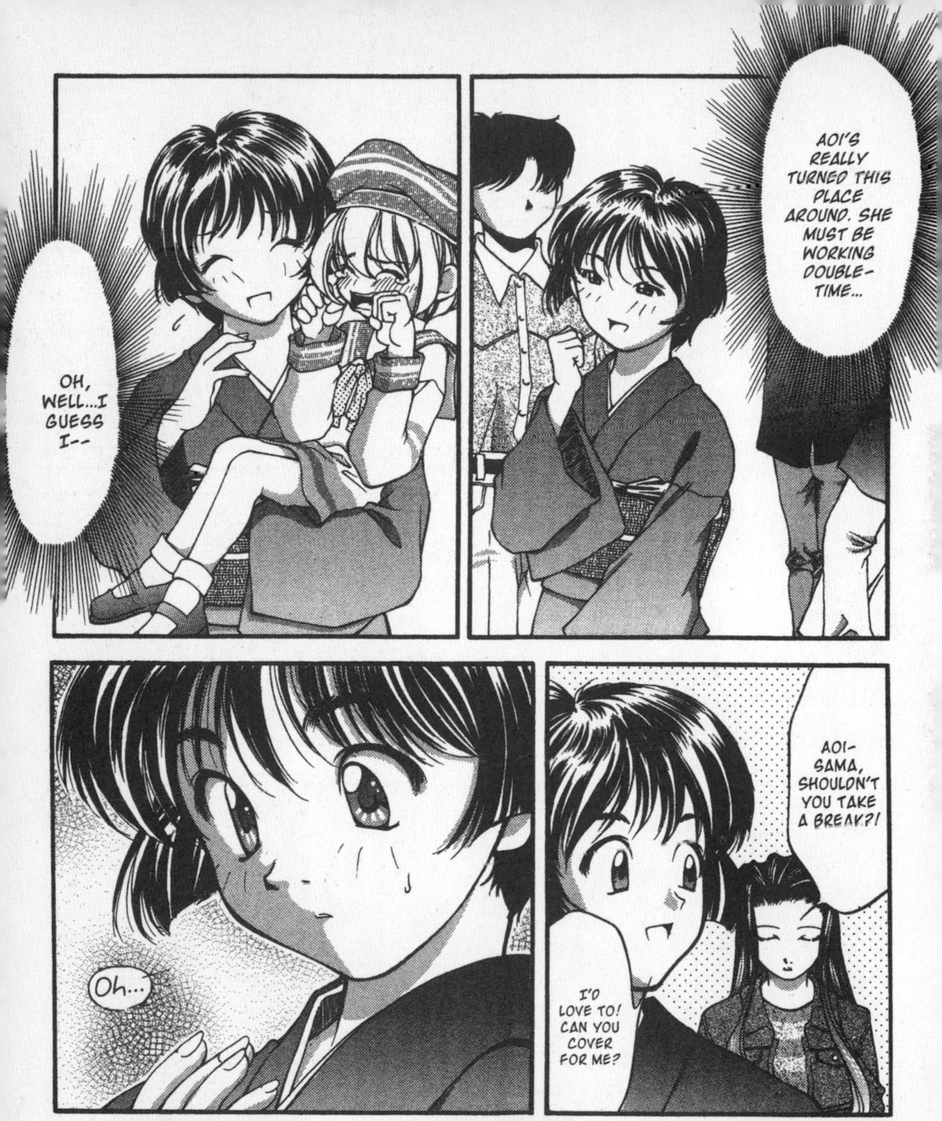
AOI'S REALLY TURNED THIS PLACE AROUND. SHE MUST BE WORKING DOUBLE-TIME...
OH, WELL...I GUESS I--
AOI-SAMA, SHOULDN'T YOU TAKE A BREAK?!
I'D LOVE TO! CAN YOU COVER FOR ME?
Oh...

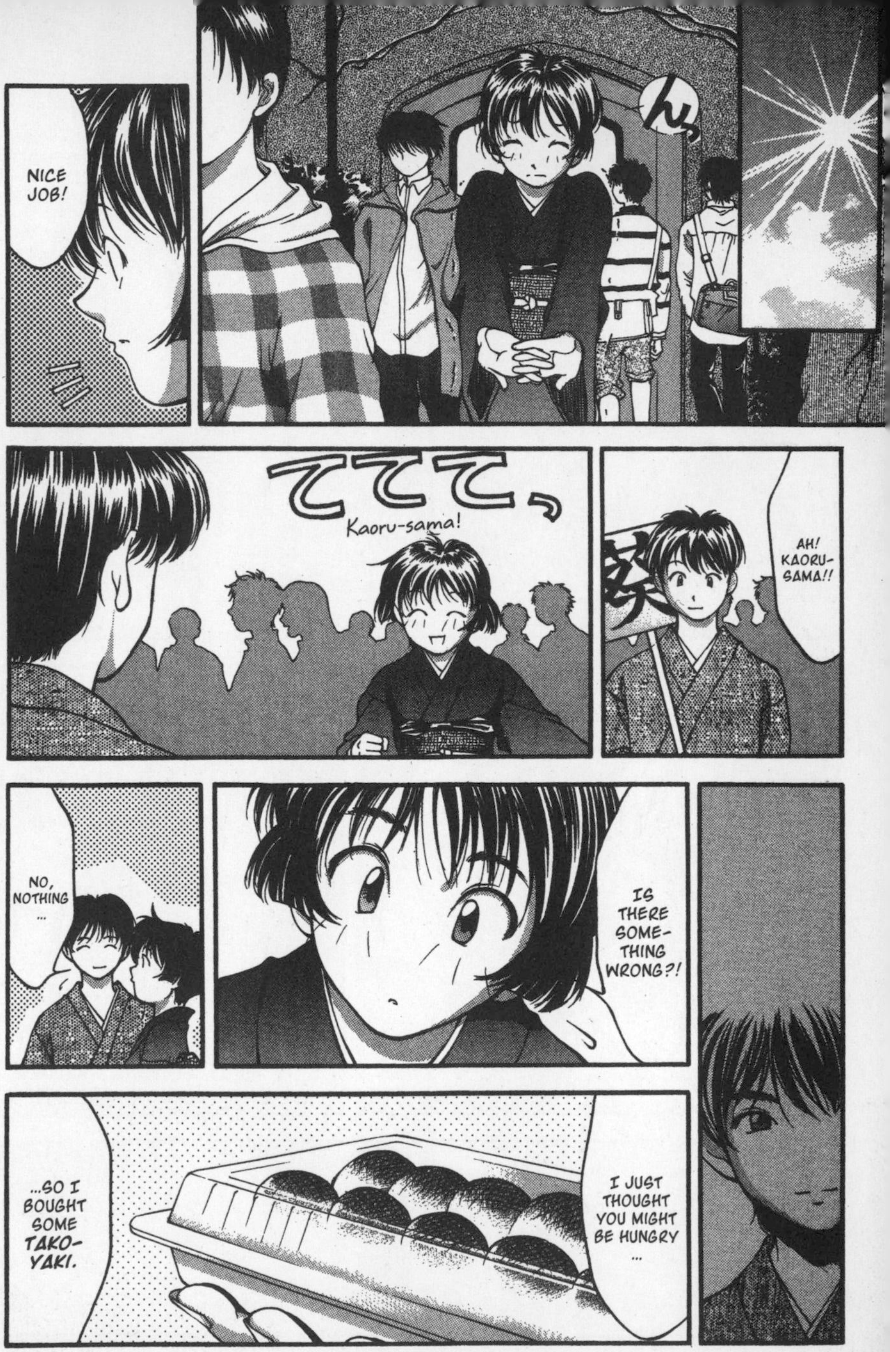
ん
NICE JOB!
てててっ
AH! KAORU-SAMA!!
Kaoru-sama!
IS THERE SOMETHING WRONG?!
NO, NOTHING ...
I JUST THOUGHT YOU MIGHT BE HUNGRY ...
...SO I BOUGHT SOME TAKO-YAKI.

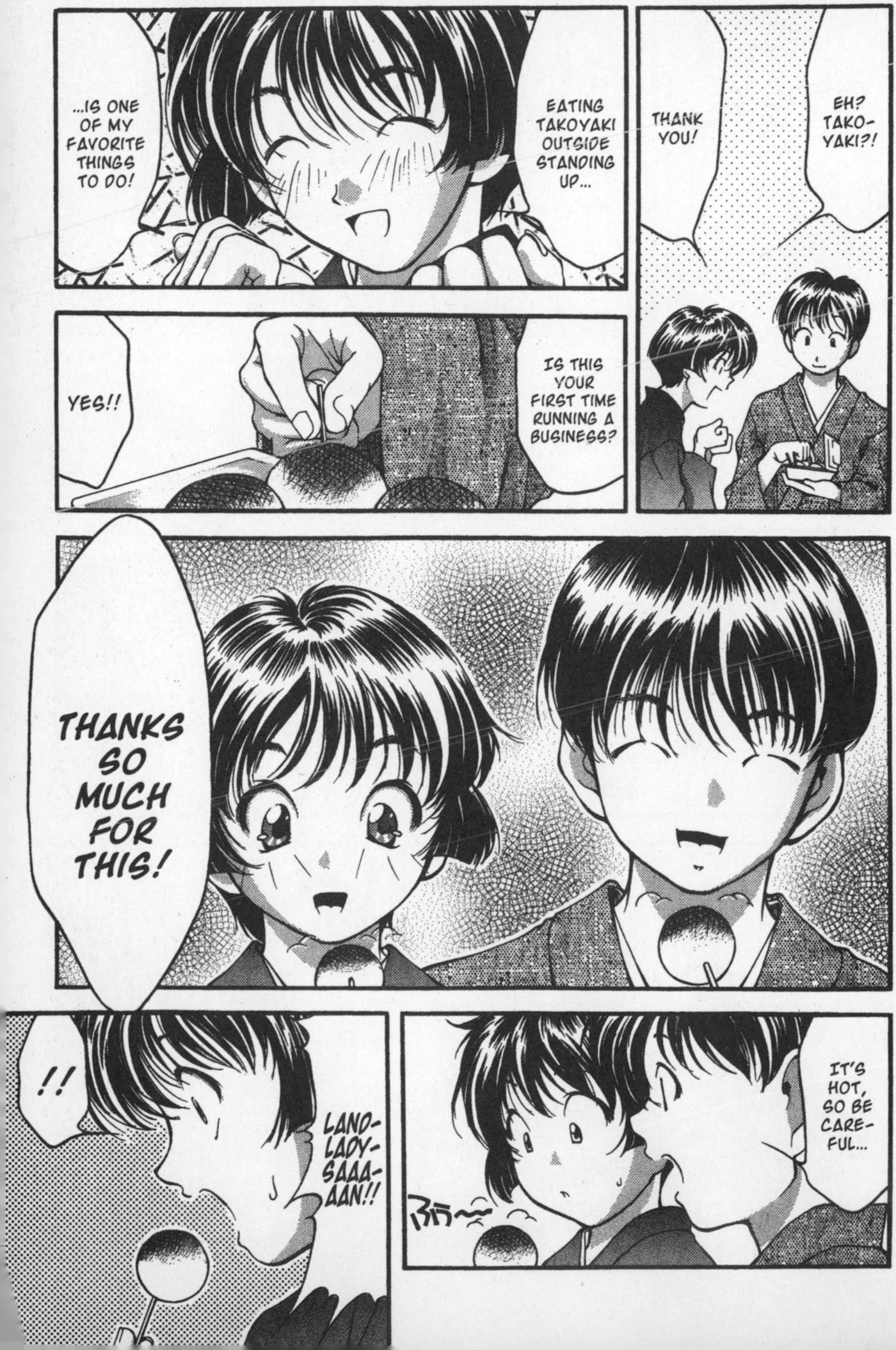
EH? TAKO-YAKI?!
THANK YOU!
EATING TAKOYAKI OUTSIDE STANDING UP...
...IS ONE OF MY FAVORITE THINGS TO DO!
IS THIS YOUR FIRST TIME RUNNING A BUSINESS?
YES!!
THANKS SO MUCH FOR THIS!
IT'S HOT, SO BE CARE-FUL...
LAND-LADY-SAAAA-AAN!!
!!

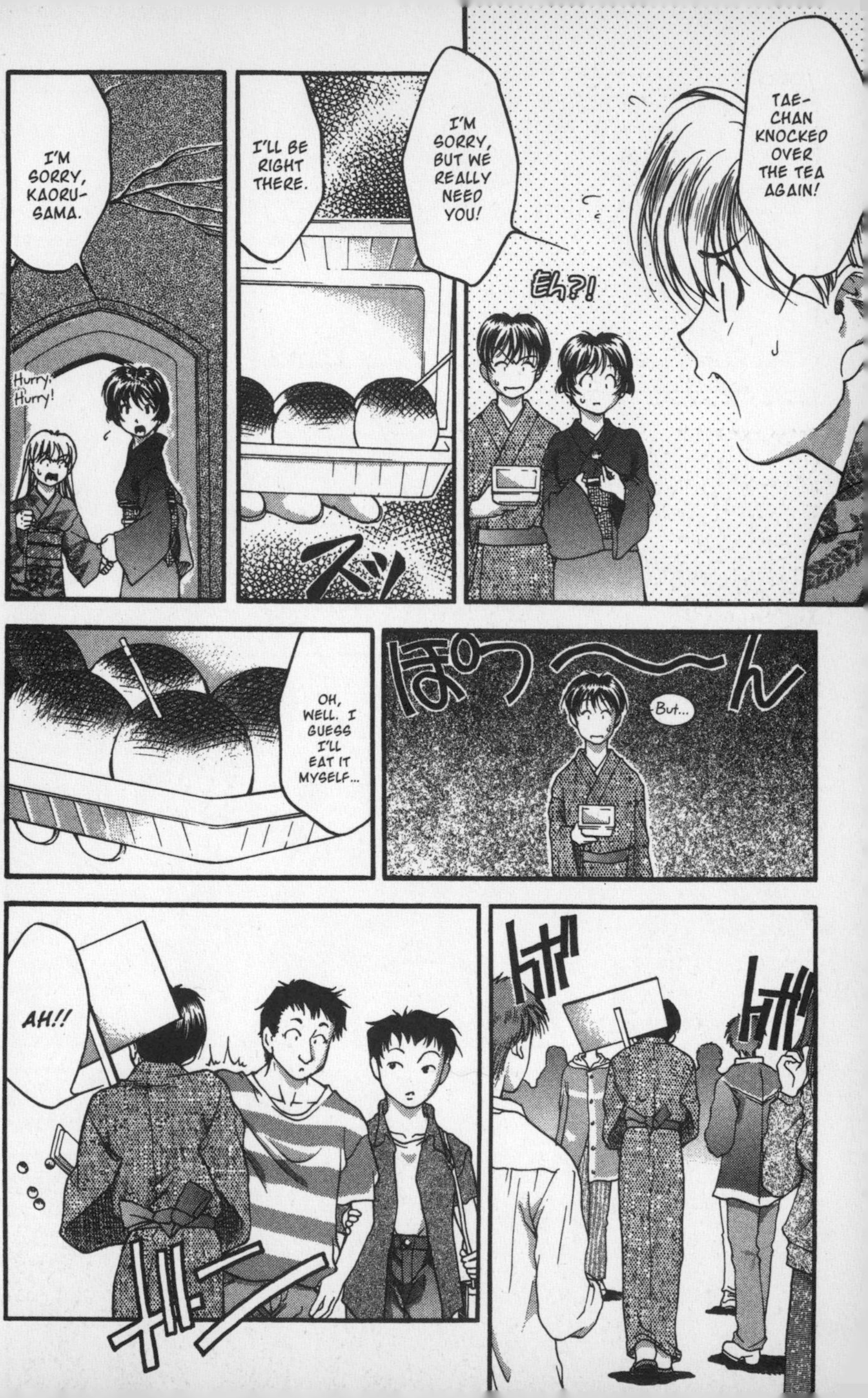
TAE-CHAN KNOCKED OVER THE TEA AGAIN!
I'M SORRY, BUT WE REALLY NEED YOU!
I'LL BE RIGHT THERE.
I'M SORRY, KAORU-SAMA.
Hurry, Hurry!
ぽつ〜ん
But...
OH, WELL. I GUESS I'LL EAT IT MYSELF...
AH!!

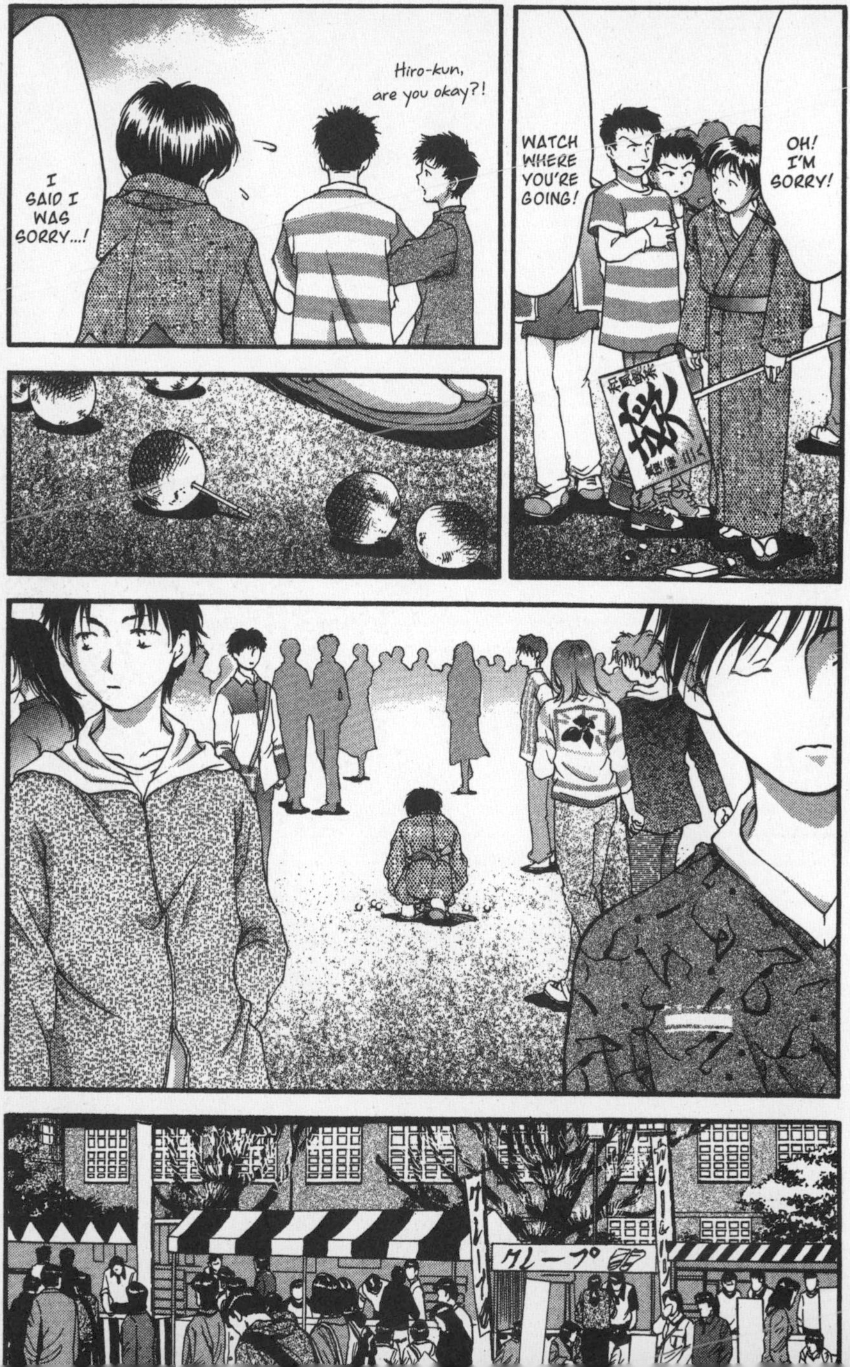
OH! I'M SORRY!
WATCH WHERE YOU'RE GOING!
Hiro-kun, are you okay?!
I SAID I WAS SORRY...!
クレープ

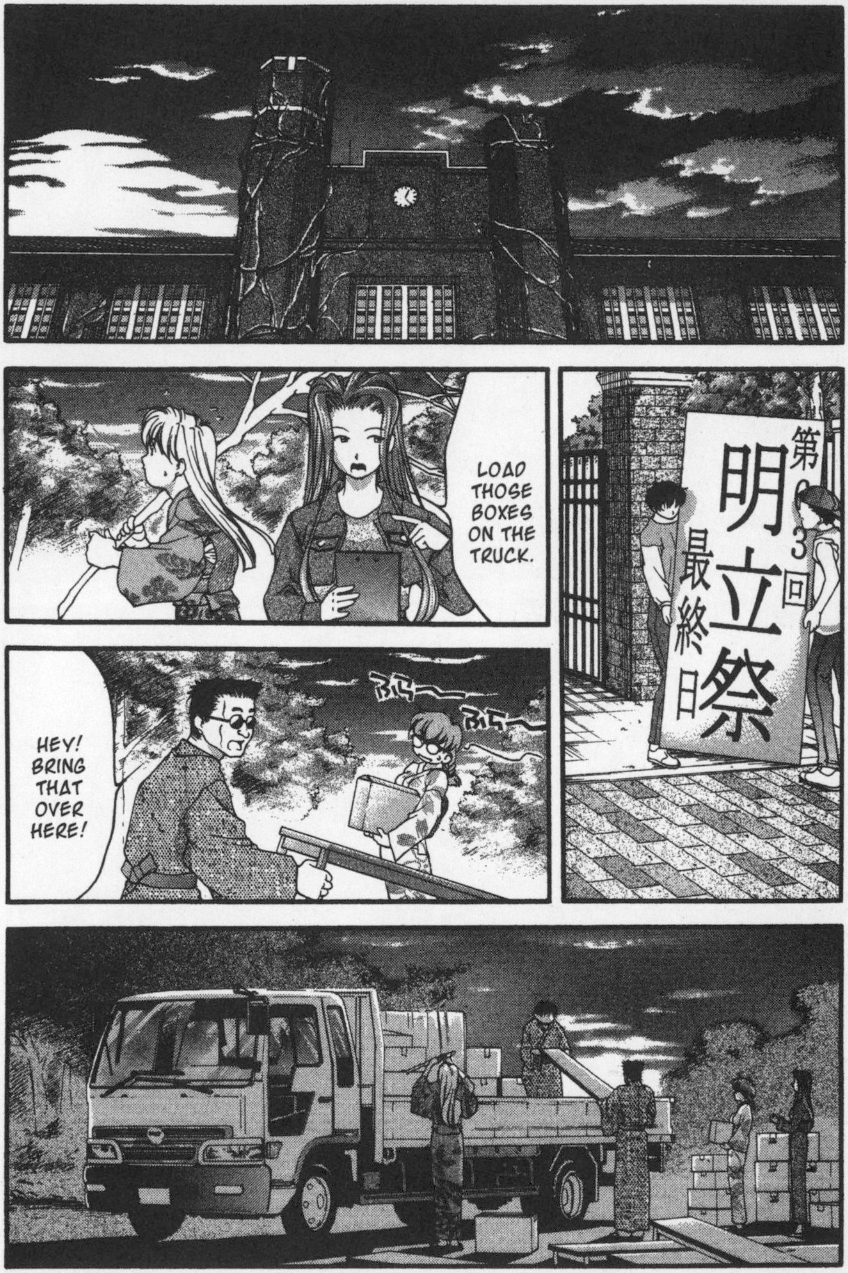
第3回
明立祭
最終日
LOAD THOSE BOXES ON THE TRUCK.
HEY! BRING THAT OVER HERE!

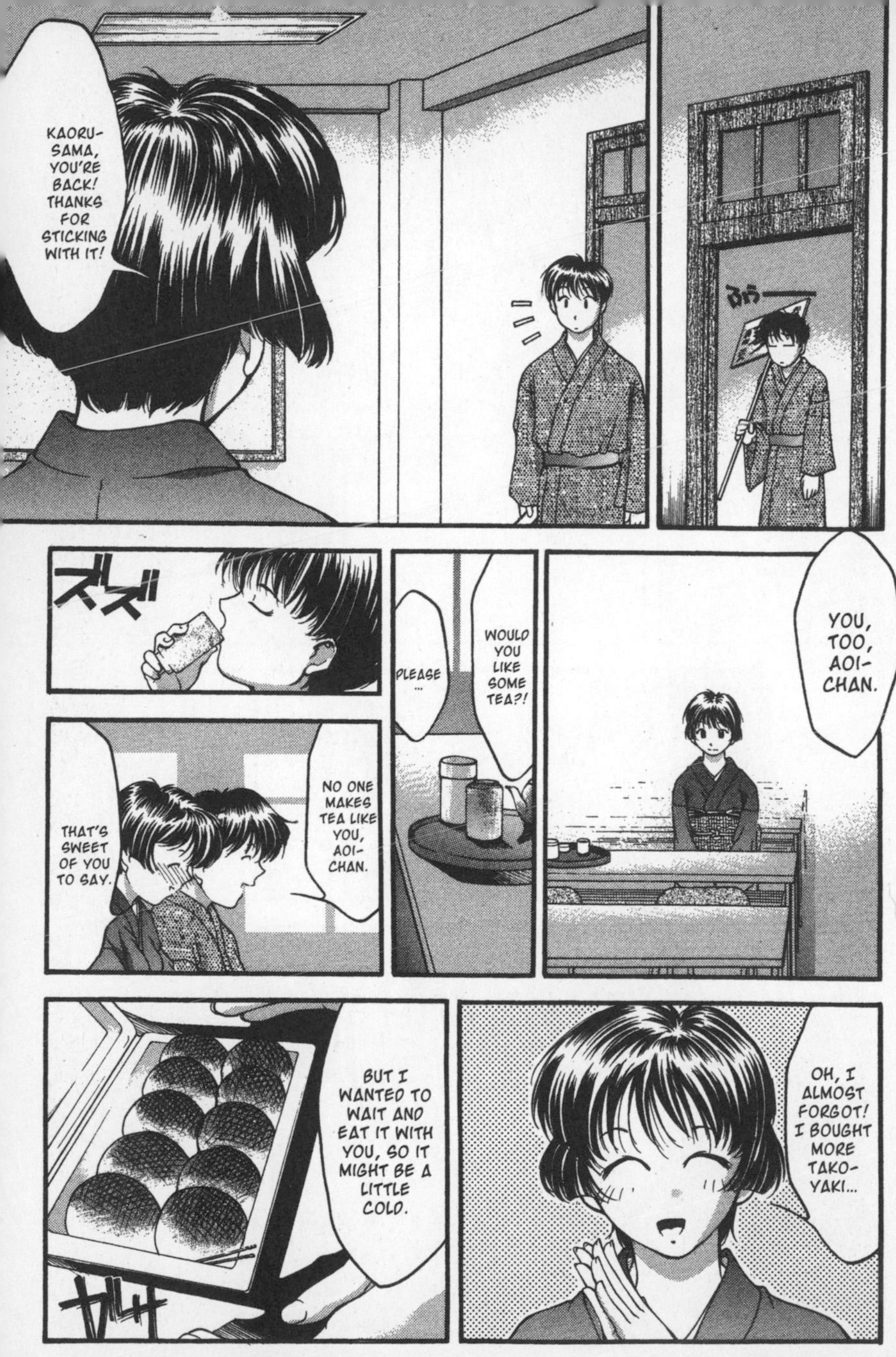
KAORU-SAMA, YOU'RE BACK! THANKS FOR STICKING WITH IT!
YOU, TOO, AOI-CHAN.
WOULD YOU LIKE SOME TEA?!
PLEASE ...
ズズ
NO ONE MAKES TEA LIKE YOU, AOI-CHAN.
THAT'S SWEET OF YOU TO SAY.
OH, I ALMOST FORGOT! I BOUGHT MORE TAKO-YAKI...
BUT I WANTED TO WAIT AND EAT IT WITH YOU, SO IT MIGHT BE A LITTLE COLD.

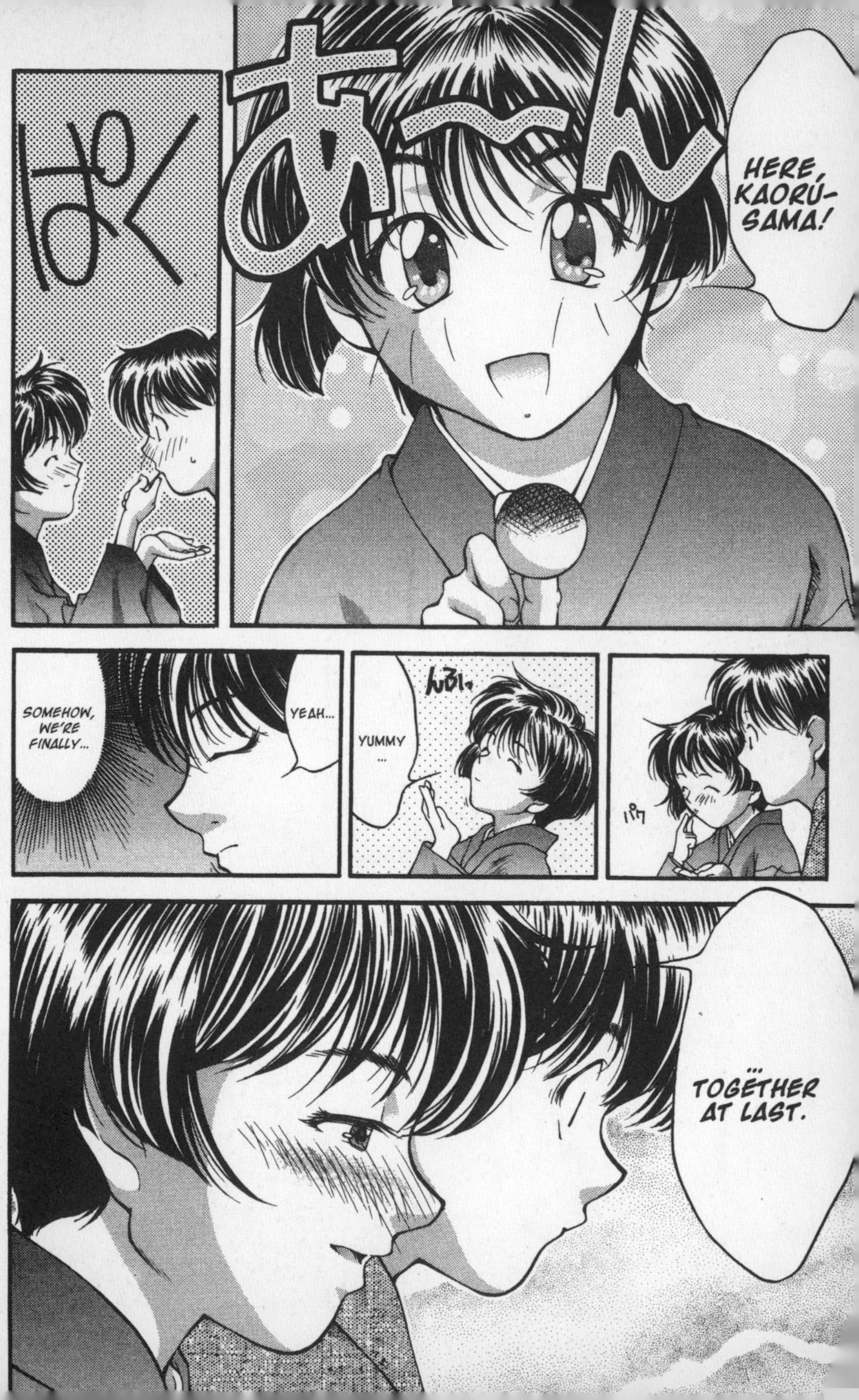
あ〜ん
HERE, KAORU-SAMA!
ぱく
パク
んふっ
YUMMY ...
YEAH...
SOMEHOW, WE'RE FINALLY...
... TOGETHER AT LAST.

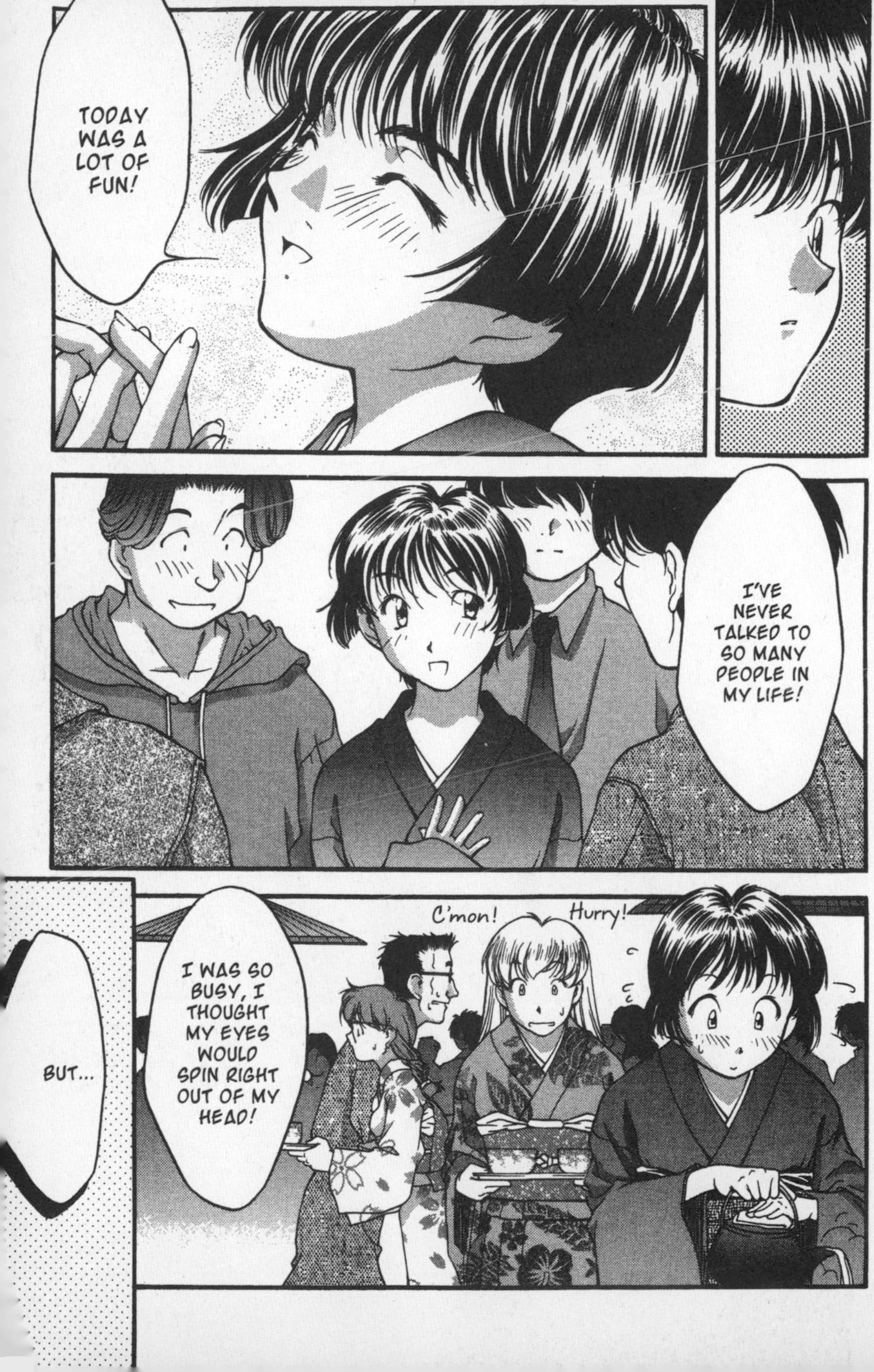
TODAY WAS A LOT OF FUN!
I'VE NEVER TALKED TO SO MANY PEOPLE IN MY LIFE!
Hurry!
C'mon!
I WAS SO BUSY, I THOUGHT MY EYES WOULD SPIN RIGHT OUT OF MY HEAD!
BUT...

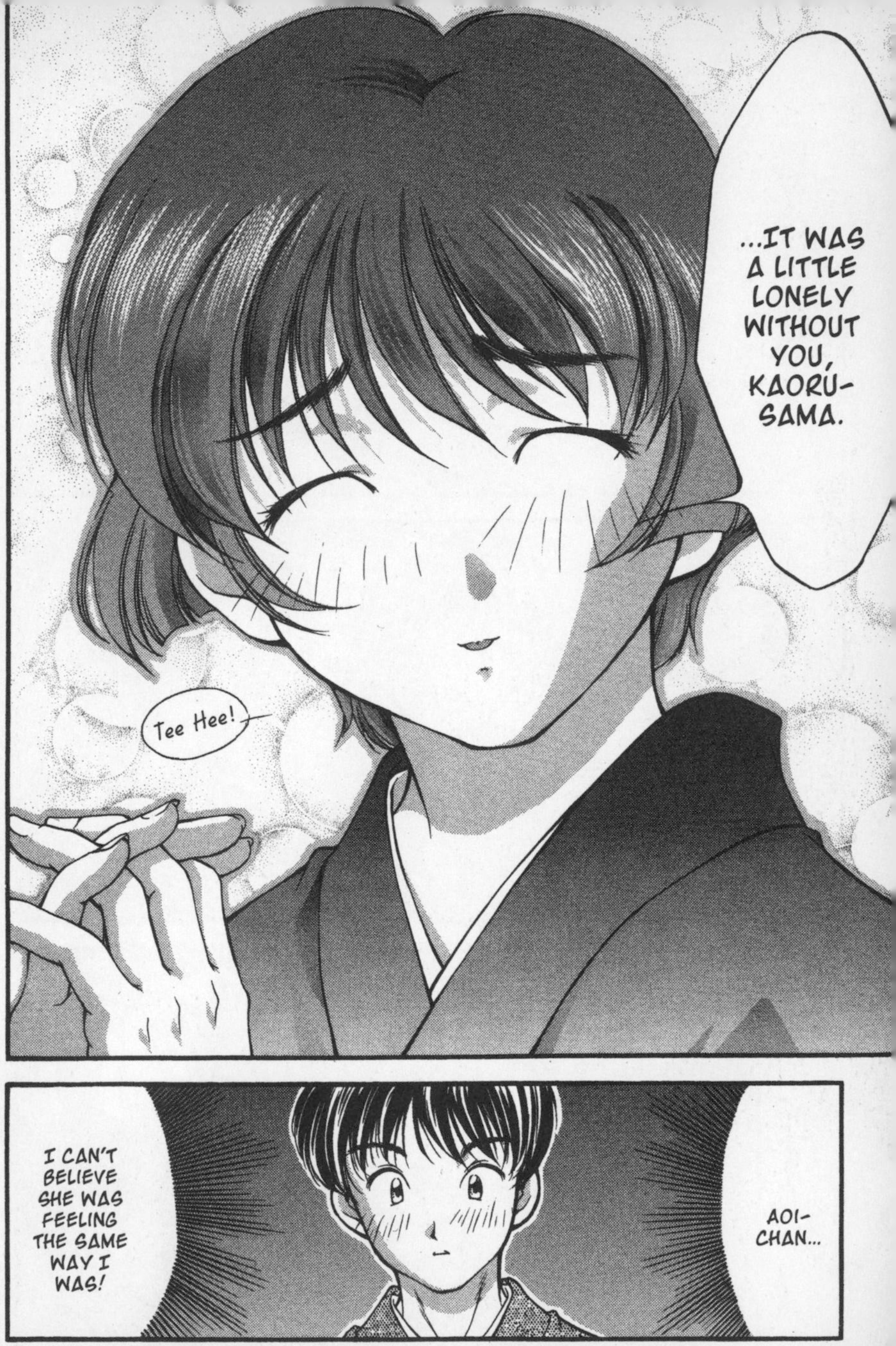
...IT WAS A LITTLE LONELY WITHOUT YOU, KAORU-SAMA.
Tee Hee!
AOI-CHAN...
I CAN'T BELIEVE SHE WAS FEELING THE SAME WAY I WAS!

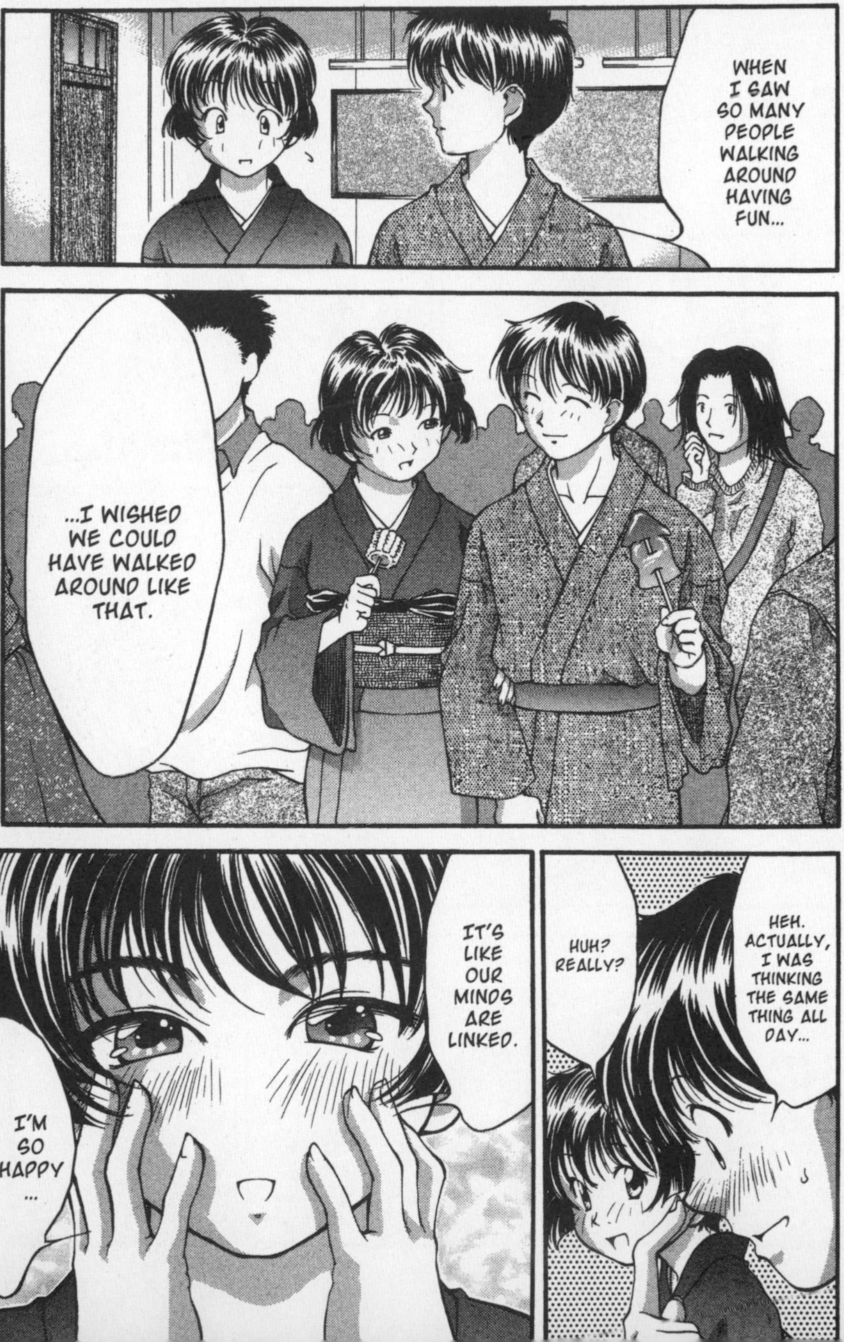
WHEN I SAW SO MANY PEOPLE WALKING AROUND HAVING FUN...
...I WISHED WE COULD HAVE WALKED AROUND LIKE THAT.
HEH. ACTUALLY, I WAS THINKING THE SAME THING ALL DAY...
HUH? REALLY?
IT'S LIKE OUR MINDS ARE LINKED.
I'M SO HAPPY ...

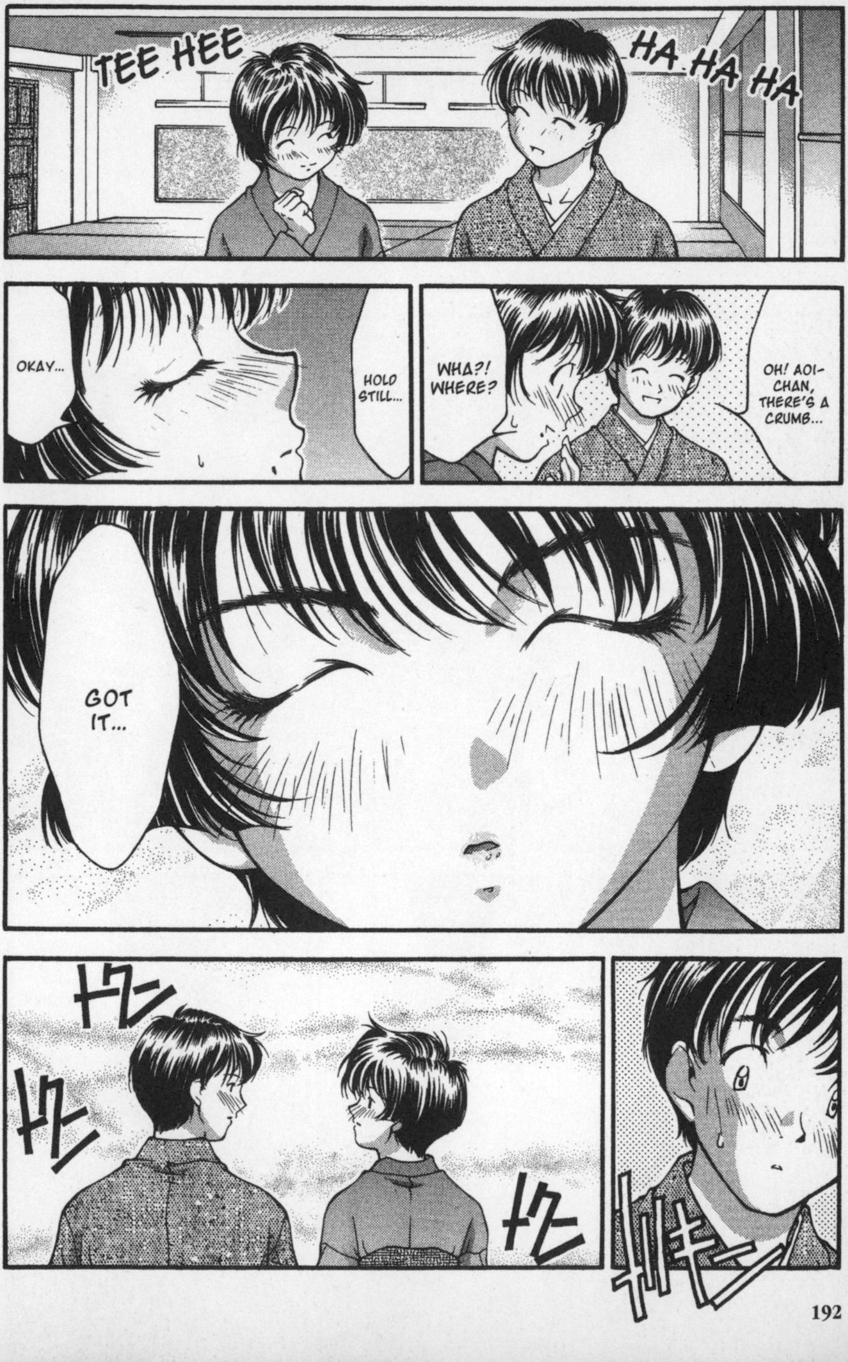
HA HA HA
TEE HEE
OH! AOI-CHAN, THERE'S A CRUMB...
WHA?! WHERE?
HOLD STILL...
OKAY...
GOT IT...
ドキーン
ドクン
ドクン
ドクン

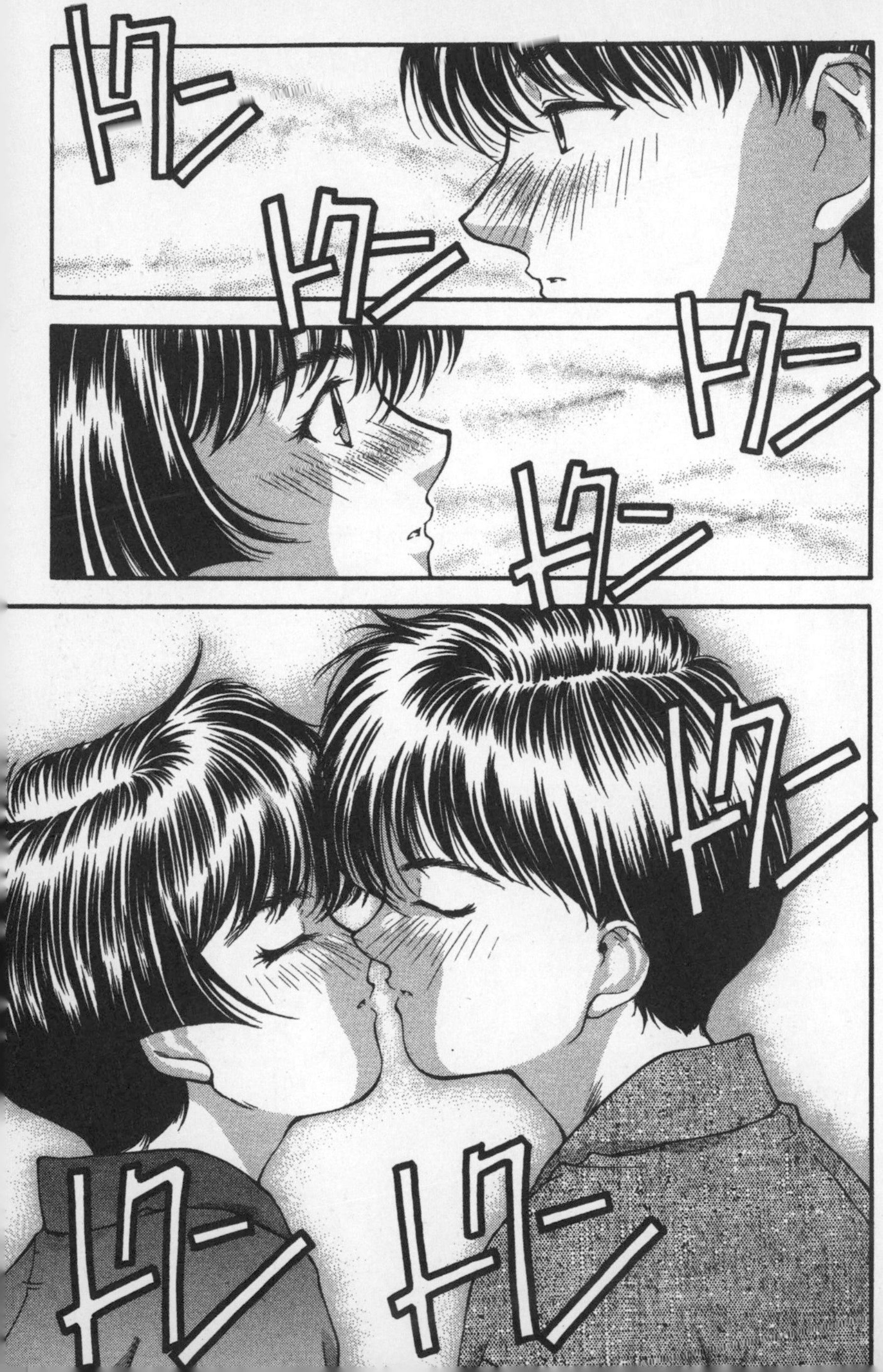
トクーン
トクーン
トクーン
トクーン
トクーン
トクーン
トクーン

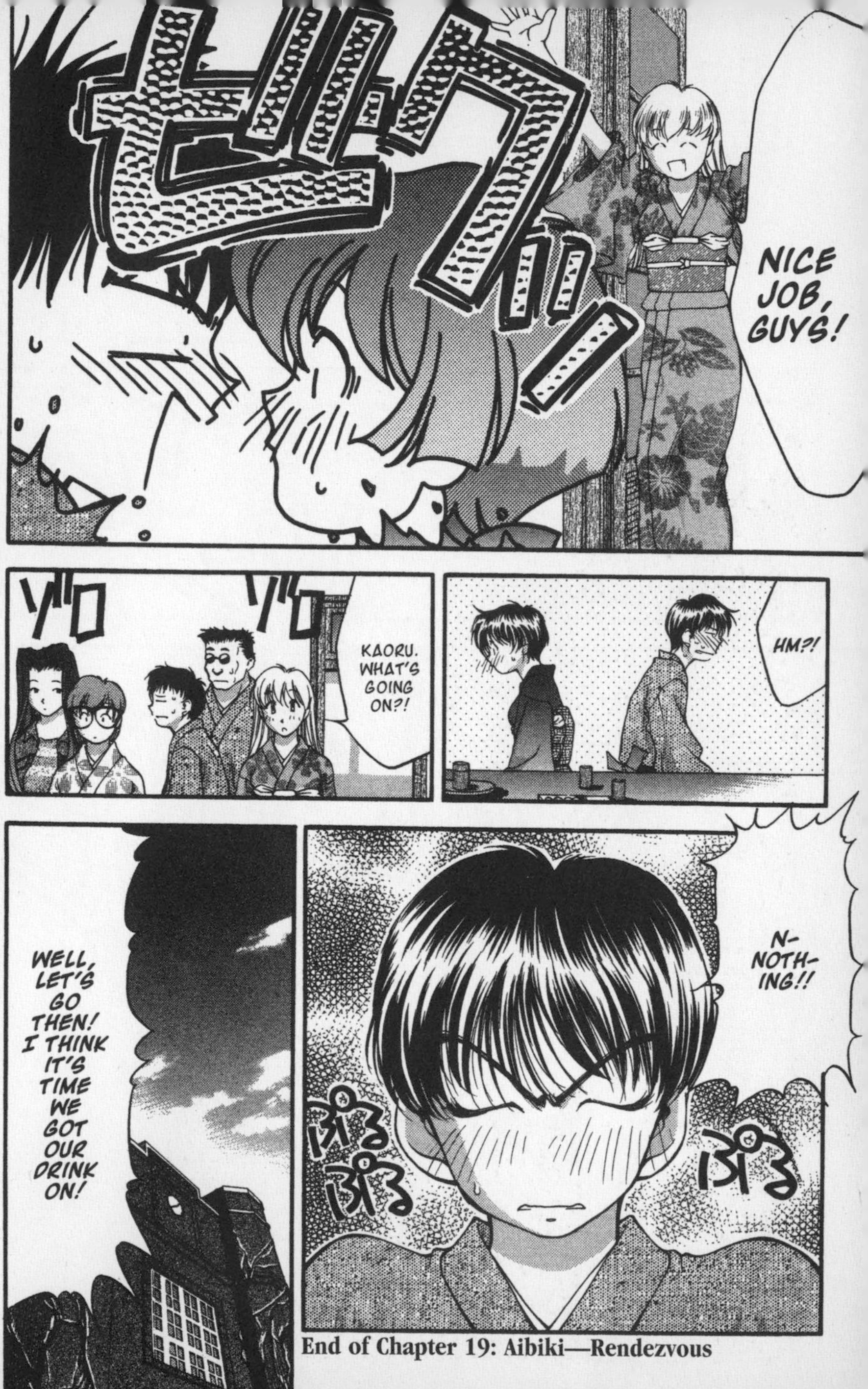
NICE JOB, GUYS!
HM?!
ゾロ
ゾロ
KAORU. WHAT'S GOING ON?!
N- NOTHING!!
ぷる
ぷるぷる
WELL, LET'S GO THEN! I THINK IT'S TIME WE GOT OUR DRINK ON!
End of Chapter 19: Aibiki—Rendezvous

Ai-Ao Theater, Part 4: Tae-chan the Maid

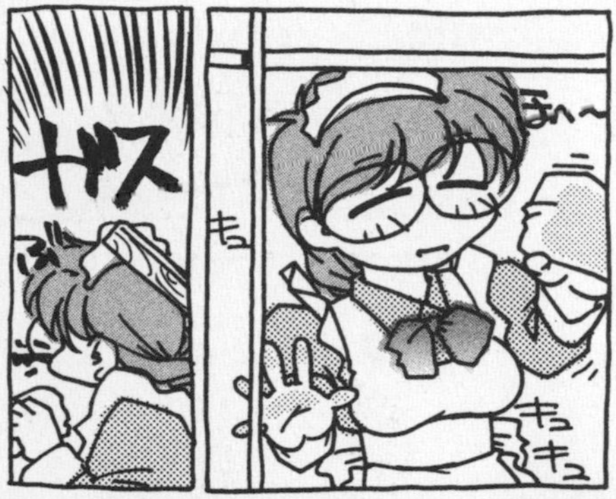
ほへ～
キュ
キュ
キュ

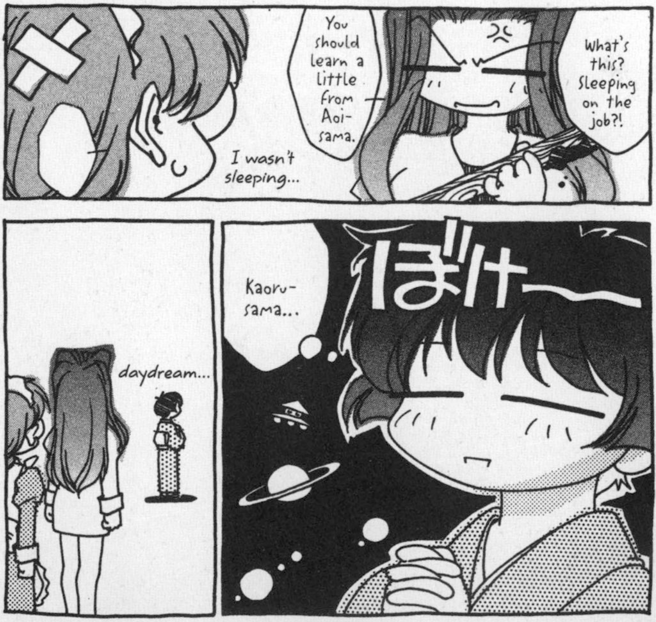
What's this? Sleeping on the job?!
You should learn a little from Aoi-sama.
I wasn't sleeping...
ぽけ～～
Kaoru-sama...
daydream...

Japan Staff

ASSIST

HIDEAKI HATTORI
HIDEKI NODA
HIROAKI SATOU
KAZUHIKO HARU
MASAYUKI KAWANO

THANKS.

MITUKAGE SYOUTENGAI
MIYUKI NARA
OSAMU MIZUTANI
RIE SUZUKI
SCHOOL IZUMI
TETUYA MISAWA

EDITOR

SYOUICHI NAKAZAWA
<HAKUSENSHA>

PRODUCER

KOU FUMIZUKI
<STUDIO LITTLE COTTON>

NEXT TIME IN

藍より青し
AI YORI AOSHI™

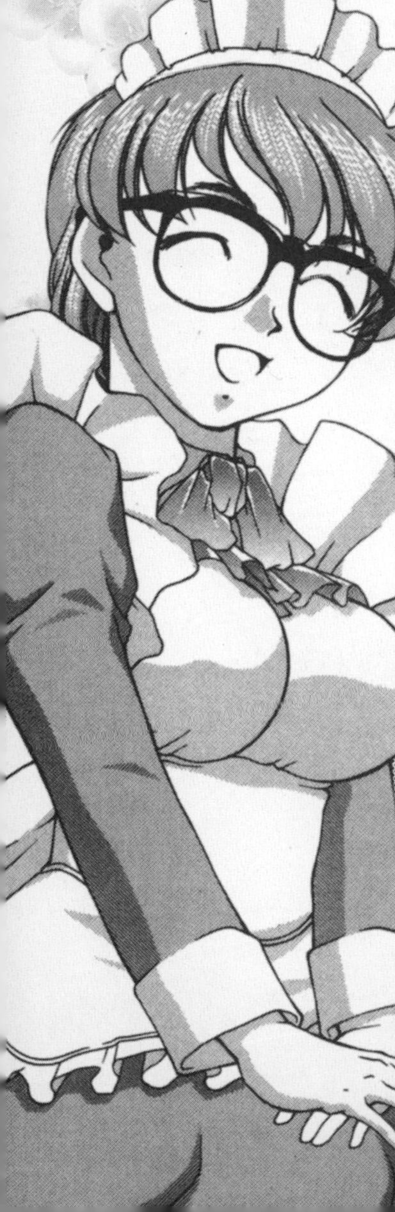

It's Christmas time at the Sakuraba boarding house, and Santa's belly isn't the only thing shaking like a bowlful of jelly. Can Kaoru slip away from the festivities long enough to spend some quality time under the mistletoe with Aoi?

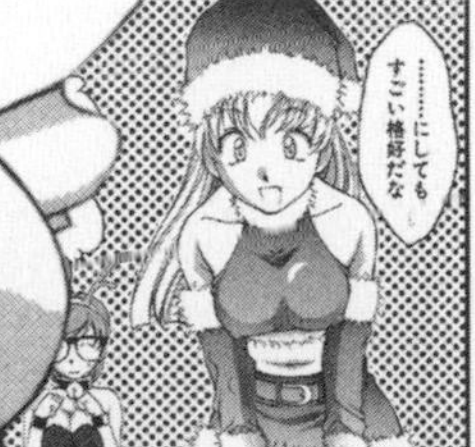
……にしても
すごい格好だな

Ai Yori Aoshi 3—
Available May 2004.

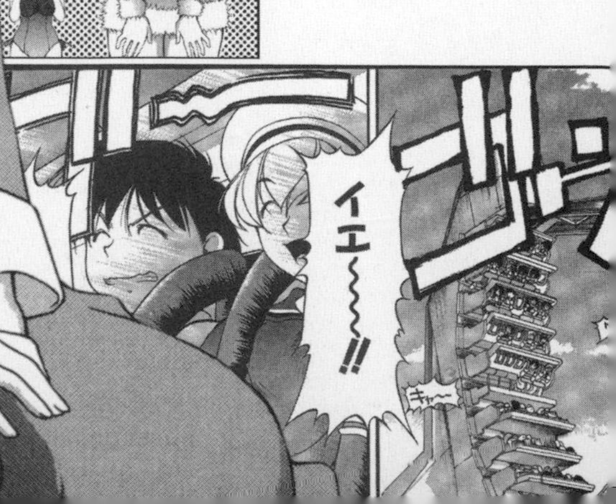
イエ〜〜〜!!
キャ〜

GLOSSARY

Tatami Mats

In Japan, floors are often covered with mats made of reeds called *tatami*. *Tatami* are so common in Japan that room sizes are measured by the number of *tatami* mats it would take to fill them. Each mat is approximately 3' x 6' in size. Kaoru's 6 *tatami* mat room is a pretty typical size for a studio apartment.

Yukata

A light, single-layered summer kimono worn by men and women. They are commonly associated with vacation resorts and hot springs.

Takoyaki

A Japanese street food of the Kansai area (southern Japan), *takoyaki* consists of bits of octopus, grilled in ball-shaped molds with a pancake-like batter. Chewy, flavorful and easy to eat, they've become a favorite dish at street fairs and cultural festivals throughout Japan.

The Way of Tea

As Tina so bluntly points out, tea ("*cha*" in Japanese) is more than just a beverage to the Japanese people—it is a way of life. Nowhere is this more apparent than in the Tea Ceremony. Traditional tea preparation and presentation is steeped in many formalities and rituals; so much so, that the serving of tea can quite literally be a religious act. The Way of Tea is based on the concepts of Harmony, Respect, Purity and Tranquility, and the complex ceremonies involved can last for four hours or more. In these modern times, the rituals of tea-making may have largely been replaced by teabags and bottled drinks, but the traditions live on and are celebrated as an important part of Japanese heritage.

Preparing Tea at Home

There are entire volumes dedicated to the rituals and nuances of Japanese tea, but if you are interested in preparing Japanese tea at home, here are the basic tools:

Matcha
The finely ground Japanese green tea powder used in the Tea Ceremony. *Matcha* is made from only the best leaves from the first days of harvest. It's stored in a tightly sealed tin called a *chazutsu*. *Matcha* is much more expensive than the teas most Westerners are accustomed to.

Tetsubin
Teapot. As an open pot and ladle might be impractical for casual tea preparation, the "modern" *tetsubin* is an acceptable alternative.

Chawan
The ceremonial bowl in which the *matcha* is stirred and from which the thick tea is served.

Chashaku
The bamboo scoop used to remove a serving size of matcha from the *chazutsu*.

Chasen
The bamboo whisk used to stir the *matcha*.

Chakin
The cloth used to wipe off teacups before serving.

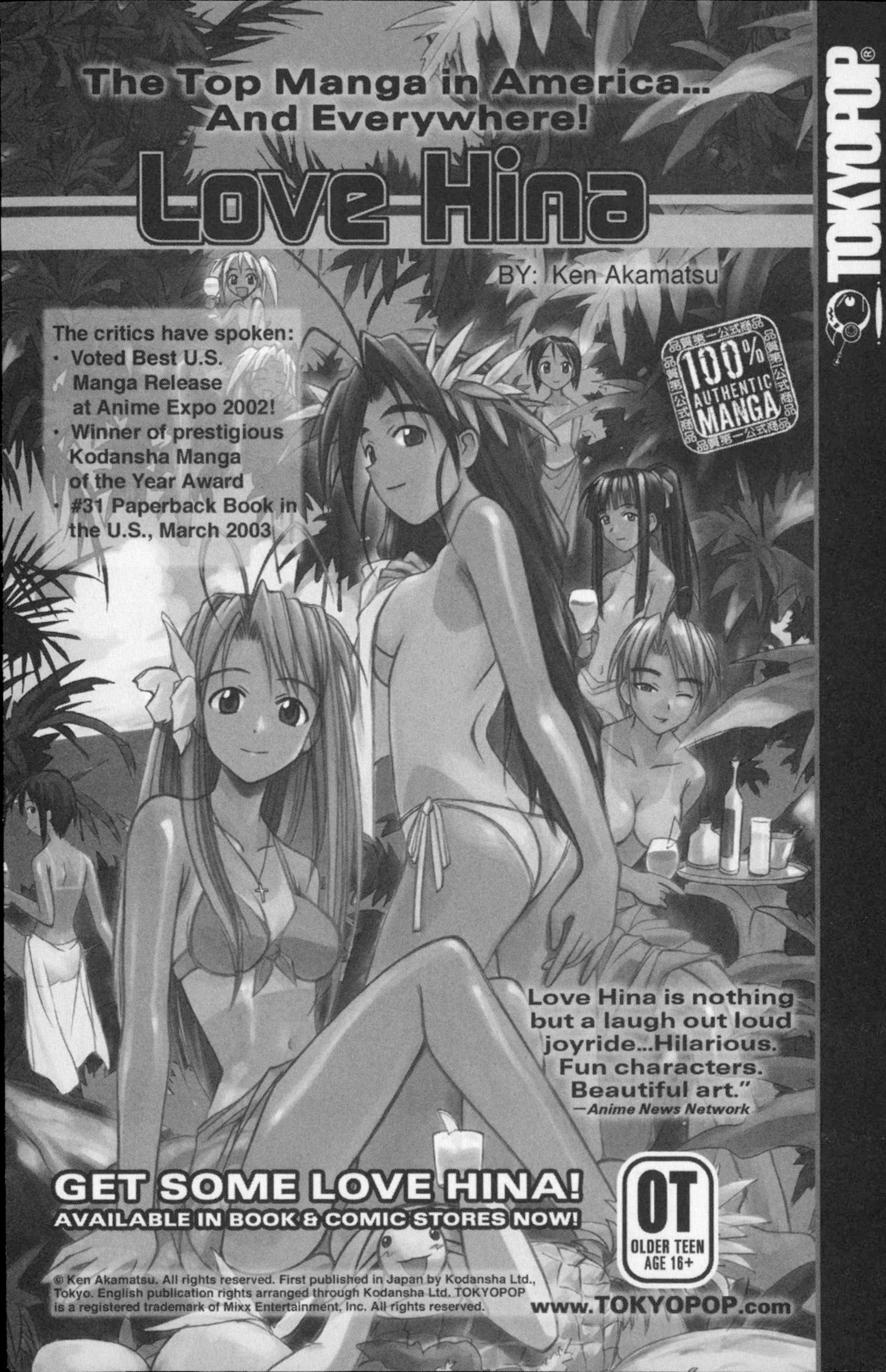
The Top Manga in America...
And Everywhere!
Love Hina
BY: Ken Akamatsu
The critics have spoken:
• Voted Best U.S. Manga Release at Anime Expo 2002!
• Winner of prestigious Kodansha Manga of the Year Award
• #31 Paperback Book in the U.S., March 2003
100% AUTHENTIC MANGA
品質第一公式商品
Love Hina is nothing but a laugh out loud joyride...Hilarious. Fun characters. Beautiful art."
—Anime News Network
GET SOME LOVE HINA!
AVAILABLE IN BOOK & COMIC STORES NOW!
OT
OLDER TEEN AGE 16+
© Ken Akamatsu. All rights reserved. First published in Japan by Kodansha Ltd., Tokyo. English publication rights arranged through Kodansha Ltd. TOKYOPOP is a registered trademark of Mixx Entertainment, Inc. All rights reserved.
www.TOKYOPOP.com
TOKYOPOP®

LAMENT OF THE LAMB ™

SHE CAN PROTECT HER BROTHER FROM THE WORLD.
CAN SHE PROTECT THE WORLD FROM HER BROTHER?

Available May 2004 at your favorite book and comic stores.

OT
OLDER TEEN
AGE 16+

© 2002 Touma Kei, GENTOSHA COMICS

www.TOKYOPOP.com

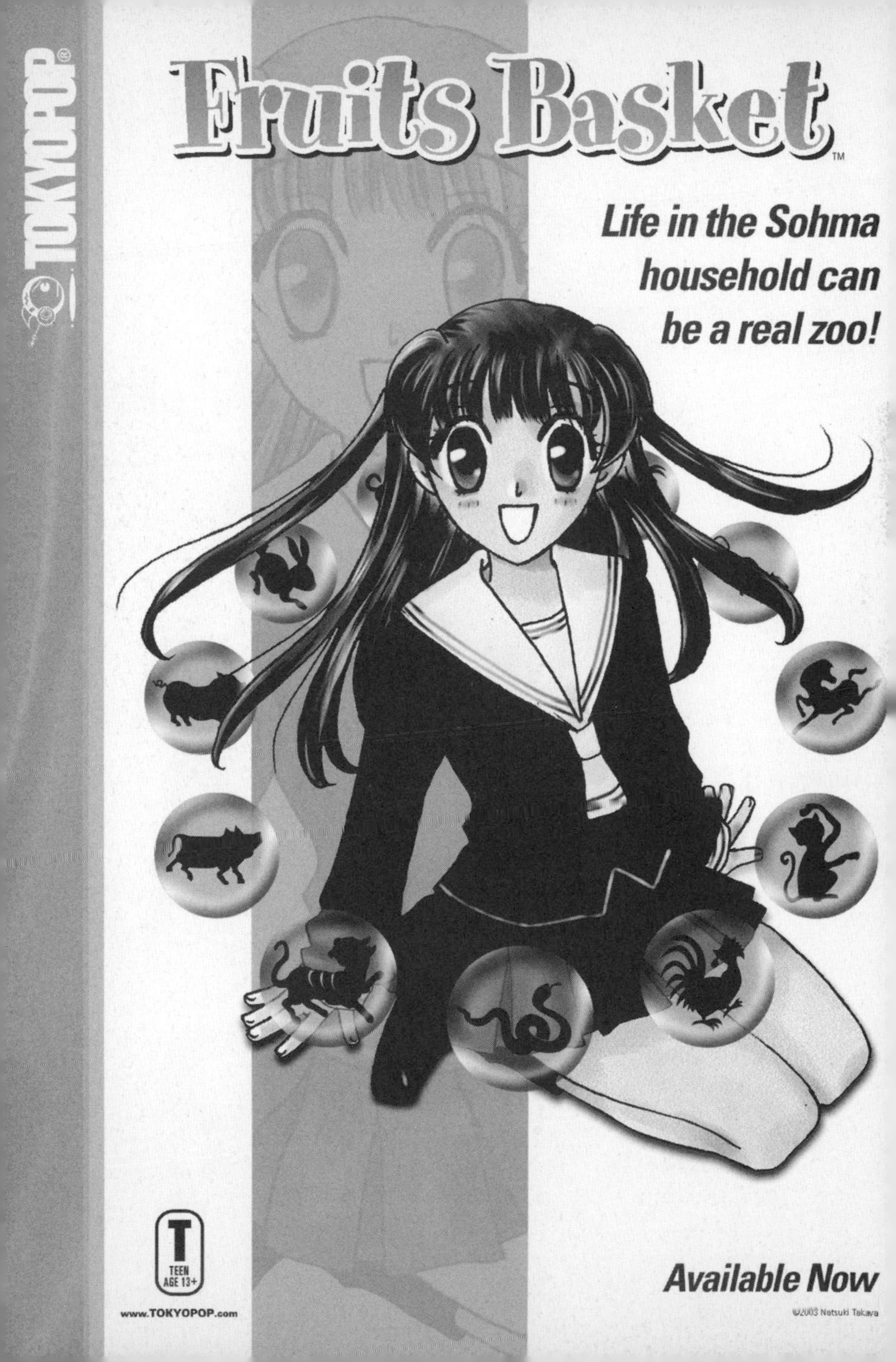
TOKYOPOP
Fruits Basket™
Life in the Sohma household can be a real zoo!
T
TEEN AGE 13+
www.TOKYOPOP.com
Available Now
©2003 Natsuki Takaya

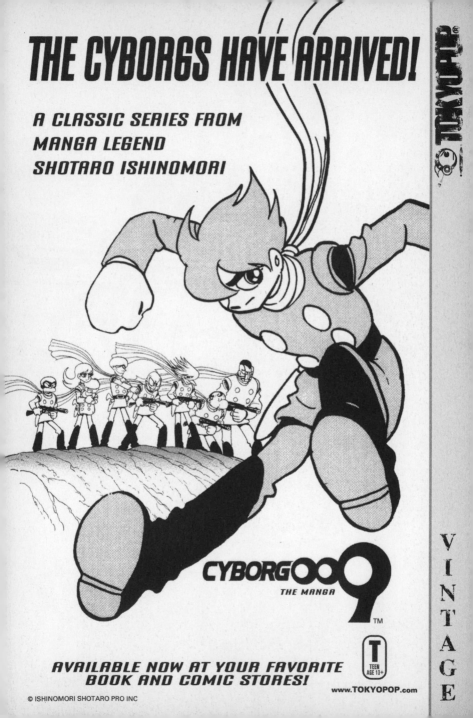

ALSO AVAILABLE FROM ✪TOKYOPOP®

REBOUND
REMOTE
RISING STARS OF MANGA
SABER MARIONETTE J
SAILOR MOON
SAINT TAIL
SAMURAI DEEPER KYO
SAMURAI GIRL REAL BOUT HIGH SCHOOL
SCRYED
SEIKAI TRILOGY, THE CREST OF THE STARS
SGT. FROG
SHAOLIN SISTERS
SHIRAHIME-SYO: SNOW GODDESS TALES
SHUTTERBOX
SKULL MAN, THE
SNOW DROP
SORCERER HUNTERS
STONE
SUIKODEN III
SUKI
TOKYO BABYLON
TOKYO MEW MEW
UNDER THE GLASS MOON
VAMPIRE GAME
VISION OF ESCAFLOWNE, THE
WILD ACT
WISH
WORLD OF HARTZ
X-DAY
ZODIAC P.I.

NOVELS

KARMA CLUB
SAILOR MOON

ART BOOKS

CARDCAPTOR SAKURA
CLAMP NORTHSIDE
CLAMP SOUTHSIDE
MAGIC KNIGHT RAYEARTH
PEACH: MIWA UEDA ILLUSTRATIONS

ANIME GUIDES

COWBOY BEBOP ANIME GUIDES
GUNDAM TECHNICAL MANUALS
SAILOR MOON SCOUT GUIDES

TOKYOPOP KIDS

STRAY SHEEP

CINE-MANGA™

ASTRO BOY
CARDCAPTORS
DUEL MASTERS
FAIRLY ODDPARENTS, THE
FINDING NEMO
G.I. JOE SPY TROOPS
JACKIE CHAN ADVENTURES
JIMMY NEUTRON BOY GENIUS, THE ADVENTURES OF
KIM POSSIBLE
LILO & STITCH
LIZZIE MCGUIRE
LIZZIE MCGUIRE: THE MOVIE
MALCOLM IN THE MIDDLE
POWER RANGERS: NINJA STORM
SHREK 2
SPONGEBOB SQUAREPANTS
SPY KIDS 2
SPY KIDS 3-D: GAME OVER
TEENAGE MUTANT NINJA TURTLES
THAT'S SO RAVEN
TRANSFORMERS: ARMADA
TRANSFORMERS: ENERGON

For more
information visit
www.TOKYOPOP.com

01.09.04T

ALSO AVAILABLE FROM 🐾TOKYOPOP®

MANGA

.HACK//LEGEND OF THE TWILIGHT
@LARGE
ABENOBASHI
A.I. LOVE YOU
AI YORI AOSHI
ANGELIC LAYER
ARM OF KANNON
BABY BIRTH
BATTLE ROYALE
BATTLE VIXENS
BRAIN POWERED
BRIGADOON
B'TX
CANDIDATE FOR GODDESS, THE
CARDCAPTOR SAKURA
CARDCAPTOR SAKURA - MASTER OF THE CLOW
CHOBITS
CHRONICLES OF THE CURSED SWORD
CLAMP SCHOOL DETECTIVES
CLOVER
COMIC PARTY
CONFIDENTIAL CONFESSIONS
CORRECTOR YUI
COWBOY BEBOP
COWBOY BEBOP: SHOOTING STAR
CRESCENT MOON
CULDCEPT
CYBORG 009
D.N. ANGEL
DEMON DIARY
DEMON ORORON, THE
DEUS VITAE
DIGIMON
DIGIMON ZERO TWO
DIGIMON TAMERS
DOLL
DRAGON HUNTER
DRAGON KNIGHTS
DREAM SAGA
DUKLYON: CLAMP SCHOOL DEFENDERS
ERICA SAKURAZAWA COLLECTED WORKS
EERIE QUEERIE!
ET CETERA
ETERNITY
EVIL'S RETURN
FAERIES' LANDING
FAKE
FLCL
FORBIDDEN DANCE
FRUITS BASKET
G GUNDAM
GATE KEEPERS

GETBACKERS
GIRL GOT GAME
GRAVITATION
GTO
GUNDAM SEED ASTRAY
GUNDAM WING
GUNDAM WING: BATTLEFIELD OF PACIFISTS
GUNDAM WING: ENDLESS WALTZ
GUNDAM WING: THE LAST OUTPOST (G-UNIT)
HAPPY MANIA
HARLEM BEAT
I.N.V.U.
IMMORTAL RAIN
INITIAL D
ISLAND
JING: KING OF BANDITS
JULINE
KARE KANO
KILL ME, KISS ME
KINDAICHI CASE FILES, THE
KING OF HELL
KODOCHA: SANA'S STAGE
LAMENT OF THE LAMB
LES BIJOUX
LEGEND OF CHUN HYANG, THE
LOVE HINA
LUPIN III
MAGIC KNIGHT RAYEARTH I
MAGIC KNIGHT RAYEARTH II
MAHOROMATIC: AUTOMATIC MAIDEN
MAN OF MANY FACES
MARMALADE BOY
MARS
MINK
MIRACLE GIRLS
MIYUKI-CHAN IN WONDERLAND
MODEL
ONE
PARADISE KISS
PARASYTE
PEACH GIRL
PEACH GIRL: CHANGE OF HEART
PET SHOP OF HORRORS
PITA-TEN
PLANET LADDER
PLANETES
PRIEST
PRINCESS AI
PSYCHIC ACADEMY
RAGNAROK
RAVE MASTER
REALITY CHECK
REBIRTH

01.09.04T

STOP!

Sumimasen! In your haste, you have opened to the back of the book. It would be most unfortunate if you were to start reading from this point. Perhaps you are new to TOKYOPOP's 100% authentic format? You see, in Japan, pages and panels read from right-to-left, and in respect for the manga-ka, TOKYOPOP keeps this format intact in its translated manga. At first it might feel bizarre reading like this, but we assure you that it will be second nature in no time! Please, so that you may properly enjoy this manga, turn the book over and begin reading from the other side. Arigatou gozaimasu!

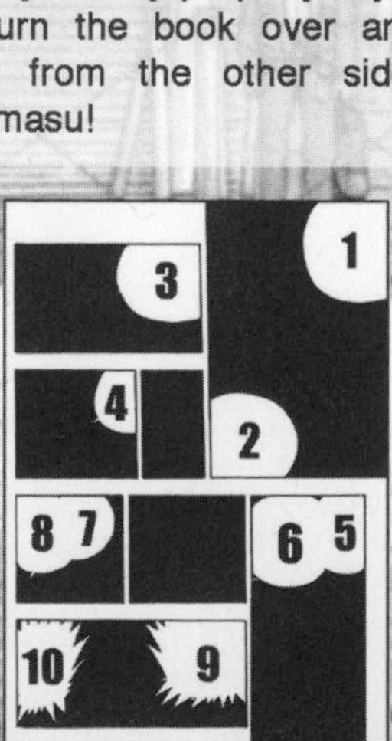
1
2
3
4
5
6
7
8
9
10

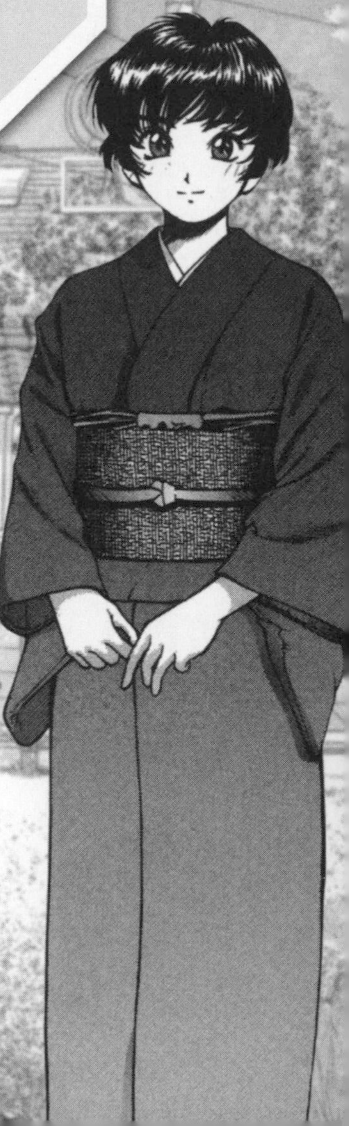

100% AUTHENTIC MANGA